No one sees what tomorrow brings, so why waste today?
If we can't laugh at the moment, why spend it in tears?

Whether you come to me or not, your happiness keeps me
*   well;*
These eyes that thirst to see you hide a storm deep within.

Stay drunk in your happiness, don't turn to someone else,
And whoever disturbs your bliss—set his home on fire.
                    Written inside the back of a truck

Truck decoration in Pakistan is a pervasive and growing form of art. After the initial bodywork and painting is done in a workshop with the artist, driver, and owner all collaborating in design decisions, the driver continues to add minor ornamental features to the truck, making it an ever-evolving work of art. Decorative features follow a recognizable pattern in their location on the truck: normally overtly religious elements go on the front, references to pop culture and commerce on the sides, and humor as well as some religious imagery (particularly elements that ward off the evil eye) on the back. The combined effect and affect is akin to a full body tattoo.

J.J.E.

Front and Back Covers: Pakistani trucks of the Punjabi style photographed at the wholesale produce market in Rawalpindi, Pakistan. The rear of the truck depicts *Buraq,* the celestial horse that carried Muhammad on his ascension to heaven (*Mi'raj*). (Photos: Jamal J. Elias)

Inside Front and Back: Side panels of Pakistani trucks of the Punjabi style awaiting final touches in a design workshop in Rawalpindi, Pakistan. The image of a young woman on the door (inside front) is opaque and renders the window useless. The other woman (inside back) is Nur Jahan, a very popular Punjabi singer. (Photos: Jamal J. Elias)

Res 43   Spring 2003

Anthropology and aesthetics

Islamic arts

Res 43   Spring 2003

Anthropology and aesthetics

EDITOR
Francesco Pellizzi

ASSOCIATE EDITORS
Remo Guidieri
Joseph Koerner
Joseph Rykwert

EXECUTIVE EDITORIAL COUNCIL
William Fash
Francesco Pellizzi
Rubie Watson

ASSISTANT EDITORS
Kirsten Swenson and Nuit Banai

EDITORIAL CONSULTANT
Ivan Gaskell (Harvard University Art Museums)

CONTRIBUTING EDITORS

Suzanne Preston Blier	Jeffrey Hamburger	Z. S. Strother
Sarah Brett-Smith	Jonathan Hay	Karl Taube
Thomas Cummins	Michael Meister	Marvin Trachtenberg
David Freedberg	Erika Naginski	Gary Urton
Dario Gamboni	Alina Payne	Irene Winter
Oleg Grabar	Victor Stoichita	Gerhard Wolf

EDITORIAL ADVISORS

Alain Babadzan	Adrienne Kaeppler	Carlo Severi
Akeel Bilgrami	C. C. Lamberg-Karlovsky	David Shapiro
Edmund Carpenter	Pamela Lee	David Stuart
Clemency Coggins	Gulru Necipoglu	S. J. Tambiah
Whitney Davis	Jeffrey Quilter	Robert Farris Thompson
Kurt Forster	Thomas Reese	Gianni Vattimo
John Hay	Marshall Sahlins	Nur Yalman

PROJECT COORDINATOR (Peabody Museum) Susan McNally
DESIGNER Richard Bartlett
COVER DESIGN From a 1981 sketch by Dan Flavin
LAYOUT Glenna Collett

EDITORIAL OFFICE
12 East 74th Street, New York, NY 10021, phone: (212) 737-6109, fax: (212) 861-7874,
e-mail: pellizzi@fas.harvard.edu

PRODUCED AND PUBLISHED BY
The Peabody Museum of Archaeology and Ethnology, Harvard University
11 Divinity Avenue, Cambridge, MA 02138

Manufactured in the United States of America
Printing by Henry N. Sawyer Company, Charlestown, Massachusetts
Binding by Acme Bookbinding, Charlestown, Massachusetts

ISSN 0277–1322   ISBN 0-87365-844-2

Editorial

What should one know about Islamic art?

OLEG GRABAR

These introductory remarks have two purposes. One concerns this particular issue of *Res,* the other focuses on a broader question concerning the values of certain kinds of knowledge.

Let me, first, explain the context which led to this group of twelve idiosyncratic essays written independently of each other. In their own individual ways, each writer responded to the request that their topics be of significance to wider issues of the history and criticism of art. It was important, we felt, to present the study of the arts in Islamic lands, ancient or contemporary, through discrete scholarly investigations rather than through programmatic proclamations or facile complaints about the sad state of the field. But it was also important to show that detailed discussions of narrow issues or magisterial elaborations of broad topics can be intellectually useful much beyond their individual constrictions. We hoped, thus, to attract the attention and interest of a wider public than that of specialists.

My second purpose is to explain why there is reason, most particularly at this juncture of scholarship and historical knowledge, to argue for the intellectual importance of an awareness of Islamic art. The field has grown enormously over the past two decades, both in the number of women and men dealing with it and in the breadth of subjects with which they deal. As scholarly activities grow, they also divide into linguistic, national, or regional groups which no longer share information and ideas with any degree of ease, thus spawning separate enclaves or chapels that are rarely in communication with each other and lack built-in mechanisms to avoid parochial isolation. This may indeed be a good moment to reflect on the accomplishments of the field, its concerns, its priorities for future work, and the ways to establish, maintain, and improve contacts between many sub-fields of study or regions of the world which are not contiguous with each other and do not share a language. The absence of contacts and awareness occurs in two ways. One is regional within the Muslim world: Mauretania and Senegal, for example, have an artistic history and an artistic identity within the wider Islamic world which are hardly known in Syria or Egypt, not to speak of Sinkiang or Indonesia, and a fascinating artistic and intellectual energy has grown in the Muslim diaspora all over the world which is as rich as it is original and yet is not well known either in the ancestral or adopted lands of the artists. The other difficulty is cultural. The critical and historical study of Islamic art is still most common among westerners writing in at least half a dozen languages rarely shared by all practitioners. Thus, intellectual discussions with broad ambitions often end up as parochial exercises. There is not much one can do about the distances separating countries, but knowledge and recognition of local artistic traditions and the ways of their understanding can be fostered and maintained, provided proper mechanisms for doing so exist and the reality of the problem is recognized.

It is not inappropriate to add that the tragic events of September 11, 2001 and the psychologically as well as physically destructive forces unleashed by these events have put a special burden on those who are spending their professional life in understanding and explaining to others any aspect of the Islamic world. Those of us who deal with the arts have the advantage of working with monuments and objects meant to please and to attract, and with a creative impulse which is as exciting and as powerful today as it was in the past. It is important to point to these activities and to these achievements at a time when, all too easily, the many, very different, and often contradictory values of a whole culture are ignored, misjudged, rejected, or misinterpreted by Muslims and non-Muslims alike.

In setting the stage for the pages that follow, this introduction is an invitation to think further about the scholarly needs of the field of Islamic art and about the expectations one can reasonably derive from these studies.

There is a paradox at the core of a scholar's life and it is a particularly troubling one for those who specialize in fields removed in time and space from the concerns and awareness of the culture that surrounds them. The paradox lies in the contradiction between two truths. One is that, *a priori,* everything is worth knowing and worth studying. Whether properly applied or not, the old Roman adage *nihil humanum a me alienum est,* "nothing human is alien to me," is the basic premise behind the commitment to the acquisition and sharing of knowledge and information which justifies institutions of higher learning and feeds the enthusiasm of scholars. This premise underlies the current hopes for a "good" globalization which would be, ideally, a technology of awareness and recognition making all cultures and all knowledge accessible with the same intensity to institutions and individuals all over the world. The point of the premise is that there is no necessary hierarchy in what should be known, and it is by regrettable accident or willful and therefore dubious choice that we know some things and not others. The other side of the paradox is that, however virtuous it may be to want to know everything, it is not feasible to do so for practical reasons. There are limits to the capacities of the intellect and, as specialized knowledge increases and subdivides itself constantly without corresponding increase in mental capacities, the proportion of the available information one can process decreases constantly.

As far as the history and criticism of the arts in Muslim lands is concerned, the paradox can be translated into a series of questions: what intellectual benefit can a historian or critic of the arts in general as well as a political or cultural historian of Islamic civilization derive from knowing something about the arts and other visually perceived data from the Islamic world? What should one read or see to become acquainted with Islamic art? In a sense these questions imply a more fundamental one: why should an educated person with or without personal connections to the Muslim world know anything about Islamic art? It is the responsibility of all practitioners in the study of that art to provide answers to these questions, but the usual answers are not satisfactory. Only too often, they require access to well-stocked libraries and visual collections or travel to places difficult to access, such as private collections, rare book rooms, or remote lands. They discourage without seducing and make much of learning a penalty rather than a pleasure. As to the question, why study all of this, it is rarely answered beyond the platitude that all things deserve to be known and I shall return to it in my conclusion.

A recent issue of *Res* provided me with the inspiration for this volume.[1] Jonathan Hay, in his

introduction, put forward a question and a theory of what he called "interculturality" and then a group of scholars discussed, in their own idiosyncratic ways, topics more or less related to the question posed. The result was neither a solution to a puzzle nor an answer to a query, but a series of considerations which enlightened the readers and, through the quality and originality of their research, served as models for future investigations. In a similar vein, the epistemological question of this issue—What should one know about Islamic art?—elicited a great variety of responses, some of which were aired at a small seminar held at MIT in May 2001 under the auspices of the Aga Khan Program for Architecture and the direction of Professor Nasser Rabbat. Some of the talks at that seminar became part of this issue. They are not answers to the questions posed earlier, but contributions to an eventual collectively achieved sense of the ways in which specialists see their obligations to their public, learned colleagues, and enlightened amateurs of art.

Let me begin by looking at my original question in the abstract. Are there features of Islamic art, whether generated by its own internal development or by historical and geographical constraints, that can be seen as constructive exemplars which modify or enrich known conclusions or known research processes for a discourse on the arts, and are not merely additional examples used to confirm otherwise well-established paradigms?

There are important topics in the history of art for which Islamic art does not provide useful or major evidence; such would be the representation of the human body or even the portrayal of nature, although within the study of Islamic art both are quite fascinating.[2] There are issues of Islamic art which have occupied the intellectual energies of many learned minds of specialists and which fill pages of printed matter that are of considerable import for the field but hardly significant for the general history of the arts. Random examples would be the evolution of glass and ceramic techniques, the spread of luster ware or of the *muqarnas,* the attributions of paintings to artists, perhaps even a popular subject like the importance of Sufism in interpreting formal developments. This is not to say that these subjects are forever assigned to the level of parochial usefulness only. Many are not and I shall

---

1. *Res* 35 (1994) dealing with intercultural China and guest edited by Jonathan Hay.

2. Kenneth Clark in his *Landscape into Art* (New York, 1949) is a rare instance of a writer on a general topic to have included Islamic examples in his discussion, and he does it very gingerly. Architectural historians have been more generous.

return to some of them shortly. It is rather that the ways in which they are presented are restrictive and their wider, cultural or art historical implications have not always been drawn out, or perhaps, at times, do not even exist.

What, then, can be identified as endowed with values of potential importance to as many scholars, students, and amateurs as possible? I am proposing four categories of topics which meet criteria of transcultural and panartistic importance: universal masterpieces, general theories of art and criticism, the culture of boundaries, and contemporary art.

The first category, "universal masterpieces," includes artistic creations of the Muslim world which are esthetically important to historians of art, independent of their individual cultural meanings. Examples are the Dome of the Rock in Jerusalem, the Taj Mahal in Agra, Sinan's architecture in Istanbul and Edirne, glazed and painted ceramics from Nishapur or Iznik, most silks and many rugs, the geometry of decoration in the Alhambra, and perhaps even the vegetal ornament known as the arabesque. In all these instances, it is relatively easy to demonstrate that the architectural examples have been noticed and admired (even critically so) by nearly all those who saw them, the objects have been used or collected for centuries all over the world, and decorative patterns attributed to Islamic art have inspired artists and philosophers since the Renaissance and have been recognized and culturally bound with the Muslim world. The assumption can be made that the appeal and interest exercised by these items do not derive simply from their historical or cultural context, but from something else, some chords struck in the minds of their viewers. It may simply be location, as the Dome of the Rock, the Taj Mahal, and in many ways Sinan's mosques occupy striking spaces and serve as unavoidable visual beacons or magnets in the cities in which they are found. Location can be more than the actual physical space occupied by a building. It can be an ideological component, as the Dome of the Rock owes some of its effectiveness to its presence in a city with deep and complex religious associations. It can also be trivial, as is the case with the Selimiye in Edirne, the undoubted masterpiece of Sinan's buildings, which is less well-known than his Istanbul creations, because Edirne is not on the circuit of tourists and visitors. But, while location may color or intensify the quality of these masterpieces, they are in fact masterpieces for intrinsic reasons of construction, decoration, and association. Such is even more obviously the case for ceramics or textiles from the Islamic world universally collected since the Middle

Ages. Until the middle of the twentieth century, their origins in the Islamic world were secondary to the technical dexterity they exhibited, or to the sensuous luxury and sensory pleasure they provided.

In dealing with these universal masterpieces, the difficulty lies in finding the appropriate equilibrium between scholarly accuracy and contemporary expectations of knowledge. I shall limit myself to examples of architecture, because the other arts have not acquired the same interest and concern among scholars or the general public. Thus the Dome of the Rock survived the Crusades because it was thought to be the *Templum Domini,* where Christ had been. The Taj Mahal has for decades been preserved, restored, and catered to because it was seen as a symbol of a husband's love for his wife, hardly the most appropriate and most significant feature of that building of great complexity. And Sinan's domes were (and still are) frequently seen as demonstrations of the greatness of Hagia Sophia, not as outstanding works of their own reflecting a very particular Ottoman culture. Often enough, all these monuments are instruments of public relations, as their pictures are used for state and city publicity and they become obligatory stops for tourists. Does it help, at the level at which these masterpieces are perceived and felt by most people, to provide them with their scientifically and contextually accurate explanations? Precision and accuracy can be confusing, as they often require considerable knowledge and sophistication and their conclusions are often ambiguous. For instance, in Islamic architecture, inscriptions are essential to the significance of a building, but the perception of writing is much less immediate than that of the painted or sculpted surfaces in Christian or Hindu arts. It is difficult to present inscriptions without expecting a knowledge of the language or script in which they are written and without an attitude that focuses on the writing found in a building, yet it is not possible to understand many monuments without them.

It is relatively easy to write about architecture from this particular point of view of masterpieces. It becomes more difficult to do so when we turn to objects, whatever the technique of their creation. We have two choices. One is to identify specific bowls, plates, rugs, pages from a book, or silks as particularly striking examples of a given type and to focus on a specific object as esthetically or intellectually exciting. The other choice is to talk only in terms of types and simply assume that luster ware or hunting rugs are always of the highest quality and deserving universal admiration.

Neither approach is really satisfactory and both require further investigation and elaboration which are beyond my purpose here.

A second category of topics starts from a different premise: There are broad and general concerns of the history of art and criticism for which the centuries of Islamic art offer significant data. No study of opposition to images, from aniconism to iconoclasm, can avoid the arguments developed by Muslim theologians, philosophers, and practitioners of science or art. Nor can it skip the formal and technical practices which derived from these arguments and from their impact, weak or strong depending on time, area, or social setting. Discussions and definitions of ornament always take into consideration the many ways in which monuments from the Islamic world were decorated, as was properly seen by nineteenth-century European theoreticians of art and of ornament.[3] The nineteenth century and much of the work done on ornament in the twentieth century concentrated primarily on individual, mostly vegetal motifs and rarely picked up on more fundamental principles of ornamental design, except for the "arabesque," which is as much a fiction of Renaissance design ideas as it is a peculiarity of Islamic art.[4] Any consideration of geometry on two-dimensional space requires handling the decoration of the Alhambra with the seventeen symmetries represented in its designs and could also involve earlier Iranian brickwork and the theories of design which grew around them.[5]

Methodological difficulties arise when we turn to two artistic themes for which Islamic art has often been utilized in art historical thinking: writing as art and abstraction. Writing was used in many different ways, from true "calligraphy," i.e., the writing of texts with the primary purpose of sensory attraction, all the way to imitations of kufic known as "kufesque" or pseudo-Kufic,[6] used in works of Islamic art as well as in the Christian world and even in China. These numerous permutations of meanings and intensity within the same formal sphere of writing are unique, with useful but quite different parallels in the Far East, the medieval Slavic world, the Latin West, and contemporary painting everywhere. The concept of abstraction is easily related to geometry and to writing, but it is also applied to vegetal ornament in much of Islamic art. Abstraction is a major feature of twentieth-century art, and a recent exhibition in Basel dedicated to "Ornament and Abstraction" showed on its posters and on the cover of its catalogue half of a Paul Klee painting next to half of a seventeenth-century Iranian iron work decorated with writing.[7] A segment from an acknowledged masterpiece of twentieth-century western painting was juxtaposed with a nice but run-of-the-mill work of Iranian metal.

On all issues dealing with surface decoration on buildings, books, or objects, the many faceted developments of Islamic art have a great deal to offer to any consideration of the arts in general. Other questions are more technical and perhaps more restricted in importance, although this may be so only because they have not been fully investigated. For instance, dome construction and methods of treating bricks are universal needs, whose Islamic instances are of particular originality, but the questions themselves are limited to the interests of narrow specialists.

Two other issues are more unusual, but, as it turns out, their elaboration for the history of art in general can profit from the study of Islamic examples. One is the important question of the ownership and transmission of works of art, of taste, and of models. The peculiar sociopolitical structure of the Islamic world, with its competing dynasties, princely courts in ever changing places, and urban centers in different regions sharing the same culture and the same tastes led to a well-documented, if not always well-studied, pattern of collecting, trading, and exchanging techniques, objects, and artisans or artists. Thus, for instance, the ways in which the technique of luster ceramics or glass spread from Iraq to Egypt but avoided northeastern Iran, or *muqarnas* architecture is found with different expressions in the Muslim West, Iraq, or Iran, can be explained in several different ways: presence or absence of competencies in effecting transfers of techniques, social or political rejection or acceptance of new ideas, or a patronage intent on favoring novelties rather than in continuing old ways.[8] The study of the manufacture of

3. The most obvious example is that of O. Jones, but for a useful general view see Frank-Lothar Kroll, *Das Ornament in der Kunsttheorie des 19. Jahrhunderts* (Hildsheim, 1987).

4. Ernst Kühnel, *Die Arabeske* (Graz, 1977).

5. M. S. Bulatov, *Geometricheskaia Garmonizatsia v Arhitektury Srednei Azii* (Moscow, 1988); Gülrü Necipoglu, *The Topkapi Scroll* (Los Angeles, 1995). Major works on this subject by A. Özdural and C. Bier are in preparation.

6. G. C. Miles coined the term "kufesque." Much has been written in recent years on the art of writing without necessary agreement. For one view see Oleg Grabar, *The Mediation of Ornament* (Princeton, 1992).

7. Markus Brüderlin, *Ornament and Abstraction* (Basel, 2001).

8. Oliver Watson, *Persian Luster Ware* (London, 1985); Yasser Tabbaa, *The Transformation of Islamic Art during the Sunni Revival* (Seattle, 2001).

great royal manuscripts in fifteenth- and sixteenth-century Iran made it possible to imagine and to reconstruct the operation of royal ateliers,[9] while the elaborate relationship between Safavid and Mughal painting and the movements of artists from Iran to India or Central Asia is a fascinating example of the ways in which new patrons use a supply of talents found elsewhere, just as happened with Italian artists and works of art moving to northern Europe in the sixteenth century. And, as a last example of procedures typical of artistic developments in many places, the ways of exchanging beautiful or cherished things, made or acquired, is well documented since the eleventh century and has been the subject of many recent investigations.[10]

In all these cases, the Islamic phenomenon is sufficiently well documented to help in designing paradigms which could be useful when we deal with other cultures, especially those in feudal Europe, Renaissance Italy, or Baroque monarchies which share with the Islamic world patterns of internal social behavior. At times, simple comparisons can enrich the understanding of both parties. At other times, it is the contrasts that do so. But, in either case, our sense of the behavior of patrons, consumers, and artists is bound to be enriched. What is required is simply to consider and present the story as documented in Islamic art in terms pertinent and useful to all fields.

My other example for the possibility of imagining an Islamic model for other artistic traditions is one which had already attracted the attention of scholars late in the nineteenth century, when Islam was proclaimed as the one religion created "in the full light of history," as used to be said: It is that a great deal is known, although there are differing opinions on the quality and veracity of the information, about the formation of holy places in Mecca, Madinah, and Jerusalem, and about the creation and evolution of the mosque in general.[11] These examples make it possible to define how the new monotheism created, over a short period of time, its sacred spaces and the ways of expressing its piety. But it is not merely a question of faith related changes or inventions. It is a matter of learning and understanding whether and how all aspects of life and culture were changed, if at all. Historians argue that a new configuration of political and religious order developed in the seventh century. But were these changes visible? Do new vestimentary patterns or different ways of public and private socializing appear whenever we posit a new period of history? What was the geography of changes, their rhythm, their social or ethnic spread? Especially in our own time of new secular, restricted, and national "sacred" public spaces, of idiosyncratic symbols and ceremonies next to sameness in clothing, music, games, and cellular phones, the relationship of these developments to places and ways of a tradition which has left a large documentation for its own religious history could be of enormous interest.

My third category of topics from Islamic art that should be everyone's concern derives from the true but rarely acknowledged fact that the Islamic world is the only cultural entity in the history of mankind to have borders or boundaries with almost all the cultural entities known before 1492: India and Southeast Asia, China, northern Eurasia, West and East Africa below the Sahara, southeastern Europe, northern Europe, western Europe; Japan alone escapes such direct contacts with the Islamic world. These other cultures, like Islamic culture itself, can be defined geographically as well as linguistically, or in terms of religious affiliation. Everywhere, artistic traditions, ideas, and objects, probably artisans as well, moved from one area to the other and did or could carry practices and provide ideas or innovations in the arts in ways that may or may not be idiosyncratic to each culture and for which I have already provided examples. There were also internal boundaries within the Islamic sphere, as Jews, Zoroastrians, Buddhists, various Christian denominations (probably also Manicheans, pagans, and shamanists) formed discrete cultural groups which either sponsored or used patterns and styles created and developed for the Muslim majority or had an art of their own, reflective of or reacting to the Islamic world. These boundaries are also chronological ones. The beginnings of Islam were bound to Late Antique forms from Spain to the Hindu Kush. Later political events such as the Crusades and the Mongol invasion, or economic exchanges with Africa, India, or the north of Europe provided different creative opportunities for the arts or witnessed upheavals which affected the arts in positive ways, as with the movement of artisans by Mongol rulers, or negative ways, as with the wanton destruction of art ordered by the Talibans of Afghanistan.

9. M. Shreve Simpson, *Sultan Ibrahim Mirza's Haft Awrang* (London, 1995).

10. Qadi ibn al-Zubayr, *Book of Gifts and Rarities,* tr. Ghada al-Qaddumi (Cambridge, 1996); O. Grabar "The Shared Culture of Objects," in Henry Maguire ed., *Byzantine Court Culture from 829 to 1204* (Washington, 1997). A recent symposium on the subject was organized at Dumbarton Oaks by Professor Anthony Cutler.

11. Much new research has dealt with the formation of mosques, for example Jeremy Johns, "The House of the Prophet and the Concept of the Mosque," in J. Johns ed., *Bayt al-Maqdis* (Oxford, 1999).

Much has been written about the presence of Islamic themes in Sicily or Armenia, on Islamic objects in Christian collections in Byzantium, Muscovy, or the West. Studies exist on *mudejar* art in Spain or the development of Indian provinces shared by Hindu and Muslim cultures.[12] To my knowledge, less has been done with Islamic art in sub-Saharan Africa. Chinese fashions in Islamic art are relatively well known, but movements in the opposite direction are less obvious, perhaps because there were fewer of them. The problem with most studies dealing with these topics is that they are descriptive and enumerative, not interpretive. One can easily imagine two kinds of interpretations. One lies in explaining why certain Islamic techniques and motifs were prized elsewhere. Was it in search for whatever we call luxury? We should probably learn to distinguish between two formal traits. The first is exemplified by the *turquerie* of the eighteenth century with an "orientalist" whiff of the Islamic culture of its model. The other is, consciously acknowledged or not, the technological superiority or higher quality without necessarily cultural implications, as with the Cappella Palatina in Palermo, the *muqarnas* architecture of Armenia, or the Islamic rugs popular for centuries. In all these examples, motifs of Islamic origin are clearly present, but there is no suggestion of Islamic cultural hegemony. Were these impacts consistent and continuous or were they accidents, as with the examples of the Robe of Roger II, the Innsbrück plate, or the tomb of Bohemond in southern Italy, all of which exhibit clearly the impact of Islamic taste and of Islamic techniques, but do not seem to have had any further consequences in the arts of these areas? The other kind of interpretation deals with the more complicated problem of how consciously these transfers were made, and the degree to which givers and receivers were actually aware of their actions. Answering some of these questions may simply not be possible for any time before the twentieth century.

I can be brief with my fourth category, because I have not engaged in it seriously, and I have not absorbed or fully considered the intellectual ways of dealing with it or acquainted myself with the small but growing number of studies devoted to it. In a nutshell, it is the question of contemporary Muslim attitudes toward the arts in general and the history of Islamic art in particular. One could take an extreme and hardly popular position and say that, from the late twentieth century onward, the study of all arts and cultures has become a universal activity and should be judged as such. Concerns with the past are not, and should not be, any more meaningful for Muslims than they are for Italians or Frenchmen and, if they are, these concerns are either restrictive and localized or else should be explained in visual terms meaningful on their own, not because they relate to the past. A local creativity with traditional themes catering to a limited public will always exist, as it is the normal outcome of any cultural center with a school of architecture or of fine arts. At the same time, creations of meaningful contemporary forms related to a specific past have occurred in some of the architecture produced in Muslim lands, around the continuing fascination with the Arabic alphabet found from Morocco to Indonesia, as well as in the art of the Muslim diaspora everywhere, and, most recently, in the transformation of miniatures into vehicles for contemporary expression.[13]

The real problem is that we do live in a world of art in which there are constantly two parallel tracks. One is universal, in the sense that artists, architects, art critics, and art historians, wherever they are, share the same tools, ideas, and modes of expression; their technical or intellectual competencies have been (or can be) recognized and accepted everywhere; their art is sold, their books and articles are read, and they are called on to build or to lecture all over the planet. The other track can easily be seen as parochial and limited, restricted to the art school of some university town, to the architectural practice of a single country, or to journals and publishing houses printing only in a local vernacular. It is easy enough to see the first track as one toward which everyone must strive, because, as with Nobel prizes, there is a national and cultural pride in international recognition. Yet such recognition rarely profits the homeland of the awarded individual. Even its educational value is weakened by the relative inaccessibility of rarefied scholars and by a necessary concern for mass audiences at the expense of more sophisticated individual instruction. The second track does bring profit to the places where it operates and its educational value is far more tangible, but it makes little sense beyond its place of origin, because of its confined setting secure in its linguistic and political separateness and unable to reach beyond a local public. The contrast between the two tracks is reflected in the awards given

12. See below the articles by F. Flood, M. Meister, C. Robinson, and T. Kaufmann. To my regret, I did not find someone to write on Islamic art and Africa.

13. I have in mind the paintings by Shahzia Sikander as in Vishaka N. Desai, *Conversations with Traditions* (New York, The Asia Society, 2001).

by the Aga Khan Award for Architecture. In these, a fascinating and usually successful equilibrium has been found between the two tracks which merits investigation in depth.[14]

The more intricate question involved in these remarks is whether such investigations in the contemporary psychological and emotional complexities of cultures other than one's own is an act of intellectual voyeurism—akin to some of the worst sins of Orientalism or of the ad hoc position papers of think tanks—or else a way to enrich all involved by recognizing and defining originality and quality in the making of works of art without succumbing to parochialism or to the constant comparisons of ethnic, national, or cultural achievements on some absurd scale, imposed from elsewhere or derived from past glories. In short, any consideration of contemporary artistic activities in the Islamic world requires at the same time a deep awareness of the varieties of contemporary artistic expressions and expectations and also a sense of a constantly evolving modern world, fickle and often cruel in its judgments, yet indispensable for any adjustments to one's own modernity.

My remarks can be construed in two ways. They can be seen as a call for publishers to sponsor short or long, attractively illustrated monographs on selected topics of Islamic art—monographs that should be accessible to anyone interested in understanding the arts of one fifth of humanity over the past 1500 years and seeking to figure out their place in the arts of humankind. Or, my remarks can be taken as a call for a profession to analyze itself, to weed the trivial from the essential, to investigate the premises within which it operates, and to situate itself within the cultural climate of our own time while heeding the requirements of a tradition of many centuries. These seem to be, at first glance, searches for relevance requested by trustees and deans of institutions of higher learning, against which I fought most of my life because I thought that scholarly programs must come from those who do scholarship, not from outsiders. But it is perhaps our own processes of scholarly work rather than the demands of a general public that should lead to the explanations and interpretations that will become both valid in their own right and accessible to the scholarly community, perhaps even beyond it to the

general public. The essays which follow are all, in their different ways, steps in that direction.

In a broader sense, they are first steps toward answering the question I posed, What should one know about Islamic art? Its intrinsic qualities of technical achievements or the unique documentation it offers for the understanding of the arts everywhere? In the deepest methodological sense, Islamic art acquires its uniqueness and its fascination through something other than individual monuments, historical or esthetic conundrums, or contemporary struggles for expression. That "something else" has been recognized, without full elaboration, by the monumental *Dictionary of Art* published by McMillan and lies in the fact that, until the nineteenth century or thereabouts, Islamic art had been neither the art of a land nor the art of a people. It does not possess, like Chinese or Greek art, roots, real or fictitious, in a specific area. Islamic art has always been the art of a culture, even if that culture expressed itself in a specific area. It is, of course, possible to consider a continuous art of Syria or of Uzbekistan, but such considerations will be meaningless without a thorough awareness of the areas surrounding these two modern countries. For the boundaries of contemporary Syria or Uzbekistan hardly correspond to anything real in the twelfth or fifteenth centuries. This originality in historical structure is not peculiar to the Islamic world. A recent theoretical reflection on the literary culture of eastern and central Europe brought out quite eloquently and quite persuasively the fascinating fact that, next to and between single-language cultures like those of Russia or Germany, a large array of lands using their own languages created a more or less continuous literature which can best be described as interactive with each other and therefore different from neighboring German or Russian literary cultures. Fascinating methods of literary analysis have been developed for the study of this literature, which may well be useful for the study of Islamic art.[15]

---

15. Marcle Cornis-Pope and John Neubauer, *Towards a History of the Literary Cultures of East-Central Europe: Theoretical Reflections* (American Council of Learned Societies Occasional paper no. 52, New York, 2002).

---

14. The excellent reports on the Aga Khan Awards, published every three years in handsome books, need now to be analyzed in depth from the many different points of view in which the awards have shown themselves to be important.

Figure 1. Humay at the gate of Humayun's castle. Manuscript painting from the *Three Masnavis* of Khvaju Kirmani, copied by Mir Ali b. Ilyas al-Tabrizi al-Bavarchi, 1396, Baghdad. Opaque pigment and gold on paper, 281 x 191 mm (painted surface). London, British Library, Add. 18113, fol. 18b. (Photo: By permission of The British Library.)

Micrographia

Toward a visual logic of Persianate painting

DAVID J. ROXBURGH

Shifting patterns of thought about Persianate painting, a movement away from the taxonomic concerns that dominated early studies, have become current in recent years. New lines of investigation have responded—probably by osmosis—to historiographic concerns in the history of art and contextual modes of historical inquiry. The results include an increased awareness of intersections among scholars, collectors, the market, and museums; a revived interest in studies of word and image; and questions about the meanings, functions, and values of book painting produced in the milieus of the pre-modern courts of Iran and Central Asia.

Art historical narratives about Persianate painting generally hold that the tradition spanned three centuries (ca. 1300–1600) and its broad outlines are readily available in synthetic studies. Long recognized are momentous changes in book painting in western Iran in the 1390s. One manuscript in particular, Khvaju Kirmani's *Three Masnavis* (dated 1396), heralds the arrival of what will become commonplace in Persianate painting. This future is manifest in vertically oriented compositions (fig. 1), a rich polychrome palette, and dense accumulations of minutely rendered details. By the mid-1390s—especially in books of poetry—the number of paintings in a book became fewer, often as few as eight: it is impossible not to notice the concentration of labor and resources that went into these richly worked images. Scholarship accords importance to such paintings precisely because of their intermediary status: more prospective in orientation, they mark the beginnings of "classical" Persianate painting.

The form of painting discernable from the 1390s was embraced and refined in the first decades of the fifteenth century, especially in Herat under the patronage of Timurid prince Baysunghur (d. 1433), a grandson of the

dynastic founder Timur (i.e., Tamerlane).[1] Baysunghur's books embody an aesthetic framed entirely in response to the visual terms of the Jalayirid tradition.[2] However, the materials are prepared fastidiously, execution becomes still more precise, and composition more rigorously controlled. By ca. 1430, Baysunghur's books had set the standard and put painting on an irreversible course. Developments in Herat represented a definitive movement away from the pictorial experimentation characteristic of fourteenth-century painting, best exemplified through the Great Mongol copy of the *Shahnama* (Book of Kings), Firdawsi's epic. Made in western Iran before 1336, paintings such as Bahram Gur fights the Karg (fig. 2) differ from the later Jalayirid and Timurid traditions by their larger painted surface area, combination of flat color with expansive areas of wash, and coding of spatial recession by overlapping planes and the bluish effect of atmospheric perspective. One can only assume that painters from the fifteenth century onward considered some aspects of the fourteenth-century pictorial language to be too indeterminate; from the last years of the fourteenth century onward, the formal aspects of painting become increasingly coherent and codified.

Although this narrative of a history of Persianate painting attends to broad changes in the formal aspects of painting, we are still left wondering, What is a Persianate painting? What are the salient visual features of Persianate paintings and how does one encounter these images? It is strange that such questions have not been pursued and that the problems they raise have been skipped over. In some respects, both painting and book—its object carrier—seem to have been taken for granted or at least to have acquired a certain measure of

I would like to thank Philippe-Alain Michaud and Sophie Makariou (Musée du Louvre); Cynthia Robinson (University of New Mexico); and Nasser Rabbat (Massachusetts Institute of Technology) for invitations to present versions of this essay. I thank Renata Holod for her insightful remarks on a draft.

1. The Timurid dynasty controlled the lands of Iran, Central Asia, and Afghanistan between the period 1370 and 1506.

2. The Jalayirid dynasty (1336–1432) succeeded the Mongols to control the regions of Iraq and Azarbayjan. The "Jalayir" tribe was probably Mongol in origin. A succession of patrons made their courts (Baghdad, Tabriz) centers of literary and artistic achievement, especially Uvays (r. 1356–1374) and Sultan Ahmad (r. 1382–1410).

Figure 2. Bahram Gur fights the Karg. Manuscript painting from the Great Mongol *Shahnama* of Firdawsi, before ca. 1336, Tabriz. Opaque pigment, gold and silver on paper, 210 x 290 mm (painted surface); 415 x 300 mm (folio). Cambridge, Mass., Arthur M. Sackler Museum, Harvard University Art Museums, Bequest of Abby Aldrich Rockefeller, accession no. 1960.190.2. (Photo: Courtesy of the Arthur M. Sackler Museum, Harvard University Art Museums, Bequest of Abby Aldrich Rockefeller.)

familiarity. This familiarity is caused in part by relying on art historical paradigms developed for other artistic traditions as well as from the way that most people encounter Persianate paintings. In either publications or exhibitions, a longstanding practice—only recently challenged—was to conceal the text adjacent to paintings. Now exhibition spaces combine cases displaying open books and framed folios mounted on the walls. The compromise endeavors to remind us that a picture seen on a wall should be seen in a book, not that this fact of Persian painting has passed without comment.[3] Scholars have yet to attend to the fact that although the Persianate painting is dense and complex, albeit in "miniature," it cannot be understood as an autonomous object analogous to an easel picture of the western European tradition.[4]

Focusing on the relationship between word and image—now emphasizing the painting's position in a book—however, can result in the opposite extreme where painting is only accounted for by its text. This more recent approach of word and image studies dates to the 1970s. One tendency of these studies has been to "match" image to text, identifying linkages between pictorial content and textual content in often quite literal and descriptive ways.[5] Indeed, some scholars think that every picture is inspired by a text, one of them proposing that Persianate paintings are "in nine cases out of ten . . . 'pictures with a story,'"[6] that their principal function—and meaning—is a story-telling one. On the question of meaning, the same author writes:

> Indeed, it would be foolish, when looking at a Persian painting or drawing, to ask the sort of question that springs to mind when we contemplate Western pictorial art: "What is the artist's message for us?" The Persian artist's message is simple and invariable: "This is the most beautiful and effective illustration I can make to this story; I hope you will like it." This humble desire to give pleasure to others comes as rather a surprise and a relief. . . . (ibid. p. 14).

This passage shows that some scholars recognize the inadequacy of Western paradigms for the analysis of Persianate painting, and that formerly assumed cultural homologies do not exist: Persianate painting is "foreign." But the assessment raises other problems by its emphases; first, the issue of the painter's volition, in an art form that was collaborative; and second, by defining the painting as essentially pleasurable and pragmatic. In the same essay, the author writes that the Persianate painting is a place to escape the "confusion, tension, and cruelty of the world around us," and urges us to contemplate "these elaborate yet uncomplicated works with the simple eyes of children . . . , delighting in their beauty of line and richness of color, and enjoying the strange stories they tell. Their beauties are all on the surface; no spiritual message or Freudian symbolism lurks beneath their exquisite forms and colors."[7] For this scholar, Persianate painting is a curative, a palliative that can restore the child within us. The painting is an experience of wonder, of seeing things in a way that is familiar to the memory yet forgotten, foreign but somehow known.

Intriguing in most writing on Persianate painting is its amnesiac quality, an insensitivity to the problems inherent to any analysis that would claim to be

---

3. As noted by Robert Hillenbrand, "The Uses of Space in Timurid Painting," in *Timurid Art and Culture,* ed. Lisa Golombek and Maria Eva Subtelny (Leiden: E. J. Brill, 1992), pp. 76–102, 77; and Thomas W. Lentz, "Pictures for the Islamic Book: Persian and Indian Painting in the Vever Collection," *Asian Art* 1, no. 4 (Fall 1988): 9–35, esp. 12–13.

4. Otto Pächt made the same point about medieval manuscripts (*Book Illumination in the Middle Ages: An Introduction* [London and Oxford: Harvey Miller Publishers and Oxford University Press, 1986], pp. 9 and 155).

5. See Jerome Clinton, "Ferdowsi and the Illustration of the Shahnameh," in *Islamic Art and Literature,* ed. Oleg Grabar and Cynthia Robinson (Princeton, N.J.: Markus Wiener, 2001), pp. 57–78.

6. B. W. Robinson, *Drawings of the Masters: Persian Drawings from the 14th Through the 19th Century* (New York: Shorewood Publishers, 1965), p. 13.

7. Robinson's comments take off from remarks made by Eric Schroeder, who Robinson quotes in full: "There is, for instance, the loitering interest of narrative in childish form subtly organized in a very mature way, and a perfected draughtsmanship which has yet something in common with children's drawings and reminds us of something we can no longer see ourselves." After discussing terms used by Muhammad Haydar Dughlat, Schroeder remarks: "They praised the craftsman qualities in their men of genius. . . . Accepting monotony and extravagance as canons, let us proceed to judge the tension, the all-over thoroughness, and the seductive human grace of the design, the cold fluency of the execution, the high polish of the finishing" (ibid., pp. 11 and 13).

It is difficult to know if Robinson and Schroeder refer to the "innocent eye," the notion common in the early twentieth century that children's art was a more objective, unfettered vision with closer access to artistic inspiration (because children lacked the extensive social conditioning of adults). The ideas are summarized in Jonathan Fineberg, "The Innocent Eye," *Art News* (April 1995): 118–125, esp. 119–120. Fineberg links the production of many vanguard artists to concepts of children's art of the time (the subject of publications and exhibitions since the late nineteenth century), but missing is an appraisal of forces that shaped notions about what was exemplary in children's art. See the review by Sue Malvern, "The Ends of Innocence: Modern Art and Modern Children," *Art History* 23, no. 4 (November 2000): 627–631. In his reference to children, Robinson seems to intend an attitude to painting that does not question what come across as unintuitive properties.

historical. Certain forces will always shape the way we write about history, and it is impossible to escape our presentist concerns. Of equal importance to paradigms that shape our perceptions about Persianate painting is the language used to describe it. Deriving from preconceptions about Persianate painting, defined as distinct from the visual modes of western visual traditions, the scholars' language also shapes our perception of these images by establishing an ambience of association for them. Adjectives such as "exquisite," "beautiful," "romantic," and "fantastic" put Persianate painting in the category of decoration and highlight the painting's power to distract us or to transport our minds, effectively deterring us from pursuing other questions about pictures.[8] Inadvertently, language can function as both symptom of and prescription for regression, reinforcing the image of the child-viewer, denying Persianate painting forms of complexity by prescribing only disinterested looking.

Contrasts remain in the study of Persianate painting: in the confounding choice of seeing painting at opposite ends of a spectrum (painting as subservient to text vs. painting as autonomous visual entity); or in uncertainties about the existence of pictorial complexity—and if it is thought to exist, then how do we define the nature of that visual intelligence? It is here that differences between the Persianate painting and immediately obvious comparative cultures of the book—western Medieval and Byzantine—become important. If part of an image's function was to embody meanings that could be decoded by means parallel to the hermeneutic procedures applied to texts, then Persianate painting certainly could not be held equal to these antecedent and contemporary visual cultures. Cycles of paintings and individual images in Persian books focus intently on the development of increasingly complex and detailed environments for their subjects, combining non-optically naturalist depictive modes with abstracted surfaces for clothing or architecture (both are representational). Virtually absent from Persianate paintings found in works of literature, history, and biography is a developed and consistent iconographic system of signs, symbols, and attributes, or a spectrum of visual modalities that would match the range evidenced in a similarly restricted category of a comparative manuscript culture. The western Medieval manuscript tradition, for example,

extends from the typological and diagrammatic modes of the mnemonic to figural narrative. Elements in this repertoire of meaning-producing systems appear to have been avoided in the pictures accompanying Persian books.[9] Although no scholar has put it quite this way, I would argue that viewers of Persianate paintings are less than sure about what they are expected to do in seeing them and that a comparativist framework is one of the root causes of uncertainty about meaning.

Limitations prevent the full elaboration of these questions in this essay, especially as they obtain to the development of image and word interaction. As one step toward them, however, I will focus here on questions related to image and word interaction in the experience of using a book, the painting's narrative structure, composition, and medium and materiality, as well as more specifically, how these aspects come together to forge a unique visual phenomenon. My emphasis on the painting in its material context responds to two facts. First of all, that the Persian art historiographic tradition does not discuss aspects of production or reception, though it does praise the painter's skill among other practitioners. And secondly, that Persianate painting has been ignored for too long and its ontology—*what* it is— incompletely considered: evidence suggests that the "whats" of Persianate painting—material and pictorial effects and the practitioners' skill—carried more than a share of cognitive value. It is also my hope that by examining elements of Persianate painting—recurring features that made it a unity over time—we will be more sensitive to the visual tradition's historical and cultural particularities, freeing it up from the constraints of comparative perspectives.

Image and word in comic books[10]

Other scholars have compared Persianate painting to the comic book, but I was initially suspicious of the comparison because their references to it were so

---

8. Also noted by Lentz (see note 3), p. 13. The aesthetic features of Persianate painting were doubly decorative—abstracted surfaces of pattern making were used for architecture and even the figurative elements of the painting ran against the mimetic tradition of verisimilitude.

9. Persianate paintings that could be interpreted as allegories or possessing visual puns, both of which become increasingly apparent in the heightened self-referential painting of the sixteenth century, remain unstudied.

10. Critical texts on the comic book are scarce, but the following are useful: Francis Lacassin, "The Comic Strip and the Film Language," *Film Quarterly* 25, no. 4 (1972): 11–23; Pierre Fresnault-Deruelle, *La Bande Dessinée: L'Univers et les techniques de quelques 'comics' d'expression française* (Paris: Hachette, 1972); Charles Wooley, *Wooley's History of the Comic Book 1899–1936: The Origin of the Superhero* (Lake Buena Vista, Florida: ca. 1975); and David Carrier, *The Aesthetics of Comics* (University Park, Penn.: Pennsylvania State University Press, 2000).

allusive as to make it difficult to understand what they really intended.[11] In the end I decided to pursue the comparison to see if the comic book could function as a heuristic device for the Persianate painting. I use the comic book as experimental evidence with full recognition that it is a quintessentially modern medium of communication—indeed, this fact configures various utilities. It is also worth repeating the obvious—modern media, like the comic book, have habituated us to certain patterns and methods of making sense of images and words. It is for this reason that I have selected examples from the most recent comic books and have not attempted to match Persianate painting to what I or anyone else might perceive as its closest kin in the history of the comic book. The objective is to begin with a comparison that is historically anachronistic as a point of entry to the Persian painting, and then to articulate its particular features—as object and image.

The principal and most obvious value of the comic book for exposing the logic of Persianate painting lies in its combination of image and word, and in its size and format. Like the Persianate book, the comic book depends on a tightly integrated sequence of images and words that are viewed in a field that measures on average 260 x 180 mm per page. The physical space in which the reader finds himself or herself immersed is comparable. One reads, sees, and makes sense of a story in a circumscribed visual field that is encountered in the format of an object—a book—that is slightly tipped up before the eyes and held in one's hands or that lies on a flat surface. The story advances as the eye scans image and word on the page and as the hand turns successive pages. Tempo changes according to such variables as text type (e.g., the difference between endlessly rhyming poetry or non-rhyming prose), and the desire to linger on an image. It is also possible to use a

Persianate book without reading, to leaf through its folios to find the paintings located at intervals between pages of text. And some paintings, such as the common double-page enthronement, had no immediate origin in a text. For both the Persianate book and the comic book the act of reading/seeing is an intimate, interiorizing experience that enlists the mind and body in a symbiotic engagement which cannot be compared to the act of viewing a painting on the vertical wall of a room.

One example can help to illustrate these various points. The next three illustrations show a sequence of six pages from Marvel Comics's *Ultimate Marvel Team-Up* issue involving Spider-Man and the Hulk. The first double-page layout (fig. 3) is in a canonical format. The first page shows a series of splintered frames—introduced by the word *RUMMBLE*—whose borders are demarcated by white margins; figures extend beyond these spatial boundaries in two places, augmenting by visual means the dialogue between staff members of the newsroom. Just when the chief reporter orders his staff onto the street to scoop the front page story (about which we are as yet unsure), we see the last two cells: at the left, figures run from the office, and at the right a trigonometry textbook lies closed on the table and papers fall over an empty stool. The swift departure of the figure causes the papers to fly into the air. All of a sudden we are on the next page and out on the window ledge of the newspaper office, many floors above ground, positioned before a running Spider-Man. A dramatic shift of perspective sets us beneath him as he fires his silky web, and a third shift takes us several floors below to see Spider-Man's descent (he is now a black silhouette). The second page is structured as three integrated bands that show different perspectives of the hero, a line of speech bubbles containing his thoughts, a mixture of duty, reflection, and anxiety. If we were in danger of being hypnotized by the medium's truth value, Spider-Man's final speech bubble snaps us out of it.

Turning this page does not provide answers (fig. 4). As yet, we are uncertain of what is causing fear and commotion on the streets below; why the citizens are running in terror; why the boss ordered his reporters to the street. Five panoramas, running across the next two pages, show the street and trace Spider-Man's descent. In the middle band, Spider-Man senses the possible cause of the commotion when he sees footprints hammered into the concrete sidewalk—"Oh boy, this isn't good"—"is that a footprint?" In the next panorama, a car is hurtled through the air causing Spider-Man to fall backward. In the very last panorama Spider-Man regains his balance and leaps into the middle distance

11. Barbara Brend, "Beyond the Pale: Meaning in the Margin," in *Persian Painting From the Mongols to the Qajars: Studies in honour of Basil W. Robinson,* ed. Robert Hillenbrand (London and New York: I. B. Tauris, 2000), pp. 39–55, 39; and Oleg Grabar, "Toward an Aesthetic of Persian Painting," in The Art of Interpreting, ed. Susan C. Scott (University Park, Penn.: Pennsylvania State University, 1995), pp. 129–163, p. 138. Marianna Shreve Simpson—who made the comparison earlier—is extremely precise, noting the textual dependence of illustrations to the Shahnama in the early years of the fourteenth century (idem, The Illustration of an Epic: The Earliest Shahnama Manuscripts [New York and London: Garland Publishers Inc., 1979], pp. 203–204). Simpson describes the illustrations in the small Shahnama as "picture stories," somewhere halfway between pictographs and paintings. She also notes that the paintings do not "by themselves narrate a progression of events in visual form."

Figure 3. Spider-Man and the Hulk. From *Ultimate Marvel Team-Up, Issue 2,* vol. 1, no. 2 (May 2001), pp. 8–9. Published by Marvel Comics, a division of Marvel Enterprises Inc. (Comic book material: ™ and © 2002 Marvel Characters, Inc. Used with permission.)

(shown in the register above). A tiny passage of green to the right—a flexing bicep—hints at what is to come.

The scene of discovery fills the third double-page as a single image—Spider-Man confronting the bellicose green Hulk amid a scene of urban destruction (fig. 5). By using the most direct compositional devices—the cartoon artist's cheap shot—we are placed below the terrifying and angry Hulk, a position we come to hold with Spider-Man (with whom the preceding pages have already made us identify by image and word).[12] This sequence of six pages underscores the temporal experience inherent in a process of reading integrated with seeing and shows us not only how the tale is told but also how it can be carried suspensefully to its conclusion.

Many other narrative structures are employed in the comic book. One is the presentation of successive images that stand alone—the images are not immediately

connected to what comes before or after, neither spatially contiguous nor in temporal sequence (they might be simultaneous snapshots of different locations). When this visual structure is used—analogous to a machine-gun-fire of image after image *brattatatata*—narrative coherence is jeopardized in favor of drama and the visual storytelling can become paratactical, akin to sentences without coordinating connectives (as in "he laughed"; "she cried"). In film it is described as "bad narrative breakdown" or "taking place off camera"[13] where the gaps between cause and effect are too big and create the potential for ambiguity. To counter this undesirable effect, the accompanying text in the comic

12. On the variation of frame size and viewing angle, see Lacassin (see note 10), p. 15.

13. As noted by Carrier (see note 10), p. 55. Think of Roy Lichtenstein's method of excerpting single cells from the comic book's sequential cell structure and making the single cell stand for the whole. The action created interpretative problems for the viewer. See Lawrence L. Abbott, "Comic Art: Characteristics and Potentialities of a Narrative Medium," *Journal of Popular Culture* 19, no. 4 (Spring 1986): 155–176, esp. 155.

Figure 4. Spider-Man and the Hulk. From *Ultimate Marvel Team-Up, Issue 2,* vol. 1, no. 2 (May 2001), pp. 10–11. Published by Marvel Comics, a division of Marvel Enterprises Inc. (Comic book material: ™ and © 2002 Marvel Characters, Inc. Used with permission.)

book becomes heavier to explain the interrelationship between successive visual cells.

Word and image in the Persian book

One of the crucial aspects of experiencing a Persianate painting is that it is seen in a book and is discovered by turning pages, most likely after reading. No illustrated Persian book matches the comic book for rate of illustration, even those literary genres (e.g., historical writing) that retained a higher rate of illustration throughout the fifteenth century and after. The comic book is a constant flow of images, a potential that the Persian book may indeed hold—after all, any number of its stories could be made into images—but never actualized. A small number of developed compositions tends to be the rule. But this distinction touches on only one aspect of difference. Another has to do with a reversal of balance between word and image. The comic book uses text to narrate dialogue or monologue (spoken out loud or said to oneself), conveying sounds

by onomatopoeia and securing meaningful communication between what we see and what we understand. Image and word are completely interdependent in this communicative discourse and indeed the distinction between the two can be blurred.[14] In the Persianate painting, however, image follows after word in a linear sequence; the text introduces and follows after the image, but it is not actually read when the image is being viewed. In other words, although the temporal experience of Persian book and comic book are similar, making sense of a comic book requires a constant shuttling between image and word. In the Persian book the act of seeing is initiated by a process of remembering the narrative just told. Moreover, that text does not prepare the viewer for what will be seen in the painting.

---

14. This occurs through the manipulation of the letter's allographic features (font, color, shape, size). The crumpled edges of *"RUMMBLE"* in fig. 3 serves as an example.

Figure 5. Spider-Man and the Hulk. From *Ultimate Marvel Team-Up, Issue 2,* vol. 1, no. 2 (May 2001), pp. 12–13. Published by Marvel Comics, a division of Marvel Enterprises Inc. (Comic book material: ™ and © 2002 Marvel Characters, Inc. Used with permission.)

So how are subjects chosen for depiction in the Persian book integrated with text? As noted earlier, Khvaju Kirmani's *Three Masnavis* (dated 1396) is held to represent the beginnings of what would become common practice in the Persian book, especially the custom of granting the book a few developed compositions. It serves as a good example of image and word integration. The book comprises three of Khvaju Kirmani's *masnavis* (a poem composed of distichs corresponding in measure and containing a pair of rhymes), the *Humay u Humayun, Kamal-nama* (Book of Perfection), and *Rawzat al-anvar* (Garden of Lights).[15] The texts are independent from each other. Of the three, the first *masnavi* is the most illustrated, having six paintings in all (the entire book contains nine). Two paintings from the first *masnavi*

(fig. 1 and fig. 6) show this technique of bracketing, of how text precedes the image and then follows after it. Although the surface area of the painting expands so considerably that the relevant text can be imperiled, the text is rarely banished from the page. We might sometimes have to hunt to find it, as in these two paintings, but it is almost always there. In both examples, the text is reduced to one couplet of poetry.[16] In the painting of Humayun revealing her female gender to Humay by removing her helmet, after their combat, the text reads "The plain-faring horse kicked up the level ground/And the turning heavens were hidden by dust."

Other paintings in the *Three Masnavis,* for example Malikshah accosted by the old woman in the *Rawzat al-anvar,* have more text embedded in them than the

---

15. London, British Library, Add. 18113, 93 fols., 320 x 235 mm (folio), 181 x 127 mm approx. (text pages). *Nasta'liq* script in four columns, twenty-five lines to the page. *Humay u Humayun,* fols. 1b–49a; *Kamal-nama,* fols. 50b–78b; *Rawzat al-anvar,* fols. 79b–93a.

16. Khvaju Kirmani, *Humay u Humayun,* ed. Kamal Ayni (Tehran: Bunyad-i Farhang-i Iran, 1348 [1969]): fol. 18b, Humay at the gate of Humayun's castle, p. 126, line 4; fol. 23a, Humay recognizing Humayun as she removes her helmet after their fight, p. 147, line 13.

Figure 6. Humay recognizing Humayun as she removes her helmet after their fight. Manuscript painting from the *Three Masnavis* of Khvaju Kirmani, copied by Mir Ali b. Ilyas al-Tabrizi al-Bavarchi, 1396, Baghdad. Opaque pigment and gold on paper, 294 x 202 mm (painted surface). London, British Library, Add. 18113, fol. 23a. (Photo: By permission of The British Library.)

previous two examples[17]—in fact, both paintings in this *masnavi* contain much more text than the paintings in *Humay u Humayun*. In the painting of Malikshah and the old woman, a broad swath of text appears to float over the pictorial space which continues behind to culminate in leafy trees and a golden sky. The five couplets immediately preceding the image describe Malikshah's desire to go hunting, and how on the edge of the Zandarud river an old woman "leapt up and took his rein," saying "'O! You world-conquering king!'"[18] The text quite literally brings us into the here and now of the narrative moment, a threshold that we cross over into the visual realm of the painting. On the next page, the text continues with the old woman's complaint about the king's tyranny and injustice. The *masnavi* section (*hikayat*) treating Malikshah and the old woman is flagged by a block of colored and larger scaled writing, a rubric summarizing the text. Immediately before it come twelve couplets that conclude the preliminary discourse on the "justice of the great" (*mazammat-i kubar*). An identical arrangement is found in the second painting in the *Rawzat al-anvar*, Nushirvan and Buzurgmihr in conversation.

The paintings in the *Three Masnavis* can be divided into two types, but both involve a literal integration between text and image, a staging of the image in which pictorial content is keyed to relevant text. First, there are those with as little as a single couplet carefully selected to serve as a transitional point leading the reader into the painting—these are often the most metaphorical or drama-laden, as in Humay and Humayun in combat.[19]

The second type uses comparatively more text and a textual passage that is a transition between structural elements of the text (moving from a discourse to its example), as in Malikshah accosted by the old woman.

The integration of image with text evidences different kinds of thought and often required significant planning. To introduce a painting with one couplet required the manipulation of the text. The text had to be slowed down to allow for a break at the right moment so that the painting could be allotted a whole page.[20] Slowing the text down required either the addition of couplets or a reduction in the number of couplets that could be copied on a single page. To achieve the desired reduction—for example, eight couplets—some hemistichs were written on a diagonal, filling a space with half as much as it could be made to contain, and the leftover spaces illuminated. Such a manipulation of tempo had the desired result of maximizing the surface area of the painting and of using the text to bring the reader into the painting.

While many Persian books show the close "keying" of image to text, equally numerous are those examples where the painting follows after the folios of text to which it is most directly connected. The danger of a contextual disconnect to the painting's legibility were averted most often than not by an introductory caption, a rubric that encapsulated the proper narrative content of the painting. Such captions appear in manuscripts of the *Shahnama*, such as the Great Mongol copy of the *Shahnama* (fig. 2), and continued to be used in books of the fifteenth and sixteenth centuries. The captions offered another means of bringing the reader into the painting, but what they also did was to enable a sequential viewing of images, or visual study of a single image, without requiring that the text be read. And given that many of these stories and their texts were already

17. Humay u Humayun, ed. Ayni: fol. 3b, Bihzad found by Humay and Azar Afruz drunk, p. 51, lines 15–18, p. 52, lines 1–4 (seven couplets); fol. 12a, Humay at the court of the faghfur of Chin, p. 94, lines 11–12 (two couplets); fol. 40b, Humay and Humayun in a garden feasting and listening to music, p. 203, lines 17–18, and p. 204, lines 1, 5–7, and 13 (seven couplets); fol. 45b, Humay, on day after the wedding, has gold coins poured over him as he leaves Humayun's room, p. 217, line 3 (one couplet). Kamal-nama: fol. 64b, Ali threatening an infidel with his sword (11 couplets). Rawzat al-anvar (Khvaju Kirmani, Rawzat al-anvar, ed. H. Kuhi Kirmani [Tehran: Majlis, 1306/1927]): fol. 85a, Malikshah accosted by an old woman, p. 66, lines 9–20, p. 67, lines 1–5 (seventeen couplets); fol. 91a, Nushirvan and Buzurgmihr in conversation, p. 92, lines 5–17, p. 92, lines 18–20, and p. 93, lines 1–5 (nineteen couplets).

18. Translations taken from Teresa Fitzherbert, "Khwaju Kirmani (689–753/1290–1352): An *Éminence Grise* of Fourteenth Century Persian Painting," Iran 29 (1991): 137–151, 143.

19. Comparing the 1396 manuscript (London) to the earliest dated manuscript of 1349–1350 (Tehran), Fitzherbert shows that the five couplets before the painting of Humay and Humayun in combat do not appear in the Tehran recension. She suggests that this resulted in

the separation from the painting of the couplet most literally connected to it (Fitzherbert [note 18], p. 143), viz., "When the love nourishing king took his dagger / The fairy-faced one drew the helmet from her head." Fitzherbert suggests that the poem's theme (the journey of a soul), told through Humay and Humayun's love, is embodied in the painting by the metaphor of the mirror image. Representing the self coming to self-recognition, it is structured visually by pairs of like things (e.g., figures, horses, trees). The painting invokes *tajnis* (alliteration), a word play that relies on the near-identical shapes of words. In this way, discursive parallels of a figurative order are established between the painting and the specific couplet selected for it (ibid.).

20. For an example, see Marianna Shreve Simpson, *Sultan Ibrahim Mirza's Haft Awrang: A Princely Manuscript from Sixteenth-Century Iran* (Washington, D.C., New Haven, and London: Freer Gallery of Art and Yale University Press, 1997), p. 64.

well known, the absolute functional relationship of text to image is questionable. I can only note the possibility of an act of seeing that was reading-free because the history of Persian reading, especially the cultural practices of reading and the diverse functions of books, remains unwritten. Yet another complication involves the metatextual dimensions of the painting, where a depicted subject can refer to versions of a story other than the one given in its object-carrier (one example discussed later is the seduction of Yusuf from a *Bustan* of Sa'di).[21]

There are other ways to think about how text and image were combined. One is through the various compositional shapes used in books; these may often be stepped, creating a visual fusion with the text columns. The picture's contents may also extend beyond the frame defined by the textblock and into the margins to create an extra-pictorial space and an extra-textual dimension for the image. In the production of most manuscripts, the text was copied on the sheet by the calligrapher before the artist began his work. In this way, the textblock established a framework for the page. It is most often the case that the dominant axes formed by the text serve as anchors for the arrangement of the picture's contents, its figures and architectural structures, as a series of vertical markers, invisible sight-lines. Pages devoted to painting and with as little as one couplet tended to follow this principle of arrangement even though there was no need to do so. Hence, in one way or another, the text is present in the painting regardless of whether or not there is a significant amount of writing.

Monoscenic composition

Persianate paintings tend to use a continuous space that infers a single temporal moment, a representation of one instant in time.[22] In this respect the Persianate painting also differs from the comic book's endless sequence of image cells, although this most common visual technique of structuring narrative in the comic

book was not unprecedented in the Persian art tradition.[23] Although monoscenic narratives appear to be a synchronous moment in time they in fact can be read as several discrete moments running continuously in a *melée* over the picture's surface. The trick is to learn how to read the images, to decipher causes and effects.

It is intriguing that the method chosen to visualize narratives in Persianate paintings was the monoscenic composition arrayed in a developed and detailed painting and not the sequence of paintings showing successive narrative moments in time. One of the aspects that made it a viable choice was the eschewal, or the non-use, of a single-point perspectival scheme to organize elements in a pictorial space. The comic book again becomes useful as a comparative tool. Obviously, comic book images—particularly at the level of the single cell—are derived from a way of showing the world that is photographic, and many of the visual tricks employed in the comic book are remediations of photography.[24] By retaining this perspectival and photographic conception, a larger number of successive image cells is essential—the narrative cannot move forward without them in much the same way that a movie would not be much of a movie with only a handful of celluloid frames. The recurring sequence of images provides constant clarification of relationships between things and it is a way of seeing to which our eyes have become accustomed. For this reason, making sense of Persianate paintings can be a challenging and counter-intuitive enterprise.

A good example is a painting from a *Shahnama* of Firdawsi (fig. 7), datable to ca. 1530 and made in Tabriz for the Safavid ruler Shah Tahmasp. It shows the nightmare of Zahhak. In this painting the tyrannical

---

21. Renata Holod examined the metatextual and metapictorial aspects of painting in Shiraz in the sixteenth century in a conference paper she presented at Harvard University in May 1999.

22. To my knowledge, Kurt Weitzmann was the first to coin the term "monoscenic" (*Illustrations in Roll and Codex: A Study of the Origin and Method of Text Illustration* [Princeton, N.J.: Princeton University Press, 1970). He defined it as "based on the principle of the unity of time and place," and continued, "Now only one single action is represented in a picture, and the increasingly expressive and individualized gestures of all the participants are related to one precise moment" (ibid., p. 14).

23. The best known example is a stain- and overglaze-decorated (*mina'i*) beaker dated to the early thirteenth century (Freer Gallery of Art, Washington, D.C.). Its three tiers show compartmentalized scenes in narrative sequence, each scene one moment from the narrative of Bizhan and Manizha. A large plate in the same ceramic technique and made at the same time, also in the Freer Gallery of Art, depicts a battle in a manner comparable to the complex monoscenic compositions of fifteenth-century book painting. These ceramics show a set of options for depicting narrative.

24. "Remediation" was coined by Jay David Bolter and Richard Grusin in their study of what they term the "double logic of remediation," the simultaneous urge for immediacy and hypermediacy in new media technologies. A large part of their book concerns the ways that new digital media "borrow avidly from each other as well as from their analog predecessors such as film, television, and photography." The combination of media results in hypermediacy (*Remediation: Understanding New Media* [Cambridge, Mass., and London: MIT Press, 1999], p. 9).

Figure 7. The nightmare of Zahhak. Manuscript painting from the *Shahnama-yi Shahi* made for Shah Tahmasp, Tabriz, between ca. 1522 and 1535, fol. 28b. Opaque pigment, gold and silver on paper, 348 x 278 mm (painted surface). Cambridge, Mass., Arthur M. Sackler Museum, Harvard University Art Museums, 0672.1983. (Photo: Courtesy of the Arthur M. Sackler Museum, Harvard University Art Museums, Private Collection.)

ruler Zahhak has just woken from a terrible nightmare in which he meets his nemesis, the hero who will bring an end to the ruler and his injustices. As Zahhak wakes, the palace trembles as if in an earthquake, waking the ladies of the harem. The palace is structured as two tall pavilions connected by an elevated walkway. The largest pavilion rises over a tiled parterre and well-tended gardens lead away from the palace. Although some sense of volume in space is conveyed by axonometry, the spatial logic of the architecture requires that we read it from changing viewpoints to be assumed by our imagination. We must accept that we can see inside the private chambers of Zahhak, and at the same time see from a side view the figures on the roof. We must understand that although the sleeping youth at the lower right straddles the axonometric steps, the man guarding the door above him is literally beyond him, and that the tipped up plane we see the youth sit on is conceived in plan view while the guard is seen from the side. Combinations of viewing perspectives—plans and elevations, interiors and exteriors—occur throughout this painting and others. These techniques permit a multiplicity of pictorial elements to come into the painting, where they create a dense matrix of information. The expectation that perspectives are not static, as in a single-perspectival scheme, allows the viewer to make sense of the composition while its careful design, the manipulation of interval between figures, and the distribution of colors across the painting, knit the image into a unified entity.

A second example of the monoscene is from a *Bustan* (Orchard) by Sa'di dated 1488 and made in Herat for Sultan Husayn Mirza, the last Timurid ruler.[25] In this painting we see a scene from the story of Yusuf and Zulaykha (fig. 8). Zulaykha, Potiphar's daughter, has fallen in love with the prophet Yusuf who was famed for

his beauty. Before the narrative moment represented in the painting, Zulaykha leads Yusuf through a series of seven rooms, each one decorated with erotic themes of lovemaking; she locks each door behind them. The scene depicted is the moment when Zulaykha professes her love for Yusuf and makes amorous advances toward him. She falls to her knees and pulls at his arm. Although Yusuf is hidden away from all witnesses, he realizes that God can still see, and hoping to maintain his chastity, he tries to escape. By some miracle, the doors that Zulaykha has locked will fly open to aid Yusuf's escape.

The painting depicts a dense and complex architectural unit that integrates text into its structure; it is another good example of how text columns can demarcate the major axes of a painting. Once again, deciphering the pictorial space requires shifts of perspective. We read some spaces as views from the outside—like the balcony—and other spaces as cross-sections that are in many respects like a doll's house. Although the seven rooms are not depicted, the complex visual rendering of a sequence of rooms, shown as an interlocking array of trapezoidal planes and vertical rectangles intersected with helter-skeltering text, stands metaphorically for the labyrinthine space that Yusuf has entered and from which he must now escape. And even after he has left this interior and finds his way out to the patio below, he must negotiate a high perimeter wall that is in itself blocked, cut short by the text panels below.

Like the painting showing Zahhak's nightmare, the painting of Yusuf and Zulaykha can be seen as a fusion of single compositional units, a series of contiguous cells that organize the picture. And yet, in each example it is the subject matter of "architecture" that necessitates this visual result. The choice of a monoscenic composition and of opening up all spaces for the eye to see allowed the painting to contain a maximum number of narrative components. In Zahhak's nightmare this allows for the full visual development of the courtly circle, that is, the ruler's harem, guards, attendants, and sundry other palace workers. The painting is populated by numerous figures. In Yusuf and Zulaykha, the content is the architecture: the multiple perspectives fragment architecture to create a metaphorical space that conveys Yusuf's anxiety. Architecture becomes a subject and thus a vehicle of visual narration; the building's fabric is fragmented into relationships of cause and effect; how architecture is made becomes a story.

This way of showing the world in painted form has critical implications for the "story-telling" dimension of

---

25. Cairo, General Egyptian Book Organization, Adab Farsi 908. *Bustan* of Sa'di, 54 fols., 305 mm x 215 mm, copied by Sultan Ali al-Mashhadi. The paintings are: a double-page painting showing a celebration at Sultan Husayn Mirza's court; King Dara and the Herdsman; The Beggar at a Mosque; A discussion at the Court of a Qadi; and The seduction of Yusuf by Zulaykha.

Of interest in this latter example is that the relevant text played a minimal role in informing the artist's depiction of the setting. Lisa Golombek noticed that the text that inspired the painting is actually by the poet Jami, a mystical allegory of Yusuf and Zulaykha completed in 1483. Golombek points out analogies between the painting and Jami's poem, where Zulaykha's palace is "more than a setting for an event. It is a mystical image, a symbol for the splendor of the material world with its seven climes represented as seven rooms" (idem, "Toward a Classification of Persian Painting," in *Islamic Art in the Metropolitan Museum of Art,* ed. Richard Ettinghausen [New York: Metropolitan Museum of Art, 1972], pp. 23–34, 28).

Figure 8. The seduction of Yusuf. Manuscript painting from a *Bustan* of Sa'di, copied by
Sultan Ali al-Katib [al-Mashhadi] for Sultan Husayn Mirza, dated Rajab 893 (June 1488).
Opaque pigment and gold on paper, 305 x 215 mm (folio). Cairo, General Egyptian Book
Organization, Adab Farsi 908. (Photo: Courtesy of Cairo, General Egyptian Book
Organization, Adab Farsi 908, and Los Angeles County Museum of Art.)

the painting. In both of these examples, the initial impression of the monoscene is of a frozen narrative moment, of the eye capturing a split second of activity.[26] This impression is particularly evident in the painting of Yusuf and Zulaykha. We see the two figures only once and at the culminating moment of seduction, and do not see successive images of Yusuf moving through room after room. The multiple figures in Zahhak's palace can also be read as an instantaneous view. And yet, the architecture in each example subdivides the space, creating the potential to read space as time, or spatial interval as time passing.[27] In so doing, the composition emphasizes duration in the beholder's experience of the image.[28]

Time as duration—and not only as instant—enters into the paintings by other means too. By representing multiple perspectives, the paintings do not control the viewer's bodily relationship to surface, as in a single-point perspectival scheme, but allow the viewer's head to move from side to side and up and down. The eye is free to roam over the painting's surface because it does not dictate a fixed position. Another critical aspect of the paintings that doubles their effect of temporal duration is the complexity of gesture, facial expression, and bodily position that we see in the figures that populate the nightmare of Zahhak and other paintings.[29] Interpreting

the actions of single figures and interactions among groups of men and women is a fundamental response. The multifaceted treatment of architecture in Zulaykha's palace produces the same visual effect. What I am proposing is that even if the painting does depict a single moment, our experience of the painting—by the power of its compositional makeup and its many details—occurs over time and reading chains of cause-and-effect is an inevitable interpretation that we apply to the image.[30] Of course, this is true of almost any image that holds the potential to become narrativized, but the intimacy of the painting seen in a book and its miniature size only amplify the effect of time passing. Quite simply put, it takes longer to see.

Medium and materiality

Medium and materiality are critical for the particular ontology of the Persianate painting. It seems accurate to generalize that, ever since the time of Baysunghur's manuscript patronage in the early fifteenth century, artists sought to refine both the materials and execution of painting.[31] Technical virtuosity and perfection of execution became of paramount importance and artists were praised for it in written sources. The preference for "micrographia" is suggested in a progress report (*arzadasht*), written ca. 1430 to Baysunghur, where the writer states: "On the day this report is being written Mawlana Ali is designing a frontispiece illumination for the *Shahnama*. His eyes were sore for a few days."[32] At the end of that century, Khvandamir, the historian and courtier to the last of the Timurid rulers in Iran, Sultan Husayn Mirza (d. 1506), described the artist Bihzad in the following way: "Through his mastery the hair of his [Bihzad] brush has given life to inanimate form / In precision of nature he is hair splitting, and this is no exaggeration."[33] "Hair-splitting" (*mu-shikaf*), an adjective applied originally to the minuteness of the painter's brushes, could equally be used as a synonym for the miracle-working artist. And nearly a century after Khvandamir, Qazi Ahmad looked back to the time of

26. Martin Dickson and Stuart Cary Welch (*The Houghton Shahnameh*, 2 vols. [Cambridge, Mass.: Harvard University Press, 1981], 1:90), describe the painting in this way, likening the nightmare of Zahhak to a moment caught by a fast camera.

27. Noted by Hillenbrand (see note 3), p. 78.

28. The perceived limitations of the narrative when represented as a single moment were noted by Lessing in 1766 (*Laokoon oder über die Grenzen der Malerei und Poesie*), where he suggested that to avert this problem the artist must "choose the instant that is most laden with significance: that which makes most clear all that has preceded and is to follow." To this proposition Husserl's phenomenology added the terms "retentional" and "protentional," described by Kemp as an awareness of the present accompanied by retentions and protentions or memories and expectations. See Wolfgang Kemp, "Narrative," in *Critical Terms for Art History*, ed. Robert S. Nelson and Richard Shiff (Chicago and London: University of Chicago Press, 1992), pp. 58–69, 64.

29. These kinds of complexities in the structuring of narrative were examined by Alois Riegl in his final study *Das holländische Gruppenporträt* (1902). Film studies were quick to develop his propositions, developing the terms diegesis, gaze structure, and scopic regime to discuss "point-of-view identifications" provided by the camera as it was inserted into a "network of glances" (perspectival presentation is the equivalent term used in literature). Riegl focused on "communicated communication," the ways that paintings can convey group cohesions only through specific kinds of relationship with the viewer ("external coherence" by including viewer; "internal coherence" by fiction of non-viewer). See Kemp, note 28, pp. 67–68.

30. Clinton is disturbed by what he sees as paintings' "dramatically intrusive" nature—how the painting "immobilizes characters and action even when the event depicted is embedded in a fluid, ongoing narrative" (see note 5, p. 67).

31. As also noted by Robinson (see note 6), p. 14.

32. Trans. in Wheeler M. Thackston, *Album Prefaces and Other Documents on the History of Calligraphers and Painters*, Studies and Sources in Islamic Art and Architecture 10 (Leiden: Brill, 2001), p. 43.

33. Ibid., p. 42.

Timur: "[Umar Aqta] wrote a copy of the Qur'an in *ghubar* writing; it was so small in volume that it could be fitted under the socket of a signet ring. . . . Umar Aqta wrote another copy, extremely large, each of its lines being a cubit in length and even longer."[34] Umar Aqta's minutely copied Qur'an was not met with favor by Timur, so the calligrapher made the opposite. These and other references in the corpus of written sources imply that the quest for minuteness of execution was an expectation and that it became one of the criteria of aesthetic judgment.[35]

In paintings from the *Chahar Maqala* (Four Discourses) of Nizami Arudi, made for Baysunghur in 1431, the paintings have become increasingly small in dimension, some as little as 102 x 72 mm. The pigment is applied with such perfect execution that no trace of the brush is left; in fact, the execution left no trace of manual production. No matter how close our eyes move to the surface of the picture—and at some point they give up from tiredness—the depicted subjects never give up their identity. Things do not melt away and become patches of factured brushstroke. It is easy to understand why some scholars have likened Persianate paintings to enamel—a hardened medium of bright colors and carefully delineated forms.

In the first decades of the sixteenth century, artists were still working within the limits of pictorial conception defined in the illustrated manuscripts of Baysunghur. In a second painting from Shah Tahmasp's *Shahnama* (fig. 9) we see King Gayumars and his court in a mountain location. The image measures 340 x 230 mm. Although the painting results from the participation of several artists, their individual "hands" have been suppressed to the point that no single element of the painting can be understood as expressive of an individual manner. The mark of the artist has been excised, banished from the act of execution. Like the paintings in Baysunghur's manuscripts, no trace of production, of manufacture, is visible—it is as if the painting came into being spontaneously. The composition of multiple figures and intricate landscape is perfectly designed, intervals between elements and the contours of figures

well considered. The restricted palette is used to unify the surface of the painting and to camouflage certain elements within it, especially the numerous animals located amid the rocks. The density of visual content squeezed into this image—with apparent ease—requires long and patient analysis.

Themes of seeing

There is a wonderful set of oppositions at work in the Persianate painting that results from a unique confluence of factors: they include the dimensions and format of the book, compositional paradigms, spatial conception, and medium and material. The Persianate painting's diagrammatic composition—stacking elements up the page's vertical axis—and its spatial code of multiple points of perspective seem to afford the eye access to everything. Nothing is concealed or positioned out of view. The minute execution of details and the clarity of overall design deepen this impression. Pictorial elements are described and their interrelationships are shown with clarity. There is no indeterminacy. All of these aspects come together to trick us into the belief that we can see everything all at once.

It is a theme of seeing that is illustrated in numerous poetic works, including such subjects as Iskandar peeping at the sirens as they sport by a lake depicted in an anthology made for Iskandar Sultan in Shiraz in 1410, and Farhad before Shirin in a manuscript of *Khusraw and Shirin,* dated to ca. 1420.[36] Both subjects share the theme of seeing—the capacity accorded some individuals to see and not to be seen. In the example of Iskandar (Alexander) and the sirens it is quite easy to find Iskandar and his companion lurking behind the rocks. In the developed and more heavily populated composition, showing the sculptor Farhad coming before the princess Shirin, it takes us longer to find the silent witnesses hidden throughout the palace.

The theme of seeing, of an individual's empowerment through the faculty of vision, occurs in numerous stories in Persian literature. And yet, running against it is the equally common theme of the duplicity of vision, of the trickery of images: the object lesson is that images are never as or what they appear to be despite their apparent claims. Curiously, the formal language of the Persianate painting might be understood as combining these two opposite conclusions. First there is a mirage of clarity, of feeling that one can know and come to

34. Qazi Mir Ahmad, *Gulistan-i hunar,* trans. V. Minorsky, *Calligraphers and Painters: A Treatise by Qadi Ahmad, Son of Mir Munshi* (ca. A.H. 1015/A.D. 1606), Freer Gallery of Art Occasional Papers 3, 2 (Washington, D.C.: Freer Gallery of Art, Smithsonian Institution, 1959), p. 64.

35. In his observations about the Persianate painting, Robinson notes the perfection of execution, following Schroeder, but emphasizes that perfectionism was desired as a means of securing the story's legibility and comprehension (see note 6, p. 13).

36. For illustrations, see Basil Gray, *Persian Painting* (Geneva: Skira, 1961), pp. 54 and 76.

Figure 9. The court of Gayumars. Manuscript painting from the *Shahnama-yi Shahi* made for Shah Tahmasp, Tabriz, ca. 1522–1525, fol. 20b. Opaque pigment and gold on paper, 342 x 231 mm (painted surface). Geneva, Collection Prince Sadruddin Aga Khan. (Photo: Collection Prince Sadruddin Aga Khan.)

understand the Persianate painting all at once. It is an intuition fostered by the monoscenic composition—which combines multiple points of perspective that deny nothing to the eye—and the rigorous execution and unifying effect of color distribution. Despite these formal features, the sheer density of information provided in the painting overwhelms the senses and resists being completely understood. This is Persianate painting's "reality effect," one often remarked on by contemporaries and misunderstood by scholars today (it is read as a culturally coded form of resemblance and not as the dialectic of the experience of seeing). Returning to the painting that we thought we had comprehended only turns up more surprises, things left unnoticed, or the inevitable connections that were never made. This is the source of the Persianate painting's power—the right of endless return. We spend time finding elements we had never noticed in previous viewings, imagining stories within stories, deciphering the actions of figures and the responses that their companions will make. Inevitably these last features opened the way to the passage of time, blocking an "all-at-once" comprehension, although the painting seemed to have acquired its existence in no time.

Signs in the horizons

Concepts of image and boundary in a medieval Persian cosmography

OYA PANCAROĞLU

Encapsulated in the categorical German term *Bilderverbot* ("prohibition of images"), the notion that figural representation does not have a rightful place in Islamic cultures is arguably the most ingrained misconception in the mainstream appreciation of Islamic art. Although the work of art historians has demonstrated the extensive production of figural arts outside the specific contexts of worship from the very rise of Islam onward, a widespread subscription to the idea of an essential socioreligious aversion to figural representation continues to cloud the conventional understanding of Islamic arts and cultures. In this view, the depiction of images is assumed to constitute a breach of religious interdictions and is usually explained in terms of social or ethnic prerogative gaining the upperhand over any spiritual concerns.[1]

Clarifying the place of figural representation in the medieval Islamic world requires going beyond the minutiae of the question of religious permissibility. One valuable avenue in this endeavor is constituted by texts that communicate the cultural fascination with images and image making. Accounts of varying lengths about sundry figural images are contained particularly in medieval geographical writings in which knowledge of the physical terrain of the earth is frequently extended to include narratives about the human-made environment.[2]

Within this genre of writing are certain types of travel literature, manuals of pilgrimage, and hybrid forms of historical accounts which shed light on the contemporary significance of cities, buildings, and images—usually statues and paintings of legendary status. While some of the accounts on images are succinct or simply incidental to the main text, others constitute passages of considerable length. Their value lies primarily in the evidence they offer for the very *concept of the image* in medieval Islamic societies, in the period—to borrow Hans Belting's meaningful expression—"before the era of art."[3]

This essay introduces a remarkable example of medieval Islamic discourse on images and image making incorporated into a late twelfth-century book of cosmography written in Persian. Dedicated to Tughril b. Arslan (r. 1176–1194), the last sultan in the dynasty of the Great Seljuks, Muhammad b. Mahmud b. Ahmad-i Tusi's *ʿAjāʾib al-makhlūqāt* ("Wonders of Creation") is a systematically organized exposition of the knowledge of creation imparted primarily by means of engaging descriptions and edifying stories.[4] The popular flavor of the text is counterbalanced by its logical structure achieved by the arrangement of the chapters according to the Aristotelian conception of a hierarchically ordered universe. Beginning with the celestial spheres, Tusi devotes individual chapters to the consecutive components of creation. Descriptions of the heavens,

---

1. Thomas W. Arnold's influential work, *Painting in Islam* (Oxford: Clarendon Press, 1928), is typical of early twentieth-century scholarship which propagated such simplistic formulae which still prevail beyond the limited sphere of scholars and students of Islamic art. For example, Arnold claimed that "with few exceptions, [. . .] disregard of the Sacred Law [vis-à-vis figural representation] found expression rather in the interior of the palace than under the public eye [. . .] The Muslim monarch, therefore, generally kept his indulgence in forbidden tastes concealed from all except his intimates" (p. 19).

2. An excellent introduction to this type of literature is André Miquel, *La géographie humaine du monde musulman jusqu'au milieu du 11e siècle. Géographie arabe et représentation du monde: la terre et l'étranger* (Paris: Mouton, 1975). One geographical work which is particularly fruitful in this regard is Ibn al-Faqīh's *Kitāb al-buldān* ("Book of Countries"), written ca. 903 [edited by M. J. de Goeje (Leiden: E. J. Brill, 1885); French translation: *Abrégé du Livre des Pays*, trans. Henri Massé (Damascus: Institut Français de Damas, 1973)].

3. Hans Belting, *Likeness and Presence: A History of the Image before the Era of Art,* trans. Edmund Jephcott (Chicago: Chicago University Press, 1994).

4. Muḥammad b. Maḥmūd b. Aḥmad-i Ṭūsī, *ʿAjāʾib al-makhlūqāt,* ed. M. Sotūde (Tehran: Tehran University Press, 1345/1966). Based on internal evidence and the dedication, the book is dated to the years between 562/1167 and 573/1194; see editor's introduction, pp. 17–19. See also Ziva Vesel, *Les encyclopédies persanes. Essai de typologie et de classifications de science* (Paris: Editions Recherches sure les Civilisations, 1986), pp. 33–34. An illustrated manuscript of the book dated 1388 is in the Bibliothèque Nationale, Paris (Suppl. persan 332); see Francis Richard, *Splendeurs persanes: manuscrits du XIIe au XVIIe siècle* (Paris: Bibliothèque nationale de France, 1997), p. 71 and Taraneh Fotouhi, "Les illustrations d'un manuscrit persan de la Bibliothèque nationale: 'Le livre des merveilles de la Création,'" *Histoire de l'Art* 4 (1988): 41–52.

the sublunar phenomena, and the physical earth with its climes and countries are followed by chapters devoted to the animal and vegetal realms. The seventh chapter entitled "The excellence of man and the wonders of his nature" (fī sharaf al-ādamī wa ʿajāʾib fiṭratihi) is a lengthy account of various aspects of the human species, including descriptions of the intellect, the soul, social classes, tribes, and nobility, followed by "human interest" sections on alchemy, medicine, predestination vs. free will, science of the soul, oneiromancy, and resurrection. The stage for this extensive chapter about the nature and experience of humankind is set in the preceding chapter, which consists of four sections entitled as follows: "The wonders of carved and painted images" (fī ʿajāʾib al-ṣuwar al-manqūr[a] wa'l-manqūsha), "Strange images" (fī al-ṣuwar al-gharība), "The mention of tombs and their wonders" (fī dhikr al-qubūr wa ʿajāʾibihā), and "The mention of treasures" (fī dhikr al-kunūz).[5] The aim of this essay is to introduce Tusi's discussion of images contained in the first two sections of the sixth chapter of his cosmography and to identify the significance of this text for understanding, at least in part, the role of images in the medieval Islamic imagination. A summary of the two sections on images is followed by an analysis of the text, and a consideration of its relationship to the remainder of the chapter and to a book of cosmography. The analysis of this significant document is conceived as a preliminary contribution to a text-based theoretical understanding of the concept of the image in the medieval Islamic world.[6]

The narrative of images

Tusi's discourse on images and image making is essentially a collection of stories and descriptions which is intended to elicit the wonder response from the reader and to support statements made in the beginning such

as: "Know that many images have been made on earth for the sake of admonition so that [people] may take heed of them."[7] This explanation of the purpose of image making is illustrated immediately by the story of the Sasanian king Khusraw Parviz, who is said to have wept at the sight of a relief carving of his legendary horse, Shabdiz, because the stillness of the likeness reminded him of death (fig. 1). Tusi follows this story with a second statement which expands the first explanation: "Know that image-making is unlawful but it affects the soul."[8] Together, these two opening statements carefully endorse image making by underscoring the didactic and affective potential of images. They prompt the reader to be cognizant of the moralizing and psychological dimensions of the accounts of images beyond their immediately entertaining or awe-inspiring effect and aside from any objection that might be raised against representational images. This cognizance of the ultimate value of images, Tusi tells the reader in the closing statement of the second section of the chapter, is a means to understand that God

> created man so that with ingenuity he is able to make such works. If all [of these accounts of images] are truthfully conveyed, then they are among the works of God. If they are fabricated, we have no proof [of that] for we have related what has been conveyed. God knows best.[9]

Between the initial announcements about purpose and the final linkage of image making to the signs of God's creation cautiously phrased like a disclaimer, Tusi

---

5. Ṭūsī (see note 4), pp. 331–369 (pp. 331–343, two sections on images; pp. 343–358, section on tombs; and pp. 358–369, section on treasures).

6. Recently, new theoretical approaches to the role of images in Islamic cultures have been undertaken but these have concentrated more specifically on the idea of portraiture rather than images per se; see for example, Priscilla Soucek, "The Theory and Practice of Portraiture in the Persian Tradition," Muqarnas 17 (2000): 97–108 and Yves Porter, "La forme et le sens. À propos du portrait dans la littérature persane classique," in Pand-o Sokhan. Mélanges offerts à Charles-Henri de Fouchécour, ed. Christophe Balaÿ et al. (Tehran: Institut Français de Recherche en Iran, 1995), pp. 219–231. There have also been new and notable studies on the concept of depiction (taṣwīr) especially in early modern Persian art historical writing; see in particular David Roxburgh, Prefacing the Image: The Writing of Art History in Sixteenth-Century Iran (Leiden: E. J. Brill, 2001).

7. Badān ka ṣurathā dar ʿālam bisyār karda-and az bahr-i mavāʿiẓ tā az ān ʿibrat gīrand; Ṭūsī (see note 4), p. 331. The word ṣurat (pl. ṣūrat-hā or ṣuvar) is used almost exclusively throughout the text to denote "image." Where the context allows a differentiation to be made between painting and sculpture (freestanding or relief) or indicates a portrait of an individual, I have translated accordingly. Otherwise, I have retained the word "image" wherever Tusi uses ṣūrat. It is also worth noting that many, but not all, of the stories related by Tusi may be readily found in both earlier and later writings ranging from the geographical and historical to the literary and art historical. For the purposes of this introductory essay, which is concerned not with Tusi as author and/or compiler but rather with his approach to the topic of images, I have left out references to his possible sources and discussion of the various versions of some of the accounts. Needless to say, a more extensive study of this chapter (as well as the entirety of the book) requires an interdisciplinary approach. I would like to thank Dominic Brookshaw for his assistance in the transliteration and translation of the Persian text.

8. Badān ka ṣūrat kardan ḥarām ast valīkan dar dil-hā ta'thīr kunad; ibid.

9. ādamī-rā āfarīnad kay ba-kiyāsat chunīn ṣanʿat-hā dānad kard. Īn jumlat agar rāst naql karda-and az ṣunʿ-i āfarīdgār būd va agar durūgh gufta-and mā-rā burhānī nabūd va ān-cha gufta-and naql kardī m va'llāhu aʿlam; ibid., p. 343.

Figure 1. Sasanian relief carving at Taq-i Bustan. (Photograph from F. Sarre, *Die Kunst des Alten Persien* [Berlin, 1923], fig. 85.)

introduces numerous statues, relief carvings, and paintings either in the context of stories reported about them or simply by providing a description of them. At first glance, this collection of stories and descriptions seems like a loosely organized gazetteer of images situated in random distant lands or past times and reported to have talismanic qualities. Tusi's writing provides only the occasional explicit statement to indicate the logical connection between the consecutive stories. However, a closer reading suggests that there are in fact loose categories of accounts which speak to various aspects of image making and that both sections are structured on the logical thematic progression of these accounts (see Appendix for outline of the two sections).

The opening statements on the didactic and affective significance of image making are accompanied by three stories which illustrate these functions. One of these, as mentioned above, depicts the potential of images to alter the emotional state of those such as Khusraw Parviz who will reflect upon them and be reminded of such eternal truths as death. The second story narrates an exchange of portraits between Alexander and Aristotle.

By noticing the facial flaws visible in their respective portraits, the great conqueror and his wise teacher question each other about the ultimate cause of these flaws and mutually derive a lesson about life. The capacity of images to convey more than just visual data is related in the third story, which relates that an Iranian king had commissioned a portrait of the prophet Muhammad during his lifetime. This portrait was subsequently used by a diviner in the service of the king to foretell the enduring triumph of the Prophet's message. Images in each of these stories trigger an intellectual or emotional response which is then used to arrive at a lesson or a truth.

The third story in this opening segment provides a transition to the next six accounts, which form a thematic group illustrating the power of talismanic images to reveal Islam as a faith of universal validity and extent. The first three accounts, situated in the time of the early Islamic conquests, are also related in a number of well-known geographical and historical writings predating Tusi. In the first story, entitled "Portraits of the Prophets" (*ṣūrat al-anbiyā'*), Tusi relates a report given by an embassy of Muslims to the Byzantine court in

Constantinople. The Byzantine emperor shows the Muslims a box containing portraits of the prophets from Adam to Muhammad painted on silk and tells them that he has secretly sworn by Muhammad. This account is followed by a short entry on the statue of an armed rider on camelback in Rome. The founder of the city is said to have warned the citizens about possible future conquerors on camelback, presumably referring to Arabs. The third story is perhaps the most widely disseminated of all; it describes the legendary locked house in Toledo. It is reported that when Lazríq (Roderic, the last Visigothic ruler of Spain) broke its many locks and entered this forbidden house, against the advice of the local deacons, he saw an image of a spear-wielding Arab on camelback and an inscription warning that once the house is broken into, the fall of Spain to the Arab armies will ensue. The prophecy is fulfilled soon thereafter.

Tusi's next story in this grouping is about three copper statues hidden in Constantinople, identified as the likenesses of Bilal, Muhammad, and Ali, each represented with some distinguishing attribute. Bilal, the first muezzin, is depicted with his hand placed on his ear. Muhammad's statue is said to carry an inscription in Greek stating: "This is the statue of the Prophet of the Last Day. Whenever a limb of this statue is broken, two-sixths of the world will be destroyed. If another limb is broken, four-sixths of the world will be devastated."[10] Ali is represented on horseback striking a serpent with a spear. The people of Constantinople hide these statues to prevent any damage from occurring to them as this is known to have triggered devastating earthquakes in the past.

The last two instances of images discussed in this grouping are each set in a comparatively lengthy story about a Muslim who is marooned in a distant land where he witnesses some form of visual testament to Islam. The first testament takes place in a far eastern land where a piece of onyx containing a human image is discovered and reported to protect against famine; it is identified by the expatriate Muslim as the likeness of Muhammad. When the king of the land learns about the identity of the image, he orders that the Muslim be expelled lest his subjects find out and abandon their own religion. The second testimony is situated in a country in the far western end of the world where, every

time a calamity occurs, the people ask for intercession from two portraits held in a church; according to the Muslim who was present at one such event, these are portraits of Adam and Muhammad.

The second section of the chapter begins with descriptions of various talismanic images in different parts of the world. These are prefaced by Tusi's reflection on the nature of such images and his reason for writing about them:

> We will relate another section on other images which are talismanic so that you will know that the Creator gives divine inspiration to His subjects to make such wonders. And you know that is from His might, not from the might of the created one, just as you do not consider writing as [coming] from the pen but from the hand of the writer.[11]

These talismanic images include a statue in Turkestan believed to make water appear in times of draught, a singing statue near India which has fallen on its side, the giant Buddha statues of Bamiyan perceived to smile when the sun shines on them (fig. 2), an Indian statue functioning as a fountain, an extraordinary colossus in Spain warning travelers with an inscription that the road ends here, and a copper statue in Alexandria pointing in the direction of Constantinople. This last statue is said to have been melted down to make coins on the order of the Umayyad caliph Abd al-Malik who died only a few days later. Tusi's narrative advances the idea that these miscellaneous wonders are conceptually unified in their mysterious testament to God's will which manifests itself through the talismanic action of statues. The pointer statues in Alexandria and Spain function as ominous and miraculous signs which test human judgment. On the other hand, the fountain statues, the singing statue, and the Buddhas of Bamiyan with their benevolent characteristics are understood to be attuned to God's goodwill toward humankind. About the Buddhas of Bamiyan Tusi relates the following:

> In the region of Bamiyan, there is a place called "Astar Bahar." They have made two statues, each one 250 cubits tall with crowns on their heads. They call one "White Idol" and the other "Red Idol." In their nose, pigeons have nests. When the sun rises, they both smile. This I have seen in many books but the meaning of their smile is not known, God knows best. This smile should not be [thought] strange

---

10. *In ṣūrat-i payghambar-i ākhir al-zamān ast har gah az īn ṣūrat-i ʿuḍvī judā shavad dudāng-i ʿālam tabāh gardad, agar ʿuḍvī dīgar judā shavad chahārdāng-i ʿālam kharāb gardad;* ibid., p. 333.

11. *Va mā faṣlī dīgar yād kunīm dar ṣūrat-hā-yi dīgar kī ba-tilism-hā karda-and tā badānī ka āfarīdgār bandagān-rā ilhām dahad kay chunīn shigiftī kunand va ān az qudrat-i vay dānī na az qudrat-i makhlūq chunān ka kitābat na az qalam bīnī balī az dast-i kātib bīnī;* ibid. p. 336.

for whatever the sun shines on cheerfulness and joviality appear in it and that thing inclines toward the sun.[12]

Tusi begins the next segment with a story tracing the tradition of portraiture and image veneration among the "infidels" (kuffār) to an apprentice of Idris who made a likeness of his master upon his death. The portrait was made from gold and placed on a throne before which the apprentice prostrated everyday. This practice was continued by his followers and became established as a tradition. Tusi's final remark in this account, seemingly uncritical of image veneration, affirms the magnitude of the tradition thus established: "Great works in the world arise from small things."[13] Yet this remark also provides the argument of the next two stories which illustrate how seemingly inoffensive acts can contain the danger of deviating from the practice of true belief. The first story exemplifying this hazard is not about images as such but about a man who gained access to the Abbasid caliph Harun al-Rashid and asked permission to burn 500 maunds of aloe at the Ka'ba. Harun's initial enthusiasm for this man's generosity turned sour when an investigation revealed that his true intention was to turn the Ka'ba into a fire-temple as he was in fact a Magian fire-worshipper. The second account in this segment tells the story of one of Solomon's wives who asked for permission to keep a portrait of her father to remember him by. Unbeknownst to Solomon, she venerated the image by prostrating before it until Solomon's counselor Asaf found out and advised him to destroy the idol. Ultimately responsible for this grave transgression in his household, Solomon was punished by losing his kingdom for forty days. Both stories demonstrate the potential pitfalls in seemingly harmless acts—whether making a likeness or burning sweet-smelling wood—if the true intention behind them constitutes a transgression of the strict monotheism of Islam. This puts a cautionary spin on Tusi's seemingly

Figure 2. Buddha statue at Bamiyan. (Photograph from A. Godard, *Les antiquités bouddhiques de Bamiyan* [Paris, 1928], pl. 10.)

---

12. *Va dar ḥudūd-i Bāmiyān jā'ī ast ān-rā "Astar Bahār" khvānand, du ṣūrat karda-and har yak davīst u panjāh arsh, tājhā bar sar nahāda, yakī-rā khing but khvānand yakī-rā surkh but, dar bīnī-i īshān kabūtar lāna dārad. Har gah āftāb bar āyad har du bakhandand. Īn dar basī kutub-hā dīda-am va ma'nā-yi khanda-yi īshān ma'lūm na, va'llāhu a'lam va īn khanda 'ajab nabāshad ka āftāb bar harcha mīāyad dar vay bashāshatī va faraḥī ẓāhir mīgardad va ān shayy ba-āftāb mayl mīkunad;* ibid., p. 337. In the aftermath of their senseless destruction in the spring of 2001, the affectionate reception of these statues in the medieval period as conveyed by Ṭūsī's account makes the tally of recent cultural casualties of war-torn Afghanistan all the more poignant.

13. *Va kār-hā-yi mu'aẓẓam dar jahān az chīz-hā-yi andak barkhīzad;* ibid., p. 338.

enthusiastic remark appended to the story of Idris's portrait and adds a critical nuance to his comment in the very beginning of the chapter about the unlawful nature of image making.

The remainder of Tusi's discourse in the second section consists of a descriptive list of various wondrous images, followed by an excursive account of the image of Khusraw Parviz's horse Shabdiz with which the chapter had begun. Tusi once again emphasizes the moralizing effect of this legendary image depicted as if alive and mentions the necessity of divine inspiration in producing it. He also provides an extensive visual description of the depiction of Shabdiz and his armed rider, clearly in reference to the celebrated relief carving at Taq-i Bustan (fig. 1). Tusi attributes this image and others in the vicinity to Farhad, providing a convenient segue to the story of this architect–sculptor in the service of Khusraw Parviz who haplessly fell in love with Shirin, Khusraw's virtuous wife, and also made a portrait of her. Another story about Shirin follows, this one regarding Khusraw's parricide Shiruya who harrasses his stepmother, the widow Shirin, to marry him. To escape his evil intentions, Shirin first deceives him and then commits suicide. "This story is related," Tusi informs the reader at the end, as if to justify this narrative digression, "for [the purpose of describing] this woman's virtue. We have adduced it for the sake of morality."[14] The section finally concludes with another list of wondrous images—these consisting mostly of animals—and Tusi's final remark, mentioned above, locating remarkable images among the signs of God and calling for due contemplation.

The testimony of images

Many of Tusi's stories and descriptions in these two sections discuss images that are peripheral to Islam in terms of either geography or chronology. Some of these clearly predate Islam while others are set in lands beyond the abode of Islam. Of course, the element of wonder is magnified as the image basks in the mysterious glow of distance from the here and now. Yet this gap between Islam and the images discussed by Tusi should not be interpreted as a device to disassociate the two. It is quite clear that Tusi wished to present the wonder of these remote images not only as manifestation of God's work through humankind but also as affirmation of Islam's universal validity and magnitude. Moreover,

the chronological distance implied in the "historical" presentation of the accounts is mitigated, at least psychologically, by the inclusion of figures such as Alexander or Solomon who are routinely seen in a positive light in Islam as true believers. Likewise, though the geographical settings may be non-Islamic, they are situated in lands such as Byzantium, the Maghrib, India, and Central Asia, which delineate the ever-moving threshold of Islam. Described as standing just beyond the edge of the world and age of Islam, many of the images included in Tusi's text, therefore, function as markers of the territorial and symbolic boundaries between divergent identities existing in contiguous spaces or times.

As an example of an image associated with the idea of territorial boundary, the colossal copper statue in Spain declaring, through its inscription, the end of the road is said to point out the limit of the known world and to stand as a warning to those who would dare to undertake a journey into the realm of the unknown. Here, the immovable image, which is remarkable for its size and craftsmanship and attributed by Tusi to the mysterious workings of divine inspiration, literally and figuratively embodies the portentous demarcation between charted and uncharted territory.[15] Conversely, the portable image is presented as a mediator of the physical distance between humans, conveying information which verbal communication can miss. The exchange of portraits between Alexander and Aristotle, who are said to be separated from each other by a great distance, is portrayed as a virtual encounter between two individuals. The portraits provoke questions resulting in serious reflection at both ends which leads to greater understanding about the important things in life. Similarly, the portrait of the Prophet commissioned by an Iranian king becomes a visual intermediary between the Prophet's message and the king's diviner who, on the basis of the portrait, foretells the victory of Islam. Through the portable image, information is gathered and

---

14. *in ḥikāyat az ʿiffat-i in zan bāz gūyand va mā in-rā irād kardim az bahr-i favāyid;* ibid., p. 342.

15. "Humankind is unable to comprehend how they made this statue since some say that it rose from the ground or came down from the heavens, for it could not have been beaten by a hammer nor poured into a mold as no human has the strength or skill to craft such a thing except for he who must have made it with the inspiration of the Creator or with prophetic miracle;" (*ʿālamiyān dar ān ʿājiz-and kay in ṣūrat-rā chūn kardand tā baʿḍī gūyand az zamin rusta ast yā az falak āmada ast, zirā ka ba-miṭraqa natavān zadan va ba-qālib natavān rikhtan, zirā ka bani ādam-rā ān qudrat va ān istiʿdād na-bāshad kay ān chunān chizī-rā batavānand sākht magar ān-kas ki ān karda bāshad ba-ilhām-i āfaridgār karda bāshad yā ba-muʿjiz-i nubuvvat;* ibid., pp. 337–338).

knowledge is expanded in ways that distinguish the importance of visual communication and narrow the physical and psychological distance between individuals and events.

On a more symbolic level, Tusi presents talismanic images hidden away in Christian or pagan lands as revealers of the preordained success of Islam in spreading far and wide. In general, the non-believers recognize and fear the power of these images but their comprehension falls short of their ultimate significance. When the images are tampered with, they display their talismanic powers. The legendary house in Spain was guarded by generations of rulers by the addition of locks until Roderic, the last Visigothic king, decided to ignore the warnings and enter it. Inside, he saw a depiction of an Arab warrior and an inscription signaling the imminent conquest of Spain. The statues of Bilal, Muhammad, and Ali in Constantinople are guarded fiercely by the locals because both inscription and experience tells them that damage to the limbs of the talismanic statue of Muhammad, labeled in Greek as the "Prophet of the Last Day," will set off a devastating earthquake. The revealed identities of these messianic images embodying Islam at the threshold also point to the appointed triumph of God's will. In the case of Spain, the triumph heralded by the revelation of the concealed image of Toledo has already come to pass. By extension, the reader may surmise that the fate of Constantinople, at the immediate periphery of medieval Islamdom and already marked by the talismanic statues of the messenger of Islam and two of his closest followers, cannot be any different. The idea seems to be that the mysterious presence of these talismanic images denotes Islam's divinely sanctioned claim on these lands whose geographically external status is bound to be transformed. Once the concealed images are exposed, the status quo will be drastically altered and the boundary will shift in favor of Islam. The same idea is conveyed in the story about the expatriate Muslim who identifies a talismanic image on an onyx as the likeness of Muhammad. He is swiftly expelled from the country by the king who fears that revealing the true identity of the talismanic image will lead to his defeat by Islam.

The presence of these images implies that Islam has already appropriated these regions but that its mission remains latent until the images and their identities are revealed and accepted. This covert yet messianic presence of the image perforates the seemingly unambiguous boundary between true belief and misguided belief, particularly in the case of Constantinople, which is home

not only to the three talismanic statues but also to the legendary chest containing portraits of the prophets from Adam to Muhammad said to be painted on silk by Daniel. The Byzantine emperor, who is the custodian of the chest, secretly reveals to his Muslim visitors that he has sworn by the portrait of Muhammad although he has kept this a secret from his army. Tusi's version of this widely disseminated story does not clarify whether the emperor knew the true identity of the last portrait and therefore consciously put his faith in Muhammad and Islam or if he simply swore by the last prophet represented in the genealogical sequence of prophetic portraits contained in the chest and had thereby unconsciously ventured into Islam. In either case, the story illustrates the role played by images in planting the seed of Islam which will certainly come to fruition once the ultimate truth of the visual testament is recognized and proclaimed. The emperor's reluctance to share the visual testament with his soldiers is perhaps meant to signify his inability to recognize the predestined nature of Islam's political, territorial, and spiritual victories over the Judeo–Christian tradition. Even as he conceals the chest, the portraits contained therein constitute an irrefutable testament to the message entrusted to Muhammad and serve as a preexistent beacon for the preordained victory of Islam. True faith as revealed to Muslims has already penetrated Byzantium; its visual presence is witnessed by the Muslim envoys but awaits recognition and restitution.

Another version of the testament provided by the sequence of prophetic portraits appears in the story of the Muslim expatriate stranded in the far western reaches of the world. This Muslim witnesses the locals showing reverence to the images of Adam and Muhammad—a visual abridgment of the sequence of prophets achieved by reference to the first and last prophet—every time a miracle or a calamity occurs in their land. The locals relate some of the calamities which occurred in the past and which ended when they prayed for the intercession of these two images. The Muslim identifies the events as miracles of the Prophet mentioned in the Koran, such as the birds who cast stones from the sky to crush the Abyssinians as they attempted to destroy the Kaʿba in the year of the Prophet's birth (Chapter 105) and the cleaving of the moon (Chapter 54: 1). His identification unites both the images of Adam and Muhammad and the accounts of the ominous events under the banner of prophetic miracle, demonstrating that the extent of the divine sanction of Islam is intelligible through deeds and images alike.

From images to tombs and treasures:
Markers of liminality

The relationship between human images and human boundaries constructed in Tusi's discourse in the first two sections of the cosmography's sixth chapter points to a remarkable interpretation of images as testimony. Indicating the temporary border between ignorance and revelation, the images stand on the brink of preordained transformation and herald the coming of a new age. The messianic character of the talismanic images, especially of those in concealment, qualifies them to be counted "among the works of God" as humans were divinely inspired to create them. At the end of the second section Tusi calls his readers to contemplate these images as signs of God, providing a pivotal segue to the last two sections of the chapter dealing with tombs and treasures. Echoing, by their very nature, the theme of concealment, tombs and treasures join images by analogy to illustrate the function of signs and boundaries in human existence.

As signs representing the deceased, tombs mark the loci of passage from this world to the hereafter and signify the one boundary which all humans will ultimately cross. Tusi devotes the first part of his narrative to tombs of the prophets from Adam to Daniel and other holy personages such as the Seven Sleepers who, as exemplary human beings and agents of God's will on earth, constitute a chain of testimony to divine inspiration and revelation. Tombs are also permanent reminders of human mortality; contemplation of tombs therefore constitutes one of the more valuable lessons in life. This is evident particularly in the remainder of the section in which tombs of such legendary kings as Alexander are discussed in the context of moralizing tales told about them. The transience of human life stands in stark contrast to the permanence of funerary memorials; in this regard, tombs teach the same ethical lessons which Tusi ascribes to the affective power of images. This aspect of tombs is reminiscent, for instance, of the story of Shabdiz's relief portrait which moved Khusraw Parviz to the point of tears because he was able to feel and understand, through the permanently motionless image, the certainty of death in contrast to the transient animation of human life. Thus, Tusi advances the idea that images and tombs similarly function as intermediaries between the visible (life on earth) and the invisible (passage to the hereafter), between what is known and what is to be revealed. For Tusi, the kind of testimony provided by tombs and images may be said to reveal their ultimate value for expanding one's understanding of the workings of God's design for humankind.

The connection established by Tusi between images and tombs by means of juxtaposition and thematic parallelism has its roots embedded in early Islamic discourse. An example from *ḥadīth* literature shows that the conceptual and physical alliance between the two had already been recognized in early Islam and debated as a matter of lawfulness. According to this *ḥadīth,* the Prophet Muhammad denounced the practice of prayer at grave sites over which tomb structures are built and decorated with paintings.[16] No doubt the connection observed between the two and the criticism leveled against such constructs was informed by the Christian cult of saints in which both relics and images were venerated as equal conduits to experiencing the presence of a deceased saint.[17] The main difference between Tusi's discourse and the Christian practice is that the former explicitly denounces the act of veneration in line with Islam's strict position on idolatry and calls instead on human reason to contemplate the lessons contained in such visual signs. Apart from this crucial difference, however, Tusi's textual juxtaposition and analogous interpretation of tombs and images are nonetheless evocative of the joint Christian cult of relics and images.

The fourth and final section of the chapter is devoted to the subject of treasures associated with legendary figures and kings such as Alexander and Kaykhusraw. Treasures by their very nature of being buried or hidden in some other manner easily speak to the theme of concealment which characterizes Tusi's discussion of tombs and images. As Tusi advises his readers, treasures are also intimately connected with acts of divine revelation:

> Know that there are many treasures in the world and all are the hereditary property of others. Many remain buried under the earth and no one can find the way to the secret [of their location] unless the Creator informs someone about it.[18]

The existence and location of buried treasures are thus revealed to individuals in their dreams or through the agency of enlightened men.

---

16. For references to the collections in which this *ḥadīth* appears, see Daan van Reenen, "The *Bilderverbot,* a new survey," *Der Islam* 67 (1990), pp. 50, 77.

17. The analogy between images and relics in medieval Byzantium and western Europe is discussed in Belting (see note 3), pp. 59–63 and 301–303.

18. *Badān ka kunūzhā-yi ᶜālam bisyār būd va hama murdarīg-i dīgarān shud va basā kī dar zīr-i khāk-hā bamānad va kas rah ba-sirr-i ān namībarad magar kay āfarīdgār kasī-rā iṭṭilāᶜ dahad bar ān;* Ṭūsī, p. 361.

The section on treasures begins with a cautionary mention of the biblical story of Qarun (Korah) as described in the Koran (Chapter 28: 76–82). Bestowed with indescribable wealth, Qarun became arrogant and thought himself invincible and was ultimately punished by God when He made the earth swallow up the transgressor and his possessions. Qarun's legendary wealth then became a hidden treasure waiting to be discovered by others. This Koranic story of admonition extends the didactic current underlying Tusi's section on tombs to the section on treasures and thereby elevates treasures to the same status as images and tombs which, if contemplated properly, reveal themselves to be signs of God to humankind. Man's relationship to treasures hidden from sight mirrors the extent of his fortune and wisdom in tandem with the vanity of the material world. On the one hand, the role ascribed to divine revelation in the discovery of treasures is an indication of the favor which God occasionally chooses to bestow on certain individuals by showing them the path to riches unattainable by ordinary humans. On the other hand, the material wealth that constitutes treasures, no matter how great, is a worldly delusion which will be revealed as such to all in death, if not before. In this connection Tusi relates the story of King Zahhak who attempted to defy the inevitable transience of the wealth that he had amassed during his tyrannic reign by carefully hiding it. Ultimately, it was discovered by others who in turn became rich.

Treasures, whether hidden or discovered, are recurrent reminders of the bounded nature of earthly existence in which material wealth passes from hand to hand but always accompanies its owner only as far as the end of life. Without the necessary wisdom, humans are deluded by the material wealth of treasures and are unable to recognize the bounty as a sign of God's design for humankind. With wisdom comes recognition and transcendence of the material limits of human life. In this regard, Tusi's juxtaposition of images, tombs, and treasures is very much in line with the contemporary poet Nizami's exploration of these three themes as crucial linked motifs in the *Haft Paykar* (completed in 1197), an allegorical romance about the Sasanian ruler Bahram Gur's journey to enlightenment.[19] In the beginning of the romance, the young prince fortuitously discovers a great treasure hidden in a cave and carts it off as material gain to his palace. After he acceeds to the throne, Bahram Gur discovers another "treasure," this one consisting of portraits of the princesses of the Seven Climes of the earth surrounding his own portrait mysteriously painted in a secret room of his palace. The beauty of the portraits compels Bahram Gur to seek out the seven princesses and to make them his brides. The king's ethical enlightenment is initiated by the moralizing tales told to him by each of his brides. At the end of his spiritual progress to wisdom, Bahram Gur is once again led to a cave from which he never reemerges and his remains are never found. In his mysterious disappearance, the king transcends the material limits of life on earth and, as one who has attained the true treasure of wisdom, gives "his kingly treasure to the cave."[20] Nizami thus uses the rich symbolism of caves and secret rooms—spaces which offer invisibility—as the loci of hidden treasures, propitious images, and as passageway to the hereafter.[21]

Nizami's conceptual manipulation of these three motifs in the allegory about human perfectibility strongly parallels and clarifies Tusi's own handling of images, tombs, and treasures as testaments to the nature of human existence in God's universal design. As a preamble to the subsequent chapter on "The excellence of man and the wonders of his nature," Tusi's sixth chapter occupies a pivotal role in his cosmography. The urge to derive lessons from images, tombs, and treasures as interrelated signs of God is part and parcel of the endeavor to discern the workings of the design of creation by drawing attention to some of the boundaries which are integral to it. This is all the more significant in the context of the cosmography which is an all-inclusive description of a harmonious universe arranged according to a divinely ordained yet humanly intelligible system of interrelated forces and structures operating on the hierarchical continuum between the heavens and the earth. Humankind, entrusted with God's revelation, occupies the central position in the hierarchy depicted in Tusi's cosmography and, in accordance with the Koranic prescription, is charged with the responsibility of discerning God's "signs in the horizons and within themselves until it is clear to them that it is the Truth" (Chapter 41: 52). By bringing together three markers of the movable limits of human experience before the chapter devoted to the nature of humankind, Tusi provides the ethical and symbolic framework necessary to understand the place of man in the design of God's creation.

19. Nizami Ganjavi, *Haft Paykar: A Medieval Persian Romance,* trans. Julie Scott Meisami (Oxford: Oxford University Press, 1995).

20. Ibid., p. 259 (chapter 52, line 27).
21. For a discussion of the symbolism invested in the structure and themes of the *Haft Paykar* see the introduction by Meisami, ibid., pp. xxiv–xxxiv.

Conceptualizing the image in medieval Islamic cultures

Tusi's sixth chapter is an exceptionally meaningful source for understanding the role played by the concept of the image in medieval Islamic thought and culture. On the basis of this preliminary analysis of the sections on images and their semantic relationship to tombs and treasures in the context of the cosmography, it is possible to discern aspects of a sophisticated, multivalent conceptualization of the image. According to Tusi, the ultimate value of images lies, in the first instance, in the lessons they impart through the catalysis of wonder. Expressed through a pious stance, Tusi's validation of images seeks to realign human reason so that the wonder of images may be perceived as instruments of ethical instruction rather than as traps leading to idolatry. He relates the danger of idolatry to a weakness of the human will and not to the images themselves. By balancing the positive effects and negative potential of images, Tusi provides more than just an apology for image making. Rather, he invites the reader to ponder the place of images in the greater scheme of God's creation and to see their affective power in a didactic and pious light.

The wonder of images is thus construed as a reflection of divine inspiration and intervention in human life. The sequence of accounts which are alternatively—and sometimes jointly—moralizing and awe-inspiring is in line with the book's mission to depict the humbling wonder of creation. To this end, Tusi posits images alongside tombs and treasures as analogous markers of liminal places and times. Images are harnessed to explore and give meaning to the movable boundaries of human knowledge and vision in contrast to the absolute nature of God's decrees. The testimony provided by these markers sheds light on the critical points of transition from the visible to the invisible or from the concealed to the disclosed, thereby broadening the perspective from which the place of humankind in the design of creation may be seen. The wondrous image, if contemplated in this light, reflects the intermediate points on the various continuums in temporal existence which affect human experience and consciousness. Tusi's discourse suggests at least four such continuums through which images were conceptualized: a geographical one between the near and the distant, a historical one between the past and the future, a mystico-religious one between ignorance and revelation, and an eschatological one between life on earth and the hereafter. In this conceptualization, images illuminate the intersection of human life with the design of a continuous creation and signify the humanly intelligible aspects of that divinely ordained design.

The complexity of meanings and functions with which images are allied in Tusi's discourse may ultimately direct us to a more nuanced and philosophical resolution of the question of figural representation in the medieval Islamic world. On the whole, Tusi's exposition on images and his contextualization of them in a cosmography shed light on contemporary ethical and epistemic perspectives on representation. As such, this text speaks first and foremost to the wide cultural relevance of images integrated into the popular imagination. The evidence provided by documents such as this one can serve to form a fundamental theoretical basis to the more perennial and practical question of Muslim attitudes to image making. Taking note of other seemingly unlikely sources in which conceptualizations of the image occur will no doubt enhance our understanding of the wonder response elicited by images of significant portent in the medieval Islamic imagination.

APPENDIX

Outline of the first two sections of the sixth chapter of Tusi's *ᶜAjaᶜib al-makhluqat.*

"The wonders of carved and painted images"

Portrait of Shabdiz in stone (p. 331)

Exchange of portraits between Alexander and Aristotle (p. 331)

Muhammad's portrait used to foretell his victory (pp. 331–332)

Portraits of the prophets painted on silk, held in Constantinople (p. 332)

Statue of camel and rider in Rome (pp. 332–333)

Locked house in al-Andalus with image of camel and rider (p. 333)

Statues of Muhammad, Ali, and Bilal in Constantinople (pp. 333–334)

Portrait of Muhammad discovered in an onyx in a foreign land (p. 334)

Intercession asked of portraits of Adam and Muhammad in a foreign land
(pp. 335–336)

"Strange images"

Talismanic statue in Turkestan providing relief in times of drought (p. 336)

A singing statue fallen sideways on the road to India (p. 337)

The two [Buddha] statues of Bamiyan which smile
   when the sun shines (p. 337)
A fountain statue in India (p. 337)
A colossal copper statue in al-Andalus declaring the
   end of the road (pp. 337–338)
Statue called "Sharahil" in Alexandria pointing to
   Constantinople (p. 338)
Portrait of Idris as the beginning of image worship (p.
   338)
Harun al-Rashid and the Magian fire-worshipper (p.
   338)
Solomon's wife worshipping her father's portrait (p.
   339)
A mobile statue in India (p. 339)
A talismanic statue of a breasfeeding woman (p. 339)
Statue of a weeping woman in Rome (pp. 339–340)
A fountain with a talismanic statue belonging to the
   Kirmanshahan (p. 340)
An obelisk with an image of a seated woman in Egypt
   (p. 340)
Statues of two girls in Palmyra (p. 340)
Image of Shabdiz made by Farhad (pp. 340–341)
Story of Shirin (pp. 341–342)
A column with an image of a duck in India (p. 342)
Statue of a sheep in Armenia (p. 343)
Statues of two lions in India (p. 343)
A silver lion mounted by a human figure holding a
   mirror in Tangiers (p. 343)
Talking images of genies in Kairawan (p. 343)

Figure 1. Simon de Barrientos (?), Santiago Matamoros (St. James as Slayer of the Moors), detail of lateral portal, church of La Compañía, Arequipa, Peru, 1654.

Islam, art, and architecture in the Americas

Some considerations of colonial Latin America

THOMAS DaCOSTA KAUFMANN

In the millennium after the Hegira Islam spread all over the Eastern Hemisphere, but traces of Islamic culture should not have been found at all in the vast areas of the Western Hemisphere ruled by the Spanish and Portuguese during the period between the first voyage of Columbus and the independence of modern Latin American states, 1492 to ca. 1820.[1] The Spanish crown repeatedly placed restrictions on the immigration of "Moors," including those newly converted to Christianity, as well as on their children and descendants.[2] From the year 1569 the Inquisition worked in the Americas to make sure that only Christians (i.e. orthodox Catholics) practiced their religion. Extensive archival data attests to the presence in the New World of the Holy Office,[3] whose widespread activity is also suggested physically by buildings known by the name of *Casa del Gran Poder,* some of the largest extant structures that are not churches or monasteries erected in places such as Sucre (formerly known as Chuquisaca and La Plata), now in Bolivia, and Cartagena de las Indias, now in Colombia.

These restrictions should have assured that the effects of Islam and its cultural products would have been absent in the Americas. But historians and art historians have often noted that the transculturation of Iberian culture in the New World also involved Islam in multiple and at times complex ways. Attitudes, ideas, and products engendered by longstanding contact with Moslems and their culture left many marks on the European colonies in the Americas.

How can it be that motifs and ideas found in art in the Americas reflect the impact of Islam? This paper assembles and comments on some of the diverse information concerning this impact, direct, and indirect, on monuments of art and architecture in the colonies of Latin America. It addresses the question of how it may be that motifs and ideas that were created in one culture may appear and be used, consciously or unconsciously, in another culture. It investigates how objects, forms, and attitudes forged in Iberia became absorbed and reused in the iconography, techniques, and forms of the cultures of the Spanish colonies. The question of Islam's impact, conscious and unconscious, on the arts of the Americas raises the more general issue of how cultural products created in one culture may be transferred to and then adapted in another.

Historians have long related the Christian (re-)conquest of the Iberian peninsula to the "discovery" and conquest of the Americas. The series of events connected with both historical phenomena have been viewed as associated aspects of European interaction with the wider world, in which Christendom ultimately expanded beyond the bounds of Europe.[4] It is notable that the year 1492 that saw the fall of the Nasirid kingdom of Granada and the expulsion (or forced conversion) of Jews and soon of Moslems from Spain also experienced the landfall of Columbus in the Bahamas. The spirit of religious crusade that led Christians against Moslems in the Iberian peninsula has thus long been regarded as contributing to the launching of Columbus's first voyage.[5] As is well known, Columbus's expedition was conceived as a missionary venture and also designed, like the Portuguese voyages that eventually led around Africa to India, to find a way to circumvent the dominions of Islam by discovering a way to the east. Military and religious rivalry between two Old World faiths has consequently been counted among the factors that attended the European "discovery" of the New World.

---

1. My thanks to a reader of this paper for *Res,* who offered some critical remarks that have been incorporated into the framing of the published version.

2. Louis Cardaillac, "Le problème Morisque en Amérique," *Mélanges de la Casa de Velásquez,* 12, 1976, pp. 283–303, especially pp. 285–291, details the royal decrees relating to restrictions on immigration of Moslems.

3. There is of course a large literature on the subject: for a comprehensive overview with reference to archives see *Historia de la Inquisición en España y América,* ed. Joaquin Perez Villanueva and Bartolome Escandell Bonet, 2 vol., Madrid, 1984ff.

4. See J. H. Parry, *Europe and the Wider World* (London, 1966 [3rd revised edition; first ed. London, 1949]), pp. 8–11.

5. See for example J. H. Elliott, *Imperial Spain 1469–1716* (Harmondsworth, 1970 [first ed. London, 1963]), pp. 60f.

Yet, as is also well known, the age-old struggle between Christendom and Islam also brought about interchange between the two cultures in Europe, including images and artifacts; here the effects are examined of how this sort of cultural exchange was also evinced in the Americas. These effects appear to be manifested, for instance, in the way the conflict with Islam may have conditioned Christians' attitudes toward what they saw in the Western Hemisphere. Europeans' encounters with other faiths and cultures in the Old World seem to have predisposed some of their responses toward alien civilizations, especially religious monuments and practices, in the New World. Early European accounts of the conquest of Peru refer to Inca shrines as mosques; Inca rulers are described as sitting in the manner of Turks and Moors; pilgrimages to Pachamac, the pre-Conquest holy site near Lima, are equated with those to Mecca.[6] Similarly the conquistadors of Mexico described the first temples they discovered as mosques.[7] According to Bernal Díaz, the first large city seen on the Mexican mainland was named "the Great Cairo" by those on the expedition of Francisco Hernandez de Cordoba.[8]

It thus seems possible to relate the appearance of the symbols of the conflict of European and indigenous peoples in the New World to the transference of attitudes and institutions that had been forged in the *reconquista* of Iberia. Most familiar among these symbols is the recurrence of the apostle St. James, *Santiago,* whose shrine in Compostella was a famed goal for pilgrims in medieval Europe. "Santiago" became part of the battle cry of the reconquest, since the saint was believed to have appeared at the battle of Clavijo (930) to intervene on the side of the Christians, leading them to victory. Hence Santiago became the battle cry of the conquistadors in the New World. The saint was also believed to have intervened to help break the siege of Cuzco by indigenous rebels under Manco Inca, when he was thought to have fallen like a ray of lightning upon the fortress of Sacsahuamán, which then fell to the Spanish.[9]

Santiago did not only appear in his familiar guise in the New World, however. The arts of the Americas replicated a familiar iconography of the saint, but they adapted his image into a form more appropriate to the geographical transposition of beliefs. The different character that he sometimes assumed raises the question of how cultural products may be transfigured in different circumstances.

On the one hand, imagery that depicted St. James as slayer of Moors (*Santiago Matamoros*) that originated in Spain traveled with the conquistadors to the New World. Matamoros became a place name for towns in the Americas, for instance in Mexico. The image of the saint on a white horse trampling down Moslems is found frequently in Spanish colonial art. This depiction appears in the art of the Peruvian viceroyalty,[10] and quite often in that of New Spain.[11]

Significantly, in the New World this image of St. James also seems to have become syncretized with an indigenous deity. Accounts and images associated with the story of the siege of Cuzco indicate that Santiago not only appeared as the Christian saint who rallies the Spanish against the infidel: he was also equated in Peru with the indigenous god of lightning, Illapa. The conflation of Santiago with Illapa thus suggests one way in which the image of St. James could be adapted in the New World as protector of Christians.

Furthermore, it is worthwhile to reconsider the image that is projected of St. James as slayer of the Moors. The picture projected of the Moor is obviously a negative one. It may be compared to the monstrous creatures being slain in works of late medieval sculpture from Northern Europe, such as the great ensembles by Bernt Notke in Stockholm or Henning von der Heide in Lübeck that show St. George on horseback in combat with a dragon. In taking the place of the dragon, the Moor stands for evil. More specifically, as in other familiar contemporaneous European imagery of serpents or hydras, the Moor may stand for the evil of heresy or disbelief.

In the Americas this negative image could also be transformed, and with it also that of the saint himself. While the image of Santiago could be syncretized with

6. According to the evidence noted in Sabine MacCormack, "The Fall of the Incas: a Historiographical Dilemma," *History of European Ideas* 6 (1985): 422–423.

7. See Tzvetan Todorov, *The Conquest of America,* trans. Richard Howard, New York, 1987, p. 108.

8. Bernal Díaz, *The Conquest of New Spain,* trans. and intro. J. M. Cohen, Harmondsworth, 1963, p. 17.

9. MacCormack, "Fall of the Incas," p. 423; Alfonso Rodriguez G. de Ceballos, "Usos y funciones de la imagen religiosa en los virreinatos americanos," in *Los Siglos de Oro en los Virreinatos de América,* Madrid (ex. cat.), 1999, p. 105.

10. See Gustavo Navarro Castro, "De Iconografie van Santiago Matamoros in Spaans-Amerika," in *America. Bruid van de zon. 500 jaar Latijns-Amerika en de Lage Landen,* Antwerp (ex. cat.), 1992, pp. 189–196.

11. Elisa Vargas Lugo, "Imágines de la Conquista en el arte Novohispano," in *Sentido y Proyección de la Conquista,* ed. Leopoldo Zea, Mexico, 1993, pp. 132ff.

an indigenous deity, the Moor could be merged with an Indian. Santiago Matamoros could thus become *Santiago Mataindios*. In numerous images St. James appears riding on a white horse, sword in hand, trampling down Indians. But how to account for this process of transformation?

The image of Santiago Mataindios appears in drawings, originating before 1560, at a time when it might be assumed that preconquest beliefs had survived and the elision of evil/heresy = Moor = Indian could be readily made. It is thus reasonable that in some recent discussions of hybridity and syncretism in the contact between Christian and indigenous beliefs the role of St. James and other Christian images in the New World has been raised. St. James has been seen as conflation of Illapa, the god associated with lightning.

Yet this interpretation seems questionable. Images of the saint shown as an enemy of the indigenous are found not only in the Andes, but also outside of contexts where the Andean god was revered. The image of Santiago Mataindios crops up in regions where preconquest ideas can not be related solely to his appearance in the guise of Illapa.[12] He appears not only in paintings and sculpture in the viceroyalty of Peru, but also in New Spain, where he was even conflated with the conquistador Cortes.[13] While this last association suggests another idea of how transculturation may occur in a Spanish colonial context—the conquistador who conquers the pagan takes on a quasi-divine aspect—the transformation also does not support the interpretation that some form of syncretism has occurred between Christianity and indigenous beliefs.

This issue of interpretation leads to a consideration of the way in which the construction of negative images in the New World may have affected its arts. Indians could be substituted for Moors as enemies of Christians, but the Moor still maintained his role as the archenemy of Christianity. Moors so appear in Andean imagery long after 1492, or even the conflicts with Moriscos in Spain, and for that matter long after open battles between Christians and non-Christians in the Americas had ceased, or rather passed over into campaigns for the extirpation of heresy. The image of the Moslem as Enemy Other figures in later seventeenth-century painting in South America, in works produced in Cuzco

and near Lake Titicaca that show King Charles II of Spain as defender of the Eucharist. Saracens, or Moors, shown wearing turbans and robes and brandishing scimitars are the most prominent among the enemies who seek to topple the Eucharist displayed in a monstrance.[14] A curious Peruvian version of this image portrays Saint Rose of Lima supporting a monstrance on her head.[15]

In the light of these traditions of pictorial imagery, which speak for a deeply rooted negative stereotype, it is also possible to reconsider the interpretation of the development of some distinctive forms of architectural iconography in the New World. These involve the problem of the so-called fortress monastery or church. As represented by numerous churches and complexes in New Spain, including those at Tepeaca, Tepoztlán, Huejotzingo, Tula, Cholula, Acolman, and many other places, these are structures whose features suggest a military character. The features include massive walls with small high windows; buttresses topped at times by small structures resembling sentry boxes; crenellated parapets placed atop the churches; ledges outside windows or roofs; and walls, again often topped by merlon cresting, around the circumference of the atrium of the convent.

The evidently military features of these buildings have provoked a raft of interpretations. For example, while some of these characteristics such as buttresses and even the massive walls of churches have obvious structural purposes, others have seemed to lend support to an inference from early ecclesiastical instructions that churches were intended to double as forts. The interpretation that the "fortress" monastery possesses a military character, however, has long been thoroughly refuted. George Kubler traced formal antecedents for these buildings to churches of the fortress type in the Mediterranean region, where they may have been intended to function as fortified churches. Kubler declared that in Mexico fortified temples were so in appearance only, and that their military aspects were merely chivalric or symbolic, and rarely utilitarian.[16] In the most extensive analysis of the question John McAndrew also concluded that "battlements and heavy

12. For the origins of the image of Santiago Mataindios, as well as its relation to Illapa, see Tersa Gisbert, *Iconografia y Mitos Indígenas en el Arte*, La Paz, 1980, pp. 197–198.

13. Rodriguez G. de Ceballos, "Usos," *loc. cit.*; Navarro Castro, "Iconografie"; Gisbert, *Iconografia*; Vargas Lugo, "Imágines," pp. 134ff.

14. José de Mesa and Teresa Gisbert, *Historia de la Pintura Cuzqueña*, Lima, 1982 (2nd ed.), vol. 2, fig. 594; *America, Bruid van de zon*, p. 434, cat. no. 245, ill.

15. *Los Siglos de Oro* (see note 9), pp. 358–359, ill.

16. George Kubler, *Arquitectura Mexicana del Siglo XVI*, Mexico City, 1983 (trans. Roberto dela Torre et. al.; 1st ed. New Haven, 1948), p. 315.

Figure 2. Franciscan Monastery of San Francisco, lateral facade of church, 1543–1580, Tepeaca, Mexico.

walls" in Mexican ecclesiastical architecture were to be interpreted more symbolically than realistically, as signs of "militant faith."[17]

More recently Rafael Cómez has elaborated another sort of interpretation of the fortress church as a symbolic expression of the monastery. Cómez has related the symbolic aspect of the Mexican *convento* to the actual defensive as well as symbolic connotation of medieval monasteries. He has noted especially in relation to the latter point some comparisons St. Benedict made of monks to soldiers, of the monastery to a military fort, and of the monastic family to a kind of military unit. Accepting Kubler's view that sees the military features of convents as a Mexican continuation of medieval forms, Cómez views these features as decorative.[18] According to him, the placement of merlons on objects such as the

bases of crosses or interior stairway railing clearly argues that they possessed a decorative, rather than a defensive function.[19]

Although apparently military motifs may thus have functioned as forms of decoration, the decorative does not of course exclude the symbolic. This seems evident not only in the recurrence of the actual forms applied to the structures of churches, but also in their ground plans. Recently it has been confirmed that a well-known surviving massive "fortress" church complex in sixteenth-century New Spain in fact resulted from the transformation of a preexisting monastic complex. At Huejotzingo the original church that preceded the present structure was apparently laid out according to a basilican plan.[20] This layout has been regarded as

17. John McAndrew, *The Open-air Churches of Sixteenth-century Mexico. Atrios, Posas, Open Chapels, and Other Studies*, Cambridge, Mass., 1965, p. 278.

18. Rafael Cómez, *Arquitectura y Feudalismo en México. Los Comienzos del Arte Novohispano en el Siglo XVI*, Mexico City, 1989, pp. 108–109.

19. See for this point McAndrew (see note 17), p. 268.

20. According to Mario Córdova Tello, *El convento de San Miguel de Huejotzingo, Puebla: Arqueología histórica*, Mexico City, 1992, cited by Clara Bargellini, "Representations of Conversion: Sixteenth-century Architecture in New Spain," in *The Word Made Image: Religion, Art, and Architecture in New Spain and Spanish America, 1500–1600* (Fenway Court 28), p. 102, n. 30.

possibly symbolic of the "Early Christian churches of Rome in the Early Christian period in New Spain."

The transformation in form from that of the preexisting church has raised the question of why the shift was made.[21] If the form of the earlier building had a symbolic significance, is it not then possible that the shift to the fortress form also involves symbolic connotations? Christian responses to Islam may well provide the basis for such a hypothesis.

In the context of what may be seen as continuously combative character shaped by conflict with the Moors, a further explanation for the meaning of the shift to a fortress plan may be proposed. The militant, fortress-like character of the plan and form of New Spanish monasteries may have involved more than decorative carryovers from medieval antecedents, or a general recollection of the idea of the church militant. Although in New Spain many conflicts with the indigenous had in effect already ended by the time of the construction of fortress churches, conflicts with Islam continued in the Mediterranean basin throughout the sixteenth century and beyond, and they involved both Spanish and Portuguese. The threat of a Turkish advance into Europe continued to exist into the eighteenth century in Europe. Spaniards were drawn into military conflict with the Ottomans, most notably in the battle of Lepanto of 1571. Conversely, Spanish and Portuguese continued Christian crusades into North Africa well into the sixteenth century, exemplified by the campaigns of Charles V at Tunis in 1535, and the ill-fated efforts of Sebastian of Portugal in Morocco, where he died at the battle of Alcázarquivir in 1578. The conflict with Islam must therefore have remained very much alive in the Iberian mentality. Many European images reflect these conflicts with the Moslem Other, including a variety of images of the Ottoman Turks.[22]

These conflicts may also have had an effect on the response to Islam in the New World. The continuing struggle with Islam has been seen as one of the reasons why so many instructions were made for restricting immigration, and seeking out Moslem heretics in the New World.[23] Is it not possible that the fortress church, like the image of Santiago Matamoros, may also

Figure 3. Juan de Alameda, Franciscan Monastery of San Miguel, main facade of church, Huejotzingo, Mexico.

represent another such response, of a church embattled with its enemies, foremost among them Islam?

Seen in this light it seems to be more than coincidence that the actual forms that parapets and merlon cresting assume in Mexican fortress churches were derived from *mudéjar* decoration. In this context the term *mudéjar* is used to describe features of ultimately Islamic provenance in a Christian context, or to mean late medieval Christian buildings in Spain with Islamic elements. While the definition of this term has also been a matter of much discussion,[24] regardless of its validity

21. See Bargellini (note 20), especially p. 95f.

22. For the variety of imagery of Turks in Europe see Alexandrine N. St. Clair, *The Image of the Turk in Europe,* New York, 1973; *Münster, Wien und die Türken,* ex. cat. Münster, 1983; *Im Lichte des Halbmondes. Das Abendland und der türkische Orient,* ex. cat. Dresden, 1995.

23. See Cardaillac (note 2), especially pp. 299ff.

24. See for this question the relatively recent discussions in Rafael Cómez Ramos, "Una approximación al arte mudéjar," reprinted in

as a description for a distinctive or coherent style it seems that the origins of some forms found in New Spain are undeniably to be sought in art in Spain, in works that have Islamic origins or antecedents, and are associated with what is usually called *mudéjar.* For example, the idea of decorating a parapet with such cresting may itself be related to *mudéjar* conceptions; the specific forms that the crenelation of parapets take, of squares with pyramid tops, are commonly found in *mudéjar* architecture.[25]

Many other such forms with *mudéjar* provenance adorn Mexican monasteries. At Huejotzingo, for example, *mudéjar* forms appear in the *alfiz,* or rectangular box enclosing an arch seen on the *posas,* the corner chapels of the atrium before the church, as well as in the mixtilinear arch of the main church portal. The ornamented portal to the church sacristy in Huejotzingo with its rug-like repetition of geometrical and floral motifs may also be related to *mudéjar* decoration.[26]

In addition to such decorative details, several structural elements in the architecture of New Spain derive from the *mudéjar,* most notably wood ceilings. These ceilings are based on the type of *par y nudillo* (rafter beam, or coupled rafter) construction found in Spanish architecture. They may be built as *alfarajes,* in which decoration is placed over the tie beams or couple beams, or they may be formed in the manner of *artesonado,* or coffered ceilings. They may adopt various decorative patterns, at times assuming interlaced patterns called *laceria.* All derive from *mudéjar* antecedents. Moreover, in a few isolated instances the ground plan of a church in New Spain emulates a mosque: in the destroyed chapel of San José de los Naturales, formerly at San Francisco, Mexico City, or in

the church at Cholula, where so-called open chapels have often been regarded as resembling a mosque in elevation or construction.[27]

Numerous artistic phenomena have been traced to *mudéjar* antecedents, not only in Mexico but also more generally in the art and architecture of Latin America. Similar materials, technique, and forms apparently deriving from the *mudéjar* appear in secular as well as ecclesiastical contexts. These include the use of techniques and materials employed for decorative purposes, among them *yeseria,* or plasterwork, *azulejos,* or tiles, and decorative brickwork; the latter, however, found rather infrequently. General forms or patterns of decoration (such as carpet patterns and arabesques) are found throughout Latin America. Certain other structural forms such as enclosed wood balconies (*ajimeces*), as seen conspicuously in Lima[28] and also in the Caribbean and its litoral, have also been convincingly traced to *mudéjar* ancestry.

Forms of *mudéjar* architecture and decoration have thus been found in most of the countries of Spanish and Portuguese America. Their examples are indeed too numerous to recount in detail here. Suffice it to say that since the pioneering work of Diego Angulo and Manuel Toussaint, the presence of such elements has gained ever more scholarly attention. They have been studied in specialized essays, in symposia, and in exhibitions.[29]

Consequently, the *mudéjar* has been recognized as an important component of Ibero–American art and architecture. It is thus relatively clear that elements derived ultimately from Islamic art, or its traditions as represented by Islamic artists, or the *mudéjar,* may be found in monastic (and parochial church) architecture

Andalucia y Mexico en el Renacimiento y Barroco. Studios de arte y arquitectura, Seville, 1991, pp. 11–20; Gonzalo Borrás Gualis, "El arte mudéjar: estado actual de la cuestión," in *Mudéjar iberoamericano. Una expresión cultural de dos mundos,* ed. I. Henares and R. López Guzmán, Granada, 1993, pp. 9–19, and Ignacio Henares Cuéllar, "Perspectiva historiográfica finisecular del mudéjar en la Peninsula, Archipiélagos Atlánticos e Iberoamérica," and Santiago Sebastián, "Existe el mudejarismo en Hispanoamérica?," in *Mudéjar iberoamericano. Una expresión cultural de dos mundos; El mudéjar iberoamericano. Del Islam al Nuevo Mundo,* ex. cat., Granada, 1995, pp. 17–33, 45–49.

25. These points are frequently made; for the argument about the source of the cresting see for example especially McAndrew (note 17), pp. 173, 267.

26. For a description of the stylistic elements in Huejotzingo, see Marcela Salas Cuesta, *La iglesia y el convento de Huejotzingo,* Mexico City, 1982.

27. For terminology see the fundamental study by Manuel Toussaint, *Arte mudéjar in América,* Mexico City, 1946. A substantial literature has grown up on *mudéjar* architecture in New Spain: for a review of the historiography and the manifestations of the phenomenon, see Rafael López Guzmán, "El mudéjar en la arquitectura mexicana," in *Mudéjar iberoamericano. Una expresión cultural de dos mundos,* ed. I. Henares and R. López Guzmán, Granada, 1993, pp. 189–212. See further for an overview *idem, Arquitectura y carpinteria mudéjar en Nueva España,* Mexico City, 1992.

28. Barbara Dalheimer, "Die geschlossenen Holzbalkone von Lima," in *Europa und die Kunst des Islam 15–18. Jahrhunderts (Akten des XXV. Internationaalen Kongresses für Kunstgeschichte. Wien 4–10 September 1983),* ed. Oleg Grabar and Elizabeth Liskar, Vienna, Cologne, Graz, 1986, pp. 87–90.

29. See for example *Mudéjar Iberoamericano. Una expresión cultural de dos mundos; El Mudéjar Iberoamericano. Del Islam al Nuevo Mundo,* ex. cat., Granada, 1995, with extensive essays and bibliography; and the edition of *Artes de México,* 2001.

and some secular examples. And these may be related to the impact, even if mediated, of Moslem culture.

The question remains of how to interpret the significance of these comparably well-known phenomena, beyond noting their ultimately Islamic roots. Undoubtedly there are many ways of accounting for monuments which appear on two continents as well as the islands of the Western Hemisphere, and were made over the course of three centuries. Obviously not all explanations apply to all such occurrences. To mention but some of the explanations that have been advanced, *mudéjar* monuments in the Americas may simply represent a transference of medieval practices that were prevalent in medieval Spain. The *mudéjar* had become a common phenomenon in Spain, because of the emulation in Christian buildings of Islamic features admired for their richness, luxury, exuberance, and dynamism.[30] Then again, it may simply be that techniques of carpentry and forms of decoration of ceilings common in Iberia may have been brought over without further thought to the New World, where they were utilized especially in circumstances where wood was readily available. In the New World wood may also have been a preferred building material in areas that were often subject to seismic shock.[31]

While such explanations may fit early instances of the *mudéjar*, other arguments may apply to the appearance of *mudéjar* elements in later periods. If they do not simply represent a carryover of earlier practices, later, especially seventeenth- and eighteenth-century instances of the *mudéjar* may be traceable to other causes. It is known, for example, that seemingly *mudéjar* features such as the design of *artesanado* ceilings in fact eventually became codified and were available in books. They may thus have been passed on by carpenters' handbooks and architectural treatises in the New World. This seems to be a viable explanation for the occurrence of phenomena related to the *mudéjar* that appear in the late sixteenth and the seventeenth century in the Americas, when treatises were known in the New World that showed how *laceria* in the manner of the *mudéjar artesonado* could be made.[32] Treatises

with these forms seem in fact to have been used in actual buildings starting already in the late sixteenth century both in Mexico and in Ecuador.[33]

Ultimately the process of assimilation may have been so complete that the appearance of *mudéjar* elements may have meant no more than the employment of traits that were generally regarded as Iberian. It has also been suggested that appearances of *mudéjar* elements in later times in colonial Latin America may have even stood for Spain itself.[34] For all these reasons, it appears to be one issue to identify a motif that has its origins in Islamic Spain, and another to suggest that its appearance in the Americas might even indirectly be linked to an understanding or awareness of Islamic art.

Nevertheless, one other explanation needs to be reconsidered. Is it possible that people of Moslem origins were actually involved in the making of monuments with *mudéjar* features in the New World? The term *mudéjar* refers initially to those under submission, in this instance to Christianity, and many unconverted Moslems who could be called *mudéjares* were still living in Christian-dominated parts of Spain at the time that the final parts of the peninsula were being conquered. These people were being persecuted and forced into baptism, in Castille in 1502, but the last mosques were closed there only in 1525, and the last Moslems forcibly baptized in Aragon only in 1526, whereafter the remains of the Moslem population in Iberia may properly be called Moriscos. Moriscos survived in Iberia until they too were forced out in 1609 and 1610.

Although contemporaneous Spanish literature denies them a place in the colonization and conquest of the Americas, Moors, either secretly still as Moslems, or like many other *nuevo Cristianos*, new Christians of Jewish origins, and then later as Moriscos as well as *mudéjares*, may have come to the New World.[35] An extreme version of this hypothesis is given by what seems to have been a Moslem legend, which in its own way curiously echoes that of the Book of Mormon. According to it, thousands of Moriscos came to the New World, where they openly declared their Islamic faith and tried to convert Amerindians, only to be persecuted and sent to

30. Pilar Mogolon Cano-Cortes, "Repercusiones del arte Mudéjar en América," in *Relaciones artísticas entre la Península Ibérica y América (Actas del V Simposio Hispano-Portugués de Historia del Arte [11–13 Mayo 1989])*, Valladolid, 1990, p. 173.

31. As seems to be suggested by several essays in *Mudéjar Iberoamericano* (note 29).

32. See Enrique Nuere, "La carpintéria en España y América a través de los tratados," in *Mudéjar Iberoamericano*, pp. 173–187; *Arquitectura y carpinteria mudéjar en Nueva España*, passim; Sebastián, "Existe," pp. 48f.

33. For a review of this question in regard to the possible issue of their use on the early *artesonado* ceiling in San Francisco, Quito, see Alfonso Ortiz Cresp, "Influencias Mudéjares en Quito," in *El Mudéjar Iberoamericano*, pp. 229–230.

34. As suggested by Marcus Burke, "*Mudéjar* and the Doctrine of Right Names," Lecture given at the 99th annual meeting of the College Art Association of America, February 21, 2002.

35. The general problem of determining how this might be is reviewed by Cardaillac (see note 2).

the scaffold by the Inquisition. The problem is that there is no evidence for these latter assertions, and little firm evidence for the presence of any openly practicing Moslems anywhere in the American colonies.[36]

Nevertheless, the names of several conquistadors indicate their Moslem descent.[37] And some Moorish customs, whether imitated by Christians or carried on by New Christians, such as the wearing of turbans, were maintained in the New World.[38] Significantly, a royal decree of 1540 that prohibited the passage of Moriscos to the New World was apparently ineffective; in any event a document of 1543 made reference to the numbers of Moorish slaves and converts who were already present in the colonies, and were a potential source of difficulty there.[39] Many slaves of Moslem faith slipped through the net in any case. The recent confirmation of the identity of the so-called *China poblana* of Mexican legend makes clear that even in the seventeenth century people of Moslem origins continued to come to the Americas, whither they may have been brought as slaves: the *China poblana* was a Mughal princess who had converted to Christianity, but who seems to have come as a slave to New Spain.[40]

The possible presence of Moslem (or rather formerly Moslem) workers or their descendants might account for some earlier appearances of *mudéjar* forms in the Americas. Spanish conquistadors, upholding the spirit of *hidalquia,* the ideal of aristocratic deportment that disdained manual labor, were notoriously unwilling to work with their hands. Besides indigenous labor, slaves would have carried out many tasks, and among them there may have been Moslem slaves, brought over from Africa as well as from southern Spain. Then again New Christians, who may have been Morisco or *mudéjar* artisans, may have carried out the work. Although the plan was not realized, there is evidence that Moriscos prized for their skills, in this instance the ability to

cultivate the silk industry, were to be brought over to the Americas.[41] It is thus possible that carpenters and ceramists also came.

Several problems, however, still attend these hypotheses. First, evidence for the presence of Moriscos or *mudéjares* is hard to obtain. In contrast with cases the Inquisition brought against Moriscos in Spain, or even against Judaizers in the New World, very few cases are recorded against suspected Moslems in the Americas. For example in contrast with the 1,759 cases brought against Judaizers in Spain, and 78 in Peru, and the 9,354 cases brought against Moriscos in Spain, only two such cases against Moors are evinced in Peru.[42] Similarly, an argument that Moriscos *were* involved in the early construction of churches or other buildings with *mudéjar* elements must follow from the possibility of giving a firm, and early enough dating for such features in these monuments. Yet few such traits seem to be firmly datable before the middle of the sixteenth century in New Spain, or even slightly later in Peru, although some such mid-sixteenth-century examples, perhaps the ceiling in the church of the Merced in Potosí, may exist.[43]

A problem for further research for historians, hardly resolved, thus remains: to ascertain the presence of actual Moriscos in the Americas,[44] as well as their possible involvement in structures with *mudéjar* features. Similarly, art historians and archaeologists must continue the difficult process of dating the constructions found in the New World. However these questions are resolved by future scholarship, the *mudéjar* features that they investigate still will attest to an extraordinary extension of the process of transculturation that occurred within the Iberian peninsula as well as the Americas. They constitute one aspect of a remarkable process of cultural exchange, whereby there appeared in the New World a variety of iconographic, formal, and technical features that may be associated with the reaction to Islam and Islamic art. This question remains of interest not only for those concerned with Islam, or with the Americas, but also for those addressing the more general problem of interpretation of cultural exchange and transformation.

36. Raymond Delval, *Les Musulmans en Amérique Latine et aux Caraïbes,* Paris, 1992, p. 27, citing an otherwise unidentified author, Ali Kettani, and for the general problem, Cardaillac, *ibid.*

37. As pointed out by Toussaint (see note 27), p. 9, n. 5.

38. See McAndrew (see note 17), p. 389.

39. The *cedula* is remarked upon by Cardaillac, "Le probleme Morisque," and a letter of 1543 indicating the problem still existed in part there, and more fully in Guadalupe Avilez Moreno, "El arte mudéjar en Nueva España en el siglo XVI," *Annuario de Estudios Americanos,* 38, 1980, pp. 656–657.

40. See Gauvin Alexander Bailey, "A Mughal Princess in Baroque New Spain. Catarina de San Juan (1606–1688), the *china poblana,*" *Anales del Instituto de Investigaciones Estéticas,* 71, 1997, pp. 37–73. Cardaillac, *ibid.,* also discusses the issue of Moslem slaves in the Americas.

41. See Toussaint, *Arte Mudéjar,* pp. 9–10.

42. According to figures published in the *Historia de la Inquisición en España y América,* vol. 1, p. 926.

43. As dated after 1570 by José de Mesa and Teresa Gisbert, *Monumentos de Bolivia,* La Paz, 1992 (2nd ed.), p. 139.

44. The last thorough study of the problem seems to have been that of Cardaillac, published over a quarter century ago; Cardaillac sees problems, and indeed the anti-Moslem mania he notes may have obscured as well as clarified evidence pertaining to the issue.

Mudéjar revisited

A prologoména to the reconstruction of perception, devotion, and experience at the mudéjar convent of Clarisas, Tordesillas, Spain (fourteenth century A.D.)[1]

CYNTHIA ROBINSON

Oh, Garden of the Valley, there do I find the Mistress of the
  Sanctuary!
Valley Garden, she who enfolds the shining blade!
Rest for a while in her shade, rest from your cares,
Rest until the dew settles upon her.
    Muhyî al-Dîn Ibn 'Arabî, Tarjumân al-Ashwâq[2]

Since the nineteenth century, the history of the visual culture of the Iberian peninsula has included the category of *mudéjar* art, architecture, and ornament. The term is derived from the Arabic *mudayyan*, which refers to those Muslims who "remained behind" after Christian conquest of the lands they inhabited. As a descriptor, however, referring to a particular category of ornament or object which "looks Islamic" but was commissioned and used by Christians, the term owes its existence to nineteenth-century Spanish art historian José Amador de los Ríos.[3] The currently accepted *mudéjar* model posits the appropriation of Islamic art by Christians, and suggests a notable intensification of the phenomenon following the (re-)conquest of the Muslim territories of al-Andalus by Christians, with the fourteenth century constituting, for many specialists, the zenith of the style or aesthetic.[4]

There are two paths generally taken to the interpretation of visual phenomena characterized as *mudéjar*. The first entails the reading of structure and/or ornament through an agonistic lens inspired by *reconquista* ideology, with Islamic art being appropriated by Christians into their "language of power." Alternately, this agonistic interpretation is suppressed and attention is focused on a generalized and rather uninformed fascination on the part of Christian royalty and elites with Muslim culture, and in particular with its palatine aspects.[5] In the case of the fourteenth-century royal convent of Clarisas, or Poor Claires, at Tordesillas (province of Valladolid, Spain), most interpretations have been made through the generalized "fascination" lens.[6] The accepted model manifests itself in the famous friendship which existed ca. 1359–1362 between Pedro I of Castile, the patron to whom we most probably owe the existence of a significant part of the structure as it stands today, and Muhammad V, Nasrî sovereign of the kingdom of Granada. Implicit is that, without this friendship and the (undocumented) interchange of artisans believed by many to have resulted from it, the Islamic motifs could

---

1. I would like to take this opportunity to thank the already considerable number of colleagues whose insights have enriched this project: Gonzalo Borrás, Jonás Castro Toledo, María J. Feliciano, Fernando Gutiérrez Baños, Oleg Grabar, Renata Holod, Michelle Lamprakos, Teresa Pérez Higuera, Francisco Prado Vilar, José Miguel Puerta Vílchez, Nasser Rabbat, and Juan Carlos Ruiz Souza. I am also grateful for the enthusiasm of Brendan Branley, Damon Montclare, Elizabeth Olton, Richard Perce, and Jessica Streit, the students who made up a seminar on *mudéjar* art and culture which I taught at the University of New Mexico during the spring semester of 2002. Their insights and contributions are present throughout this essay; some are footnoted where appropriate.

2. Ibn 'Arabî, *Tarjumân al-Ashwâq* (Beirut: Dâr Sâder, 1998), pp. 87–89. My translation.

3. See José Amador de los Ríos, Pedro de Madrazo, *El estilo mudéjar en arquitectura: discurso* (1872; reprint Valencia: Librerías "Paris-Valencia," 1996).

4. Specialists are not in agreement as to whether the *mudéjar* phenomenon constitutes a style, or merely an aesthetic choice. The

history of the debates surrounding this question are discussed in succinct detail in Gonzalo M. Borrás Gualis, "El arte mudéjar: estado de la cuestión," in *Mudéjar iberoamericano: Una expresión cultural de dos mundos* (Granada: Universidad de Granada, 1993). See also ibidem, "El mudéjar como constante artístico," *Actas del I Simposio Internacional de Mudejarismo* (Teruel: Diputación Provincial, 1981).

5. Whichever of the two interpretive tactics is chosen, most of the extant scholarship communicates the idea that all mudéjar art is the same. This assumption has resulted in a notable paucity of monographic studies of individual buildings; rather, the first inclination on the part of scholars of *mudéjar* art appears to be to establish relationships between buildings or regional schools.

6. For this interpretation of Tordesillas and of *mudéjar* palaces in general, see most recently María Teresa Pérez Higuera, "Los alcázares y palacios hispano–musulmanes: paradigmas constructivos de la arquitectura mudéjar castellana," in Miguel Angel Castillo Oreja, ed., *Los Alcázares Reales: Vigencia de los modelos tradiconales en la arquitectura áulica cristiana* (Madrid: Fundación Banco Bilbao de Vizcaya, 2001), pp. 37–57.

not have been incorporated into the Christian building's ornamental program.[7]

Rather than enriching the monument's interpretation, however, Tordesillas' association with "Islamic art" would appear to have stymied it. The majority of extant studies seem to be in tacit agreement that, once an object or a building has been accorded the label of *mudéjar*, no further interpretation is required: the motifs in question—architectural forms and types, "pseudo"-kufic inscriptions, vegetal ornament, geometric interlace, etc.—acquire their meaning through their association with Islamic art, but in paradoxical fashion this association until recently has constituted license to consider those very elements to be without meaning.[8] Moreover, the widely accepted characterization of the

mudéjar as a Christian (or Jewish) appropriation of Islamic art appears, rather ironically, to have distracted art historians to the point that the figural components of programs such as that of Tordesillas are marginalized in the discussions.

This essay will offer an interpretation of parts of the Tordesillas ornamental program which are dated to the fourteenth century, and thus to the period most immediately surrounding the foundation of the convent. Both figurative and ornamental components will be assessed with equal attention, and it will be argued that these categories of elements are mutually dependent for the creation of meaning: paintings and ornament were produced as part of a coherent program. For the evaluation of Tordesillas's non-figural components, paradigms which have figured in recent discussions surrounding the signification potential of non-figural ornament in an Islamic context will be used.[9] These strategies will be coupled with iconographic evaluation and other practices of inquiry most common to the study of Western medieval art history. In the end, however, each discourse will be shown to be, alone, inadequate to the evaluation of such a phenomenon as Tordesillas, which is neither one nor the other, nor even both at once. It is something different entirely, a cultural artifact whose understanding has in fact been greatly impeded by the separation of Eastern and Western fields of inquiry and analytical tools.

Furthermore, this essay will suggest the use of a particular group of motifs in devotional imagery, literature, and practice in Jewish, Christian, and Islamic spheres in a specific geographical region (Iberia) at a particular chronological moment (late thirteenth–late fourteenth centuries), with, on the one hand, the creation and interpretation of Islamic vegetal ornament having been strongly impacted by a centuries-long interaction with Christianity and Judaism and their practitioners, and, on the other hand, the cultural associations of such quintessentially Christian iconographic themes as the Epiphany (or, the Adoration of the Magi) having been deeply affected and changed by the same *convivencia*.[10] I will also propose that this

7. This direct connection cannot at present be definitively demonstrated through documentation. The argument has been made numerous times for Tordesillas, but in the end we simply do not have definitive proof one way or another; on this question, see especially Pedro J. Lavado Paradinas, "Mudéjares y moriscos en los conventos de Clarisas de Castilla y León," *VI Simposio Internacional de Mudejarismo, Teruel, 16–18 Septiembre de 1993* (Teruel: Instituto de Estudios Turolenses, Centro de Estudios Mudéjares, 1994), pp. 393–406 and illustrations, and most recently Juan Carlos Ruiz Souza and Carmen Rallo Gruss, "El Palacio de Ruy López Dávalos y sus bocetos inéditos en la Sinagoga del Tránsito: Estudio de sus Yeserías en el Contexto Artístico de 1361," *Al-Qantara* vol. XX, fasc. 2 [1999], pp. 275–297. Moreover, it is now a commonplace view in the scholarship that Muslims themselves are not necessary to the manufacture of such ornament. Nevertheless, the unexamined association of it with Islam (and thus presumptions concerning its ultimate impenetrability to a Christian viewer, however well acquainted with such structures) remains intact.

8. This issue was brought to the forefront of the discourse on Islamic art by Oleg Grabar in *The Mediation of Ornament* (Princeton, N.J.: Princeton University Press, 1992); in this publication, Grabar's discomfort with the idea of an association between specific ornamental motifs and more or less specific referents was apparent. Nevertheless, this is precisely the line of inquiry which has proceeded most directly from this seminal publication. First was Gülru Neçipoğlu, *The Topkapi scroll: Geometry and ornament in Islamic architecture: Topkapi Palace Museum Library MS H. 1956;* with an essay on the geometry of the *muqarnas* by Mohammad al-Asad (Santa Monica, Calif.: Getty Center for the History of Art and the Humanities, 1995). Equally insistent on the importance of context and cultural factors in the interpretation of Islamic ornamental languages is Yasser Tabbaa, *The Transformation of Islamic art during the Sunni revival* (Seattle: University of Washington Press, 2001); the introductory chapters of both Neçipoğlu's and Tabbaa's studies offer concise and incisive observations on the historiography of the problem. On the other hand, Valérie Gonzalez, *Beauty and Islam: Aesthetics in Islamic art and architecture* (London; New York: I. B. Tauris; London: in association with the Institute of Ismaili Studies; New York, N.Y.: St. Martin's Press, 2001), takes a universalizing approach emblematic of much earlier scholarship: written sources are taken into account, but the criteria of selection does not include a demonstrable relevance to cultural life at the Nasrî court during the mid-fourteenth century. Also key to a discussion of aesthetics in medieval Islamic culture is José Miguel Puerta Vílchez, *Historia del pensamiento estético árabe: Al-Andalus y la*

estética árabe clásica (Madrid: Ediciones Akal, 1997). Finally, Cynthia Robinson, *In Praise of Song: The Making of Courtly Culture in al-Andalus and Provence, 1005–1135 A.D.* (Leiden: Brill Academic Press, 2002) offers an extensive contextual interpretation of the ornamental program of Zaragoza's Aljafería as it existed under the Banû Hûd.

9. See the preceding note.

10. For this term and its importance to the study of late medieval Iberian visual culture, and culture in general, see Thomas Glick's introductory essay to Jerrilynn D. Dodds, Thomas F. Glick, and Vivian

group of motifs is one whose coalescence was generated not by the appropriation of a category of motifs, or of an aesthetic by one tradition from another entirely separate from it, but by the participation of specific groups from among the practitioners of all three traditions (namely, those attached to the Castilian court) in the creation of a devotional language, literature, practice, and visual tradition which is both specifically Iberian and strikingly different from those prevalent at contemporary moments elsewhere in Europe and the Islamic world. The elaboration of this premise here will lay the foundation for a larger reevaluation, with Tordesillas as point of departure, of the *mudéjar* phenomenon in a future study.

As is true of most *mudéjar* convents,[11] Santa María la Real de Tordesillas[12] began its life as a palace, but was officially donated in 1363 to the second Franciscan Order, the Clarisas, or "Poor Claires."[13] Although the

process through which palace was transformed into convent is not fully known, the heavy concentration of economic activity documented in what remains of the convent's archives points toward the decade of the 1370s as key; the documents also hint at the possibility of other additions or renovations for the 1360s, the period most immediately surrounding the donation of the convent to the Clarisas. On the other hand, some areas of the structure underwent changes throughout the early modern period, resulting in effacement of much of the building's late-fourteenth-century physiognomy. The church, for instance, including both the choir at the western end and the funerary chapels, is most probably to be dated to the fifteenth or perhaps early sixteenth century, but it is practically certain that this later structure replaced a late-fourteenth-century one.[14]

The areas of interest to the present study include the Capilla Dorada (Golden Chapel),[15] the contiguous Patio Mudéjar, and the vestibule (see figs. 1–7). Also dating to the fourteenth century are the Baños Árabes (Arab Baths), located to the east of the church, although these latter do not form a central focus in this interpretive

B. Man, eds. *Convivencia: Jews, Muslims, and Christians in medieval Spain* (New York: G. Braziller in association with the Jewish Museum, 1992), pp. 1–9; Glick's essay contains concise discussion of the historiography of the *convivencia* model, as well as citations of pertinent bibliography.

11. See Balbina Martínez Caviro, *Mudéjar toledano: Palacios y conventos* (Madrid: Vocal Artes Gráficas, 1980).

12. On Tordesillas, see Juan Agapito y Revilla, "Restos del arte árabe y mudéjar en Santa Clara," *Boletín de la Sociedad Castillana de Excursiones* (1905–1906); Clementina Julia Ara Gil and Jesús María Parrado del Olmo, *Catálogo Monumental de la Provincia de Valladolid*, Tomo XI, *Antiguo Partido Judicial de Tordesillas* (Valladolid: Diputación Provincial de Valladolid, 1980), pp. 284 ff.; Eleuterio Fernández Torres, *Historia de Tordesillas*, ed. facsímil, 4. ed. (Valladolid: Ámbito Ediciones, 1993); Carmen García-Frías Checa, *Convento de Santa Clara, Tordesillas* (Madrid: Patrimonio Nacional, 1999); ibidem, *Guía del Real Monasterio de Santa Clara de Tordesillas* (Madrid: Patrimonio Nacional, 1992); Pedro J. Lavado Paradinas, "Palacios o conventos: Arquitectura en los monasterios de Clarisas de Castilla y León," in *Actas del Congreso Internacional "Las Clarisas en España y Portugal*," vols. I–IV (Salamanca, 1993), II, pp. 715-752 ; ibidem, "Mudéjares y moriscos;" Rafael López Guzmán, *Arquitectura Mudéjar: Del Sincretismo Medieval a las Alternativas Hispanoamericanas* (Madrid: Manuales Arte Cátedra, 2000), esp. pp. 295–320; Pérez Higuera, *Arquitectura Mudéjar en Castilla y León* (Valladolid, 1993), pp. 91–99; Juan Carlos Ruiz Souza, "Santa Clara de Tordesillas. Nuevos datos para su cronología y estudio: La Relación entre Pedro I y Muhammad V," *Reales Sitios* 130 (1996), pp. 32–40; ibidem, "El Patio del Vergel del Real Monasterio de Santa Clara de Tordesillas y la Alhambra de Granada. Reflexiones para su estudio," *Al-Qantara* 20 (1998), pp. 61–81; ibidem, "Santa Clara de Tordesillas. Restos de dos palacios medievales contrapuestos (siglos XIII–XIV)," in *V Congreso de Arqueología Medieval Española*, 2 vols. (Valladolid: Junta de Castilla y León, 1999), II, pp. 851–860; Leopoldo Torres Balbás, "El baño de Doña Leonor de Guzmán en el Palacio de Tordesillas," *Al-Andalus* (1959).

13. On the Clarisas and the mendicant orders in Spain and the Iberian peninsula in general, see *Actas del Congreso Internacional "Las Clarisas en España y Portugal"*; P. Manuel de Castro y Castro,

OFM. "Monasterios hispánicos de clarisas desde el siglo XIII al XVI," *Archivo Iberoamericano* 49 (1989), pp. 77–122; José García Oro, *Francisco de Asís en la España Medieval* (Santiago de Compostela: Consejo Superior de Investigaciones Científicas; Liceo Franciscano, 1988); Antonio Linage Conde, "Las órdenes religiosas en la Baja Edad Media: Los mendicantes," *Historia de la Iglesia en España*, II (Madrid, 1982); Ignacio Omaechevarría, OFM, *Católogo de monasterios de monjas franciscanas de vida contemplativa* (Burgos, 1973); ibidem, *Las clarisas a través de los siglos. Apuntes para una historia de la Orden de Santa Clara* (Roma, 1975).

14. See the publications listed in note 12 for full discussion of the arguments put forward concerning the phases of construction, renovation, and intervention at Tordesillas, especially Lavado Paradinas, "Mudéjares y moriscos." Ruiz Souza, "El Patio del Vergel" also contains useful discussion concerning the palace's archaeological history. The present location of the church is believed by many originally to have been the reception hall of Pedro I's palace (constructed sometime after 1350 and before 1363) which faced outward toward the river to the building's south. Fragments of polychromed stucco ornament containing geometric interlace, *muqarnas,* and stylized vegetation which appeared during relatively recent restorations in the archway portal which today serves as entrance into the church from its north side. These would seem to confirm the existence of a previous structure, quite possibly the proposed reception hall; see especially Ruiz Sousa, "Dos palacios medievales." For other brief comments on this issue, see Pérez Higuera, *Arquitectura Mudéjar en Castilla y León*, p. 94, also cited by Rafael López Guzmán, *Arquitectura Mudéjar: Del Sincretismo Medieval a las Alternativas Hispanoamericanas* (Madrid: Manuales Arte Cátedra, 2000), p. 295.

15. See Ruiz, "Dos palacios medievales." This space is likely to have been constructed at the very end of the twelfth century or during the first years of the thirteenth by the bishop of Palencia, an uncle of Alfonso VIII's.

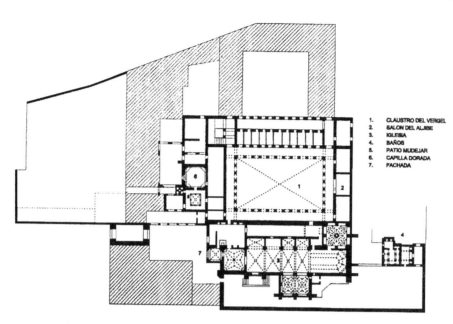

1. CLAUSTRO DEL VERGEL
2. SALON DEL ALJIBE
3. IGLESIA
4. BAÑOS
5. PATIO MUDEJAR
6. CAPILLA DORADA
7. FACHADA

Figure 1. Plan of Santa María la Real, Tordesillas (prov. Valladolid, Spain). Fourteenth century. After Lampérez.

study.[16] On the basis of a combined consideration of physical, documentary, and circumstantial evidence, it is possible to suggest that these areas, despite the chronological proximity in which their construction and/ or alteration was carried out, provide evidence of two distinct phases in Tordesillas's building history. This suggestion, in turn—one which has not, to my knowledge, been made—will permit the differentiation of two equally distinct phases of the convent's devotional life.

The first of these phases marks the period most immediately surrounding the palace's donation to the Clarisas in 1363, and includes both the Patio Mudéjar, which was probably constructed at this time (Ruiz argues convincingly on stylistic grounds for the dating of its ornamental program to the years immediately preceding the palace's donation), and—by virtue of its close relationship to the patio—the Capilla Dorada. The patio (figs. 3–5) was, again according to Ruiz's

16. This structure has traditionally been attributed to the patronage of Leonor de Guzmán, consort and concubine of Alfonso XI (d. 1350), and has thus served some scholars as justification for the proposal of an earlier date corresponding to that king's reign for the entire complex. Ruiz ("Santa Clara de Tordesillas. Nuevos datos."), however, has proposed that the heraldic evidence most often adduced in favor of this argument has been misread, and that the arms displayed in painted form in the baths are in fact those of Queen Juana Manuel, wife of Enrique II Trastámara of Castilla, thus suggesting a construction, or perhaps renovation, date of post-1369; others dispute this interpretation, and for the moment the issue remains unresolved but, as shall become clear in the following pages, Juana Manuel is by far the patroness whose desires and agenda are most clearly reflected in the documentary record preserved for Tordesillas, and the suggestion should be given serious consideration. While the baths will not be the focus of detailed analysis here, they are in fact key to what I shall propose as a second phase of fourteenth-century royal intervention. As for their dating, the baths were extant, but perhaps in need of repair, during the reign of Enrique II (1369–1379), the period in which the convent was so extensively affected by Juana Manuel's patronage. In the exchange (trueque) document which records the queen's

acquisition of the "casas de los baños" the term "adobar" appears. This implies that it was the queen's intention to restore those structures and make them suitable for the purposes for which she intended them. See Jonás Castro Toledo, Colección diplomática de Tordesillas, 909–1474 (Valladolid: Servicio de Publicaciones de la Diputación Provincial de Valladolid, 1981), document issued at Tordesillas, dated 15 February 1377, pp. 110–111; the document is not reproduced in Castro's collection. It is found in the convent's archives, ASCT Caja 1/7, and may be viewed in microfilm at the Archivo General del Palacio de Oriente, Madrid. The document in which this donation is recorded (Tordesillas, 26 September 1377) is mentioned in Castro Toledo, Colección diplomática, no. 170, p. 119; ASCT Caja 1/8, and Margarita González Cristobal, Inventarios documentales de Santa Clara de Tordesillas, 1316–1936 (Madrid, 1987), no. 81, p. 24. Neither scholar transcribes the document, and it is most unfortunately missing both from the microfilmed copies of Tordesillas documents at the Palacio de Oriente and, apparently, from the convent itself. It is possible that it is currently in restoration, or alternately that it has been lost. The document bore Juana Manuel's seal, and is recorded as being in good condition by both Castro Toledo and González Cristobal. It is to be hoped that it will reappear.

Figure 2. Santa María la Real, Tordesillas, vestibule, north wall, with images of Santiago and St. Christopher. Ca. 1380 A.D. Casa Amatller, Foto MAS.

arguments, probably a solution to the joining of what were originally two separate palaces.17 I would take Ruiz's argument a step further, and examine his assumption that the patio and its program of ornament, having probably been carried out in 1361,18 belong to the palace (as opposed to the convent) phase of the building's existence. Indeed, rather than the result of a decision made with the palace as secular space in mind, I believe that the patio's construction represents— whether it was undertaken in 1361, and thus immediately before the donation, or sometime shortly after that event—one of the first steps toward the transformation of palace into convent. Thus, patrons' decisions concerning its ornamental program, carried out in a style on whose classification as mudéjar all scholars agree, allow us to posit devotional significance for this space and the motifs with which it is adorned. The patio and its ornament must be evaluated not as an adaptation of secular spaces for sacred purposes (and thus as palace leftovers with no inherent meaning), but rather as part of a coherent program which both contained significance of its own and affected that of the

spaces immediately contiguous to it, dictating the women's religious experiences there.

The tiny patio's northern wall offers, amid its lace-like draping of dense, rhythmic coils of strikingly naturalistic stucco vegetation, an entrance into the Capilla Dorada (figs. 6–7); the doorway is bordered on the patio side by an inscription which links the space to the Virgin.19 By

17. See Ruiz, "Dos palacios medievales" and, with Carmen Rallo Gruss, "El Palacio de Ruy López Dávalos."

18. The justification of this argument constitutes one of the principle foci of his essay, "El Palacio de Ruy López Dávalos."

19. This inscription is not discussed in any detail in any of the publications on the convent which I have consulted to date. Scholars are, however, in general agreement as to its reading: ". . . *SANCTE M[ARIE] . . . ET LIBERATIONE M . . . VIRGO CLEMENTES VIRGO PIA VIRGO DOLCIS* [?] . . ." The corpus of inscriptions which inform the interpretation of *mudéjar* monuments is actually quite a large one, but the phenomenon has not received focused attention as such in the scholarship. Many of the inscriptions in question (e.g., those of Santa Clara la Real in Toledo; the Taller del Moro and the Seminario Mayor in the same city; the fourteenth-century palace of Pedro I of Castille in Seville) are religious in character and serve to so designate spaces which might not otherwise receive such an interpretation (given the similarities of their spatial disposition and ornamental programs to other rooms or salons with "secular" purposes). Indeed, these inscriptions appear to "behave" much like the inscriptions in Arabic which serve to define the iconography and create the symbolic matrices of a building, or a part of one, in the Hispano–Islamic context. For the inscriptions of the Toledan buildings, see Martínez Caviro, *Mudéjar toledano*. For Seville, particularly interesting are the inscriptions which mark the chapel in Pedro I's *Alcázares Reales* in Sevilla; see Ana Marín Fidalgo, *El Alcázar de Sevilla bajo los Austrias,* 2 vols. (Sevilla: Guadalquivir, 1990), I, p. 84.

Figure 3. Patio Mudéjar, Santa María la Real, Tordesillas. Ca. 1360. Casa Amatller, Foto MAS.

Figure 4. Patio Mudéjar, Santa María la Real, Tordesillas, detail. Ca. 1360. Casa Amatller, Foto MAS.

passing through the archway, Tordesillas's inhabitants, along with, on occasion, their royal or noble guests,[20] would leave behind the vegetal world of the patio for an intimate space populated by images. The chapel is a small, square room topped by a smooth, rounded dome ornamented with geometric *lacería* which emanates in sixteen points from the dome's center in a star-like pattern, and terminates in two rows of eight-pointed stars, their edges formed on three sides by the juxtaposition of four-part knots at the sixteen-sided dome's edges.[21] The

dome is supported by four complex squinches referred to in Spanish architectural terminology as *trompas;* these latter form the basis for the dome's sixteen sides, and are typical both of Nasrî and *mudéjar* construction vocabularies.[22] Walls are articulated by a series of overlapped horseshoe-shaped and polylobed arches which echo the variety of architectural features found in the patio. Horseshoe-shaped arcades appear to spring

20. See Angela Muñoz Fernández, *Beatas y santas neocastellanas: Ambivalencias de la religión y políticas correctoras del poder, ss. XIV–XVI* (Madrid: Comunidad de Madrid, 1994); ibidem, *Mujer y experiencia religiosa en el marco de la Santidad medieval,* Colección Laya, no. 2 (Madrid: Asociación Cultural Al-Mudayna: Instituto de la Mujer, Ministerio de Cultura, 1988); ibidem, *Acciones e intenciones de mujeres: vida religiosa de las madrileñas (ss. XV–XVI),* Series "Mujeres en Madrid" (Madrid: Horas y Horas: Comunidad de Madrid, Dirección General de la Mujer, 1995).

21. As noted by López Guzmán (*Arquitectura mudéjar,* pp. 173 ff.; 318), and as much more fully discussed by Ruiz, small, square, and domed spaces in Christian palace–convents are clearly linked to the concept of the *qubba* (literally, a dome; by extension, a small domed space often with commemorative or funerary associations) in Islamic architecture. Ruiz has offered convincing arguments concerning the linking of *muqarnas* domes particularly with funerary purposes and spaces in a *mudéjar* context (see Juan Carlos Ruiz, "La Cúpula de Mocárabes y el Palacio de los Leones de la Alhambra," *Anuario del*

Departamento de Historia y Teoría del Arte [Universidad Autónoma de Madrid] vol. XII, 2000, pp. 9–24 and ibidem, "La planta centralizada en la Castilla bajomedieval: entre la tradición martirial y la qubba islámica. Un nuevo capítulo de particularismo hispano," *Anuario del Departamento de Historia y Teoría del Arte* vol. XIII, 2001, pp. 9–36). See also Pérez Higuera, *Arquitectura Mudéjar,* pp. 121–138.

22. Ara Gil and Parrado del Olmo, *Catálogo Monumental,* p. 294, quoting Lampérez, describe the dome as of *estirpe Toledano* and *policromada y dorada.* The dome's affiliations with the Toledan regional school of *mudéjar* architecture and/or ornament, as well as the idea of its originally having been painted (or, perhaps, decorated with ceramic tile, as in the case of the Capilla de San Jerónimo at the Toledan convent of La Concepción Franciscana, dating to the early years of the fifteenth century; see Martínez Caviro, *Palacios y conventos*) and gilded (all traces of such ornamentation have today disappeared), are both intriguing and worth further consideration in light of points I make in the conclusion concerning the activity of important personalities in the newly created Jeronymite order in and around both Tordesillas and Toledo during the period in question; see below.

Figure 5. Patio Mudéjar, Santa María la Real, Tordesillas, detail. Ca. 1360. Casa Amatller, Foto MAS.

The Epiphany scene on the chapel's north wall is the only readily legible segment of two distinct fourteenth-century painting programs to have been preserved. Fernando Gutiérrez Baños, however, on the basis of detailed examination of the faintly preserved traces in other areas of the space, has proposed that the later of the two cycles was dedicated to the Virgin, including the Annunciation and the Visitation, and the extant Epiphany, as well as more iconic images of Saints Peter and Paul. This later cycle of images most probably included the Coronation. Although no firm date may at present be associated with the first program of images, it is probable that it belongs to the period of interventions most immediately surrounding the palace's donation to the Clarisas; at any rate, it is logical to suppose that it was finished well before the 1380(s) date, to be discussed briefly below, suggested by the vestibule's inscription.[24] The materials used in the second cycle would be different from those employed in the first, and thus the preservation of the Epiphany and the almost complete disappearance of the rest of the images from the second cycle would be explained.[25] Of the first cycle, the Epiphany alone was retained at the moment of the second cycle's execution.

As observed earlier, the second phase of fourteenth-century construction and/or alteration at Tordesillas is indicated in the documentary record by evidence of intense economic activity throughout the decade of the 1370s, as well as the presence in the archive of a tightly knit succession of papal bulls and privileges, also issued

from the tier of polylobed forms below them; these latter provide frames for the images. Despite the probable earlier date of the chapel itself, its program of wall paintings is almost certainly to be dated to the mid-fourteenth century, possibly to the years immediately preceding the convent's foundation. Patrons' subsequent decisions not to alter the structure indicate that it, along with certain of its images, was important in later phases of the building's life as well. Others of the images, on the other hand, were substantially altered following the moment of the program's original conception. The image of the Crucified Christ, for instance, which occupies the central *mihrab*-like niche of the chapel's east wall, dates to the sixteenth century and is thus much later than the rest of the program; no definite information exists concerning what was originally there.[23]

---

23. See Ara Gil and Parrado del Olmo, *Catálogo Monumental,* pp. 294–296; also dating to the sixteenth century, according to these authors, is the bust-length portrait of a bishop just to the south of the central niche on the east wall containing the crucifix.

---

24. The cornice of the vestibule originally bore an inscription in Spanish, most of which has been destroyed. Above the Annunciation, however, appears the word *ochienta,* suggesting a completion date sometime during the 1380s for the program of images. Personal communication from Fernando Gutiérrez Baños; on a subsequent to the palace, I was able to confirm this reading for myself.

25. Personal communication from Fernando Gutiérrez Baños, who is currently completing a much-needed dissertation on fourteenth-century painting in Castilla-León, in which a detailed stylistic analysis of the Tordesillas images will appear. Prof. Gutiérrez also believes, on the basis of evidence provided by costume, that the Epiphany scene might be dated as early as the 1340s, in which case one would be able to argue for religious activity at Tordesillas much prior to its formal establishment as a convent of Clarisas. This, moreover, would not be terribly uncommon, as many houses and palaces functioned as the informal setting for devotional activities for long periods of time—sometimes decades—before their donation to a particular religious order; see publications cited in earlier notes by Muñoz and numerous of the convents discussed by Martínez Caviro in *Palacios y conventos.* I would like to sincerely thank Prof. Gutiérrez for his suggestions concerning these problematic cycle(s) of paintings and for sharing his ideas with me.

Figure 6. Capilla Dorada, Santa María la Real, Tordesillas. Fourteenth century. Casa Amatller, Foto MAS.

during the 1370s, which relate to the changes to be discussed below. At this time, Tordesillas was under the patronage of Queen Juana Manuel. According to the documentary record, the Queen's interest in the convent appears to have begun immediately following the murder of Pedro I by Juana's husband, the bastard Enrique, and the consequent ascent of the Trastámara to the throne in 1369; indeed, we might, given the importance Tordesillas had possessed for Pedro I, to be discussed in greater detail below, view the commencement of Juana's interventions there as something of a Trastámara *prise de pouvoir*. Included in the building activities belonging to this phase is the transfer, at Juana Manuel's request in 1373, of the body of Leonor de Guzmán, Enrique's mother and royal "concubine" of Alfonso XI, to Tordesillas's *capilla mayor*, evidence of a clear intent on the part of Trastámara women to make of Tordesillas a royal pantheon.[26] Also

part of this second phase is the probable construction, and certainly the ornamental program, of the vestibule. Indeed, an enlargement of the church which included the *portales*, a space which corresponds at least in part to the vestibule, is mentioned in the same document as the *translatio* of Doña Leonor's body.[27] It was in the context of the *translatio* and the dynastic self-presentation of which it formed part that the vestibule was ornamented with the cycle of images, which reside among a framework of polylobed arcades and bands of *mudéjar* ornament and pseudo-kufic inscriptions, still found there today. In addition, the second program of images from the Capilla Dorada probably belongs to the second phase in the structure's devotional life, and would thus have been carried out at a moment contemporary to the decoration of the vestibule. These painting cycles represent the finishing touch to a coherent renovation and iconographic program carried out under the patronage of Queen Juana Manuel, parts of which focused on desert or hermit saints.

26. See Castro Toledo, *Colección diplomática,* letter from Don Gutierre, archbishop of Palencia, dated 15 November, 1373, no. 112, pp. 97–98; ASCT, caja 6, expt. 5. Leonor had been unceremoniously imprisoned and then discreetly "dispatched with" a few years earlier at the orders of Alfonso XI's "legitimate" spouse, the jealous and humiliated María de Portugal, who was Pedro I's mother. As for the idea of Tordesillas as royal pantheon, it does not appear to have ever come to full fruition, as both Juana Manuel and Enrique are buried in their funerary chapel at the cathedral of Toledo. I have not yet located a copy of Juana Manuel's will, and thus am unable to say whether or

not this accorded with her wishes. In addition to Enrique's mother, however, his sister, Juana de Castro (who, according to documentary evidence, lived for a time at the convent) and her daughter, Leonor, who professed as a nun at Tordesillas, did receive burial there in the *capilla mayor.* Their bodies rest today in a crypt below the chapel.

27. Ibid. Concerning the termination date of the vestibule's program of painting, see above, note 24.

Figure 7. *Adoration of the Magi,* Capilla Dorada, Santa María la Real, Tordesillas. Fourteenth century. Casa Amatller, Foto MAS.

This second phase also included the construction of rooms, now disappeared, for Queen Juana as well as for her sister-in-law, Juana de Castro. The structures (Doña Juana's was erected first) possessed two *tornos,* one for the reception of "necessary things" (food, water, etc.) and one which would allow Juana to sustain *conversaciones espirituales* with the nuns. It seems that both Doña Juana and Queen Juana harbored ambitions to become at least part-time *emparedadas* (lit., hermits who are "walled in," usually in a room attached to a church or a shrine), a desire which would be entirely consonant with the ideals of the Jeronymite order, whose importance to this second phase of building and of devotional life at Tordesillas will be briefly explained in the paragraphs to follow.[28] It was, moreover,

specifically these ideals and ambitions which would have informed both the choice of the iconographic and ornamental program for the vestibule and the changes carried out in the Capilla Dorada; their study, however, due to limitations of space, must be left for a future date.

Finally, although they were probably not initially constructed during the 1370s, the Baños Árabes form a key part of this second phase of activity at Tordesillas. As observed earlier,[29] Ruiz has suggested that the coat of arms displayed on the walls of the structure, which has traditionally been interpreted as belonging to Leonor de Guzmán, is in fact that of Queen Juana Manuel. This appears all the more likely in light of the fact that the queen went to great lengths, in a *trueque,* or exchange, involving the donation of an annual sum of 9,000 maravedis in tax revenues to the convent, to acquire the baths for herself.[30] The reasons for this become clear when, only a few months later, she donates the "casas de los baños" to the convent of Santa María de Aniago.

The importance of this donation has been overlooked, largely because the relationships which impelled it were dissolved upon the queen's death. They are, however, capital: it seems likely that, during the latter years of the 1370s, Queen Juana was seriously contemplating, together with a certain Fray Pedro "de Aniago," a Jeronymite reform for her convent. Fray Pedro's presence in the documents of the convent's archives has gone largely unremarked.[31] This is certainly

---

28. See Castro Toledo, *Colección diplomática,* Bull of Gregory IX, dated 30 September 1376, no. 130, pp. 106–107; cf. Arch. Vaticano

Reg. Vat. Ex lib. 2, f. 119. Queen Juana followed suit almost exactly two years later: ibid., bull of Urban VI dated 6 October 1378, and issued in Rome; ASCT caja 6, expt. 8. Permission to the queen had in fact been granted by Gregory IX almost a year earlier (2 December 1377), but the bull was never dispatched as a result of that pope's death (ibid., p. 129). My suggestion is based both on the description of the rooms in the papal bull and on the fact that a bull was necessary in the first place—the simple addition of a room or rooms would not normally require papal permission, as it was quite common for royal and noble women to retain *casas* within convents which they either founded or patronized. On the phenomenon of *emparedadas* in late-medieval Iberia, see the studies by Angela Muñoz cited above in note 20. The phenomenon has been difficult to trace for the fourteenth century, and is most often presented as a development of the fifteenth. Thus the examples provided by Queen Juana and her sister-in-law provide us with valuable evidence of the phenomenon's early acceptance and practice among members of the highest level of court society.

29. See note 26.

30. For a listing of the relevant documentary sources concerning the *trueque,* see above, note 16.

31. Castro Toledo, *Colección diplomática,* Rome, 6 October 1378, no. 190, ASCT Caja 6/7 with copy, p. 129. In this bull, Juana Manuel was given papal permission to revise the convent's *Constituciones,*

due to the fact that, in the shadow of the sweeping reforms carried out by observant branches of the Franciscan order in the decades that followed, during which Tordesillas as a reformed observant convent was held up to its neighbors as an example, this first tentative step toward change in the convent's life has been forgotten. Fray Pedro de Aniago, however, is none other than Fray Pedro Fernández Pecha, one of the founders of the Jeronymite order, formally constituted in 1373.[32] Prior to her donation of the Tordesillas's baths to nearby Santa María de Aniago, Juana Manuel had in fact purchased and donated the abandoned convent at Aniago to the Jeronymites, with the understanding that the new foundation would be under the leadership of Fray Pedro who, in return, promised to pray for the queen's soul. In the documents in which these transactions are recorded, Fray Pedro appears unequivocally as "Fray Pedro de Guadalajara," the name taken by the former courtier to Pedro I upon his spiritual conversion.[33] As shall be seen in the conclusion to this essay, in addition to other implications of great interest for the study of late-fourteenth-century devotional culture in Iberia, the idea of the creation of a specifically Jeronymite program of meaning at Tordesillas provides a second layer of signification for the patio-and-chapel complex, one which explains why these two elements of the palace–convent's already-extant structural and ornamental program might have appealed to the queen and her spiritual counselor.

Interpretive directions

Let a little water be brought, and wash your feet,
and rest yourselves under the tree . . .

Genesis 18.4

Before undertaking the analysis of the patio-and-chapel complex, some observations might be offered concerning the overall nature of Tordesillas's fourteenth-century visual program. Although negative evidence should be used with caution, it does not seem that, during the decades immediately following its donation to the Clarisas, Tordesillas's visual culture included images of the sort which would become common in the Iberian peninsula after the middle of the fifteenth century, and which were already plentiful in other European contexts in the mid-fourteenth century, in which the devotional and contemplative significance of the human Christ's sufferings, not only on the cross but also during the days preceding the Passion, are emphasized through graphic depiction.[34] The almost complete absence of such imagery from conventual contexts in Castilla-León during the thirteenth and fourteenth centuries would appear to distinguish these Clarisas from their sisters elsewhere in Europe.

---

together with Fray Pedro. Given that this bull was issued on the same day as the one in which the queen is given permission to erect and inhabit the rooms discussed earlier, we may almost certainly speak of a reform with a distinctly Jeronymite flavor.

32. In some of the documents recording Tordesillas's relationship to Aniago, Fray Pedro Fernández Pecha appears as "Fray Pedro de Aniago." This is in fact logical from a local scribe's point of view, because at that point Fray Pedro was living at Aniago. It is without doubt this multiple identification of Fray Pedro in the documents (indeed, to further complicate matters, in documents concerning another Jeronymite convent which he founded, La Sisla, near Toledo, he appears as "Fray Pedro de la Sisla") which has thus far hindered scholarship's realization of his association with Tordesillas.

33. Archivo Historico Nacional (AHN), Clero, *carpeta* 3.404/6, for the donation, 3.404/7 for the bishop's confirmation. In 3.404/8, Fray Pedro's purchase of the *monte*, or "mount" of Aniago is recorded. This particular purchase may have had symbolic as well as practical importance for the Jeronymites; more on this matter in the larger study of which this essay forms part. In 1382 (1.304/11), the Jeronymites sold Aniago back to the council of Valladolid. The sale shortly follows Juana Manuel's death and most probably marks the end of Fray Pedro's relationship with the convent.

34. Although my survey of museums throughout Castilla and León is still incomplete, I would venture to suggest that the same might be argued for the majority of Clarisan establishments in Castilla-León during the thirteenth and fourteenth centuries. The only late-thirteenth- or early-fourteenth-century Iberian Franciscan monastic context for which I am aware of the existence of an extensive Passion cycle of the sort commonly found elsewhere in Europe at this time is in La Concepción Franciscana in Toledo. Although the monastery was later given over to Clarisas, it began as a male establishment; see Martínez Caviro, *Mudéjar Toledano*, pp. 43–96; I would also suggest that the dating for this cycle is very much open to debate, and that at least parts of it might in fact have been produced much later than the thirteenth century. Nicolás Francés is reported to have carried out a monumental cycle of paintings dedicated to the theme of the Passion in the cloister of the cathedral of León sometime during the 1430s, and this is one of the earliest examples from Castilla-León which we have record; see Chandler Rathfon Post, *A History of Spanish Painting* (Cambridge, Mass.: Harvard University Press, 1930–1966), 8, pp. 152–169. Shortly thereafter, or possibly at the same time, Nicolás Francés was almost certainly at work on the *retablo* for the funerary chapel of Juan II's *contador mayor*, Fernán López de Saldaña, for which he secured papal permission to construct at Tordesillas. The chapel was built between 1430 and 1435, and the *retablo* is probably to be dated to this period. The painter was responsible for both sides of the doors, on which scenes from the life of the Virgin and the Infancy and post-Resurrection miracles of Christ appear, and which protect the centerpiece, a sculpted Passion sequence, most probably produced in Flanders. See Frías Checa, *Convento de Santa Clara*, pp. 63–69. Relationship between the proposed Passion cycle by Nicolás Francés at León and the Tordesillas *retablo* will be examined in a chapter of the larger study of which this essay forms part.

St. Francis's history of contemplation of painted wooden crucifixes similar—according to its representation at Assisi by Pietro Lorenzetti—to mid-thirteenth-century works by Giunta da Pisano and Coppo di Marcovaldo is a very familiar one, and inspired similar practices in his followers.[35] Indeed, the thirteenth and fourteenth centuries represent the coming of age, in so-called European contexts, of the *devotional image,* and Hamburger, van Os, and others have argued that the mendicant orders, particularly in their feminine manifestations, were significant in the development through their patronage activities.[36] Critically important to the reception and "use" of these images are narrative meditations written by significant figures in the Franciscan First Order, particularly the *Meditationes Vitae Christi* composed during the mid-to-late thirteenth century, previously attributed to St. Bonaventure. This text, although it had a powerful effect on a much wider audience, was intended specifically for the devotions of members of the Second, or female, Franciscan Order. The meditations guide the devotee in the visualization of the humiliations and sufferings of Christ as he passes through the various stations of the Passion. The nun is instructed to look, to see, to contemplate, to feel, and ultimately, to empathize and to emulate, through the use of both vision and visualization.

As observed, there is a striking *lack* of evidence for Iberian Clarisas until the fifteenth century (again, particularly in Castille; the situation in eastern regions of the peninsula appears to have been a bit different) for the use of images related to devotional exercises which elicited physical empathy with the human Christ's sufferings.[37] Certainly not coincidentally, the earliest manuscript copies of "Pseudo-Bonaventure"'s *Meditationes* appear to date well into the fifteenth century for the Iberian peninsula. Even allowing for the margin of error constituted by the well-known scarcity of manuscript and documentary material preserved in Iberia, compared to the richness of such documentation in other European contexts, the lack of evidence for the presence of the text, coupled with the almost complete absence of the sorts of devotional imagery which generally accompany its use, is worth noting.[38] To put the matter another way, it seems that Clarisan devotions in the northwestern regions of the Iberian peninsula were, at least initially, very different from those practiced in better-known contexts, and this at a moment precisely corresponding to the acknowledged "heyday" of "The *Mudéjar.*" But was fourteenth-century Clarisan devotional culture in the Iberian peninsula devoid of devotional imagery? As shall be seen, I do not believe that it was. Rather, it had elaborated its own set of devotional "phonemes" which may, in fact, also have been generalized among royal and noble lay audiences as well. These, however, operate on premises very different from those which are suggested by the *Meditationes,* and these differences respond to the very particular elite culture from which many early Clarisas proceeded. Why this difference in the Iberian peninsula?

This question is intimately linked to another: What sort of devotional literature were the Clarisas reading? What, in a broader sense, was the intellectual and devotional culture of women who were likely to profess

35. See, for example, Anne Derbes, *Picturing the passion in late Medieval Italy: Narrative painting, Franciscan ideologies, and the Levant* (Cambridge; New York: Cambridge University Press, 1996).

36. See Hans Belting, *Likeness and presence: A history of the image before the era of art;* translated by Edmund Jephcott (Chicago: University of Chicago Press, 1994); Jeffrey Hamburger, *The Rothschild Canticles: Art and mysticism in Flanders and the Rhineland circa 1300* (New Haven: Yale University Press, 1990), and ibidem, *The visual and the visionary: Art and female spirituality in late medieval Germany* (New York: Zone Books; Cambridge, Mass.: MIT Press, 1998); Henk van Os, *The art of devotion in the late Middle Ages in Europe, 1300–1500;* with Eugène Honée, Hans Nieuwdorp, Bernhard Ridderbos; translated from the Dutch by Michael Hoyle (Princeton, N.J.: Princeton University Press, 1994).

37. Nothing of the sort is discussed, for instance, in the relatively recent four-volume set of conference proceedings, *Las Clarisas en Espana y Portugal.* Contrast with the devotional culture reconstructed for Italian Clarisas during the earliest centuries of the order's existence by Jeryldene M. Wood, *Women, art, and spirituality: The Poor Clares of early modern Italy* (Cambridge; New York: Cambridge University

Press, 1996). In Manuel de Castro, OFM, *Manuscritos Franciscanos de la Biblioteca Nacional de Madrid* (Madrid: Dirección de Archivos y Bibliotecas, 1973), we find only one example from the fourteenth century in which a narration of Christ's life and passion is specifically offered to Franciscans as material for meditation. This is Castro's no. 483, "Pseudo-Bonaventure," *Liber Meditationem,* Biblioteca Nacional (BN) Ms. 12797, pp. 503–504.

38. An entirely different matter, and one beyond the scope of this study, is that of the composition of verses dedicated to an exposition of the *Vida de Cristo* in Castilla-León during the latter quarter of the fifteenth century and the effects of these texts on the production of images, and vice versa. On this matter, see Keith Whinnom, *Medieval and Renaissance Spanish literature: Selected essays,* eds. Alan Deyermond, W.F. Hunter and Joseph T. Snow (Exeter, UK: University of Exeter Press with the Journal of Hispanic philology, 1994), pp. 143–155, and, for *retablo* paintings which may be related to this phenomenon, see María Pilar Silva Maroto, *Pintura hispanoflamenca castellana, Burgos y Palencia: obras en tabla y sarga,* vols. I–III (Valladolid: Junta de Castilla y Leon, Consejeria de Cultura y Bienestar Social, 1990). The *Vita Christi* composed by the Catalan Francesc Eximenis in the earliest years of the fourteenth century does not appear to have significantly impacted devotional life in Castilla-León until much later, if at all.

as nuns in royally patronized and sponsored convents such as Tordesillas? The Clarisan order is by definition a contemplative order. Therefore, to state the obvious, these women must have been contemplating something, and they must have been doing so in tandem with, or at the very least, in relation to, some sort of devotional exercises and/or meditations involving the use of words—a convent which received as much royal patronage as did Tordesillas would almost certainly have had a largely literate set of inhabitants. The work of Ángela Muñóz,[39] although primarily focused on a period slightly later than ours, suggests that a particular characteristic of women's monastic establishments in Iberia is that they operated on terms which involved direct and intimate connections with royalty and/or noble patrons with close connections to the royal court; this is borne out by one very well-documented Clarisan context from Cataluña, that of the convent of Pedralbes, established by Elisa de Moncada.[40] This intimate interaction between convent and patrons resulted in rather sui generis manifestations of devotional practice and taste, which varied from convent to convent and almost always reflected the devotional concerns and practices of these patrons.[41]

The Patio Mudéjar, Pedro I, and Ibn al-Khatîb

> When Rabbi Abba saw a tree whose fruit turned into a bird and flew away, he wept and said, 'If men only knew to what these things alluded,
> they would rend their garments down to their navels because this wisdom is now forgotten!'
> —The Wisdom of the Zohar[42]

Scholarly attention has focused particularly on the relationship to Tordesillas of the much-romanticized couple constituted by Pedro "el Cruel" (also known as "el Justiciero," although the popular imagination exhibits

a definite preference for "el Cruel") and his beautiful concubine, who died young enough to satisfy even the most romantic at heart. Indeed, the royal patroness tacitly agreed by scholarship to be most likely to have impacted both the convent's devotional life and the images and programs of ornament which were chosen for it is María de Padilla (d. 1361), in whose memory the donation was made (Juana Manuel, despite her documented presence at Tordesillas for extended periods of time, generally fades into the background beside the more flamboyant María). This focus, in turn—given that the palace, until the moment of María's death, had no apparent religious affiliation or function—has informed scholars' readings of Tordesillas's structural and ornamental programs as meaningful in a secular sense, rather than a religious one, and it is this bias which I wish to interrogate here.[43]

Although it was in fact María's daughters (at the instigation of Pedro I) who founded the convent, in almost all discussions of Tordesillas María's name figures heavily. A close scrutiny of the dates involved, however, indicates María's greatest impact on Tordesillas-as-convent was in fact produced by her death.[44] Moreover,

---

39. See note 20.

40. Juan Bassegoda Nonell, *Guía del monestir de Pedralbes* (Barcelona: Edicions de Nou Art Thor, 1978); Anna Castellano i Tresserra, *Pedralbes a l'edat mitjana: història d'un monastir femení* (Barcelona: Ayuntament de Barcelona, Institut de Cultura: Publicacions de l'Abadia de Montserrat, 1998).

41. The same has been suggested by Pedro Cátedra specifically in terms of the reading and devotional materials used by female religious in late-medieval Iberia. Pedro Cátedra, "Lectura femenina en el claustro (España, siglos XIV–XVI)," en *Des femmes et des livres: France et Espagne, XIV–XVII siècle,* ed. D. Courcelles and C. Val Julián, Études et rencontres de l'École des Chartes, París, 1999, pp. 7–53.

42. *The wisdom of the Zohar: An anthology of texts,* systematically arranged and rendered into Hebrew by Fischel Lachower and Isaiah Tishby; with extensive introductions and explanations by Isaiah Tishby;

English translation by David Goldstein (London; Washington, D.C.: The Littman Library of Jewish Civilization, 1991), pp. 671–672, "Trees and Herbs," Zohar II, 15b–16b, *Midrash ha-Ne'elam.*

43. Certain documents in the convent's archive do indicate that María ordered some repairs to be carried out in "her" palace during the 1350s, but there is no indication of what exactly these were; there is no indication of her involvement in such activity after 1356. See Castro Toledo, *Colección diplomática,* letter from Doña María de Padilla, dated 11 January 1356, and issued in Tordesillas, no. 87, pp. 73–74, A.H.P Valladolid, s. leg., ni f.

44. María, on the other hand, was extremely influential in the formation of the devotional culture of the convent of Astudillo (province of Palencia), also of the Clarisan order, which she both constructed and founded in 1353. See Anacleto Orejón Calvo and María Valentina Calleja González, *Historia de Astudillo y del Convento de Santa Clara* (Palencia: Diputación Provincial de Palencia, 1983); Pedro J. Lavado Paradinas, *Carpintería y otros elementos típicamente mudéjares en la provincia de Palencia, partidos judiciales de Astudillo, Baltanás y Palencia* (Palencia: Instituto Tello Téllez de Meneses, 1975). According to Castro Toledo (*Colección diplomática,* introduction, p. XXXIII), the earliest phases of Tordesillas's existence as a convent are closely connected to Astudillo, as many of the nuns' names known for both establishments indicate the direct involvement of the earlier institution in the foundational stages of Tordesillas. Moreover, the two convents received their papal bulls at the same time. The visual culture and devotional climate of Astudillo will present an interesting point of comparison (in terms of both similarities and differences) for Tordesillas, to be undertaken as a chapter of the larger study of which this essay forms part. I would here offer my gratitude to Madre Celina and Madre Ester, as well as the other Clarisan sisters at Astudillo, who so kindly received me during my visit in May 2002.

María's daughters, Beatriz and Isabel, by whom the donations on which the convent was founded were made, were equally insignificant in the direct formation of Tordesillas's devotional culture, given that both were very young children at the time the donation was made, and that neither ever lived at the convent, either as a formally professed Clarisa or (as in the case of Juana Manuel) as a (very) interested and involved royal patron. Rather, it must be argued that the initial impulses which shaped the convent's earliest devotional life came not from María or her daughters, but from Pedro I.

The idea of the king's direct participation in the formation of the convent's devotional life is not one which is generally discussed in the literature on *mudéjar* convents. Nevertheless, as clearly indicated on the one hand by the convent's foundational documents, and on the other by reforms undertaken at Tordesillas between 1378 and 1382 which involved limiting (!) to five the number of male visitors who could enter the convent's cloistered area on a given visit, providing the male in question was the *infante* or his son, it is clear that men—from the secular as well as the religious sectors of society—participated to a much greater extent in this sphere of religious life than is generally imagined.[45] Indeed, it is widely known that the king's will, redacted in 1362, states his desire that Tordesillas be donated to the Clarisas. This fact would seem to indicate the possibility that ornamental and structural choices belonging to the years immediately prior to the 1363 donation (during which the Patio Mudéjar was almost certainly constructed) were made according to a sacred agenda as well as a secular one.

Tordesillas' Patio Mudéjar is, as has been observed, characterized by a program of ornament almost entirely vegetal in nature, some of which is disposed in a wide band of cartouches connected by smaller quatrilobed medallions which runs just beneath the roofline and covers approximately one-third of the wall space; the rest covers the spandrels and wall space above the arches, columns, and capitals which surround the small, open square of space at the patio's center. This vegetation, as has also been observed, is strikingly naturalistic in appearance (figs. 3–5):[46] each cartouche features a specific motif—grape leaves and vines, pomegranates, flowering plants—which stands out clearly against a dense and uniform background of stylized leaves.[47] More striking still is the fact that the visual and sensory impressions conveyed together by the space, superstructure, lighting, and ornamental program

45. For the foundational documents, see Castro Toledo, *Colección diplomática*, pp. 176–186. Visits from the royal family and members of their entourages clearly constituted a theme which was of concern to Fray Fernando de Illescas, named visitor of the convent by Clement VII in a bull issued in Avignon, 16 May 1380; Castro Toledo, *Colección diplomática*, no. 295, ASCT Caja 6/16, p. 136. The subject is discussed in some detail in a letter produced after 3 August 1382 from Fray Fernandez to the abbess of Tordesillas (then María González de Guadalajara, another potential connection to Jeronymite circles since Guadalajara was where the order first came into being), *Colección diplomática*, no. 220, ASCT Caja 8/6; the contents of the document are transcribed by Castro Toledo. The Franciscan attempts to establish limits which he feels are reasonable, without curbing the privilege unduly (as he was certainly aware of the connections between visits allowed and royal patronage received): "*Yten el sennor ynfante, sy entraren sus fijos con él . . . E don Alfonso, fijo del ynfante, si quisiere entrar, reçebitle con quarto personas varones, e a los otros sus fijos con cada tres . . .*" Given that this letter is issued in the context of a reform undertaken by Fray Fernando at the behest of the pope, one may only assume that these frequent royal visits were viewed as a problem, and that those allowed inside had been even more numerous in the past.

46. This naturalism in terms of the rendering of vegetation may be witnessed in the *mudéjar* ornamental programs of numerous structures dating roughly to the second half of the fourteenth century (and in some Islamic ones as well, namely in the Alhambra's *Sala de la Barca;* although it seems a bit absurd to do so, scholarship insists on categorizing Muhammad V's salons in the Alhambra as Islamic, and Pedro I's at Seville as *mudéjar*). This naturalism is often, even in the most recent publications, explained (away) as a manifestation of "Gothic influence"; see, to give just one example, Martínez Caviro, *Palacios y conventos,* pp. 202 ff. Finally, as noted by Pérez Higuera, *Arquitectura Mudéjar,* pp. 93–99, any interpretation of the Patio Mudéjar must take into account the restoration carried out in 1904 by Enrique María Repullés (clearly noted in the convent's archives; see González Cristóbal, op. cit., no. 1912, 1902–1904, ASCT Caja 345/4 and /5, p. 298. The restoration is also mentioned in Ara Gil and Parrado del Olmo, *Catálogo Monumental,* p. 293). Although any restored monument must certainly be approached with caution in interpretive terms, I feel that, given the striking similarities of Tordesillas's vegetation with programs of ornament in Toledo and Seville, at least parts of which survive in their original states, it would seem possible to proceed with the process of interpretation based on Tordesillas's ornament in its current state. More importantly, it is probable that Tordesillas's naturalistic vegetation was among the earliest produced; see the discussion in the article by Ruiz and Rallo, "El Palacio de Ruy López D ávalos."

47. Interestingly—and of potentially great importance for future developments of this topic—the separation of plants into like kinds is the basis for a section of commentary on Ecclesiastes 7:14 in *The Wisdom of Zohar,* pp. 671–672: "Rabbi Judah said: What is the meaning of the verse 'God made one corresponding with the other'?" See the quote with which this section began; the passage continues: "For Rabbi Jose said: 'The trees through which wisdom [the mystery of he Godhead] is revealed, for example, the carob, the palm, the pistachio, and so on, have all been constructed according to a single combination. All those that bear fruit, apart from apples, are part of a single mystery, but the paths are separate' . . ." The possible links to Jewish thought and aesthetics manifested by a program of *mudéjar* ornament such as that of Tordesillas has not been taken into consideration in any of the extant scholarship.

of the tiny patio impart sensations similar to those one would experience in a small, intimate, and lush garden.[48] Sunlight softly illuminates its center, spilling in through the rectangular opening provided, *impluvium*-like, in the palace's roof, and throws the shallow galleries behind the four arcades into cool shadow. The elevation of the arcades surrounding the patio is composed of marble columns topped by capitals which, given their somewhat archaic appearance, are probably reused. Columns and capitals support arcades of horseshoe (on east and west sides) and polylobed arches (on north and south). The wall space provided by the *intrados* of arches, from springing to roofline, is entirely covered on both interior and exterior with vegetal ornament that is disposed along a roughly circular grid and carefully designed to accommodate both polylobed and horseshoe-shaped arches; several echo the motifs contained in the cartouches. All of the plants are in bloom: intricate curls of branches or vines bear, alternately, berries, fruits, or flowers. On the exterior faces of the arcades, the areas surrounding the arches are bordered by vertically placed rectangular fields containing vines which bear bunches of ripe grapes. Standing at the center of the Patio Mudéjar, one feels that one is indeed within a *hortus conclusus,* or perhaps in a bright clearing or glen which has appeared suddenly in the midst of a cool, shaded forest, whose trees are represented by the eight columns and by the dense network of leaves, branches, vines, flowers, and fruits which they sustain.

Most striking of all, however, is the fact that the patio manages to convey this impression without the presence of a single living plant. Architecturally, the space is in fact of a curious nature. It is too small to have been intended to function as a garden; moreover, none of the archaeological literature notes the presence of irrigation channels or other features which would make it a suitable place for plant cultivation. In addition, the convent possesses a large cloister (El Patio del Vergel) which, according to Ruiz, in its earliest fourteenth-century manifestation most probably resembled the Alhambra's Patio de los Leones in layout (irrigation

channels, fountains, etc.) and possibly function.[49] The smaller patio is experienced as something of a curious pause in a trajectory toward the chapel, and was not necessary to include for the building to function architecturally. In other words, the Patio Mudéjar does not fulfill a practical need of any sort; rather, its purpose must be sought in its physical presence, the visual and sensory effects it provides, and the fact that it is very clearly intended to preface a viewer's experience of the Capilla Dorada.

The chapel is entered from the doorway on the northern side of the patio, framed by the inscribed invocation of the Virgin, mentioned earlier. From the threshold between patio and chapel, the Epiphany on the north wall of the Capilla Dorada is clearly visible. This image is of special significance to the convent—all the more so if, as proposed by Gutiérrez Baños, it is the only one among a first cycle of images conserved and incorporated into the second—and, as shall be seen, it has a particularly symbolic relationship with the Patio Mudéjar. The crowned Virgin sits upon a cushioned throne adorned with protomes in the form of beasts' heads. Although the painting is severely damaged in places, it is possible to identify one diminutive musician–angel hovering to the Virgin's left; it is logical to assume that at least one other angel, pendant to the visible one, would be present on her right. The scene is framed by voluminous white curtains, pulled back to reveal the Queen of Heaven, holding her Son and seated against a backdrop of red patterned textile hung as a curtain. The Christ Child is haloed, and is represented as an adult in miniature: the proportions of head to body are not those of a baby or young child, and he is draped in gray-blue robes which leave bare his left shoulder and most of his torso, its musculature starkly delineated as if to represent that of a young adult male. Furthermore, and in sharp contrast to the images of tender affection between Mother and infant Son which are common both in the late thirteenth- to fourteenth-century iconography of the

48. López-Baralt, *Asedios a lo Indecible,* esp. Ch. 1, "El 'Cántico Espiritual' del Simurgh," pp. 22–145, for extended discussions of the specific type of metaphor which affects the viewer/hearer in the same way as might the subject of the comparison; this approach to metaphor is rightly singled out as particular to Arabic and Hebrew literature, and as relatively atypical of western languages and thought. This is in line with the way metaphor is analyzed in the context of Arabic poetry from very early on.

49. See Ruiz Souza, "El Patio del Vergel," "Santa Clara de Tordesillas"; and Lavado Paradinas, "Mudéjares y moriscos." Both authors discuss the quasi-iconographic importance of water (and, hence, of fountains and irrigation systems) in the Islamic architecture of the Iberian peninsula, and particularly of the Alhambra, noting the similarity of Tordesillas's *Claustro del Vergel* in its original state to these structures, as has recently been revealed by archaeological investigation. Again, Kabbalistic commentary is of interest and of potential importance. See Hames, "Conversion via Ecstatic Experience," p. 192: "This meeting between the human and divine intellects is likened by the Kabbalists to the breaching of a pool from which the divine influx in the form of speech (the word) pours like flowing water."

Mediterranean and in the iconography typical of northern and central Europe, the Child turns away from his mother's breast in order to gaze at and gesture to the king who kneels before him in adoration. The royal sage offers a gift in the form of a cylindrical object topped by a ring of golden orbs or coins.

The gestures of the king's left arm and hand—the arm lifted in an almost circular arc, fingers appearing to grasp his crown, perhaps in order to offer it as well—would appear to indicate a moment of visionary enlightenment, or perhaps even ecstasy. The king's face is turned fully toward the Christ Child, and the rays surrounding the head of the latter also indicate the out-of-time nature of the scene depicted. The Virgin, in turn, rather than feeding, caressing, or offering a toy or piece of fruit to her son, appears to gaze either toward the King or directly toward the viewer. Visible just above the upper border of the curtains are architectural elements which resemble tracery, topped by three discs, one black, one red, and one clear. These might possibly be associated with concepts relating to the Holy Trinity, or with the sun and moon often included in the Crucifixion iconography of the earlier middle ages. Finally, although the left side of the image is the most damaged, it is possible to discern the star which has led the kings to the birthplace of the Lord, clearly drawn against the backdrop of white curtain. The most unusual (and therefore arguably the most significant) feature of this Adoration, however, is the diminutive tree which the Virgin holds in her hand. The tree grows out of a craggy mound of earth, and at the very tip of its topmost leafy branches a small bird of indeterminate color is in the process of perching, its wingtips caressed by the baby's fingers.

The possible Iberian precedents for this Epiphany—images which show clear and demonstrable links to it either in terms of style or iconography or both—are few. One is a small panel painting of the Coronation of the Virgin, with clear connections to French- or French-inspired manuscript illumination of the mid-to-late thirteenth century, which belongs to the Clarisan convent at Astudillo, founded in 1353 by María de Padilla. The convent possesses no record of the painting's entry into the collection; it is possible that it formed part of a nun's dowry. Given the probably strong connections between Astudillo and Tordesillas during the earliest years of the latter's existence as a convent, it is conceivable that the manner in which the earlier image was executed was taken into account at Tordesillas. It is important to note, however, that no programs of mural painting are known to have existed at

Astudillo; if the Astudillo Coronation informed the program of paintings in the Capilla Dorada, the latter represents a significant enlargement of what was probably an image intended for more private, personal devotions.

A second category of related imagery is offered by a series of Epiphany scenes produced during the latter years of the thirteenth century and the first half of the fourteenth. Most of these are found in the Catedral Vieja of Salamanca, and all are traceable to funerary contexts; the distinctly votive function sketched out in the convent's foundational documents (prayers are to be offered for the souls of Doña Maria, the deceased *infante* Alfonso, the two *infantas,* and the King himself), in whose wording Pedro I certainly had a hand, would make this link all the more significant.[50] Particularly relevant because of its similarity to the Tordesillas image is the ornament of the tomb of "Doña Elena" who died in 1272 (fig. 8).[51] The tomb is placed into a niche topped by a pointed arch; typically for Castillan tomb sculpture of the period, the sarcophagus includes a life-like *yacente* (*gisant*) of "Doña Elena" and a representation, on its front, of a funeral scene, including the ascent of the *dinfunta*'s soul, carried by two angels. The area encompassed by the arched recession into which the tomb is placed is treated to create the impression of a monumental burial topped by a dome. Five ribs divide the area into four elongated triangles; one of the center two of these triangles contains the Epiphany (in the other are shown two of the sages from the east). Flanking the Epiphany and the kings on the left is a page leading the kings' horses through a verdant and leafy forest; on the right, a woman, who is almost certainly the deceased, reclines on what appears to be a

---

50. Indeed, although there is at present no solid evidence to support this suggestion, the possibility of funerary associations for the Tordesillas chapel are not to be ruled out. Given the strong emphasis placed on the votive purposes of the convent's foundation in the documentary sources connected to that event, in fact, the possibility would appear to be a strong one.

51. On Dona Eleña's tomb, see Daniel Sánchez y Sánchez (La Catedral Vieja de Salamanca (Salamanca: Ilustrísimo Cabildo de la Catedral de Salamanca, 1991), pp. 97–104; see also J. J. Martín González and J. M. Pita Andrade, Castilla la Vieja; León, I, Tierras de España (Madrid; Barcelona: Publicaciones de la Fundación Juan March; Editorial Noguer, 1975), p. 268, fig. 225. Queen Juana Manuel was, in fact, involved to some extent with the cathedral of Salamanca (ACS, cajon 16, legajo 3, no. 3 bis, records a donation by Juana Manuel to the cathedral in 1369 of 3,000 maravedis in portazgo taxes; earlier royal personages such as María de Molina also made similar donations), and thus it is possible that she or someone else closely involved with Tordesillas may have seen and admired the tomb images.

Figure 8. Tomb of Doña Elena, Catedral Vieja, Salamanca, 1260–1300. Casa Amatller, Foto MAS.

funeral bier and observes the scene of adoration taking place before her.

The Tordesillas Epiphany is similar enough to the Salamancan renditions of the theme, and particularly to the scene as depicted on Doña Elena's tomb, to argue for a direct relationship between the two on formal grounds. More importantly, however, the particular iconographic elements of the Tordesillas Epiphany—tree, bird, ecstatic posture of the king, curtains—would seem to gain additional significance through the comparison, for it is precisely on these points that the two images differ. In other words, what would seem to be an acknowledged iconographic type has been edited for the purposes of its use at Tordesillas.

The tree and the bird are the most important changes brought about by this editing. These elements must have a reason for being present in the Tordesillas image, and they must be related to some specific component of the convent's, or its patrons', devotional life. Furthermore, this idea must be an important one, otherwise a tried-and-true iconographic type would not have been altered. The topos which might first come to an art

historian's mind, particularly if schooled in the tradition of Christian iconography, is that of the Tree of Jesse. This theme was widely used throughout the second half of the twelfth century and all of the thirteenth, in Iberia as well as elsewhere in the European and Mediterranean world. Factors which contributed to its popularity were many, and certainly among the most important were the more central role the Virgin was given in devotions both elite and popular, both monastic and lay, and the desire to visually represent, through the invocation of Old Testament authorities, both her and her son's royal lineage, and her central role on the incarnation of the Word.

If one carefully considers the Tordesillas image, however, the identification of the tree as a Tree of Jesse is difficult to sustain. Traditionally, the tree appears to grow out of a sleeping Jesse's side, and viewers familiar with the story would identify it as Jesse's dream vision. Jesse, however, is nowhere to be found in the Tordesillas image. Nor does the tree grow from any part of the Virgin's body (an unlikely possibility, but one which might argue for the identification of it with the Tree of

Jesse). Furthermore, neither the Virgin and Child nor the other Old Testament ancestral figures which represent their kingly lineage are present among its branches. The bird, at its top, is alone. The tree, in good "Semitic" fashion, to borrow a phrase from Luce López-Baralt, may *allude* to the Tree of Jesse, just as, as shall be seen, it alludes to and/or evokes many other things and concepts, but if this is the case, the Tree of Jesse is hardly the most important of these associations, and the link is not made through the sort of clearly legible iconographic clues commonly placed as aids to identification and study in objects of Christian visual culture. Indeed, the Virgin—whose arresting gaze is, as has been noted, directed toward the viewer, most probably a nun—delicately balances the tree in her hand, and appears to offer it specifically and deliberately to the viewer's gaze. Given the vegetal frame from which the image would first have been viewed from the patio, through the doorway, the conclusion that trees and vegetation are being offered insistently to the nuns as objects for their contemplation (or, as *devotional images*) is difficult to escape.

Another possibility which might now come to the Christian iconographer's mind is that of the Tree of Life. As shall be seen, this identification is indeed a sustainable one, but not in the generalized fashion the motif is often invoked in art historical writing (particularly in discussions of non-western art, where everything, it would seem, providing it has lots of leaves and a central stem, is potentially identifiable as a Tree of Life). Rather, the sublimation of the idea of Christ's cross, and thus his crucifixion, into the metaphor of a verdant, living tree is one which is *specific* to the devotional context suggested here.[52] Although it finds resonances with other Mendicant evocations of the theme in Italy and Cataluña, the Tordesillas image differs from these in ways which are crucial to its meaning, which were certainly deliberate, and which effectively constitute a rejection of the dominant tendencies in image production and use in the larger context of Franciscan visual culture. Nevertheless, we may account for the presence of the tree, at least to some extent, by

acknowledging its association with the Tree of Life.

But we are left with the problem of the bird. The bird is necessary neither to the iconography of the Tree of Jesse nor to that of the Tree of Life as it is described in the scriptures.[53] The nightingale (*filomena*) is the subject of meditative poetry by St. Bonaventure, Spanish and Portuguese translations of which are attested for the Iberian peninsula. These, however, are late, and they are not identified with a context linked to Tordesillas or to its patrons.[54] One possibility is that the bird refers to the Holy Spirit.[55] It is not, however, specifically represented as a dove, and moreover, is certainly not an element commonly included in representations of the Epiphany (it is, on the contrary, as is well known, much more common to find a dove as a symbol for the Holy Spirit in representations of the Annunciation). The Tordesillas bird may be related to an apocryphal text in which Jesus, in analogous fashion to his Father, fashions clay birds and then breathes life into them.[56] This association,

---

52. For an extensive study of the Tree of Life as a central motif in Italian Franciscan art and thought, see the essay by Rab Hatfield, "The Tree of Life and the Holy Cross: Franciscan Spirituality in the Trecento and the Quattrocento," in Timothy Verdon and John Henderson, eds., *Christianity and the Renaissance: Image and Religious Imagination in the Quattrocento* (Syracuse, N.Y.: Syracuse University Press, 1990), pp. 132–160. Here Hatfield argues that the Tree is to be equated with Christ's cross, and its fruits with Christ. As is Wood's, his interpretation is closely based on St. Bonaventure's Lignum Vitae.

53. Passages in which it is mentioned are as follows: Genesis 2:9, 3:22, 24; Proverbs 3:18, 11:30, 13:12; 15:4; 4 Ezra 2:12, 8:52; Maccabbees 18:16; Revelation 2:7, 22:2, 14, 19.

54. The Biblioteca Nacional (BN) in Madrid houses a Spanish translation of Bonaventure's lyrical poem on the nightingale, or *filomena* (BN 2244); particularly relevant is the closing verse, "del Rey supremo logras las bodas/y en ella juntas las delicias todas." See Manuel de Castro, OFM, *Manuscritos Franscicanos de la Biblioteca Nacional de Madrid* (Madrid: Servicio de Publicaciones del Ministerio de Educación y Ciencia, 1973), no. 123, p. 125; cf. BN Mss. 2244, ff. 327–338. The manuscript, however, dates to the seventeenth century, so we certainly cannot attribute this image to knowledge on the part either of Pedro I or the nuns of Bonaventure's poem. Similar sources were also important in Portugal at the same time. See Jose de Freitas Carvalho, "Das ediçoes de S. Bonaventura em Portugal nos seculos XVI, XVII e XVIII. Semantica de uma influencia na historia da Espiritualidade Portuguesa," *Archivo Ibero–Americano* 47 (1987), nos. 185–188, pp. 134–159.

55. As is common in representations of the Annunciation, Baptism, Pentecost, etc. The case of the Tree of Life, however, is different, as neither birds nor references to the Holy Spirit are necessary to its representation. In the Tree of Life mosaic program of the apse of the church of San Clemente (Augustinian canons) in Rome, dated to the early thirteenth century and discussed by Hatfield ("Tree of Life and the Holy Cross"), the verdant foliage forms a backdrop to a representation of the crucifix at the image's center (Christ's cross here being thus unequivocally equated with the tree). On the cross are represented twelve birds, one of which disappears into the thick growth of foliage which surrounds the cross/tree's base. The twelve birds might possibly represent the twelve apostles, with Judas equated with the disappearing bird. At any rate, the similarities between this image and the Tordesillas Epiphany do not surpass the superficial, and the latter certainly responds to more local concerns.

56. See Rocío Sánchez Ameijeiras, "Las artes figurativas en los monasteries cistercienses medievales gallegos," in Jorge Rodrigues and Xosé Carlos Valle Pérez, eds., *Arte de Cister em Portugal e Galiza =*

however, while it (like that of the Tree of Jesse for the tree) may be intended to be evoked by the bird, is clearly not the primary one. The bird is not held in the Christ Child's hand;[57] rather, his fingers caress its wingtips. Furthermore, it, like the tree held by the Virgin, appears to be offered or indicated—this time to the ecstatic king; the Child's teaching or speaking gesture is clearly directed to him—as an object for contemplation or study, and the fact that it is perched (or perhaps *in the process of perching,* as its wings are spread as though for flight) among the very topmost branches of the tree can hardly have been intended to escape the sage's attention, just as it attracts ours. It could be, and almost certainly is, an allusion to the individual soul of the believer, but the specific association between bird and tree is not satisfactorily accounted for by this identification.

There is, however, a treatise which contains the key both to the mystery of the tree held by the Virgin and to that of the ecstatic bird (ecstatic because of the Christ Child's caresses?) at its topmost branches. The treatise, entitled *Rawdat al-ta'rîf bi-l-hubb al-sharîf* (The Garden of Knowledge of Noble Love),[58] *is,* in effect, a meditative tree. It was written at a moment and by a person whose association would allow us—but for the barriers traditionally agreed to be constituted by faith and by language—to argue for the *Rawdat's* position as the devotional text most immediately relevant in thematic terms to the Tordesillas image. The famous friendship with the Nasrî Sultan was not the only relationship which Pedro I cultivated with members of the Granadan elite. He is also known, during the years immediately preceding his daughters' donation of the palace to the Clarisas, to have maintained correspondence with Ibn al-Khatîb, one of the most trusted advisors of Muhammad V. Ibn al-Khatîb was a

courtier, a historian, a polymath, and, most importantly for this study, a Sufi mystic and the author of the *Rawdat al-ta'rîf,* an extensive guide designed by its author to aid in the practice of devotions particular to his *tarîq.*[59]

Ibn al-Khatîb's meditative tree, moreover, is expressly presented to readers as a *tashbîh,* as an *image* of a tree, complete with roots, trunk, leaves, and branches, indeed as a contemplative image (much in the fashion of the tiny tree offered by the Queen of Heaven to the nuns of Tordesillas) whose use will allow their souls to ascend from the roots of spiritual cleansing to the heights of spiritual ecstasy and mystical union. Through an ascending mental and spiritual consideration of its branches, twigs, shoots, and leaves, a contemplative might reach, as does the tiny bird (mentioned twice by Ibn al-Khatîb as "shouting with joy") caressed by the Christ Child, the heights of mystic ecstasy. One further association for this curious image which will be important for arguments to be made further on, is that of the enthroned Virgin with the *Sedes Sapientiae* (Seat of Wisdom). These associations for the enthroned Virgin have been put forward and argued extensively for other earlier and contemporary European contexts,[60] and her association here with wisdom and knowledge—indeed,

Arte del Cister en Galicia y Portugal (Lisboa: Fondación Pedro Barrié de la Maza; Fundação Calouste Gulbenkian, 2000), pp. 116 and 121. Many thanks to Prof. Sánchez for this suggestion.

57. Several other images belonging to a late fourteenth- and early-fifteenth-century Iberian context depict the bird as held securely in the Christ Child's hand (e.g., Museo Diocesano de Barcelona 22, *Virgin and Child with Sta. Oliva and S. Benedict,* from the Benedictine priory church of Sta. Maria, also known as Sta. Oliva del Penedès, dating to ca. 1360). An almost identical example, the early-fifteenth-century *Maiestas Mariae* from the workshop of Pere Serra (?), is the central panel of a *retablo* belonging to the cathedral of Tortosa; see J. Sureda I Pons, *La pintura gòtica catalana del segle XIV* (Barcelona: Els Llibres de la Frontera, 1989), pp. 93 and 110. The bird in the Tordesillas image clearly is meant to transmit a different message.

58. Ibn al-Khatîb, *Rawdat al-ta'rîf bi-al-hubb al-sharîf,* 2 vols., ed., Muhammad Kattânî (al-Dâr al-Baydâ': Dâr al-Thaqâfah, 1970).

59. Pedro I's relationship with Ibn al-Khatîb is in fact documented in the chronicle sources for that king's reign compiled by the chancellor Pero López de Ayala. See Cayetano Rosell, ed., *Crónicas de los Reyes de Castilla, Biblioteca de Autores Españoles* (B.A.E.), vol.66, Madrid 1953. Discussed are two supposed letters which Pedro I sent to the Granadan courtier (thus implying that the latter was able to read and communicate in Castilian, as we have no indication whatsoever of documents or correspondence being produced in Arabic in Pedro's chancery). Pero López refers to the Granadan as "Benahatin," which is beyond reasonable doubt a "Castilianization" of Ibn al-Khatîb. The passages in question are: año 1367, cap. XXII, y año 1369, cap. III. Ahmad Mujtar al-Abbadi, "El reino de Granada en época de Muhammad V," Madrid 1973, pp. 70–71, confirms the identification of the personage mentioned by Ayala with Ibn al-Khatîb. Many thanks to Juan Carlos Ruiz for bringing these citations to my attention.

60. Viz., the series of enthroned Virgins figuring as the centerpieces of panel paintings and altarpieces produced in Italy and Cataluña throughout the thirteenth and fourteenth centuries; portal sculptures and manuscript illuminations from a French context; earlier Iberian representations in sculpture of the Virgin enthroned and holding her Son which often form the focus of pilgrimage activity, etc.—the parallels are numerous, and the association of our Virgin with this concept would seem an indisputable one. For Italy, see Hayden B. J. Maginnis, *Painting in the age of Giotto: A historical reevaluation* (University Park, Pa.: Pennsylvania State University Press, 1997), where extensive bibliography is given. A recent discussion of the phenomenon and its relationship to contemporary developments in Jerusalem is found in Daniel H. Weiss, *Art and Crusade in the age of Saint Louis* (Cambridge; New York: Cambridge University Press, 1998).

with a particular kind of wisdom and knowledge—will round out the series of associations proposed here for this image.

Both bird and tree are motifs which would have been familiar to any Muslim mystic, particularly one who had lived and studied in medieval Iberia. The bird, as discussed by López-Baralt, is especially common,[61] but the particular form taken by Ibn al-Khatîb's tree appears to require more explanation, because of the visual sense in which it—in contrast, for example, to Ibn ʿArabî's much more abstract _Shajarat al-Kawn_ (Tree of Creation)—is presented to readers: indeed, it is urged on them as a subject, first, for visualization and then as a tool for contemplative and mystical ascent. Ibn al-Khatîb's treatise, in fact and because of its presentation as tree, is touted as "original and unique" by later writer al-Maqqarî. The originality perceived by the Muslim, however, who writes at a significant chronological and psychological distance from the fourteenth century, may find an explanation in the practical certainty—given Ibn al-Khatîb's extensive dealings with royal Castilian Christians, who in the fourteenth and fifteenth centuries were great readers of devotional treatises written by Ramon Llull[62]—of the Muslim's knowledge of works on similar themes by Christian (not to mention, as shall be seen, Jewish) authors. The _Rawdat_ does indeed exhibit striking similarities with other Islamic works produced in an Iberian context, including the poetic corpus of Ibn ʿArabî (particularly the _Tarjumân al-Ashwâq,_ mentioned in an allusive fashion by the Granadan in the introduction to his "Garden"), as well as his _Shajarat al-Kawn._[63] Even more relevant, however, are Ramon Llull's _Llibre del gentil e dels tres savis, Libre de contemplació en Deu,_ and _Llibre d'Amic e amat,_ as well as others of his essays which present knowledge and enlightenment of a decidedly mystical cast deliberately and specifically in the form of a tree.

Finally, as many readers must have been thinking for some paragraphs now, of importance is St. Bonaventure's _Lignum Vitae._ The _Rawdat's_ relationship to this particular work, however, is a complex and conflicted one; indeed, the two treatises, when taken together, might almost be said to constitute a set of antitypes. In Bonaventure's treatise, readers are instructed thus: "picture in the spiritual faculty of your mind a certain tree, whose root shall be watered by the font of a perpetual spring. . . ."[64] On the basis of this image, they are then told to visualize the tree's twelve fruits, which are unified into one—Christ's body. Ibn al-Khatîb's instructions to his pupils begin in an almost identical fashion. An initial impression of similarities between Ibn al-Khatîb's treatise and Bonaventure's, however, is quickly rectified, for the Granadan assiduously avoids references to pain and suffering, certainly in deliberate contrast to the necessity, in the Franciscan's model, of the devotee's empathetic experience of the pain and humiliation of the Lord's crucifixion. Instead, the _Rawdat_ offers more diffuse admonitions toward penitence, tempered by passionate assurances of the joyful, even ecstatic results which these efforts will yield (and in this, the Sufi's _tarîq_ is remarkably similar to early Jeronymite contemplative practices, but this is truly another story).

Thus, the Islamic components which Ibn al-Khatîb's treatise brings to bear on the Tordesillas Epiphany are not exactly pure. Indeed, the Granadan Sufi's meditative tree shares with all of the texts mentioned (save Bonaventure's), to which list should be added the Zoharic commentaries to be discussed briefly below,

61. See López Baralt, _Sufi Trobar Clus,_ ibidem, _Asedios a lo Indecible,_ and Annemarie Schimmel, _Mystical dimensions of Islam_ (Chapel Hill: University of North Carolina Press, 1975).

62. Indeed, this has been firmly demonstrated for the fifteenth century by Helen Nader, _The Mendoza family in the Spanish Renaissance, 1350–1550_ (New Brunswick, N.J.: Rutgers University Press, 1979), p. 97 ". . . the Counts of Benavente [who were _converso_ Jews] . . . quickly adapted to Christian culture and became famous in fifteenth-century Castile as poets and men of letters. Part of their reputation rested on their library, which reflects the taste of both the Counts of Benavente and their Castilian admirers, educated but not particularly aware of the Renaissance. . . . The greatest number of books by a single author are those of the thirteenth-century religious philosopher, Ramon Llull." Thanks to David McKenzie for bringing this citation to my attention. Although this phase of the project is far from complete, a glance through de Castro, _Manuscritos Franciscanos de la Biblioteca Nacional,_ followed by a consultation of Philobiblon, has yielded a substantial number of copies of works by Llull datable to the fourteenth century.

63. Ibn ʿArabî, _Tarjumân al-Ashwâq_ (Beirut: Dâr Sader, 1998); ibidem, _Shajarat al-Kawn = L'Arbre du Monde,_ intro., trans., and notes,

Maurice Gloton (Paris: Les Deux Océans, 1998); Ramon Llull, _Llibre del gentil e dels tres savis,_ ed., A. Bonner, in _Nova edició de les obres de Ramon Llull,_ 2 (Palma de Mallorca, 1993), pp. 5–210; ibidem, _Le Livre du Gentil et de Trois Sages,_ version française médiévale complétée par une traduction en français moderne, trans., Armand Llinarès (Paris: Presses Universitaires de France, 1966); ibidem, _El Libro del Amigo y Amado_ (Madrid: Tipografia Yagües, 1900); Ibn al-Khatîb, _Rawdat al-taʿrîf._

64. _Lignum Vitae,_ in Bonaventure, _Decem Opuscula,_ 5th ed. (Quaracchi: Collegio di S. Bonaventura, 1965), p. 138, quoted and translated in Hatfield, "Tree of Life and the Holy Cross," p. 141. An empathetic narration of Christ's life and sufferings is also intimately wed to the structure of Ubertino da Casale's slightly later _Arbor vitae crucifixae Jesu_ (Turin: Bottega d'Erasmo, 1961), composed in 1305. See Hatfield, op. cit., p. 158, n. 23.

most if not all elements of an allegorical or symbolic paradigm which might be sketched as including *locus amoenus,* water, trees (of various sorts), vines, and other carefully specified varieties of vegetation, bird, and Lady (the Virgin; Llull's *Intelligence,* Ibn ᶜArabî's mysterious Mistress of the Sanctuary—*rabbat al-hamâ*). All, moreover, deploy these elements, as recently expounded by Hames,[65] in a manner so that they might, if considered by an informed reader (ideally, a mystic), serve as a contemplative guide toward the achievement of ecstatic experience and union with the divine.[66] Thus, although Iberia's fourteenth-century devotional imagery cannot be shown to be directly related to texts such as the *Meditationes* more commonly in use elsewhere in Europe, it finds striking echoes in the metaphorical, allusive, loving, and joyful paradigms evoked by these texts, through which the pain and agony of the Passion are, literally, subsumed into the metaphors of love-, wine-, and garden-description verse.[67]

As stated, I believe that the Patio Mudéjar was originally intended to serve a religious function. It then follows that the naturalistic vegetal idiom particular to it was chosen with this function in mind.[68] As also noted,

the patio was probably constructed as a solution to the problem of how to connect the chapel to the rest of the convent, and thus it might be said that the patio was conceived with the already-extant chapel and its first program of images in mind. Like the iconographic modifications to traditional representations of the Epiphany, the decision to use a naturalistic vegetal idiom in the ornament of Tordesillas's Patio Mudéjar was deliberate. It came, however, not from a desire to appropriate a "Granadan" language of (secular) power,[69] but from an awareness, on the part most likely of Pedro I, that these motifs "meant" something very specific. Although it is indeed a stretch to imagine Pedro I entering Tordesillas's cloistered area accompanied by Ibn al-Khatîb, it is not so difficult to imagine him bringing along a few of the Granadan Sufi's ideas. As discussed by Dodds and many before her, then, the connection which produces Islamic influence in these *mudéjar* structures is indeed the court (through which sphere we may explain Pedro I's association with Ibn al-Khatîb). The currency of exchange, however, is not, in the case of these particular motifs, one of a language of power. Rather, it is a specific and significant devotional idiom intimately connected to devotional practices directly associated with the most elite sphere of Iberian society and meaningful to Muslims, Christians, and Jews alike.[70]

---

65. Again, see Hames, "Conversion via Ecstatic Experience," and now, *The art of conversion: Christianity and Kabbalah in the thirteenth century* (Leiden: Brill, 2000).

66. Also important to a more detailed consideration of the "iconographies" of Tordesillas, then, will be methodologies and models suggested in recent work on ritual uses of poetic, allegorical, metaphorical, and narrative forms, including their composition and performance. See Harvey J. Hames, *The art of conversion;* Luce López-Baralt, *Sufi Trobar Clus* and *Asedios a lo Indecible;* María R. Menocal, *Shards of love: Exile and the origins of the lyric* (Durham: Duke University Press, 1994); Michael Sells, *Stations of desire: Love elegies from Ibn ᶜArabî and new poems* (Jerusalem: Ibis Editions, 2000) and ibidem, *The Mystical Languages of Unsaying* (Chicago: University of Chicago Press, 1994). Limitations of space only permit that these texts be mentioned here; the larger study of which this essay forms part will include a detailed comparative analysis of the texts in question (their common language of metaphor, symbols, and meditative and communicative strategies).

67. It is interesting to note that Llull's *Book of the Gentil and the Three Sages* has a tradition of illustration which quite probably stems back to the original, and the processes of contemplation and the organization of enlightenment and knowledge are virtually identical to those which characterize Ibn al-Khatîb's. Moreover, drawings of a "sacred tree" are mentioned in the introduction to the edition of the text consulted here as being present in ms. copies of the *Rawdat* housed today in Istanbul; I have not yet been able to view a copy of these images.

68. Recent work by Ruiz (see "Nuevos Datos") has again focused on the relationship between building (Tordesillas) and couple (Pedro I and María de Padilla), on the importance of Pedro's intimate friendship with Muhammad V, and on the probable exchange of artisans which

resulted from this relationship (see, on this, Ruiz and Rallo Gruss, "El Palacio de Ruy López Dávalos"). Ruiz rightly argues that this relationship would have strongly impacted the aesthetic decisions made at Tordesillas; he also proposes the specifically Granadan connections which are the consequences of this relationship as a counterargument to (rather vague) assertions made by previous scholars who have seen primarily influence of the "Toledan *mudéjar*" in Tordesillas's program of ornament. I believe that both associations are relevant, but full discussion of this point must be left for future studies.

69. The suggestion is made by Dodds, *Convivencia,* pp. 113–131. This is not to deny that power is part of it: rather, it almost certainly is, and Schlomo ha-Levi did indeed derive a large part of his power through his association with Pedro I's court. Anyone, moreover, who had the funds and the permission to construct a sumptuous building for the purposes of religious activities had power, and in the large majority of cases, this power might be argued to derive directly from the king. Given recent research, however, we may now begin to be much more specific in our interpretations: according to findings by Ruiz and Rallo Gruss discussed in previous notes, the construction and ornamentation of the synagogue almost certainly predates the construction of Pedro I's Alcázares in Sevilla, thus making a derivative interpretation of the synagogue vis-à-vis the Sevillan palace problematic to say the least.

70. Conversely, if applied to a parochial church, this language would have had little meaning for its parishioners, which is perhaps why we find no early examples of naturalistic *mudéjar* vegetation from such contexts.

Figure 9. Sinagoga del Tránsito, Toledo, detail. Ca. 1360. Casa Amatller, Foto MAS.

Connections to this latter group of thinkers may now be explored. Tordesillas's Virgin, in her manifestation as *Sedes Sapientiae* (indeed, she proffers to her viewers a very specific sort of *sapientia,* contained in the diminutive tree she gracefully balances in her hand), finds a Jewish sister in Toledo. She appears, or so the building's inscription program tells us, in the dense and relatively abstract rendition of vegetal motifs on the walls of the Sinagoga del Tránsito. This association is one which both strengthens the case for an intimate connection having been envisioned from the start between chapel and patio, and provides the basis for the present interpretation of the patio's program.

The extant program of ornament which exhibits the greatest similarities to Tordesillas's Patio Mudéjar is, in fact, that of the Toledan synagogue which dates between 1357 and 1362. The similarities are striking, particularly with regard to the more naturalistic panels of vegetation which adorn the second-floor chamber which was most probably the women's gallery (fig. 9).[71] The link which both connects the two programs of ornament and, in my opinion, accounts for the striking similarities between them, is the Hebrew personification of Wisdom in the Proverbs—*khokhmah.* According to kabbalistic traditions, she is not only Wisdom, but Divine Wisdom, direct emanation from *Ein Sof,* the primary principle, and the source of Intelligence, or *Binah.* She is not, however, represented in human form, but rather, in an associative manner similar to that argued here for the Epiphany's tree and which will also be proposed for the Patio Mudéjar, as the Tree of Life:[72] on the synagogue's eastern wall, near where the holy Arc of the *torah* was kept, we read (Hebrew Proverb III, verse 18), "She is a tree of life to those who lay hold of her/those who hold her fast are called happy."[73]

The synagogue was built under the patronage of Schlomo ha-Levi Abulafia, one-time treasurer of Pedro I and member of one of Toledo's wealthiest and most prominent Jewish families. Although this fact is less discussed in the art historical literature on the synagogue, Schlomo ha-Levi was also a member of a family with a long history of kabbalistic practice and

71. For discussion of the possible dating of this structure, as well as a new suggestion regarding this matter, see Ruiz and Rallo, "El Palacio de Ruy López Dávalo."

72. Juan Joseph Heydeck, *Las Inscripciones Hebreas de la Sinagoga Toledana de R. Semuel ha-Levi* (Toledo: Fuensalida, 1978). Thanks, again, to Damon Montclare for bringing this citation to my attention.

73. *Khokhmah's* representation on this wall, which surrounds the most holy of all areas in the synagogue, is more abstract than in other areas of the structure, a distinction which was certainly meant to differentiate this wall from the others.

Figure 10. Seminario Mayor (formerly house of Ruy López Dávalos), Toledo, detail of frieze, late fourteenth century. Photo courtesy of the Seminario Mayor and Juan Carlos Ruiz.

writing.[74] Thus, Schlomo ha-Levi is connected with a tradition of a devotional/ecstatic language which makes intense and extensive use of plant, garden, water, flower, and tree metaphors taken directly from the holy text as the basis for extended exegesis.[75] This fact, coupled with well-founded arguments recently put forward by Ruiz concerning a probable fourteenth-century date for Toledo's "other" synagogue, the abstractly and starkly ornamented Santa María la Blanca, allows us to justify a specificity of intention in the use of such strikingly naturalistic vegetation in ha-Levi's "palatine chapel."[76]

Earlier, it was noted that Tordesillas's little patio reminds us of gardens, glens, trees, flowers, and fruit all at once. I also believe that, on the basis of its association with the program of the Toledan synagogue, it is possible to argue that it represented the Virgin, here incarnated directly into the visitor's experience of the patio as garden, glen, flowers, fruit, and trees. Through this allusive manner of representation, dialogue is established between the patio and the diminutive tree which she, appearing again in her human form, holds in the visionary version of the Epiphany represented on the walls of the Capilla Dorada. The Virgin, then, as collection of shifting, paradigmatic, and lyrical evocations of garden themes, is thus directly linked to her son through his representation as Tree of Life crucified upon the Tree of Knowledge.[77] All connections, however, to pain and suffering are sublimated—to co-opt, yet again, López-Baralt's felicitous phrase—in good "Semitic" fashion. I am reminded of a devotional exercise of Ramón Llull's which employs poetic metaphor to—literally—transform Christ's deathly pallor and the drops of red blood upon it into jewel-like flowers of the most

74. See the introductory pp. to Heydeck, *Las inscripciones hebreas,* where a long line of illustrious and kabbalistically inclined ancestors is traced for Schlomo ha-Levi Abulafia. These include Semuel ha-Levi Abulafia (born in Burgos in 1224; died in Toledo in 1283), courtier of Alfonso X, who wrote extensively in the genre of biblical commentary; his writings show marked kabbalistic tendencies. His *Osar ha-Kabod* ("Treasure of Glory") includes the first known citations from the *Zohar.*

75. Lachower, Tishby and Goldstein, *The wisdom of the Zohar,* see esp. pp. 360–370; Mosés de León, *Sefer ha-Rimmon = The Book of the Pomegranate,* trans., ed., and intro., Elliot R. Wolfson (Atlanta, Ga.: Scholar's Press, 1988).

76. Many thanks, first, to Damon Montclare for giving me permission to incorporate into the arguments made in this essay parts of his findings concerning Schlomo ha-Levi and the relevance of Zoharic material to the Sinagoga del Tránsito from his semester research paper produced in our seminar on *Mudejarismo* and, second,

to Juan Carlos Ruiz for sharing his as-yet unpublished paper on the Toledan synagogues with me ("Sinagogas Sefardíes Monumentales en el Contexto de la Arquitectura Medieval Hispana").

77. See Hatfield, "Tree of Life and the Holy Cross," p. 135.

delicate perfume, with petals of pure white and glorious crimson. The same metaphors, a few pages forward, and in a manner remarkably similar to the Patio Mudéjar's vines and fruits and in a sublimation remarkably *dis*similar to the symbolic language proposed by Hatfield for an Italian Franciscan context, are also used to evoke the Virgin.[78]

But how can the Virgin (who, besides, is nowhere "visible" to "western" eyes anywhere in the patio) be tree, vine, *hortus conclusus,* Mother of God, Queen of Heaven, and *Sedes Sapientiae* all at once? The answer lies in the fact that Iberia was home, in the fourteenth century as it had been for centuries, to a different sort of iconography, in addition to that most commonly associated, at the very least since Panofsky's seminal publications, with the "reading" of Christian images. This Iberian iconography is one intimately embedded in the poetics of metaphor particular to the Arabic and Hebrew languages, never shown off to better advantage than in a lyric about love, wine, or nature, all of which, as is well known, were embraced by both Muslim and Jewish seekers of union with the divine (it might be argued, particularly among Iberian members of these groups) as they attempted to articulate their desires, aspirations and ecstatic experiences. Christian exegesis, on the other hand—with the exception of the well-known associations of the Virgin with the *hortus conclusus* articulated through Song of Songs and its

commentaries—most commonly signals the garden as the scene of first temptation and later betrayal (indeed, Eve's betrayal of God foretells Judas's of His Son).[79] Moreover, even allowing for the positive associations of garden motifs permitted by this tradition, Christian references both exegetical and visual to the Garden of Eden most often dwell on the loss of Paradises. This is in stark contrast, certainly, to the Islamic tradition, for which the garden represents unequivocally the beatific state to come, and which finds extended echoes in the Zoharic commentaries discussed here. Indeed, the Zohar, as does Ibn al-Khatîb in his treatise, clearly signals the garden as the *locus amoenus* of mystical union. It would seem safe to argue that Tordesillas is clearly in the Semitic camp on this issue: its gardens and trees are first and foremost evocative of positive and joyous associations. Although the more dolorous significations may well lie beneath the surface, it is left to the individual viewer to infer or extrapolate them. This, indeed, might have been carried out through techniques of mental visualization which would have pleased Ibn ʿArabî himself: the sheikh from Murcia is known to have advocated bringing forth the devotional image in the mind, rather than on a piece of cloth or wood.[80]

Many would perhaps insist on the relevance of Bonaventure's *Lignum Vitae* here: surely it is more likely to have informed the production of contemplative imagery for these Clarisas, as we know it did in an Italian

---

78. The devotional treatise in question is Llull's *Les cent noms de deu* ("The 100 Names of God"), which I have consulted in manuscript form in BN Mss. Microfilm 3631; texts discussed here are found on ff. 5r–8v. This copy dates to the fifteenth century, but it is extremely interesting in the possibilities it offers us of connecting it directly to a female devotional context. On f. 15 v., one of the ms.'s characteristically ornate initials (more typical are vegetal themes) literally transforms itself into a woman's head. She does not wear monastic dress but, rather, is dressed in the height of early-fifteenth-century fashion. Clearly the manuscript was owned by, and probably conceived for a female member of the nobility. It eventually made its way to the library of the cathedral of Toledo, and from there to the BN. For the Italian *comparanda,* see again Hatfield, "Tree of Life and the Holy Cross," pp. 135 ff. He concentrates particularly on representations of the *Lignum Vitae* by Pacino di Bonaguida and Taddeo Gaddi. There are also Catalan interpretations of the more common Franciscan visual exegesis of these themes, probably influenced by the Italian examples: e.g., a *Lignum Vitae* which evidences clear parallels to Bonaventure's text from the Capella dels Dolors of the parochial church at L'Arboç, completed some time around 1330; a similar image is found in the church of the Dominican convent at Puigcerdà. Although they have not survived, documentary sources record representations of the *Lignum Vitae* in the Franciscan convent of Barcelona and in the church choir of the closely connected Clarisan establishment at Pedralbes. See Sureda i Pons, *Pintura gòtica,* pp. 23–24.

79. This is borne out in Jeryldene Wood's analysis of Pacino di Bonaguida's 1331 *Lignum Vitae,* which she has convincingly placed within a Tuscan Clarisan context (see *Women, art, and spirituality*). In this image, the garden is given a rather dubious role, as it is represented as the scene of the first temptation and the subsequent expulsion. The painter does not expend a great deal of effort in his rendition of the garden, thus signaling its position of lesser importance in the altarpiece as a whole. Even in the case of biblical texts which contain the potential for an unabashedly positive exegesis of the garden (e.g., the *Cantica Cantorum*), more Northern renditions of its illustration tend to concentrate on the narrative elements potentially contained in the poetic text, and relegate the garden and its elements to a sphere of importance which is very much secondary. See, for example, Jeffrey F. Hamburger, *The Rothschild Canticles: Art and Mysticism in Flanders and the Rhineland circa 1300* (New Haven: Yale University Press, 1990).

80. This aspect of Ibn ʿArabî's thought, as well as other related concepts such as representation and abstraction (*tashbîh* and *tanzîh,* respectively), are discussed by ʿAbd al-Wahhab Meddeb in "La imagen y lo invisible. Ibn ʿArabî: Estéticas," in *Los dos horizontes* (*Textos sobre Ibn ʿArabî*) (Murcia: Editora Regional, 1992), pp. 259–269. For some of the sheikh's views on the question of images in a Christian context, see *al-Futûhât al-Makîya,* ed., Ahmad Shams al-Din, 4 vols. (Beirût: Dâr al-Kutub al-ʾIlmîyah, 1999), I, pp. 337–343.

context—indeed, we have Pacino di Buonaguida's *Lignum Vitae* to prove it. My answer is that I have not yet found the use of Bonaventure's Lignum Vitae attested for a Castilian Clarisan context at this early date; like Pseudo-Bonaventure's *Meditationes,* it finds scant representation in the documentary record.[81] Moreover, as observed, in order to ascend Bonaventure's tree one must first pass, along with the Saviour, through the intense physical sufferings of the Passion; the accompanying imagery usually reflects the path mapped out. The garden in Pacino's painting is, indeed, the soil in which the tree grows, but it is a tree upon which the Crucified Christ hangs, amid fruit-like roundels containing extensive and evocative narrative representation of his life and Passion. It is also explicitly presented as the setting of the original sin.

It can be no accident that Tordesillas's program is evocative of the lush beauty of gardens, their plants heavy with fruit, to be enjoyed amid the delightful sounds of fountains; might this not be because Tordesillas's inhabitants knew, through their association with Pedro I and his court, of Ibn al-<u>Kh</u>atîb's tree, or of the Zoharic interpretation of the garden, and preferred their discourse of joy and love? Here, as is so often the case, the Virgin appears almost to meld into—even to take pride of place over—her son. In this case, however, it is very much an Iberian Virgin. She is indeed the mother of the Christian god, but she is also the embodiment both of a sacred garden similar to Ibn ʿArabî's, and of a Divine Wisdom expressed in terms almost identical to that contemplated, certainly with joy, by Schlomo ha-Levi.

Conclusion: A Jeronymite manuscript in the Biblioteca Nacional

> Our couch is green, the beams of our house are cedar; our rafters are pine . . . and over our doors are all choice fruits. . . . Look! There he stands behind our wall, gazing in at the windows, looking through the lattice!
> —*Song of Songs, 1:17, 7:13, 2:9*

The evocations of gardens, perfumes, fruits, and lush vegetation analyzed in this essay cannot help but lead us toward a consideration of the Song of Songs, and yet this text has yet to be mentioned in connection with Tordesillas's Semitic iconographies. It is now, however, possible to bring this rich trove of garden and vegetal imagery to bear in this context. As mentioned earlier, during the final years of the 1370s, and until the queen's death in 1381, Tordesillas's devotional life underwent a dramatic and—until now—unacknowledged reform under the patronage of Juana Manuel, whose projects were carried out in such close collusion with Fray Pedro de Guadalajara (or, "de Aniago") that we may speak of a specifically Jeronymite agenda of change. What the end results of this program might have been had it been brought to full fruition, it is impossible to say, for Fray Pedro disappears from the documentation at a moment shortly before the queen's death.

Nevertheless, it is possible to suggest the sort of spiritual exercises that Fray Pedro would have proposed (or, perhaps, *did* propose) to his protégées at Tordesillas, and to affirm that these were based not in empathetic meditations on the physical sufferings of Christ's Passion, but on a sublimation of this agony into a spiritual union affected through meditations on the Psalms and the *Cantica Cantorum.* These exercises, which in effect are presented as an "ascent" based initially on certain of the Psalms, are articulated in the sections devoted to these books in a manuscript of biblical commentary preserved in the Biblioteca Nacional. Selected biblical verses appear in Latin in columns in the center of the page and are glossed, on the left, in Latin and on the right, in almost word-for-word translation of the Latin commentary, in Castilian. The Old Testament and its commentary occupy a far greater number of pages than does the New (in which very little attempt is made to elicit viewers' empathetic experiences through vivid evocations of the Passion); the entirety is preceded by a selection of St. Jerome's prologues translated into Castilian.[82]

---

81. For the thirteenth and fourteenth centuries, in fact, it is sparsely attested in Iberia in general. Castro, *Manuscritos Franciscanos,* only records one copy of it: no. 2, p. 15.

82. The manuscript in question is BN Mss. 10232, identified in the BN's catalogue as a *"Bible moralisée."* Given limitations of space, it will not be possible to do more than sketch the directions of interpretation suggested by this association. This manuscript and its devotional message will be the object of a detailed study in a chapter of the larger study of which this essay forms part. For the moment it is interesting to note the way in which the verses which narrate the Passion are explicated (esp. ff. 199r–202v). When discussing those who weep over the Saviour's fate as he bears his cross toward Calvary, the anonymous author comments, in a tone difficult to avoid terming matter-of-fact, *"los que lloran a Jesu Cristo en via cruces s(ignifican) los que lloran los efectos y no las causas de la iglesia corrupta."* A further cry from the affective nature of more familiar Franciscan piety would be difficult to find. Likewise, the Last Supper is handled in a manner which suggests that the interior or hidden sense of the verse, rather than its immediate narrative significance, was of interest: the *cenaculo* signifies *". . . aquel que transciende la sup(er)ficie dela letra por entendimiento . . . ,"* to be contrasted with *". . . aquel que anda en la letra," "(quien) faze paschua en la cosa baxa"* (f. 195r).

The large coat of arms belonging to Castilla-León, which graces the verso side of its second folio, clearly attests to the manuscript's royal ownership and its commonly accepted fourteenth-century date, coupled with a clear association to the Jeronymites apparent through references to themes dear to the order sprinkled throughout the commentary text, leaves only a twenty-seven-year margin of error.[83] The public to which the glosses are addressed clearly was extremely knowledgeable of the holy scriptures (one thinks here of the high level of literacy generally accepted for royalty and nobility in the later years of the middle ages, and of the admonitions continually made by San Jerónimo himself to his followers concerning the necessity of unceasing and detailed study of the holy text), as the verses are unnumbered. The manuscript's audience is also one which the author wishes to convince, first, of the desirability to royalty of monastic and almost certainly Jeronymite advisors and, on the other, of the convent and particularly the mountain hermitage as the places most conducive to leading a rewarding spiritual life.[84] One likely conclusion which we might draw here is that the manuscript was commissioned by, or perhaps given to, Juana Manuel, and it is certainly possible that its author was Pedro Fernández Pecha.[85]

In this commentary, moreover, paradise—a place which, tellingly, is discussed in far greater detail in the Jeronymite's explications of the Psalms and the *Cantica Cantorum* than it is in his New Testament commentary—is not the heavenly city of Jerusalem but a garden in which the Tree of Life grows, and the faithful enjoy communion with the saints and martyrs, whom they contemplate joyfully in their manifestations as jewel-like flowers and fruits.[86] This evocation, in fact, is remarkably similar to what would appear to be a late-fourteenth-century Toledan representation of Paradise (see fig. 10), dating to the final third of the fourteenth century.[87] It might be reiterated here that Queen Juana and Fray Pedro saw fit to preserve both the chapel Epiphany and the ornamental program of the Patio Mudéjar. It is not difficult to understand their reasons.

---

83. As will be remembered, the Jeronymite order was officially founded in 1373. Gemma Avenoza has proposed (in 2001) a date between 1390 and 1400 for the ms.: see the database PHILOBIBLON, www. sunsite.berkeley.edu/Philobiblon, Ms. BN 10232, BETA/2450, BETA Manuscript or Print / MANID 2450. Information was retrieved from the site on 29 September 2002.

84. Passages which argue for a close association to the Jeronymites include, on f. 32 r., an extensive discussion of the penitence of Mariam, Moses' sister (implicitly constructing an analogy with the nuns; references to penitence are frequent in the ms., but interestingly enough are not concentrated in the New Testament commentary); the interpretation offered of Saul's false message to King David (f. 48r–48v: commentary on the verse "*Rex achis multu diligens* D[avi]d" is "*Achis que amava a david s(ignifica) a los buenos principes que aman a los Buenos clerigos en su compania*"); and especially the commentary offered on a verse from the narration of the Nativity offered in Mark: "*hic virgo filium suum reclinavit in presepio*" is interpreted as a sign that hermitages and monasteries were the most desirable places for leading a successful spiritual life ("*Esto significa que los verdaderos fijos de la iglesia estan en los encerramientos de los monasteries humilmente y otros en las cuevas de las mo(n)tanas asi como los hermitanos . . .*"). Caves in the mountainous environs of Toledo, interestingly, were the chosen dwelling places of Fray Pedro and his brother, along with other companions, during the years immediately preceding the formal foundation of the Jeronymite order. For a history of the order from its earliest days, see José de Sigüenza, O.S.J., *Historia de la Orden de San Jerónimo*, 2 vols., ed. and preliminary study, Francisco J. Campos y Fernández de Sevilla (Valladolid: Junta de Castilla y León, 2001).

85. Another possibility is Juana's son, Juan I, whose generous patronage of the Jeronymites is well documented. Juan I ascended to

---

the throne in 1380 upon his father's death. If Avenoza's proposal for the ms.'s date is accepted, we must also consider Enrique III as a possible patron; Juana and Juan, however, are probably more likely, given their close connections to the order.

86. E.g., f. 3v., in Prologue IV: ". . . descripcion del varon justo: como david, el arbol de la vida q(ue) es en parayso, lo comparase entre las otras virtudes . . .". Interestingly, here (in contrast to the Italian Franciscan context evoked by Hatfield in "Tree of Life and the Holy Cross") an overt symbolic relationship between Christ and the Tree of Life is not established. Also, in commentary on Cantica Cantorum (f. 114r–114v), specifically the verse which begins, "veni in ortum meum soror mea . . . ," we find the following statement: "Aqui dize (Jesucristo) ala egl(es)ia las tuyas palabras son oydas por cuanto tome carne en el mi huerto co(n)viene a saber en el cielo empireo el cual es sobre todos los cielos onde es el huerto de los deleytes . . .". Although much more work is needed on this point, I would offer the initial observation that Christ is saying that he "took flesh" (tomé carne) in Paradise, in the highest heaven, which is a "Garden of Delights." Might it be that readers are being asked to wait until they reach the "cielo empireo" before contemplating Christ's holy flesh? If so, the discourse then becomes even more radically different from Bonaventure's. Moreover, in a passage from the same page, the fruits of the "huerto de los deleytes" are not the events of Christ's Passion, but the holy martyrs who have already ascended to this place of greatest joy. Like apples, they are red on the outside (the only reference made to their passion), and white on the inside, and the perfumes they exude are indescribably heavenly.

87. Although Ruiz and Rallo ("El Palacio de Ruy López Dávalos") insist on a very specific date for this ornament—1361—I prefer to leave a wider margin for its establishment, as I do not view the involvement of Granadan artisans as necessary to its production. As far as we know, the Seminario Mayor did not belong to the church or to any monastic order during the fourteenth century; see Martínez Caviro, *Mudéjar toledano*, pp. 197–208. Another fascinating possibility for the Toledan monument, and for others like it, is that as a result, for example, of the close relationships maintained by the Jeronymites with, not only those religious, both male and female, under their care, but also with lay persons with whom they interacted on an intimate basis, such concepts could have become more relevant to secular patrons as well. This is a matter in need of further investigation.

López-Baralt's investigations into the Semitic roots of San Juan de la Cruz's reading of the *Cantica Cantorum* have revealed the tip of an iceberg.[88] The idea of a sudden renewal of such connections, however, is problematic in the sixteenth century when relations between confessional groups were problematic at best, and a consciousness and celebration of these connections on the part of male and female religious, is problematic (as López-Baralt readily acknowledges). Rather, San Juan's verses represent the continuation of a tradition whose past has yet to be fully uncovered, but is demonstrably linked, in the case of Tordesillas, to the Jeronymites, as it almost certainly is in other examples.[89] If, on the one hand, it becomes more and more difficult to argue for direct Islamic influence as the fourteenth century finishes and the fifteenth begins, we may, on the other hand, find these strands again, like the meandering vines of the Patio *Mudéjar* itself, preserved (under different names, to be sure) in the devotional life of the newest and most radical of the monastic orders, the only one to have, as many Jeronymite scholars remind us, come into being on Iberian soil.[90]

88. See *Asedios a lo Invisible.* The importance of the Song of Songs in an Iberian context has also been confirmed for a female Cistercian context. See A. Nascimento, "Osculetur me osculo oris sui: uma leitura a várias vozes ou dramatizaçao do Livro dos Cantares num manuscrito cisterciense de Arouca," in *Actas do IV Congresso da Associaçao Hispânica de Literatura Medieval (Lisboa)* (Lisboa: Ediçoes Cosmos, 1991), pp. 49–55. The ms. in question is a lectionary from the monastery of Arouca, a copy of the *Cantar de los Cantares,* interspersed with singular rubrics which imply, according to the author, a "quasi-theatrical" reading practice for the text, in which it is logical to suppose that the nuns would have participated. Many thanks to Gemma Avenoza for this reference. It might be possible to make a similar suggestion for BN Mss. 10232: utterances of Bridegroom and Bride are identified by rubrics: "*vox sponsi*" and "*vox sponsa.*"

89. Indeed, Fray Pedro's *Soliloquios* almost certainly represent a precedent for San Juan's verses inspired in his understanding of the Song of Songs. For the *Soliloquios,* see Rafael Lapesa, "Un ejemplo de prosa retórica a fines del siglo XIV: Los Soliloquios de Fray Pedro Fernández Pecha," in *Studies in Honor of Lloyd A. Kasten* (Madison: Hispanic Seminary of Medieval Studies, 1975), pp. 117–128.

90. The Jeronymite order in Spain has received renewed attention recently, but the territory still to be explored is vast. As an introduction to the subject see F. Javier Campos y Fernández, *La Orden de San Jerónimo y sus monasterios. Actas del simposio,* 2 vols. (San Lorenzo, el Escorial: Real Colegio Universitario Escorial María Cristina, 1999); Amalia López-Yarto, José María Prados García, and Isabel Mateos Campos, *El arte de la orden jerónima: historia y mecenazgo* (Madrid: IBERDROLA, 1999); José Antonio Ruiz Hernando, *Los monasteries jerónimos españoles* (Segovia: Caja Segovia, 1997).

Figure 1. General view of the Umayyad mosque from the southeast.

The dialogic dimension of Umayyad art

NASSER RABBAT

In the second half of the seventh century C.E., an Umayyad elite, proud of its Arabic heritage and new Islamic identity, established the center of its empire in Bilad al-Sham (the Roman Oriens or the Holy Land, which comprises modern-day Syria, Lebanon, Jordan, and Israel/Palestine). There, the Umayyads came into contact with a still-active late antique artistic tradition—the Postclassicism of modern scholarship—which was essentially heir to the Hellenistic and Roman artistic continuum. They also found traces of historic cultures of the land and some new innovations and adaptations introduced by formerly Hellenized and lately Christianized local peoples (such as the Nabateans, Palmyrenes, Ghassanids, Lakhmids, and many others).[1] How the art of the Umayyads, and by extension that of the whole nascent Islamic culture, responded to the artistic encounter with Postclassical art in Bilad al-Sham has been the subject of debate among scholars for more than a century. Was the reaction a break with or a continuation of that artistic heritage? Or was it perhaps more fluid and more complex than either of these two antithetical possibilities?

Opinions have varied over time. Many scholars of the late nineteenth and early twentieth century insisted on a rupture with Postclassical art in Bilad al-Sham which, in their view, produced a disarticulated and less expressive Umayyad art.[2] This reading, which stemmed from ideological rather than scholarly considerations, survived far longer than did its biased and compromised source, the bluntly eurocentric cultural stratification of the colonial age.[3] Other scholars accepted the continuity explanation, but saw in the transition from late antiquity to early Islam some degeneration in quality and artistic sensibility. They attributed the decline to the prevalence of copying in the making of Umayyad monuments with little understanding of the architectural and artistic qualities or iconographic content of their putative models.[4]

A more critical generation of Islamic art historians attempted in the second half of the twentieth century to soften the negative effect usually associated with the notion of copying by proposing an intentionality to it, thus restoring to the Umayyads a certain cultural and artistic agency.[5] These scholars posited a selective appropriation process, by which the Umayyads instead of merely parroting the monuments of classical art are supposed to have rejected those aspects of the art that they did not like or considered to be offensive to their beliefs, whereas they purposely adopted those other aspects that pleased them or served them in enhancing their image. Further recent refinements on the copying

---

Earlier versions of this essay were delivered in the symposium, "Exploring the Frontiers of Islamic Art and Architecture," sponsored by the Aga Khan Program For Islamic Architecture, which I organized at MIT in May 18–19, 2001, and in the Islamic Art Circle, School of Oriental and African Studies, University of London, on January 16, 2002. I would like to thank Oleg Grabar and Erika Naginsky for their valuable comments on the final paper. I would like to dedicate this essay to the memory of Margaret Sevcenko (1931–2002), irreplaceable friend, editor, and mentor.

1. A comprehensive study of the state of research on the question of Eastern Christian art is Mahmoud Zibawi, *Eastern Christian worlds* (Collegeville, Minn.: Liturgical Press, 1995); see also John Boardman, *Classical art in eastern translation: a lecture delivered at the Ashmolean Museum, Oxford, on 27th May, 1993* (Oxford: Leopard's Head: 1993).

2. Jules Bourgoin, *L'art arabe* (Paris: Firmin Didot, 1867); Michel Écochard, *Filiation de monuments grecs, byzantins et islamiques: une question de géométrie* (Paris: Librairie Orientaliste Paul Geuthner, 1977); Archibald Campbell Dickie, "The Great Mosque of the Omeiyades, Damascus," *Palestine Exploration Fund: Quarterly Statement 1897* (1897): 268–282; René Dussaud, "Le Temple de Jupiter Damascénien et ses transformations aux époques chrétienne et

musulmane," *Syria* 3 (1922): 219–250; R. Phenè Spiers, "The Great Mosque of Damascus," *Palestine Exploration Fund: Quarterly Statement 1897* (1897): 282–299; idem, "The Great Mosque of the Omeiyades, Damascus," *The Architectural Review* 8 (1900): 80–88, 103–114, 58–69; Charles Wilson, "Extracts from Diary of Captain Wilson in 1865, Making plan and taking photographs of the Mosque of Damascus," *Palestine Exploration Fund: Quarterly Statement 1897* (1897): 299–301.

3. A recent sweeping critique asserts that the art historical bias obtains in the Islamic as well as the pre-Islamic period by denying the originality of the Arabic and Syriac contributions to the art of Postclassicism and early Christianity and by subsuming them under the Western term, Byzantine; see Shakir Lou'aybi, *al-Fann al-Islami wa-l Masihiyya al-'Arabiyya, Dawr al-Masihiyyin al-'Arab fi Takwin al-Fann al-Islami* (Beirut: Riad al-Rayyes Books, 2001), 9–41, and esp. 63–71.

4. One of the most bizarrely ardent proponents of this interpretation is Giovanni Teresio Rivoira, *Architettura musulmana; sue origini e suo sviluppo* (Milan: U. Hoepli, 1914), translated by G. M. Rushforth as *Moslem architecture; its origins and development* (London: Oxford University Press, 1918). For an analysis of Rivoira's Romanocentric frame of interpretation, see Annabel Jane Wharton, *Refiguring the post classical city: Dura Europos, Jerash, Jerusalem, and Ravenna* (Cambridge: Cambridge University Press, 1995), 3–12.

5. Oleg Grabar, *The Formation of Islamic Art* (New Haven: Yale University Press, 1973, reprt. 1987), is the foundational study for this direction.

model have posited a dual cultural process of selection and translation, whereby the Umayyads recognized the need to make their art understandable and expressive to two audiences: their own Islamic, Arabic-speaking followers and the "other" local Christian subjects or the formidable Byzantine opponents.[6] This approach has shifted the focus from intercultural to intracultural exchange and introduced the notion of reception in interpreting the motive behind Umayyad art and architecture.

Seldom emphasized, however, is that the Umayyads did not come from a cultural void. Not only did they bring with them a budding Islamic dogma with its sacred texts, tentative world views, and a still-developing legal framework with its allowances and prohibitions. They also cultivated a genuine culture with deep roots in the pre-Islamic heritage of the vast area that they shared with other Arabs inside and outside Arabia. Arabic cultural heritage had engendered some favorite forms of expression—poetry in particular, but also a more general fondness for the emphatic pictorial potential of words and the inherent structural capacity of rhyme—and a set of seemingly well-developed tastes, attitudes, and religious convictions, and perhaps even pictorial conventions.[7] Nor were the Umayyads ignorant of the composite cultures of late antique Bilad al-Sham. In fact, they were quite familiar with them long before the rise of Islam. Both regular trade with Byzantine Bilad al-Sham and extended contacts with local Christian Arabs had exposed the Umayyads, as the leading merchants of Quraysh, to the visual culture of late antiquity, or at least to an Arabized version of it, as reproduced by the Ghassanids and others.[8]

These cultural and artistic preferences and sensibilities, which are still not completely mapped out, must have had a substantial effect on the development of Umayyad art and architecture. They predisposed the Umayyads toward some forms of expressions rather than others and toward a number of the different peregrinations of late antique art in Bilad al-Sham as well as affected the mode by which they appropriated them when they became the rulers of the new Islamic empire. Rather than mimetic, the appropriation process was dialogic, that is, it went beyond borrowing, copying, or reproducing to consciously engage the extant artistic traditions in an exchange that resulted in an original art form. The elements in this nascent Islamic art chosen from the antique art of Bilad al-Sham were understood for what they were and what they represented at the time for the inhabitants of Bilad al-Sham. Once selected for the new monuments, they were either used in the intended way, or imbued with new meanings and values, or deliberately and knowingly adapted to enrich, complement, highlight, or compete with new elements introduced by the Umayyads either from a shared Arabic cultural heritage or from the still-developing Islamic symbolism and world views.[9]

6. Finbarr Barry Flood, *The Great Mosque of Damascus: Studies on the Makings of an Umayyad Visual Culture* (Leiden: EJ Brill, 2001), is the most elaborate articulation of this interpretation.

7. Research in this area made substantial advances recently, see especially: José Miguel Puerta Villchez, *Historia del Pensamiento Estético Árabe; Al-Andalus y la Estética Árabe Clásica* (Madrid: Ediciones Akal, 1997), 49–69, for a compilation and analysis of all relevant pre-Islamic Arabic texts dealing with beauty; Shirbel Dagher, *Madhahib al-Husn: Qira'a Mu'jamiyya-Tarikhiyya lil-Funun fi al-Arabiyya* (Amman: Royal Society of Fine Arts, 1998), analyzes the sense of beauty in the classical Arabic culture through a thorough reading of the relevant terms in the earliest Arabic lexicon, *Kitab al-'Ayn* of al-Khalil al-Farahidi. For another discussion of beauty as expressed in poetry among the pre-Islamic Arabs see the concise and rather deterministically materialist study of Fu'ad al-Mir'i, *al-Wa'i al-Jamali 'ind al-'Arab Qabl al-Islam* (Damascus: al-Abjadiyya, 1989).

8. The history of the Arabs in the late Jahiliyya and early Islam is still badly known and hotly contested. For an introduction to the topic, see Henri Lammens, *Études sur le siècle des Omayyades* (Beirut:

1930); reviewed and critiqued by K. S. Salibi, "Islam and Syria in the Writings of Henri Lammens," in Bernard Lewis and P. M. Holt, eds., *Historians of the Middle East* (Oxford: Oxford University Press, 1962), 331–342; see also Sulayman Bashir, *Arabs and others in early Islam* (Princeton, N.J.: Darwin Press, 1997); see also the scathing review of W. Madelung, "Review of Suleiman Bashear, *Arabs and Others in Early Islam,*" *Journal of the Royal Asiatic Society* 9, 1 (April 1999): 150–152; F. E. Peters, The Arabs and Arabia on the eve of Islam (Brookfield, Vt.: Ashgate, 1998). An Arabist viewpoint is Salih Ahmad al-'Ali, "Imtidad al-'Arab fi-Sadr al-Islam," *Majallat al-Majma' al-'Ilmi al-'Iraqi* "Qism 1," 32, 1–2 (Jan. 1981): 3–56; "Qism 2," 32, 3–4 (Oct. 1981): 3–62; also Ihsan Abbas, *Tarikh Bilad al-Sham min ma qabla al-Islam hatta bidayat al-ᶜasr al-Umawi, 600–661* (Amman: Lajnat Tarikh Bilad al-Sham, 1990). Irfan Shahid has had a long-term project writing the history of the Arabs in classical times. He has systematically been publishing his series in this order: Irfan Shahid, *Rome and the Arabs: A prolegomenon to the study of Byzantium and the Arabs* (Washington, D.C.: Dumbarton Oaks, 1984); *Byzantium and the Arabs in the fourth century* (Washington, D.C.: Dumbarton Oaks, 1984); *Byzantium and the Arabs in the fifth century* (Washington, D.C.: Dumbarton Oaks, 1989); *Byzantium and the Arabs in the sixth century* (Washington, D.C.: Dumbarton Oaks, 1995). See also his collected articles on the subject, *Byzantium and the Semitic Orient before the rise of Islam* (London: Variorum Reprints, 1988); also, "Ghassan *Post* Ghassan," in C. E. Bosworth et al., eds. *Essays in Honor of Bernard Lewis: The Islamic World from Classical to Modern Times* (Princeton, N.J.: The Darwin Press, 1989), 323–336.

9. My theoretical framework shares with the model of translation advanced by Oleg Grabar and elaborated by Finbarr Barry Flood the insistence on an active role played by the Umayyads in shaping the art

The outcome was an Umayyad art and architecture that was consciously shaped by a dialogue with the late antique traditions of Bilad al-Sham, and to a lesser extent other traditions, as a way to selectively endow the Umayyads' rising culture with historical continuity, territorial rootedness, and the ability to compete in a crowded visual space. Not only were the artistic and architectural forms and decorative schemes of the Umayyad structures informed more by that dialogue than by straightforward borrowing, copying, or even translating, but so too were the evolving Umayyad aesthetic preferences and architectural and iconographic repertoires. To begin to understand Umayyad art and architecture, it is thus no longer sufficient to identify their extracultural models, be it antiquity or otherwise, and to decipher the channels of appropriation they traversed or the transformations they underwent. The inquiry itself has to be recast to take into consideration the possibility that the Umayyads saw themselves not as outsiders but as active players in the artistic production of Postclassical Bilad al-Sham, as continuators and legitimate heirs by virtue both of their former and present associations with the culture and their current position as rulers of the land. This role was not limited only to selecting from the repertoire of late antiquity (which has been often asserted from as early as the 1960s), but also in supplementing, enlarging, and transforming that repertoire with their own expressive elements and interpretive tools. According to this thesis, the Umayyads and their local Arab allies were cognizant both of the Postclassical art they inherited and of the necessity to alter the forms and functions of that art in order to give them new meanings that reflected the emerging culture to which they now belonged. The resulting Umayyad art and architecture were thus self-consciously and simultaneously classicizing and revolutionary from a conventional classical perspective. They were classicizing because, in some instances, they were appropriating without alteration extant artistic and architectural elements and patterns with full understanding of their import. They were revolutionary because, in some other instances, they were mixing and matching, modifying and transposing, and scaling and distorting elements from the heterogeneous artistic traditions of Postclassicism and pre-Islamic Arabic

culture to chart a new, or perhaps more accurately a post, Postclassical artistic direction.

In this paper, I will analyze one defining instance of this process of dialogic adaptation in Umayyad art and architecture that goes beyond the search for influence, precedent, or correspondence. My example is the decorative scheme of the first imperial mosque, the Great Mosque of Damascus, especially the famous mosaic decoration (*fusayfusa'*) and the no-longer-extant inscriptions which originally ran along its *qibla* wall. These two potent iconographic elements seem to have been manipulated together by the Umayyad patrons to create a coherent set of images and messages, not the least of which is their claim to a world empire.[10] The only other surviving Umayyad monument which bears comparison to the mosque of Damascus, the Dome of the Rock in Jerusalem, can be read in a similar manner despite the controversy surrounding its study which fails to see the imperial impetus behind its construction. This cultural, and rather secular, interpretation of the Dome is hidden underneath the mystical, messianic, and religious overlays engendered by the history of its site and induced by contemporary ideological claims and counterclaims by both Muslim and non-Muslim commentators.[11]

The Great Mosque of Damascus still occupies the center of that old historic city and functions as its main congregational mosque (fig. 1). It was built between 706 and 715 by Caliph al-Walid ibn 'Abd al-Malik as the jewel in the crown of a long list of congregational mosques built or refurbished in all major Umayyad urban centers, including Aleppo, Jerusalem, Mecca, Medina, San'a in Yemen, and possibly Fustat, the Islamic capital of Egypt, and Qayrawan, the capital of Islamic Ifriqiyya (modern-day Tunisia and Libya). These mosques

produced in their name, but differs from it in the conceptualization of that role. The model of translation seems to imply that the receiving culture of the Umayyads was already clearly different from the Postclassical cultural amalgam of Bilad al-Sham as to require translation for it; see Flood (note 6), 10–12, 203–206.

10. Garth Fowden, *Empire to Commonwealth: Consequences of Monotheism in Late Antiquity* (Princeton, N.J.: Princeton University Press, 1993), argues that late antiquity had both a direction and a sense of direction that was understood by the Romans, Persians, Christians, and Muslims. He supports this interpretation through the analysis of many Umayyad monuments, particularly the Dome of the Rock and Qusayr 'Amra. See also Maria Georgopoulou, "Geography, cartography and the architecture of power in the mosaics of the Great Mosque of Damascus," *The Built Surface, Volume 1, Architecture and the Pictorial Arts From Antiquity to the Enlightenment,* Christy Anderson, ed. (London: Ashgate, 2002) pp. 47–74.

11. I sketched the background of the shift of emphasis from the royal/imperial to the religious/transcendental in apprehending the Dome of the Rock soon after its completion in the early Umayyad period in two articles published some years ago: "The Meaning of the Umayyad Dome of the Rock," Muqarnas 6 (1990): 12–21; and "The Dome of the Rock Revisited: Some Remarks on al-Wasiti's Accounts," *Muqarnas* 10 (1993): 67–75. I hope to address the question of the artistic means used in this transformation in a future study.

are thought to have formed an integral part of the Umayyad plan to create prominent signs of the Caliphate's rising imperial status. The plan started with Caliph 'Abd al-Malik ibn Marwan (685–705), al-Walid's father, who managed during his tumultuous reign to subdue many rebellions and reunify the fractured empire, Islamicize the coinage, Arabicize the administration, and build the first Islamic monument, the Dome of the Rock in Jerusalem in 692. Al-Walid's building program, which was at times entrusted to his governors in the far-flung provinces, seems to have been a continuation of his father's imperial vision on a monumental scale. The Great Mosque of Damascus, constructed in the imperial capital, seems to have been the cornerstone and the epitome of that building program.

The mosque of Damascus was built on a site that had been occupied by a succession of religious structures for more than a thousand years: First an Aramean temple of the god Hadad; second, a Roman temple of Jupiter Damascenes; and finally a Byzantine church dedicated to St. John the Baptist which is supposed to have stood in the western side of the temenos leaving the eastern side empty. The early Muslims are believed to have appropriated only that unused space for their congregational prayer, leaving the church to the Christian Damascenes. The routine explanation of this division, which came under critical scrutiny in recent years, is that only half of the city of Damascus was conquered forcibly by the Islamic army, thus allowing the Muslims to appropriate only half of the temenos, while leaving the second half in the hands of the local Christian community. We know very little about the sharing arrangement, if such was the case in the first place, and even less about the kinds of architectural modifications the early Muslims introduced to their section of the temenos. This rather awkward situation lasted for almost seventy years, until al-Walid decided to seize the church and the other half of the temenos and to incorporate them into a new imperial mosque.[12]

The mosque in fact filled the entire temenos area, employing various components of the demolished older structures in its outer walls and porticos, and maybe other areas inside. Its plan and façades reveal a very logical and architecturally economic transformation of the old space into a monumental hypostyle mosque, employing minimal modification and rebuilding. A long prayer hall, three aisles deep, runs along the full length of the temenos on the southern side. A central and higher transversal aisle, with a central dome that has been rebuilt several times since the Umayyad period, cuts across the prayer hall marking the central axis and leading toward the main *mihrab* on the southern, *qibla* wall. In the two outer extremities of the *qibla* wall, the stumps of the older Roman towers were reused as bases for new minarets. The third minaret, situated approximately in the center of the northern wall of the temenos, appears to have been added by the Umayyads. A one-aisled portico runs along the inner sides of the three walls of the temenos not occupied by the prayer hall. It is composed of a superimposed double arcade, the lower one made of reused columns supporting semicircular arches, and the upper and shorter one of a double-arch pattern corresponding to the span of the lower arches (fig. 2).

Our primary sources inform us that gilded mosaic scenes once adorned the entire wall surfaces of the mosque, both inside the prayer hall and in the porticoes surrounding the courtyard. Only fragments in four areas have been preserved, making it very difficult to imagine how the mosque must have looked originally. But that the surviving fragments are so haphazardly dispersed around the structure at least confirms the textual reports claiming that mosaics initially covered all of the mosque's surfaces. They are in the vaulted roof, walls, and arcade of the western entrance; the interior and exterior of the western portico and arcade; the spandrels of the grand arches and pilasters of the central transept; the eight sides of the strange octagonal structure located in the western end of the courtyard (known as the *khazna*, treasury) (fig. 3); and in patches inside the central transept of the prayer hall.[13] The mosaics were all heavily and sometimes gaudily restored, or even redone, in the second half of the twentieth century, especially in the last few years when the mosque underwent a rather vain cosmetic facelift (fig. 4).

The mosaic fragments suggest that the whole composition was a series of pastoral scenes of picturesque buildings and entire suburbs and villages, set in some fanciful landscape and devoid of humans or animals. It goes without saying that the aniconic nature of these scenes is very striking indeed for anyone used to the vibrantly animated mosaic scenes teeming with humans and animals which adorn a huge number of small Byzantine churches in Syria, Jordan, Lebanon, and

12. A review of the debate over the origins of the Mosque is K. A. C. Creswell, *Early Muslim Architecture* 2 vols. (Oxford, 1932), 1: 150–252; a more recent overview is idem, *A Short Account of Early Muslim Architecture*, ed. James W. Allan (Cairo: American University Press, 1989), 46–72.

13. Eustache De Lorey, "Les mosaïques de la mosquée des omayyades à Damas," *Syria* 12 (1931): 1–24.

Figure 2. The northern portico of the Umayyad mosque. Photograph by the author.

Palestine, as well as the more monumental imperial churches in the metropolitan centers of the empire. This unusual feature has been consistently interpreted as an early signature of a new preference at work: the aniconic and strictly afigural Islamic art of later epochs. But that still leaves us with scenes that, despite their lack of figural representations, are attempting to communicate something to the viewer through the variety, complexity, and arrangement of their pastoral compositions and the staggering diversity of architectural types they display.

Buildings in the surviving mosaics appear either clustered in groups or dispersed in the landscape. Many compositions are framed by gigantic, realistically rendered trees. Some rise on the slope of a hill. Others, such as the famous Barada scene on the inside wall of the western portico, sit along a river that flows in a realistic manner (fig. 5). The buildings arranged in groups appear to be houses that belong to the type usually identified as the *villa rustica:* simple, cubical, tower-like structures, some with gabled roofs, others with flat ones, that were common in the Roman countryside. They are all represented at an angle, and grouped as if in a village following the contours of the natural setting surrounding them. Aside from playful patterns of light and shadow, most of the houses are devoid of ornamentation except for a simple door and high rectangular windows (fig. 6).

The buildings arranged in more scattered fashion are almost all of classical derivation and are all represented frontally and set in lush vegetation, which sometimes appears as if it were meant both to frame them and to separate them from each other, implying perhaps that they are independent scenes or distinct settings (fig. 7).

Figure 3. The *khazna* (treasury) in the mosque's courtyard. Photograph by the author.

The buildings encompass a wide array of types: gateways, porticoes, towers, bridges, excedrae, *tholoi* (circular temples), and palaces. Most of these examples can be matched with a classical prototype, and the extensive work of Marguerite van Berchem, Barbara Finster, and Geoffrey King, among others, has established a fascinating mixed typology of models. However, none of the Umayyad representations is completely realistic. In fact, many appear rather surreal.

Most of the structures are heavily ornamented with columns, fluted and decorated pillars sometimes joined with curtains tied toward the bottom, balustrades, curved gables, shell roofs sometimes studded with pearls, and naturally rendered acanthus scrolls that grow in the most unexpected places, such as in the tympanum of an arch or on the capitol of a column. Some structures are two-storied, the lower story almost always supported on columns and arches in ways that totally defy the laws of perspective, although it is difficult to say whether the awkward foreshortening and spatial dislocation are the result of naive application of perspective principles or simply the result of different conventions of representation. Some of these

representations were most probably intentionally disarticulated simultaneously to reveal their interior and exterior elements, which then could be recomposed along some convention of classical perspective to reveal their form and function (fig. 8). This has been shown to have been the case for other late classical architectural compositions such as the famous funerary floor mosaic of Tabarka in Tunisia representing the *Ecclesia Mater,* or the *palatium* of Theodoric on the wall of the fifth-century basilica of St. Appolinaire Nuovo in Ravenna (fig. 9).[14]

The remains of the mosaics of the Umayyad mosque have attracted a great deal of scholarly interest. They have been thoroughly examined, classified, and analyzed, and have stylistically been ascribed to the Postclassical, Mediterranean artistic *koiné*.[15] They have generated numerous interpretations, and—something rare in the study of Islamic art and architecture—provoked scholarly debate over their origin, the identity of their makers, and their intentions. Modern scholars who have studied them have either used Qur'anic associations to see Islamic paradisiacal connotations in them, or have adduced cosmographical explanations that relate more to the pre-Islamic, Christian, and even Roman symbolic languages.[16]

14. Noël Duval, "Représentations d'eglises sur mosaïques," *La Revue du Louvre et des Musées de France,* 22, 6 (1972): 441–448; idem, "La représentation des monuments dans l'antiquité tardive, a propos de deux livres récents," *Bulletin Monumental* 138, 1 (1980): 77–95; idem, "La représentation du palais dans l'art du Bas-Empire et du haut Moyen-Age d'après le Psautier d'Utrecht," *Cahiers Archéologiques* 15 (1965): 244–253; idem, "La mosaïque du 'Palatium' de S Apollinaire le Neuf," *Corso di cultura sll'arte ravennate e bizantina* 25 (1978): 93–122; Tadeusz Sarnowski, *Les représentations de villas sur les mosaïques africaines tardives* (Wroclaw, Poland, 1978).

15. The most comprehensive study of the mosaics is Marguerite van Berchem, "The Mosaics of the Dome of the Rock at Jerusalem and of the Great Mosque in Damascus," in K. A. C. Creswell, *Early Muslim Architecture,* 1: 324–372; Eustache De Lorey, "L'Hellénisme et l'Orient dans les Mosaïques de la Mosquée des Omaiyades," *Ars Islamica* 1 (1934): 22–45. More recent studies include Geoffrey R. D. King, "The Origin and Sources of the Umayyad Mosaics in the Great Mosque of Damascus" (4 vols.), University of London, PhD (1970); Barbara Finster, "Die Mosaiken der Umayyadenmoschee von Damaskus," *Kunst des Orients* 7, 2 (1972): 83–136; Myriam Rosen-Ayalon, *The Early Islamic Monuments of al-Haram al-Sharif: An Iconographic Study* (Jerusalem, 1989), 46–69; Flood (note 6), 15–56.

16. For a paradisiac explanation, see Klaus Brisch, "Observations on the Iconography of the Mosaics in the Great Mosque at Damascus," in Priscilla Soucek, ed., *Content and Context of Visual Arts in the Islamic World* (Philadelphia, 1988), 13–20; for a cosmographic one, see Georges Marçais, article "Fusayfisa'," *Encyclopaedia of Islam,* 2d ed., 2: 955–957. An asessment of the various interpretations is Flood (note 6), 31–35.

Figure 4. The external arch of the transversal aisle of the mosque after the restoration of its mosaic scenes. Photograph by the author.

My argument is that these scenes cannot be understood by resorting to a single source, whether Islamic or classical. They do not reflect a single, dominant message, but rather form a part of an expressive program with multiple complementary and stratified themes stemming from the various sources that the Umayyads turned to in this formative period. Some of these themes may have been cosmographic and eschatological in nature and some might have been inspired by Qur'anic imagery. Others appear to have been appropriated and modified from the artistic and symbolic vocabulary used in Byzantine Bilad al-Sham before the coming of Islam. Others still might have been new or imported inventions that appear to have seeped into the local Christian repertoire, the result being either a direct or an oblique alteration of the decorative scheme of some of the post-Islamic churches built in Palestine, Jordan, and Syria.[17] All these possible meanings, however, should have been relevant to the long-term Umayyad imperial program of Arabicization and Islamization begun by 'Abd al-Malik, al-Walid's father, and should have been discernible to the viewer visiting the mosque in the early eighth century, if not necessarily understood to their finest details. This hypothetical

17. The most authoritative study is Robert Schick, *Christian Communities of Palestine from Byzantine to Islamic Rule* (Princeton, NJ: Darwin Press, 1996). Maria Georgopoulou (note 10), p. 61, mentions the corrected dates for some of the Jordanian and Palestinian churches with architectural mosaics which puts them around the time of the completion of the Umayyad mosque's mosaics. She also suggests the possibility that a branch of the Damascus workshop may have worked on these churches as well.

Figure 5. Part of the Barada scene on the wall of the western portico. Photograph by the author.

viewer need not have been exclusively Muslim. But it is untenable to suppose, as some scholars have suggested, that the patrons of the mosque may not have had a Muslim viewer as their prime ideological target.

My analysis of the meaning of these mosaic scenes takes as its point of departure the proposition that Islamic sources that described the building and decoration of the mosque and the circumstances surrounding its construction have not been thoroughly and appropriately utilized, despite the many modern studies devoted to it. This inadequate handling of primary sources goes beyond the normal and expected omission of some relevant phrases or the misreading of others to two basic assumptions that prevailed among students of early Islamic history in general. The first assumption was that these often seemingly disparate and disconnected narratives—both those that are historically probable and those that were obviously invented—do not represent the intentions, aspirations, and beliefs of their alleged protagonists, the early Muslims, and therefore are not interpretable historical documents. The second assumption, more particular to the field of art history, was that reports on the architecture and decoration of early mosques and other commemorative

Islamic structures reveal no notion of intended meaning. This presumption arose not because intentional messages did not exist, but because they appeared in ways unrecognizable to a mind trained in looking for meaning in pictorial or figural representations and not necessarily in stylized architectural, verbal, or abstracted and ornamental ones.

The first presumption has caused a major debate in Islamic studies that still rages on with no constructive resolution in sight. The doubters managed to shake the historiographical complacency among students of early Islamic history, which they attributed either to dogmatic acceptance on the part of believers or sheer laziness or inadequate training on the part of secular scholars. But they did not succeed in offering convincing methodological alternatives for reconstructing early Islamic history and culture. In fact, their criticism comes across as suffering from ideological assumptions similar to those they accused their antagonists of accepting without questioning, though theirs seem to lead in the opposite direction.[18] The second presumption, that of

18. Patricia Crone and Michael Cook, *Hagarism: The Making of the Islamic World* (Cambridge: Cambridge University Press, 1977), is

the absence of iconography, has begun slowly to change in recent decades. Starting with a study on the Dome of the Rock by Oleg Grabar published in 1959, followed by an essay by Erica Dodd on the iconographic import of writing in early Islamic architecture in 1969, the assumption that an Islamic symbolic meaning was absent from the decoration of the Umayyad monuments was finally laid to rest.[19] A new method was proposed which saw in the use of Qur'anic inscriptions an attempt to evoke emphatic images in the mind of the Muslim receiver beginning in the earliest Islamic monuments. Several monographic studies followed which explored both denotative and connotative aspects of writing in Islamic architecture, and firmly anchored Islamic iconography as a distinct area of research within the wider domain of the history of Islamic art and architecture.[20]

The new dimension of interpretation has inevitably permeated later research projects on the Umayyad mosque. Recent studies had to be cognizant of the role played by Qur'anic inscriptions in defining Islamic iconography, and many tried to employ this notion in formulating their interpretation. But they faced two obvious and interrelated problems. The first is the absence of original inscriptions in the Great Mosque of

Figure 6. Example of a rural scene in the mosaic. Photograph by the author.

Figure 7. Detail of an urban example from the Barada scene. Photograph by the author.

perhaps the most notorious revisionist history. For a review of the different modern attitudes toward early Islamic historiography, see 'Abd al-'Aziz al-Duri, *The Rise of Historical Writing among the Arabs,* trans. L. Conrad (Princeton, N.J.: Princeton University Press, 1983) (especially the introduction by Fred M. Donner, vii–xvii); also the more extensive Fred M. Donner, *Narratives of Islamic origins: The beginnings of Islamic historical writing* (Princeton, N.J.: Darwin Press, 1998).

19. Oleg Grabar, "The Umayyad Dome of the Rock in Jerusalem," *Ars Orientalis* 3 (1959): 33–62; Erica C. Dodd, "The Image of the Word: Notes on the Religious Iconography of Islam," *Berytus* 18 (1969): 35–62.

20. An introductory list includes: Oleg Grabar, "The Inscriptions of the Madrasa-Mausoleum of Qaytbay," in D. K. Kouymjian, ed., *Near Eastern Numismatics, Iconography, Epigraphy and History: Studies in Honor of George Miles* (Beirut, 1974), 465–68; Richard Ettinghausen, "Arabic Epigraphy: Communication or Symbolic Affirmation," in Kouymjian, *Near Eastern Numismatics,* 297–317; W. E. Begley, "The Myth of the Taj Mahal and a New Theory of its Symbolic Meaning," *Art Bulletin* 61 (1979): 7–37; Erica Dodd and Shereen Khairallah, *The Image of the Word: A Study of Quranic Verses in Islamic Architecture,* 2 vols. (Beirut, 1981); Caroline Williams, "The Cult of the 'Alid Saints in the Fatimid Monuments of Cairo. Part 1: The Mosque of al-Aqmar," *Muqarnas* 1 (1983): 37–52; idem, "The Cult of the 'Alid Saints in the Fatimid Monuments of Cairo. Part 2: The Mausolea," *Muqarnas* 3 (1985): 39–60; Yasser Tabbaa, "The Transformation of Arabic Writing: Part 1: Qur'anic Calligraphy," *Ars Orientalis* 21 (1991): 119–48; idem, "The Transformation of Arabic Writing: Part 2: The Public Text," *Ars Orientalis* 24 (1994): 119–46; Irene Bierman, *Writing Signs: The Fatimid Public Text* (Berkeley: University of California Press, 1998).

Figure 8. A tholoi representation showing both interior and exterior of the structure. Photograph by the author.

Figure 9. The Palace of Theodoric representation in St. Appolinaire Nuovo. Photograph by the author.

Damascus as it stands today. The second is the profusion of pictorial representations of pastoral and architectural mosaic scenes with no traces of writing in them, which certainly were intended to carry some meaning and which conceivably could be taken as an indication that nascent Islamic iconography was a continuation of classical pre-Islamic practices.

Attempts to reconcile these two apparent drawbacks were inspired indeed. Barbara Finster in 1970–1971 embarked on a search for any reference in the sources to any original inscriptions in the mosque and came up with impressive finds. She established without doubt that the Umayyad mosque initially had the *Fatiha* (or the Opening of the Book) and at least three complete suras—79, *al-Nazi'at* (Those who Drag Forth); 80, *'Abasa* (He Frowned); and 81, *al-Takwir* (The Overthrowing)— inscribed on four superimposed plaques on its *qibla* wall in addition to a foundation text that included a strong and explicit attestation of faith. She noted that the general themes of these three early Meccan suras are eschatological—God's miracles of creation, the Day of Judgment and its signs, the torment that God prepared for the unbelievers in Hell and the rewards of Heaven, and the ultimate truth of the Muhammadan revelation—

and used them to emphasize and supplement the paradisiacal interpretation of the mosaics previously advanced by other scholars who had studied them.[21] She then proceeded to other Qur'anic, hadith, and even historic texts, which are not attested to have been inscribed inside the mosque or even recited in connection to it, to decode some of the more cryptic mosaic representations.[22]

Following Finster's study, many scholars noted the general themes of the three suras in their analysis of the Mosque's decoration. They seem to have found in them the license to move to other Qur'anic verses that deal with Paradise, and to use them as the basis for their readings of the mosaics.[23] Yet, this attempt to supplement

21. Finster (note 15), pp. 118–121; Flood (note 6), 222–223, lists the major themes.

22. Such as the image of the studded mihrab with little twisted colonnettes as described by Ibn Jubayr, which Finster (note 15), p. 123, sees in a mosaic of the western *riwaq*.

23 Brisch (note 16), 16–18, sees in the mosaic scenes literal and direct renderings of several Qur'anic texts about Paradise and even of the presumed early-eighth-century Islamic conception of Paradise. He, for instance, explains the absence of human figures by postulating that

the available data with extraneous texts to corroborate an a priori paradisiacal interpretation is highly problematic. It ignores a fundamental rule of historical research by transposing evidence and by leaping from the verified inscriptions in the mosque to other Qur'anic texts simply on the assumption that they all dealt with the same theme and therefore must be interconnected. But more critical from an art historical perspective is the attempt to establish a direct cause-and-effect relationship between the Qur'anic descriptions of Paradise and the details of the mosaic representations. This theory assumes that the mosaic scenes of the Umayyad mosque are not only symbolic or ideal representations of Qur'anic Paradise but virtually literal ones; it in fact blurs the distinction between the signified and the symbol. Such a theory not only belongs to an outdated tradition in the study of iconography, but also totally overlooks the allegorical nature of the Qur'anic narratives.[24]

The most questionable conjecture in the scholarly readings of the epigraphic evidence so far is that most of them subordinate it to the interpretation of the mosaic representations. They begin from a theoretical position that presupposes a single, monolithic, and all-inclusive meaning of the mosque's decoration as a whole, architectural representations and Qur'anic inscriptions included. This is simply not borne out by the evidence in the primary sources, nor does it take into account the iconographic formulations to emerge in Western medieval art and architecture, which can serve as a useful point of departure for our interpretation. In his influential, path-breaking article, Richard Krautheimer reminded us of exactly the opposite, namely of the medieval pattern of "multi-think" which was reflected in the layers of meaning in medieval art and architecture, some messages only dimly visible, and some even contradictory.[25]

Thus, although the presence of Qur'anic inscriptions in the Umayyad mosque has already been established, their meanings in that instance and their relationship to the mosaic scenes have not been really and independently investigated. My interpretation will rest on two simple queries. One is to find out what early Muslim commentators saw in the mosaics. The second is to reconstruct the scope of ideas and images that entered into the emotional and intellectual makeup of an eighth-century Muslim denizen of Bilad al-Sham, which in turn will allow us to understand how he might have perceived the meaning of the mosque's mosaic scenes.

The one contemporary report we have dealing with the inscriptions is a poem composed by al-Walid's court poet, Nabighat Bani Shayban, at an unknown date but not long after the completion of the mosque.[26] This poem has been noted by other scholars who refer to a hemistich that says that the Qur'anic inscriptions contain "the promises of our Lord and his threats," thus verifying the historical assertions in later texts.[27] But the poem mentions the mosaics many times as well. Some parts appear to be praising the luxurious materials used to paint the surface of the tesserae to achieve their colors and their luminosity. This obviously subordinates the subject matter of the scenes to the general effect of their surface finish. But there are two distiches which appear to be speaking specifically to what is represented. The first refers to the decoration of the mosque's courtyard as being covered with marble, and adds that it is surrounded by "al-Sham," possibly meaning that the scenes represent either the city of Damascus or the entire country of Bilad al-Sham, the seat of the empire. The next distich speaks of "its"—and it is not clear whether the reference is to the mosque or al-Sham— position as the omphalos of the earth (surrat al-ard), surrounded by rivers and open fields. Could this be what al-Nabigha saw in the mosaics?

مبطن برخام الشام محفوف   فكل إقباله والله زينه

وقد أحاط به الأنهار والريف   في سرة الأرض مشدود جوانبه

فيهن من ربنا وعد وتخويف   فيه المثاني وآيات مفصلة

---

the scenes must have been meant to depict Paradise as it stood then and there, i.e., before the Day of Judgment when it will become the abode of the faithful.

24. For a concise critique of the method of a pioneering figure in the study of iconography, Erwin Panofsky, see Paul Crossley, "Medieval Architecture and Meaning: the Limits of Iconography," *Burlington Magazine* 130, 1019 (Feb. 1988): 116–121. For a discussion of Qur'anic narratives, see Muhammad Arkoun, *Lectures du Coran* (Paris: Éditions Maisonneuve et Larose, 1982).

25. Richard Krautheimer, "Introduction to an 'Iconography of Medieval Architecture'," *Journal of the Warburg and Courtauld Institutes* 5 (1942): 1–33; reprinted with a postscript that emphasized the same point in *Studies in Early Christian, Medieval and Renaissance Art* (London and New York, 1969), 115–150.

26. Nabighat Bani Shayban, *Diwan*. Ahmad Nasim, ed. (Cairo: Dar al-Kutub, 1932), 53–54.

27. Finster (note 15), p. 118; Brisch (note 16), p. 16.

Unfortunately, we have no other Umayyad sources. In fact, even post-Umayyad Islamic sources rarely offer any explanation for these architectural scenes, although every visitor who wrote about the mosque noted the mosaic revetments and expressed delight in their diverse colors and shimmering effects. The earliest report comes from the geographer al-Muqqadasi (fl. 966–1000), who says in passing that they depict trees, cities, and villages, and that they have writing, without identifying any of them.[28] The foremost medieval historian of Damascus, Ibn 'Asakir (1105–1176), is the first to mention the composition of the Qur'anic inscriptions in his comprehensive bibliographic compendium, *Tarikh Madinat Dimashq.* He locates them on the *qibla* wall of the prayer hall and states that the foundation inscription, which had disappeared long before his time, was inscribed in black on gold on three plaques. The four suras, with a text at least five times longer than the dedication were, according to Ibn 'Asakir, inscribed on a fourth plaque. This may indicate that the suras were inscribed in a smaller script, or that the fourth plaque was in fact a continuous band running along the full length of the *qibla* wall. This is a different arrangement than that found in the Dome of the Rock built only twelve years earlier, where the Qur'anic inscriptions run around the dome's drum and the circumference of its surrounding arcades.[29] Ibn 'Asakir speaks very proudly of the mosque's mosaics. He collects together all the previous reports on their acquisition, value, and cost, and copies a poem composed after a fire in 1069 devastated the mosque. In this poem, the variety and enchanted nature of the trees represented are extolled, but the architectural scenes are not once mentioned.[30]

By contrast, the encyclopedic geographer, Yaqut al-Hamawi (1179–1229), reports that the porticoes of the mosque contain representations of every city as well as every kind of tree in the world.[31] He attributes this report to the famous essayist al-Jahiz (d. 869), but when he himself describes the mosaics he praises the intricate depictions of plants and trees, but says nothing about the representations of the cities. The famous cosmographer, Sheikh al-Rabwa al-Dimashqi (1256–1327), who was Damascene by birth, widens the scope of the scenes by adding castles and seas to Muqaddasi's list and gives them an Islamic stamp of approval by remarking that they contain no representation of forbidden subjects (i.e., human figures).[32] Another Damascene, the biographer Ibn Shakir al-Kutubi (d. 1362), pushes the Islamic cosmographical interpretation to its logical conclusion by saying that the mosaics "depict the Ka'ba's likeness (*sifat*), set above the *mihrab,* and the images of cities and villages, each represented with all that it produced of trees remarkable for their fruits or their flowers or other objects."[33] His text was reused in several later Damascene sources such as al-'Ulmawi in his description of Damascus (written 1566) and al-Busrawi in his *Tuhfat al-Anam fi Fada'il al-Sham* (ca. 1595).[34]

Al-Kutubi is the first to specify that the central part of the scenery depicts the holiest Islamic center, the Ka'ba, which spatially and ritually represented to the Muslims the center of the world. He also implies a certain pictorial differentiation between the illustrations of cities based on what he terms their distinct products of fruits, flowers, or other objects, which indeed are elaborately diverse in the mosaic compositions. Abu al-Baqa' al-Badari, a little-known Egyptian chronicler writing in 1494, develops this idea further by claiming that each of the cities and villages is represented with the wonders (*'aja'ib*) that distinguish it, which he reads as characterizations of their locales.[35] He thus seems to have relegated all the unexplainable architectural details and mysterious landscapes and fantastic plants with jewel-like fruits we see today in these scenes, and which we cannot comprehend, to the category of *'aja'ib.* For medieval authors, the term *'aja'ib* (sing. *'ajib*) seemingly

28. Al-Muqqadasi, *Ahsan al-Taqasim fi-Ma'rifat al-Aqalim,* ed. M. J. de Goeje (Leiden: E. J. Brill, 1906), 157; English translation in van Berchem (see note 15), 1: 163.

29. Flood (note 6), p. 204, estimates the total length to be 628 m. [four times the length of the *qibla* wall], as opposed to 240 m. in the Dome of the Rock.

30. Ibn-'Asakir, *Tarikh Madinat Dimashq,* 19 vols. (reproduced from MS in al-Zahiriyya in Damascus), ed. M. al-Tarhuni (Damascus, 1980?), 1: 311–113; French translation by Nikita Élisséeff, *La déscription de Damas d'Ibn 'Asakir* (Damascus, 1959), 57–59.

31. Yaqut al-Hamawi, *Mu'jam al-Buldan,* 6 vols. in 11 parts, ed. F. Wüstenfeld (Leipzig: in commission bei F. A. Brockhaus, 1866–1870), 8: 465.

32. Sheikh al-Rabwa al-Dimashqi, *Nukhbat al-Dahr fi 'Aja'ib al-Barr wa-l-Bahr,* ed. M. A. F. Mehren (Leipzig: Otto Harrassowitz, 1923), 193.

33. Ibn Shakir al-Kutubi, *'Uyun al-Tawarikh,* trans. Henri Sauvaire, "La Description de Damas," *Journal Asiatique* 3, 7 (1896): 369–372; English translation in van Berchem (note 15), 1: 161, no. 9.

34. 'Abd al-Basit al-'Ulmawi, *Mukhtasar Tanbih al-Talib;* Shams al-Din al-Busrawi, *Tuhfat al-Anama fi Fada'il al-Sham,* both published in Henri Sauvaire (note 33), p. 422; English translations in van Berchem (note 15), p. 163.

35. Abu al-Baqa' al-Badari, *Nuzhat al-Anam fi-Mahasin al-Sham* (Beirut: Dar al-Ra'id al-ʿArabi, 1980), 25. Ahmad Taymur Pasha, *al-Taswir 'Ind al-'Arab,* Z. M. Hassan ed. (Cairo: Lajnat al-Ta'lif wal-Tarjama wal-nashr, 1942) 4, reported the story of al-Badari and traced its probable origin to al-Muqqadasi, although he did not note the introduction of the identification of the Ka'ba.

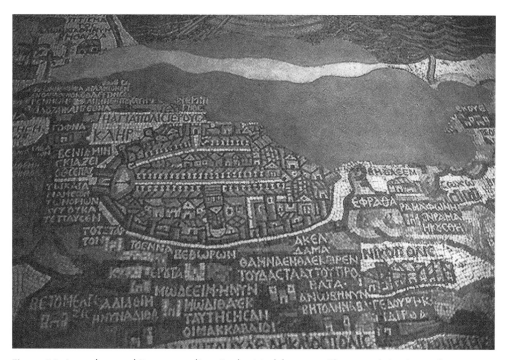

Figure 10. Jerusalem and its surroundings in the Madaba map. Photograph by the author.

spanned the whole range of cognitive reactions to the extraordinary and unusual.[36] For al-Badari, the accuracy of representation does not seem to have been important as long as the scenes suggested different cities distinguished by legible marvelous attributes and arranged in a certain order around the Ka'ba. Ibn Shakir and his successors apparently saw in the mosaics an iconographic, global depiction of the countries of Islam, probably disposed in some hierarchical order on the two sides of the Ka'ba's scene along the porticoes of the mosque.

The idea that the stylized architectural scenes represent various cities or villages probably existed throughout the early and medieval periods from Nabighat Bani Shayban to Ibn Shakir and others. Verisimilitude, as we understand it today, between architectural representations and actual cities was not regarded as important, nor was it achievable by the existing techniques and means. What counted, however, was that the scenes were plausible and decipherable representations of different cities. Slight differences in conception and composition between the various scenes would have been sufficient for contemporary viewers to identify particular locations or structures and to read in them a broader theme, such as the world or the empire or the cosmos. The patron needed only supply the intended messages, most probably verbally, and the pictorial vehicle, the mosaic scenes, that broadly engendered the messages to be accepted by his audience.[37]

This reading of the mosaics in the Umayyad mosque, in which architecture and nature present a complete image of the world, is further supported by the evidence

36. See the discussion of the concept of 'aja'ib in Qur'anic studies in Mohammed Arkoun, "Peut-on parler de merveilleux dans le Coran?" in his Lectures du Coran, 87–144. For a recent survey of the field, see Caroline W. Bynum, "Wonder," American Historical Review (February 1997): 1–26. For the relationship between geography and 'aja'ib in medieval Islamic texts, see André Miquel, La Géographie humaine du monde musulman jusqu'au milieu du 11e siècle, 4 vols. (Paris, 1967–1988), 2: 484 ff. For a concise discussion of 'aja'ib with thematically arranged examples from various artistic and literary media see the catalogue of the exhibition, L'Etrange et le Merveilleux en terre d'Islam, Musée du Louvre 23 April–23 July 2001 (Paris: Éditions de la Réunion des Musées Nationaux, 2001).

37. A modern positivist sensibility could never accept such an interpretation, and, in fact, van Berchem (note 15), 1: 163 rejects the medieval commentators who claim that they can see in the images in the mosaics of the Umayyad mosque the depictions of different locales.

of similar practices from the classical period to late antiquity. Reducing the representation of cities to single buildings is in fact an old iconographic device. Examples abound. One of the most celebrated early paradigms was the Domus Aurea built by emperor Nero around the year 64 C.E. and described by Suetonius in *The Lives of the Caesars,* where he states that "There was a pond, too, like a sea, surrounded with buildings to represent cities, besides tracts of country, varied by tilled fields, vineyards, pastures and woods, with great number of wild and domestic animals."[38] Mosaic examples from the Byzantine period—such as the Church of St. John (531) in Jarash (Gerasa), the Church of St. John in Khirbet al-Samra (634), the Church of the Acropolis in Ma'in in Jordan (719–720), and most importantly the Madaba mosaic pavement map of the Holy Land (dated to the second half of the sixth century) with Jerusalem at its center surrounded by other locales and geographical elements—seem quite specifically to represent the world of Christian faith consecrated through time by events from biblical and church history (fig. 10). They provide clear and immediate precedents for the Umayyad mosaics, with one difference: the Byzantine scenes come with epigraphic identification of the represented cities, while the Umayyad ones lack identification.[39] Because of this ambiguity, Richard Ettinghausen ascribed to them an "idyllic" iconography and read into them a message of universal power in the geographic extent of Umayyad or Islamic dominion.[40]

Finally, I come to my original argument about the influence on the mosque's decorative scheme of the cultural dialogue established by the Umayyads with the various Postclassical cultures of Bilad al-Sham. A secular interpretation of the mosaic scenes is in keeping both with the established representational traditions of the region and with an indefinite reading of their exact connotation—in other words, whether they represented Damascus, the region, the Umayyad empire, or the entire world. Furthermore, such an interpretation stresses the value of Krautheimer's hypothesis concerning the layered and vague meanings of medieval artistic

production. My interpretation of the Qur'anic inscriptions, set intentionally above the mihrab in the *qibla* wall, is that they added a layer of meaning—a meaning specifically selected by the new interlocutors—to the already existing ones engendered by the mosaics. In fact, these inscriptions may be considered the Islamic contribution to the range of possible narratives that the continuous band of architectural and natural representations might have induced in the mind of an eighth-century viewer: the city, the region, the empire, the world, or an ideal world.

The major import of the inscriptions—as I see them—is that they presented the conclusion of these cumulative narratives, as it were. They were the reminder that the world, real or idyllic, will come to an end, for the essential theme of the three suras is not the hereafter but the end of this world and the Day of Judgment. The most frequently evoked images in these three suras—according to the earliest commentator on the Qur'an we have, Muqatil ibn Suleiman (d. 767), who was a near contemporary of al-Walid—are those of the disruption of the natural laws and the destruction of the world as the fulfillment of God's initial design.[41]

The mere fact that the Umayyads decorated the mosque the way they did means that they acknowledged the connotative power of the classical conventions of representing architecture and nature on mosaic. In this, they were no different from any of the other local communities in Palestine and Syria which used the same medium to decorate their churches. But the Umayyads chose for their contribution to this narrative another medium of expression of Islamic provenance: the Word of God, most probably inscribed using the same technique as the scenes, gold mosaic on a dark background. The Umayyads also positioned the inscribed text as an apogee—as the last part of the decorative scheme one sees upon entering the mosque and moving toward its *qibla.* Such a reading of the general scheme argues for an intentional sequence in the display of messages on the part of the Umayyads, one which takes into account the usual procession from outside the mosque, passing its porticos, then the interior of the prayer hall, until one reaches the most ritually important spot in front of the *qibla* wall. Inscribing the Qur'anic texts on the *qibla* wall seems to suggest that the place where the experience of the mosque culminates is where its narrative concludes.

38. Suetonius, *The Lives of the Caesars,* ed. and trans. J. C. Rolfe (Cambridge, Mass.: Harvard University Press, 1979), 2: 135–137; see William L. MacDonald, *The Architecture of the Roman Empire: An Introductory Study* (New Haven, 1982), 31–32, and no. 24 for discussions of this important passage.

39. See, for example, Michele Piccirillo, *I mosaici di Giordania* (Rome, 1986), 172–174, for three illustrations of cities from a church in Gerasa; 175–176, for two from Khirbet al-Samra; 178–180, for five city representations from Ma'in.

40. Richard Ettinghausen, *Arab Painting* (Geneva: Albert Skira, 1977), 22–28.

41. Muqatil ibn Sulayman al-Balkhi, *Tafsir Muqatil ibn Sulayman,* 4 vols., ed. 'Abd Allah Mahmud Shihatah (Cairo: Mu'assasat al-Halabi, 1969–1987), 4: 571–581.

Clearly such a reading on my part presupposes a viewer familiar both with classical and late antique artistic tradition, which was still permeating the city and the region, and Qur'anic exegesis. This viewer should be at home in the urban setting that revels in the pictorial opulence of late classicism and its local translations as well as in the cultural Arabic milieu that acknowledges the supremacy of the Qur'an in delivering divine messages and that appreciates the power of words in general to convey the meaning of images. But this, as I have been arguing all along, is precisely the kind of viewer an Umayyad patrician would have been. To expect him to have been able to see a set of classically inspired images in their actual context and to recognize them as exact representations of Qur'anic textual descriptions at this early stage of the development of Qur'anic hermeneutics and Qur'anic imagery is the anachronistic reading.

Pillars, palimpsests, and princely practices

Translating the past in sultanate Delhi

FINBARR B. FLOOD

In the traditional master narratives of South Asian history, the conquest of northern India by the army of the Ghurid sultan Ghiyath al-Din Muhammad (r. 1163–1203) in the last quarter of the twelfth century figures a profound rupture in the cultural fabric of the region. Many of the monuments erected in the wake of the conquest appear to confirm this, for they make extensive use of architectural elements that predate the conquest and are assumed to have been purloined from temples destroyed in its wake. The idea of the trophy looms large in published discussions of these monuments, largely on the basis of a practice of reuse that has never been subjected to any serious analysis. Analysis has been obviated, in large measure, by the widespread perception that reuse offers support for the lurid and highly formulaic tales of looting, spoliation, and desecration found in the medieval texts that have been privileged in the construction of histories (and even art histories) of the period.[1]

In addition to the circularity of such an approach, the disciplinary divisions written into Orientalist discourse on South Asia at its inception frustrate the assumption of a diachronic approach to the material culture of the region.[2] Yet some of the objects and buildings in which the past is instantiated for us today were already antique in the early pre-modern period. Enduring through time and dynastic change, such artifacts often ensured continuity in the process of imagining and re-imagining the past, providing a focus for the "necessary sedimentation of meaning that accumulates as part of the process of historical change."[3] The palimpsest nature of such artifacts was intrinsic to their role as sites for an ongoing process of "translating" the past, a process that frequently encompassed a physical displacement. This was a past that inhered not only in objects, however, but also in the practices and rituals associated with them. The act of physical appropriation might itself be palimpsest upon earlier reuses of the same or similar objects, thus serving to construct a dynamic continuity between contemporary practices and their historical antecedents.

This is the case with a number of pre-Islamic commemorative pillars (*stambha*s or *lat*s) that were re-erected in Delhi during the thirteenth and fourteenth centuries. Essentialist notions of Islamic cultural practices have combined with traditional disciplinary divisions to obscure the transcultural nature of these pillars, which were central to the self-conscious articulation of an imagined relationship between the sultans of Delhi and the Indian past. The relocation of the pillars appears to reference a past that encompassed both the mythic kings of a dimly perceived Indian antiquity and the more immediate predecessors of the Delhi sultans, who provide a precedent for the reuse (that is, reinscription and/or relocation) of similar pillars.[4] The existence of indigenous precedents for such

Much of the research for this paper was undertaken in 2000–2001, when I held an Ailsa Mellon Bruce Senior Fellowship at the Center for Advanced Study in the Visual Arts, the National Gallery of Art, Washington D.C. It was written while I was a Smithsonian Senior Fellow at the Arthur M. Sackler Gallery in Washington, D.C., in 2002. I am grateful to both institutions for their support. Many of the themes discussed here will be dealt with at greater length in my forthcoming book on the looting, gifting, and reuse of cultural artifacts within the Ghurid sultanate.

1. For a critique of this position see Alka Arvind Patel, "Islamic Architecture of Western India (Mid 12th–14th Centuries): Continuities and Interpretations" (D.Phil. thesis, Harvard University, 2000), pp. 325–358.

2. Finbarr Barry Flood, "Refiguring Iconoclasm: Image Mutilation and Aesthetic Innovation in the Early Indian Mosque," in *Negating the Image: Case Studies of Past Iconoclasms,* ed. Anne L. McLanan & Jeffrey Johnson (London: Ashgate Press, forthcoming); idem., "Transcribing Ruins Inscribing Difference: Architectural Photography as Ethnographic Practice in Colonial India," paper presented to the symposium "Photography in the Islamic World, 19th–20th Centuries," Arthur M. Sackler Museum, Harvard University, December 8, 2000.

3. Annie E. Coombes, "Translating the Past: Apartheid Monuments in Post-Apartheid South Africa," in *Hybridity and its Discontents: Politics, Science, Culture,* ed. Avtar Brah & Annie E. Coombes (New York & London: Routledge, 2002), p. 175.

4. As will become clear below, "reuse" here implies a historicist gesture in which "the 'second user' was aware of his or her posterior status:" Anthony Cutler, "Reuse or Use? Theoretical and Practical Attitudes Toward Objects in the Early Middle Ages," in *Ideologie e Pratiche del Reimpiego nell'Alto Medioevo,* Settimane di Studio del Centro Italiano di Studi sull'Alto Medioevo 46, (Spoleto: Presso la Sede del Centro, 1999), pp. 1056–1057.

Figure 1. Iron pillar and *qibla* screen, Ghurid Friday Mosque, Delhi.

reuses of the past suggests that there was much greater continuity in the characteristic cultural practices of Indian rulers between the pre- and postconquest periods than has previously been acknowledged. What have been read as trophies at first glance, on closer inspection appear to offer evidence for transculturation in the ritual practices of the earliest Delhi sultans.

The earliest instance of reuse following the conquest is evidenced by a seven-and-a-half-meter-high iron pillar standing in the courtyard of the Friday Mosque built after the Ghurid conquest of Delhi in 1192, the mosque known today as the Quwwat al-Islam (fig. 1). The pillar, which stands on the axis of the mosque, directly in front of the prayer hall, is crowned with a fluted bell capital and a molding consisting of three superimposed *āmalakas* and a square pedestal, now empty (fig. 2). It can be counted among a number of commemorative columns often referred to in inscriptions as pillars of fame (*kirtistambhas*) or pillars of victory (*jayastambhas*), which were erected by medieval Indian rulers to memorialize their architectural patronage, donations to temples, or military and spiritual victories.[5] So deeply embedded in the rituals of medieval Indian kingship was the notion of a pillar of victory that the term was sometimes used metaphorically, to refer to other types of

Figure 2. Detail of the iron pillar showing its capital.

---

5. John Faithful Fleet, "Mandasor Pillar of Yasodharman," *The Indian Antiquary* 15 (1886): 255, 257; E. Hultzsch, *South-Indian Inscriptions,* vol. 3, part 1 (Madras: Government Press, 1899), pp. 52, 64, 69; Henry Cousens, "The Iron Pillar at Dhar," *Archaeological Survey of India Annual Report* (1902–1903): 207–208; Michael D. Willis, "Religious and Royal Patronage in North India," in *Gods, Guardians, and Lovers, Temple Sculptures from North India A.D. 700–1200,* ed. Vishaka N. Desai & Darielle Mason (New York: The Asia Society, 1993), p. 54, fig. 17; Ram Nath, *Jain Kirtti-Stambha of Chittorgadh [c. 1300 A.D.]* (Jaipur: The Historical Research Documentary Program, 1994), pp. 8, 13, 55, 59, 61. In addition to those which survive, such pillars are frequently mentioned in royal inscriptions: John Faithful Fleet, "Sanskrit and Old-Kanarese Inscriptions No. 185. Mahakuta Pillar Inscription of Mangalesa," *The Indian Antiquary* 19 (1890): 16, 19; Rai Bahadur Hira Lal, "Khairha Plates of Yasahkarnadeva-[Kalachuri] Samvat 823," *Epigraphia Indica* 12 (1913–1914): 216; Radhagovinda Basak, "Rampal Copper-Plate Grant of Srichandradeva," Epigraphia Indica 12 (1913–1914): 140. To suggest that the victory commemorated by such pillars, "was one of a more spiritual nature than politico-military character" (Patel, see note 1, p. 213), is to ignore the abundant epigraphic evidence for their erection in association with military campaigns, including victories over *Turushka* or Turkish armies. I have suggested elsewhere that the tradition of commemorating victories by the erection of pillars had an impact on the manner in which Ghaznavid and Ghurid sultans memorialized their own triumphs: Finbarr Barry Flood, "Between Ghazna and Delhi: Lahore and its Lost Manára," in *Cairo to Kabul: Afghan and Islamic Studies Presented to Ralph Pinder-Wilson,* ed. Warwick Ball & Leonard Harrow (London: Melisende, 2002), pp. 102–112.

Figure 3. Gupta inscription on the iron pillar.

objects or structures that memorialized martial triumphs or territorial conquest.[6] Such pillars were considered an appropriate locus for royal inscriptions, and a Sanskrit text inscribed upon the Delhi iron pillar (fig. 3) tells us that it was originally dedicated as a standard (*dhvaja*) to a Vishnu temple by the fourth- or fifth-century ruler Chandra, whose military prowess the inscription celebrates.[7]

The Delhi column is unusual because it is iron rather than stone and survived so long without being melted down, but it is by no means unique. Fragments survive of a much larger iron pillar, over thirteen meters in length and bearing a Sanskrit inscription, which was re-

6. For example, Aditya Chola (r. 850–871) had the head of his defeated Pandya rival set up in the Chola capital as a pillar of victory: Rao Sahil K. Krishna Sastri, *South-Indian Inscriptions,* vol. 3, part 3 (Madras: Government Press, 1920), pp. 387, 420. After a military victory in the early eleventh century, Rajendra Chola marched golden vessels of Ganges water back to his capital on the heads of captured prisoners. There he created a vast artificial lake, referred to in contemporary inscriptions as a "liquid pillar of victory": Vidya Dehejia, *Art of the Imperial Cholas* (New York: The Asia Society, 1990), p. 79.

7. T. S. Burt & Alexander Cunningham, "Lithographs and translations of inscriptions taken in ectype by Captain T. S. Burt, Engineers: and of one, from Ghosí taken by Captain A. Cunningham, of the same Corps," *Journal of the Asiatic Society of Bengal* (1838): 629–631; Garcin de Tassey, "Description des monuments de Dehli," *Journal Asiatique,* 5th series, 15–16 (1860): 226–229; Alexander Cunningham, *Four Reports Made During the Years 1862–63–64–65,* Archaeological Survey of India Reports, vol. 1, (Delhi & Varanasi: 1871; reprint Indological Book House, 1972), pp. 170–174; Carr Stephens, *The Archaeology and Monuments of Delhi* (Simla & Calcutta, 1876), pp. 17–24; John Faithful Fleet, *Inscriptions of the Early*

Gupta Kings and Their Successors, Corpus Inscriptionum Indicarum, vol. 3 (Varanasi: Reprinted by the Indological Book House, 1970), pp. 139–142; J. A. Page, *An Historical Memoir on the Qutb: Delhi,* Memoirs of the Archaeological Survey of India No. 22, originally Calcutta, Government of India, 1926 (Delhi: Reprinted by Swati Publications, 1991), pp. 44–45. For a complete copy of the inscription see Ram Nath, *Monuments of Delhi* (New Delhi: Ambika Publications, 1978), Inscription 1. There is some debate as to whether the Chandra mentioned on the pillar is Chandragupta I or II, or indeed any Gupta ruler: Vincent A. Smith, "The Iron Pillar of Delhi (Mihraulí) and the Emperor Candra (Chandra)," *Journal of the Royal Asiatic Society* (1897): 1–18; M. M. Havaprasad Shastrí, "King Chandra of the Meharauli Iron Pillar Inscription," *The Indian Antiquary* 42 (1913): 217–219; R. D. Banerji, "A Note on King Chandra of the Meharauli Inscription," *Epigraphia Indica* 14 (1917–18): 367–371; J. Ph. Vogel, "Facts and Fancies about the Iron Pillar of Old-Delhi," *Journal of the Panjab Historical Society* 9, no. 1 (1923): 82–86; Dines Chandra Sircar, "Digvijaya of King Chandra of the Meharauli Pillar Inscription," *Journal of the Asiatic Society of Bengal,* Letters 5 (1939): 407–415. The pillar was originally surmounted by an animal figure, which most scholars (e.g. Smith, ibid., p. 18) have assumed was removed when it was placed in the mosque; this was not necessarily the case, however, given that animal figures proliferate throughout the mosque.

Figure 4. Fragments of an iron pillar outside the Mosque of Dilawar Khan, Dhar.

erected in front of a mosque at Dhar in central India in 1404 (fig. 4).[8] The Dhar column has been interpreted as a pillar of victory (*jayastambha*) erected by a local Paramāra ruler in the twelfth or thirteenth century.[9] A much smaller pillar in the form of a trident dated Samvat 1468 (A.D. 1412) stands in front of the Achalésvar temple on Mount Abu in Rajasthan (fig. 5), and is reportedly cast from the arms abandoned by a defeated Muslim army.[10]

It has generally been assumed that the erection of the pillar was contemporary with the foundation of the Delhi mosque by Qutb al-Din Aybak, the slave general of the Ghurid sultans, in 1192.[11] According to the

fourteenth-century *Târîkh-i Fîrūz Shāhī* of Shams-i Siraj 'Afif, however, the pillar was set up in this position not by Qutb al-Din Aybak, but by Shams al-Din Iltutmish. Iltutmish was a former Turkish slave who had risen through the ranks of the army in the service of Aybak, before acceding to the Indian sultanate that had emerged after the death of the last of the Ghurid sultans with effective control over the empire, in 1206. The date at which the pillar was installed is unknown, but it was presumably after the accession of Iltutmish in 1211, and possibly around or before 1229, when the area of the mosque was more than tripled, one of numerous architectural projects sponsored by the sultan.[12]

8. Wheeler Thackston, *The Jahangirnama, Memoirs of Jahangir, Emperor of India* (New York: Oxford University Press, 1999), p. 235.

9. Cousens (see note 5), especially p. 210; B. V. Subbarayappa, "Dimensions of Iron Technology in India up to the end of the 18th Century," *Journal of Central Asia* 3, no. 2 (1980): 25; J. Burton-Page, "Dhār. Monuments," *The Encyclopaedia of Islam,* new ed., vol. 2 (Leiden: E. J. Brill, 1965), p. 219. Among the inscriptions carved after the pillar had fallen from its original position is one recording the halt of the Mughal emperor Jahangir, who mentions the pillar in his memoirs: Thackston (see note 8), p. 235.

10. Cousens (see note 5), p. 207.

11. Anthony Welch & Howard Crane, "The Tughluqs: Master Builders of the Delhi Sultanate," *Muqarnas* 1 (1983): 127, 133; Anthony Welch, "Architectural Patronage and the Past: The Tughluq

Sultans of India," *Muqarnas* 10 (1993): 319–320; Catherine B. Asher, "Appropriating the Past: Jahāngīr's Pillars." *Islamic Culture* 71, no. 4 (1997): 8.

12. Finbarr Barry Flood, "Persianate Trends in Sultanate Architecture: the Great Mosque of Bada'un," in Bernard O'Kane, ed., *Festschrift for Robert Hillenbrand* (Edinburgh: Edinburgh University Press, forthcoming). Some have argued that the pillar was already standing before a temple on this site, and was incorporated into the mosque as it stood: de Tassey (see note 7), pp. 228–229; D. S. Triveda, *Viṣṇudhvaja or Qutb Manār* (Varanasi: The Chowkhamba Sanskrit Series Office, 1962), p. 251; Sunil Kumar, "Qutb and Modern Memory," in *The Partitions of Memory: The Afterlife of the Division of India,* ed. Suvir Kaul (New Delhi: Permanent Balck, 2001), pp. 142, 176 n. 3. The text states quite clearly, however, that the *minâra buzurg*

Figure 5. Iron pillar in the form of a trident, Achalesvar Temple, Mount Abu.

The reuse of the Delhi iron pillar in the early thirteenth century inspired the actions of later Indo–Islamic rulers, who similarly relocated antique pillars as part of their architectural patronage. Ghiyath

al-Din Tughluq (r. 1320–1325) may have included a pre-Islamic pillar in the mosque which he built at Tughluqabad, but 'Afif makes it clear that it was the precedent set by Iltutmish that inspired the reuse of as many as ten antique pillars by one of his successors, Firuz Shah Tughluq (r. 1351–1388; figs. 6 and 7);[13] many

13. Afif (see note 12), pp. 313–314; H. M. Elliot & John Dowson, *The History of India as Told by its Own Historians,* 4 vol., originally London: 1867–1877 (Delhi: Reprinted by Low Price Publications, 1990), vol. 3, p. 353. For the suggestion that an Ashokan pillar was reused earlier in the mosque of Tughluqabad, see Mehrdad Shokoohy & Natalie H. Shokoohy, "Tughluqabad: the earliest surviving town of the Delhi Sultanate," *Bulletin of the School of Oriental and African Studies* 57, no. 3 (1994): 548. Firishta lists ten monumental pillars among the works of Firuz Shah Tughluq, but this may be an exaggeration: John Briggs, *History of the Rise of the Mahomedan Power in India,* 4 vol., originally London: 1829 (New Delhi: Oriental Books Reprint Corporation, 1981), vol. 1, p. 270. Those that survive are at Fatehabad and Hisar in Haryana, and Firuzabad and Meerut in Delhi. The latter two can be associated with the activities of Firuz Shah through contemporary textual evidence, while the former two are attributed to the activities of the same sultan through their architectural context or epigraphic content: James Prinsep, "Interpretation of the most ancient of the inscriptions on the pillar called the lát of Feroz Sháh, near Delhi, and that of the Allahabad, Radhia and Matthia pillar, or lát, inscriptions which agree therewith," *Journal of the Asiatic Society of Bengal* 6 (1837): 566–609; de Tassey (see note 7), pp. 229–234; E. Hultzsch, *Inscriptions of Ashoka,* Corpus Inscriptionum Indicarum, vol. 1 (Oxford: Clarendon Press, 1925), pp. xvii, 107; B. C. Chhabra, "Aśokan Pillar at Hissar, Panjab," *Vishveshvaranand Indological Journal* 2 (1964): 319–322; James Prinsep, *Essays on Indian Antiquities,* vol. 1 (Varanasi: Reprinted by the Indological Book House, 1971), pp. 324–325; Welch & Crane (see note 11), p. 133; Mehrdad Shokoohy, *Haryana I: The Column of Fīrūz Shāh and other Islamic Inscriptions from the District of Hisar,* Corpus Inscriptionum Iranicarum Part IV: Persian Inscriptions down to the Early Safavid Period, vol. XLVII: India, State of Harayana (London: 1988), pp. 15–22; Mehrdad Shokoohy & Natalie H. Shokoohy, *Ḥiṣār-i Fīrūza: Sultanate and Early Mughal Architecture in the District of Hisar, India* (London: Monographs on Art, Archaeology and Architecture, South Asian Series, 1988), pp. 32–33; Welch (see note 11), pp. 318–320; William Jeffrey McKibben, "The Monumental Pillars of Fīrūz Shāh Tughluq," *Ars Orientalis* 24 (1994): 105–118. A fifth pillar in Jaunpur was erected by Ibrahim Na'ib Barbak, Firuz Shah's half-brother, by order of the sultan: de Tassey (see note 7), pp. 231–233; Alexander Cunningham, *Report on Tours in the Gangetic Provinces from Badaon to Bihar, in 1875–76 and 1877–78,* Archaeological Survey of India Reports, vol. 11 (Varanasi: Reprinted by the Indological Book House, 1968), pp. 105–106; A. Führer, *The Sharqi Architecture of Jaunpur,* Archaeological Survey of India Reports, vol. 11 (Calcutta: 1889), pp. 26–27; Z. A. Desai, "Inscription from the Jaunpur Fort Mosque," *Epigraphia Indica Arabic and Persian Supplement* (1974): 23. It has recently been argued that the Jaunpur pillar was not antique, but was carved ex novo: McKibben, ibid., p. 110. In view of the conjunction of antique and contemporary elements in the Fatehabad and Hisar pillars (the antique parts of which may once have belonged together), this is quite possible. Although it has sometimes been assumed that the Allahabad pillar (see Asher, note 11) was also moved by Firuz Shah Tughluq, there is no evidence for this.

in the Delhi mosque was erected (*bar- avarda*) by Iltutmish: Shams-i Siraj 'Afif, *The Tarikh-i-Firoz Shahi,* ed. Maulavi Vilayat Husain (Calcutta: Asiatic Society, 1888), p. 314. The terms employed might equally refer to the Qutb Minar (see note 22), but since the passage occurs amid a lengthy discussion of Firuz Shah Tughluq's reuse of antique pillars, it is safe to assume that the reference is to the pillar in the Delhi mosque rather than its minaret. That the pillar was set up again in the thirteenth century seems to be supported by the archaeological evidence, since the column is supported by a series of iron bars soldered with lead, which rest upon the surface of a floor assumed to be that of the temple that previously stood on the site of the mosque: Smith (see note 7), pp. 4–5.

of these were re-erected within, or in close proximity to mosques. In the following century, pre-Islamic iron pillars were re-erected outside congregational mosques at Dhar (fig. 4) and Mandu in Malwa, probably in imitation of Iltutmish's gesture.[14] The re-erection of the iron pillar by Iltutmish may also have been a factor in the later reuse of an Ashokan pillar at Allahabad fort by the Mughal emperor Jahangir (r. 1605–1627), although there is no evidence for this having been associated with a mosque. Catherine Asher has demonstrated that in its Mughal incarnation, the pillar was associated with a "chain of justice," a chain-hung bell by means of which those seeking justice from the ruler would make their presence known.[15] This was a feature of Sasanian kingship as memorialized in Persian texts, but was also common in medieval Indian courts, for reference is made to it in several royal inscriptions.[16] According to Ibn Battuta, the palace of Iltutmish in Delhi had such a chain.[17] Although the subject awaits further investigation, it is quite possible that the inspiration for Jahangir's chain derived from indigenous kingship traditions mediated via the precedent of Iltutmish as memorialized in pre-Mughal histories. As we shall see shortly, the reuse of the pillar itself points to the continuation of a practice that was well established in South Asia long before the Ghurid conquest in the twelfth century. Whatever contextually specific meanings each instance of reuse acquired, culturally and chronologically the relocation of the iron pillar by Iltutmish can be seen as a pivotal act, linking the actions of later Islamicate rulers with a preconquest tradition of reuse.

Although the Delhi mosque was constructed using large quantities of spolia (fig. 8), the inclusion of the iron pillar in the mosque was merited on something other than utilitarian grounds, for it fulfills no structural function. Iltutmish's re-erection of the iron pillar in a mosque constructed in the wake of the Muslim conquest using an abundance of temple spolia has usually been assumed to reflect the pillar's value as a trophy and its consequent ability to memorialize *Muslim* victory over

Figure 6. Ashokan pillar from Meerut re-erected by Firuz Shah Tughluq, Delhi.

the conquered Hindu population of Delhi.[18] This assumption may be influenced by the European practice of re-erecting ancient obelisks looted from colonial possessions in metropolitan capitals, but it is also part of

14. Michael Anthony Brand, "The Khalji Complex at Shadiabad Mandu" (D.Phil. thesis, Harvard University, 1986), pp. 218–219.

15. Asher (see note 11), pp. 1–2, pl. 1.

16. For two twelfth-century examples see E. Hultzsch, *South-Indian Inscriptions,* vol. 2, part 3 (Madras: Government Press, 1895), p. 311, n. 3; idem. *South-Indian Inscriptions,* vol. 3, part 2 (Madras: Government Press, 1903), p. 185.

17. H. A. R. Gibb, *The Travels of Ibn Baṭṭūṭa A.D. 1325–1354,* vol. 3 (Cambridge: Cambridge University Press, 1971), p. 630.

18. See, among others, Burton-Page, who states that the pillar was "doubtless placed there by the builders not only as a curious relic but also as a symbol of their triumph over the idolaters": "Dihlī," *The Encyclopaedia of Islam,* new ed., vol. 2, (Leiden: Brill Ltd., 1965), p. 260. See also Welch (note 11, p. 320), where the iron pillar is described as "a trophy celebrating Islam's 1192 victory in north India"; Hillenbrand [*Islamic Architecture, Form, Function and Meaning* (New York: Columbia University Press, 1994), p. 158], where the small scale of the pillar, juxtaposed with that of the adjacent minaret, is said to be evocative of Muslim victory. Similarly, Catherine Asher refers to the reuse of pre-Islamic pillars in Delhi during the thirteenth and fourteenth centuries "to proclaim the supremacy of Islam": Asher (see note 11), p. 8. Carl Ernst, in an article that criticizes the traditional

Figure 7. Pillar inscribed with the genealogy of Firuz Shah Tughluq, Fatehabad.

Figure 8. Ghurid Friday Mosque of Delhi, general view.

a broader belief in an essentially Muslim penchant for triumphal gestures involving the reuse of artifacts and monuments identified as non-Islamic.[19] The attribution of static sectarian identities to medieval objects and

buildings is standard in traditional discourse on South Asian art and architecture.[20] Thus the iron pillar in Delhi is often referred to as the "Hindu" iron pillar, an object in direct opposition to the adjacent "Islamic" minaret (fig. 9),[21] ignoring the fact that the terms *stambha* (pillar) and *minār* (minaret) were used interchangeably to refer to the same objects by medieval Indians, Hindus, and Muslims.[22] Within such a paradigm, the presence of "Hindu" materials in a "Muslim" context is necessarily ascribed to the promulgation of sectarian victory rhetoric.

In the case of the Delhi mosque, scholars have turned to its epigraphic program to provide a cultural and historical context for the reuse of Hindu and Jain elements in its construction. Most frequently cited are a number of Qur'anic inscriptions that place a strong emphasis on the rejection of idolatry, and a problematic Persian foundation inscription above the eastern

---

essentialist view of Muslim responses to the relics of the Indian past, concludes more neutrally that the iron pillar is part of "the triumphant political use of trophies": Carl W. Ernst, "Admiring the Works of the Ancients. The Ellora Temples as viewed by Indo-Muslim authors," in *Beyond Turk and Hindu: Rethinking Religious Identity in Islamicate South Asia,* ed. David Gilmartin & Bruce Lawrence, pp. 98–120. (Gainesville: University Press of Florida, 2000), p. 98 and n. 1. Interpretations that foreground Muslim victory (as opposed to victory) are implicitly based on an assumed hostility toward reused objects conceived of in sectarian terms, is also manifest in scholarship dealing with the re-erection of antique stone pillars in the fourteenth century by Firuz Shah Tughluq. See for example the interpretation of Firuz Shah's pillars as representing "his triumph over India's jahiliyya": Welch (see note 11), p. 320.

19. Finbarr Barry Flood, "The Medieval Trophy as an Art Historical Trope: Coptic and Byzantine 'Altars' in Islamic Contexts," *Muqarnas*

18 (2001): 41, 63–64. See also Cousens's (as in note 5, p. 210) unsubstantiated assumption that the Dhar pillar was "thrown down by Muhammadans," in spite of the evidence for its re-erection by the Muslim patron of the adjacent mosque. Earlier, Prinsep had asserted that at some point between the fourth century and the fourteenth, the Ashokan pillar at Allahabad was "overthrown again by the idol-breaking zeal of the Musalmán": James Prinsep, "Notes on the facsimiles of the various inscriptions on the ancient column at Allahabad, retaken by Captain Edward Smith, engineers," *Journal of the Asiatic Society of Bengal* 6 (1837): 968.

20. For a critical survey of the relevant material see Patel (as in note 1).

21. Welch & Crane (see note 11), p. 134; John Irwin, "Islam and the Cosmic Pillar," in *Investigating Indian Art: Proceedings of a Symposium on the Development of Early Buddhist and Hindu Iconography held at the Museum of Indian Art, Berlin, May 1986* (Berlin: 1987), p. 134.

22. The pre-Islamic *lats* and *stambhas* incorporated into sultanate mosques are referred to as *minārs* in fourteenth-century Persian texts (e.g. 'Afif [see note 12], p. 314), which can equally compare the minaret of the Delhi mosque to a stone pillar (*sutūn*): Nath (see note 7), p. 28. Conversely, the Qutb Minar is identified as a *jayastambha* and *kirtistambha* in contemporary Sanskrit inscriptions: Pushpa Prasad, *Sanskrit Inscriptions of the Delhi Sultanate 1191–1256* (New Delhi: Oxford University Press, 1990), pp. xxx, 2–3, 18–19. The absence of any functional minarets in the royal mosques in which the pillars were re-erected (at Firuzabad and Hisar) suggests that they were intended to replace freestanding minarets such as the Qutb Minar, an impression reinforced by the decoration of some of the pillars: Shokoohy & Shokoohy (see note 13), p. 33. As Ram Nath ("The Minaret vs. the Dhvajastambha," *Indica* 7, no. 1 [1970]: 29) remarks, "the idea is more symbolic than functional," with the *lat* acquiring a role as the "conceptual equivalent" to the *minār:* McKibben (see note 13), p. 112. Formal similarities between pillar and minaret apparently enabled these to be identified in the eyes of contemporaries, for the identification of tall structures associated with Indian religious monuments (temple *śikaras,* for example) as *minārs* is found as early as the ninth century in Arabic texts: Ahmad b. Yahya al-Baladhuri, *Kitāb Futuḥ al-Buldān,* ed. M. J. de Goeje (Leiden: 1866), p. 437.

Figure 9. The iron pillar and the Qutb Minar, Delhi.

entrance to the mosque, which appears to refer to the desecration of twenty-seven temples and the reuse of their elements in its construction.[23] However, not all the materials comprising the monument are spolia, and even with regard to the mosque's structural components the whole question of reuse is more complex than has usually been assumed.[24] The dangers of reading material culture exclusively through the lens of textual rhetoric (whether Qur'anic or historical) are amply demonstrated by the survival of contemporary Ghurid coin issues that continue to feature images of Hindu deities.[25] This pragmatic continuity is in stark contrast to the rhetoric of religious orthodoxy that permeates contemporary texts and inscriptions, which make little reference to the sorts of compromises with preexistent traditions witnessed in the numismatic evidence.

We should also be aware of possible shifts in the meaning of the Delhi mosque, even over relatively short periods of time. One such shift may have occurred between the foundation of the mosque in or around 1192 and the massive extension that it underwent during the reign of Iltutmish. There are indications that the eastern "foundation" text dates from the latter period rather than the former, and it may have been set in place as part of a massing of signs of various sorts within the mosque during the reign of Iltutmish.[26] The Qur'anic injunctions against idolatry within the mosque (and especially the Qutb Minar) once found a material counterpart in a number of stone and metal Hindu icons looted during Iltutmish's campaigns of conquest in Ujjain (1233–1234), and resituated along the approach to the mosque where they could be trampled by those entering it.[27] The display of the Ujjain loot harks back to earlier Islamicate precedents (recalling Mahmud of

Ghazni's treatment of the Somnath *linga,* for example), and can be ascribed to the ability of the looted icons to index the expanding frontiers of Iltutmish's empire very publicly in the first mosque of the imperial capital.[28] While such a reuse of Indian artifacts might support the idea that the iron pillar was intended to commemorate "Muslim" victory, it should not be assumed that all the objects garnered within the mosque had the same semantic function. The rejection of idolatry can hardly be equated with a rejection of Indian culture in general, as is too often assumed,[29] and it is far from obvious that the pillar was capable of functioning as an index of idolatry in the same way that looted Hindu icons could. Moreover, there is nothing to suggest that the iron pillar was seized during one of Iltutmish's military campaigns, and it is unmentioned in the thirteenth-century sources that associate the installation of looted icons in the Delhi mosque with the theme of imperial victory.

The idea that the iron pillar was an Islamic trophy finds no support in medieval references to it, the earliest of which date from the fourteenth century. Ibn Battuta, writing after a visit to the Delhi mosque in or around 1333, gives the most extensive description of the pillar:

> In the center of the mosque is the awe-inspiring column of which [it is said] nobody knows of what metal it is constructed. One of their learned men told me that it is called *Haft Jūsh,* which means 'seven metals' (sic), and that it is composed of these seven. A part of this column, of a finger's length, has been polished, and this polished part gives out a brilliant gleam. Iron makes no impression on it. It is thirty cubits high, and we rolled a turban round it, and the portion which encircled it measured eight cubits.[30]

In the *Ta'rīkh-i Fīrūz Shāhī* we are told that fifty years later the Central Asian conqueror Timur was similarly awed by the pillars re-erected in Delhi by order of Firuz Shah Tughluq (figs. 6 and 10).[31] A reference in Elliott and Dowson's translation of the same work to these

---

23. Page (see note 7), p. 29; Anthony Welch, "Qur'an and Tomb: The Religious Epigraphs of Two Early Sultanate Tombs in Delhi," in *Indian Epigraphy, Its Bearing on the History of Art,* ed. Frederick M. Asher and G. S. Gai (New Delhi: Oxford and IBH Publishing Co., 1985), pp. 260–264; Hussein Keshani, Anthony Welch, and Alexandra Bain, "Epigraphs, Scripture, and Architecture in the Early Delhi Sultanate," *Muqarnas* 19, (2002):12–43. For a discussion of the grammatical oddities in the foundation inscription see Patel (as in note 1), pp. 101–114.

24. See Flood (forthcoming, as in note 2).

25. Hirananda Sastri, "Devanāgarī and the Muhammadan rulers of India," *Journal of the Bihar and Orissa Research Society* 23 (1937): 495. This fact is ignored by the epigraphic studies cited in note 23, as are recent studies of the monument that question the privileging of Qur'anic epigraphy above all other modes of evidence.

26. Finbarr Barry Flood, *Translating India: Art and Transculturation in a Medieval Afghan Polity* (forthcoming), chapter 8.

27. H. G. Raverty, *Ṭabaḳāt-i-Nāsirī: A General History of the Muhammadan Dynasties of Asia, including Hindustan,* 2 vol.,

originally Calcutta, 1881 (New Delhi: Reprinted by the Oriental Books Reprint Corporation, 1970), vol. 1, pp. 623, 628.

28. Finbarr Barry Flood, "Between Cult and Culture: Bamiyan, Islamic Iconoclasm, and the Museum," *Art Bulletin* 84/4 (2002):650–651.

29. See Flood (forthcoming, as in note 2).

30. Gibb (see note 17), p. 622. On the "seven metals" see Iqbal Khan, "Views of Abul Fazl on the 'Birth' of Metals," in *Art and Culture: Felicitation Volume in Honour of Professor Nurul Hasan,* ed. Ahsan Jan Qaisar & Som Prakash Verma (Jaipur: Publication Scheme, 1993), pp. 105–109.

31. 'Afif (see note 12), p. 314; Elliott & Dowson, (see note 13), vol. 3, p. 353; Welch (see note 11), p. 319. That the inscriptions on many of the surviving pillars stress their enduring nature and indicate a desire to evoke awe is hardly serendipitous: Fleet (1886, see note 5), p. 257; idem., (1970, see note 7), p. 148.

Figure 10. Re-erected Ashokan pillar, Kotla Firuz Shah, Firuzabad.

pillars being moved to Delhi "as trophies" is not borne out by the published Persian text, where their value as wonders (*ʿajaʾibān*) is instead stressed.[32] So far as surviving fourteenth-century accounts go, awe and mystery rather than triumph and victory are the keynotes in the reception of these fragments of the Indian past.

In a rare dissension from the tendency to ignore the transcultural nature of the pillars reused in Delhi, William McKibben notes that Iltutmish "may have appropriated the iron pillar for the Quwwat al-Islam mosque in part to glorify the achievements of past civilizations and affirm the ideological beginnings of Islamic rule in India by aligning himself with pre-Islamic sovereigns."[33] A similar interpretation of Jahangir's later reuse of two pre-Islamic pillars was offered by Catherine Asher, who very plausibly read the inscription of Jahangir's royal lineage on the Allahabad pillar as an attempt to link Mughal rule "to both the Timurid tradition and to deeply rooted Indian traditions."[34]

In both cases, while the meaning of the reused pillars is considered in relation to their connection (however vague) with the pre-Islamic history of India, the practice of reuse itself and its cultural antecedents remains unexamined. If one considers the antique pillars reused in sultanate Delhi diachronically, however, it quickly becomes apparent that many of them had already acquired complex genealogies through reuse and reinscription in preceding centuries. Just as Egyptian pharaohs or Byzantine emperors inscribed their names on columns and pillars that were already antique, medieval Indian rajas were apparently prone to reinscribing existing commemorative pillars in order to commend their own glorious deeds to history.[35] Some of these inscriptions correspond with the re-erection of the pillars during different phases of reuse, a fact that must

32. ʿAfif (see note 12), p. 308; Elliott & Dowson (see note 13), vol. 3, p. 350.

33. McKibben (see note 13), p. 113.

34. Asher (see note 11), p. 7.

35. The pharaonic obelisk now in New York was, for example, inscribed by three different pharaohs between 1461 B.C. and 933 B.C.: Bern Dibner, *Moving the Obelisks* (Norwalk, Conn.: Burndy Library, 1952), p. 44. See also the dedication to the Byzantine emperor Phocas (r. 602–610) on a column set up in the Roman forum in the third century by the emperor Diocletian: Marlia Mundell Mango, "Imperial Art in the Seventh Century," in *New Constantines: the Rhythm of Imperial Renewal in Byzantium, 4th–13th Centuries,* ed. Paul Magdalino (London: Variorum, 1994), p. 110.

cause us to reconsider the idea that the re-erection of the iron pillar constituted a specifically Islamic mode of commemorating victory.

In the case of the Delhi iron pillar, although attention has been focused on the Gupta temple in which it first stood and the Ghurid mosque in which it eventually came to rest, in fact these only mark the beginning and end of its history. Among a number of less well-preserved inscriptions recorded on the column in the nineteenth century was one that referred to the foundation of Delhi by the Tomar ruler Anang Pal in Samvat 1109 (A.D. 1052).[36] On epigraphic grounds it has been assumed that this is a contemporary inscription, carved at Anang Pal's behest more than six centuries after the column had first been dedicated. Some of the temple material reused in the Delhi mosque is of similar date, and it has been suggested that the iron pillar was taken from its original location and re-erected within a temple built by the Tomar ruler in 1052, at the time that the pillar was reinscribed.[37] On the basis of numismatic evidence, however, the date of Anang Pal's reign has recently been put at ca. 1130–1145.[38] Since no attempt seems to have been made to correlate the epigraphic and numismatic evidence, this redating requires further research. If the later date is correct, however, the error in the date inscribed on the column suggests that the inscription is anachronistic and cannot therefore be used as evidence for the reuse of the pillar by Anang Pal in the eleventh century.

The complicated genealogy of the Delhi column is by no means unusual. On the contrary, inscriptions on a number of reused antique pillars tell the same story. The Allahabad pillar reused by Jahangir in the early seventeenth century illustrates just how complex the life histories of such pillars could be.[39] Reconstructing its

travails from the multiple texts that it bears in different languages and scripts, the pillar was first inscribed in the third century B.C. by the Mauryan emperor Ashoka (although it may even have been erected earlier),[40] then reused in the late fourth century A.D. by the Gupta raja Samudra, when it was carved with a list of his accomplishments and those of his ancestors.[41] The same pillar was re-erected once again in 1605, and carved with a Persian text celebrating the lineage of Jahangir.[42] Such documented instances of reuse may be but the tip of the iceberg, since those reusing the pillars may not always have inscribed them, and even inscriptions are liable to wear and erasure over time.[43]

While the reuse and reinscription of antique columns by later Indian rulers provides a general context in which to locate Iltutmish's appropriation of the iron pillar, the reuse of an antique pillar in the vicinity of Delhi in the decades before the Ghurid conquest points to more immediate precedents. The pillar in question is one of five surviving from the architectural program of Firuz Shah Tughluq, and still stands where it was re-

36. Cunningham (1972, see note 7), p. 151; (see note 7), p. 45.

37. Cunningham (1972, see note 7), p. 153; Carr Stephens (see note 7), pp. 23–24; Smith (see note 7), pp. 13–15; Syed Hasan Barani, "History of Delhi to the time of Timur's invasion," *Islamic Culture* 12, no. 3 (1938): 313.

38. John S. Deyell, *Living without Silver, the Monetary History of Early Medieval North India* (New Delhi: Oxford University Press, 1999), pp. 153–154, 157–167, table 14.

39. T. S. Burt, "A description, with drawings, of the Ancient Stone Pillar at Allahabad called Bhim Sén's Gadá or Club, with accompanying copies of four inscriptions engraved in different characters upon its surface," *Journal of the Asiatic Society of Bengal* 3 (1834):105–121; Prinsep (see notes 13 & 19); Hultzsch (1925, see note 13), pp. xix, 156; John Irwin, "'Aśokan' Pillars: A Reassessment of the Evidence," *The Burlington Magazine* 115 (1973): 706–707, fig. 3; idem., "The Prayága Bull-Pillar: another pre-Aśokan Monument," *South Asian Archaeology* 1979 (1981): fig. 15b; idem., "The Ancient

Pillar-Cult at Prayága (Allahabad): its pre-Aśokan Origins," *Journal of the Royal Asiatic Society* (1983): 253–280.

40. For conflicting views about this see A. Ghosh, "The Pillars of Aśoka—their purpose," *East and West* 17 (1967): 275, and Irwin (1981, see note 39), pp. 335–337. Although Irwin argues that the Allahabad pillar has stood on the same site since the time of Ashoka, earlier writers pointed out the likelihood that it had fallen and been re-erected, since the texts on the pillar include both horizontal inscriptions which would have been legible when it was erect, and vertical inscriptions presumably carved when the pillar had fallen: Prinsep (see note 19), p. 968; Krishnaswamy Rao Sahib & Amalananda Ghosh, "A Note on the Allahabad Pillar of Aśoka," *Journal of the Royal Asiatic Society* (1935): 703–704. The same is true of the Dhar pillar. Hultzsch (1925, see note 13, p. xx) suggests that the pillar stood in its original location when reinscribed in the Gupta period, but was subsequently moved by the Mughals.

41. John Faithful Fleet, *Inscriptions of the Early Gupta Kings and Their Successors*, Corpus Inscriptionum Indicarum. vol. 3, (Varanasi: Reprinted by the Indological Book House, 1970), pp. 1–12.

42. Burt (see note 33), pp. 107–108; Prinsep (see note 19), p. 968; James Fergusson, *History of Indian and Eastern Architecture* (London: John Murray, 1876), p. 53; Asher (see note 11).

43. Burt (see note 39), p. 109; Prinsep (see note 19), p. 969; Chabbra (see note 13), p. 320. I am confining my remarks here to inscriptions that mention historical rulers, or which may be considered "official," and therefore offer some evidence for dating phases of reuse. The equally interesting, but less chronologically useful, graffiti left by merchants, travelers, and tourists would be an interesting subject for a separate study: Cunningham (1972, see note 7), p. 167; Stephens (see note 7), p. 24; J. A. Page, *A Memoir on Kotla Firoz Shah*, Memoirs of the Archaeological Survey of India No. 22 (Calcutta: Government of India, 1937), p. 29; idem. (1991, see note 7), p. 45; Chhabra (see note 7), pp. 320–321; Prasad (see note 22), pp. 32, 40–42.

erected in 1357, at the center of an extraordinary pyramidal structure in the heart of Firuz Shah's new capital, Firuzabad, just north of Ghurid Delhi (fig. 10). When re-erected in this position, the pillar was crowned with a golden *kalaśa*, a gesture which offers incidental evidence of continuity in Indian royal ritual, for such golden vases were often provided by medieval Indian rulers to crown the summit of temple *śikaras*.[44]

The Firuzabad pillar predates the monument which it now graces by over fifteen hundred years, for it may already have been standing in the third century B.C., when it was inscribed with an edict of the Buddhist emperor Ashoka, written in Prakrit in *brahmi* script.[45] Just below this original dedication is a Sanskrit inscription carved in *devnagari* script a millennium and a half later, in 1164 (fig. 11). The inscription records the conquests of prince Visala Deva, Vigraharaja IV of the Chauhan dynasty which had taken Delhi from the Tomars a few years previously and still ruled most of northwestern India at the time of the Ghurid conquest three decades later.[46] In an ironic twist, plays concerning Visala Deva's battles against the *Turushkas* or Turks (including one written by the raja himself) were found inscribed on stones later reused in the Ghurid

Friday Mosque at Ajmir.[47] The defeat of a *Mleccha* (barbarian, presumably Ghurid) army is also among the victories mentioned in the inscription carved on the Firuzabad pillar at Visala Deva's command. Since it is unlikely that this pillar remained in one spot for fifteen centuries, it seems probable that it was re-erected when it was reused in the late twelfth century by Visala Deva to commemorate his military victories.[48]

In eleventh- and twelfth-century Sanskrit texts, pillars of fame are, along with the pedestals of religious images and copper plates, among the loci considered appropriate for royal inscriptions.[49] The manner in which existing pillars were reinscribed, however, indicates a desire to highlight their function as palimpsests. On the Allahabad pillar, inscriptions of different dates and scripts are interlineated.[50] In other cases, such as the Firuzabad pillar, the Prakrit and Sanskrit inscriptions are juxtaposed in such a way that the later Sanskrit inscription frames the earlier Prakrit (fig. 11). The two texts are further distinguished not only by their differing lengths but also by a striking difference in script. Just as medieval Indian rulers could seek to link themselves with illustrious predecessors by citing earlier eras in their inscriptions, it seems likely that the

44. Page (1937, see note 43), pp. 5, 41; 'Afif (see note 12), p. 312; Elliott & Dowson (see note 13), vol. 3, p. 352. The *kalaśa* was surmounted by a globe and crescent similar to those which seventeenth-century visitors still saw on the Meerut pillar, another of the pillars moved by Firuz Shah: William Foster, *Early Travels in India 1583–1619* (Oxford: Oxford University Press, 1921), p. 157. The provision of a terminal *āmalaka* and *kalaśa* on the Jaunpur pillar and on that at Fatehabad further heightens the parallels with the crowning elements of the temple: Cunningham (1968, see note 13), p. 106; Shokoohy (1988, see note 13), p. 17. Jahangir later crowned the Allahabad pillar with a *kalaśa:* Irwin (1987, see note 20), p. 136, n. 28. For the gifting of the *kalaśa* in pre-sultanate India see Sahityacharya Pandit Bisheshwar Nath Reu, "Jalor Inscription of the Time of Paramâra Vîsala, dated V.S. 1174," *The Indian Antiquary* 62 (1933): 41. It is possible that the *kalaśa* was intended as an aniconic substitute for the animal figures that had earlier crowned many of these columns, although the two often appeared in conjunction: John Irwin, "'Aśokan' Pillars: A Reassessment of the Evidence—IV: Symbolism," *The Burlington Magazine* 118 (1976): 738, fig. 8.

45. Hultzsch (1925, see note 13), pp. xv–xvi, 119; Irwin (1973, see note 39), p. 709.

46. Henry Colebrooke, "Translation of one of the Inscriptions on the Pillar at Dehlee, called the Lat of Feeroz Shah," *Asiatick Researches* 7 (1808): 175–182; F. Kielhorn, "Delhi Siwalik Pillar Inscriptions of Visaladeva; the Vikrama Year 1220," *The Indian Antiquary* 19 (1890): 215–219. For a complete copy of the two inscriptions see Nath (1978, as in note 7), Inscription 2. On the identity of Visala Deva and Vigraharaja IV see Dasharatha Sharma, *Early Chauhān Dynasties,* 2nd ed. (Delhi: Motilal Banarsidas, 1975), p. 67; Deyell (see note 38), p. 167.

47. F. Kielhorn, "Sanskrit Plays, Partly Preserved as Inscriptions at Ajmere," *The Indian Antiquary* (1891): 201–212; Har Bilas Sarda, *Ajmer: Historical and Descriptive* (Ajmir: Fine Art Printing Press, 1941), pp. 76–78.

48. The precise context from which the Firuzabad pillar was brought to Delhi in the fourteenth century is not entirely clear, even if we know that it came from somewhere near Topra: Page (1937, see note 43), p. 29. The *Sīrat-i Fīrūz Shāhī* states that Visala Deva found the pillar standing in front a temple there (ibid., p. 34), which led Cunningham to assume that it was inscribed by Visala Deva while still in situ: idem., (see note 7), pp. 162, 167. The fact that when found the pillar was, like many Ashokan pillars, set upon a foundation stone might support the idea that it was in its original location: John Irwin, "'Aśokan' Pillars: A Reassessment of the Evidence—II: Structure," *The Burlington Magazine* 116 (1974): 719, fig. H. The replication of this arrangement in Firuzabad demonstrates, however, that the same system could be used in secondary contexts.

49. Basak (see note 5), p. 140.

50. Hultzsch (1925, see note 13), p. 156; Irwin (1981, see note 39), figs. 15b, 16b; Asher (see note 11), pp. 6–7. Prinsep (see note 19, p. 967) dismisses the interlineations on the Allahabad pillar as "merely a series of unconnected scribblings of various dates, cut in most likely by attendants on the pillar as a pretext for extracting a few rupees from visitors." Note that a later Persian inscription on the same pillar overlays part of an earlier text: O. P. Kejariwal, *The Asiatic Society of Bengal and the Discovery of India's Past* (New Delhi: Oxford University Press, 1988), p. 170. Similarly, the Persian inscription on the Fatehabad column overlies an earlier faded inscription in an unidentified Indic language: Shokoohy (1988, see note 13), pp. 17–18.

Figure 11. Detail of Ashokan and Chauhan inscriptions on the Firuzabad pillar.

act of reinscribing or re-erecting the pillars was intended as a synecdochal appropriation of the valorized pasts to which various antecedent texts bore witness.[51]

This self-consciousness with regard to script, inscriptions, and reinscriptions contrasts with most instances of reuse in the sultanate period, where (with one exception—fig. 7) there is a noticeable absence of Arabic or Persian inscriptions.[52] This is surprising, since

51. Ronald B. Inden, *Imagining India* (Bloomington & Indianapolis: Indiana University Press, 2000), pp. 249–250. Conversely, an ascendant power might seek to assert its dominance by rejecting the era in common use, as when the Chalukya raja Vikramaditya VI abolished the Śaka era and began using his own Chalukya one: K. P. Jayaswal & R. D. Banerji, "The Hathigumpha Inscription of Kharavela," *Epigraphia Indica* 20 (1929–1930): 75. On the relationship between calendars and conquest and power see Alfred Gell, *The Anthropology*

of Time: Cultural Constructions of Temporal Maps and Images (Oxford & Providence: Berg, 1992), pp. 312–313.

52. The earlier exception is the pillar at Fatehabad (fig. 7), which is inscribed with a thirty-six-line Persian biographical genealogy of Firuz Shah Tughluq. In a rare coincidence between epigraphic content and

the pre-Islamic inscriptions on the pillars reused in the fourteenth century were noticed, remarked on, and (where possible) translated by contemporaries, as we shall see shortly. While it is difficult to account for the apparent reticence to inscribe the columns reused in sultanate monuments, the difference between epigraphic and anepigraphic phases of reuse might conceivably reflect different conceptions of time. If the careful juxtaposition of inscriptions attesting to phases of use and reuse evokes the cyclical and repetitious nature of historical time in preconquest traditions, then perhaps the later reluctance to inscribe these ancient artifacts served to assert the status of Islam as the end of the line rather than another in a series.[53]

Despite this seeming reluctance to inscribe the pillars that came to grace the monuments of the Delhi sultans, it is clear that some of them had previously been transported around the north of the subcontinent over the course of a millennium or more. During this time they were erected and re-erected, inscribed and reinscribed by rulers of different dynasties and different

faiths. That this fact has been overlooked is largely due to the neglect of (or selective quotation from) the inscriptions on these remarkable artifacts within an academic tradition partitioned in ways that make it difficult to deal diachronically with objects crossing rather arbitrarily defined cultural or taxonomic boundaries.[54] Yet its importance for understanding the reuse of such artifacts by Indo–Islamic sultans can hardly be overstated. The cumulative weight of the evidence discussed above suggests that the ritual practices of medieval north Indian kings encompassed not only the erection of commemorative pillars but also the appropriation of those erected by royal predecessors. Based on the evidence of the Firuzabad pillar, we can be certain that the Chauhan rulers of Delhi were reusing antique pillars less than three decades before the Ghurid conquest of the city. Moreover, in addition to epigraphic evidence for the reuse of antique pillars in the preconquest period, medieval inscriptions also attest to the looting and destruction of the victory pillars erected by contemporary rivals.[55] The reuse of such pillars, whether those of a contemporary or a long-dead predecessor, was thus an intrinsic part of the ritual practices of medieval South Asian kings.

Seen in this light, Iltutmish's re-erection of the iron pillar in the Friday Mosque of Delhi has little to do with cultural rupture and everything to do with cultural continuity. This was no mere appropriation of spolia designed to suggest a *symbolic* continuity with pre-Muslim kingship, but the *actual* continuation of a practice associated with medieval Indian kings. The gesture may have been intended to commemorate the victories of the Ghurids and their successors, but it did

---

geographic location, many of the events that facilitated Firuz Shah's rise to power discussed in the inscription took place in this very area: Shokoohy (1988, see note 13), pp. 17–18. The Jaunpur pillar bears the foundation text of a mosque built in 761/1360, but this pillar may not be antique: McKibben (see note 13), p. 110. For the inscription of Jahangir's titles and lineage on the Allahabad pillar see Asher (note 11), p. 4.

53. Like their Indian equivalents, the various models of medieval Persianate historiography emphasize recurring patterns in human history: Julie Scott Meisami, "The Past in the Service of the Present: Two Views of History in Medieval Persia," *Poetics Today* 14, no. 2 (1993): 253, 261, 270–271; idem., *Persian Historiography to the End of the Twelfth Century* (Edinburgh: Edinburgh University Press, 1999), pp. 283–285; Gerhard Böwering, "Ideas of Time in Persian Mysticism" in *The Persian Presence in the Islamic World,* ed. Richard G. Hovannisian & Georges Sabagh (Cambridge: Cambridge University Press, 1998), p. 179. A major difference, however, is the fact that, in Persianate historiography, such patterns occur within a history that proceeds "from a finite beginning—the Creation—to a preordained end": Meisami (1999), p. 285. Historical accounts of the pre-Islamic past in medieval Persian chronicles "come to full closure," unlike their Islamic counterparts: Mohammad Tavakoli-Targhi, "Contested Memories: Narrative Structures and Allegorical Meanings of Iran's Pre-Islamic History," *Iranian Studies* 29, nos. 1–2 (1996): 152, 154–155. See also John Irwin's interesting suggestion that the Qutb Minar and the iron pillar in the Delhi mosque represent different facets of time, "one mytho-historical, the other actual": Irwin (1987, see note 21), p. 142. For a European parallel, see Ottonian reuse of pagan and early Christian artifacts to reflect the concept of a *culminatio,* "the Ottonian fulfillment of the concept of a cumulative and culminating Christian history": Irene H. Forsyth, "Art with History: The Role of Spolia in the Cumulative Work of Art," in *Byzantine East, Latin West: Art-Historical Studies in Honor of Kurt Weitzmann,* ed. Christopher Moss & Katherine Kiefer (Princeton: Princeton University Press, 1995), p. 158.

54. Thus while Prakrit scholars have focused on the Ashokan inscription, Sanskritists have tended to highlight Gupta and later texts, while Islamicists have dealt with both as anomalies, whose presence in a mosque could be best explained by falling back on the standard explanation of trophy value. William McKibben, for example, in an extensive account of the pillars reused in sultanate architecture does not discuss the content of the pre-Islamic inscriptions. While he mentions some of the inscriptions on the Firuzabad pillar in passing (see note 13, p. 117, n. 39), he omits any reference to the crucial inscription of Visala Deva.

55. For the looting of a victory pillar see the inscription of the Pallava king Vijaya-Nandivarman III recording his seizure of the pillar that stood at the center of Vatapi (modern Badami), the capital of his defeated Chalukya rival: Rao Sahib H. Krishna Sastri, *South Indian Inscriptions,* vol. 2 (Madras: Government Press, 1916), p. 511. See also the destruction of the twin victory pillars (*raṇastambhas*) erected by the Rashtrakuta raja Kaka or Kakara III by the western Chalukyan ruler Taila II in the tenth century: Fleet (1886, see note 5), pp. 255, 257; Vogel (see note 7), pp. 88, 90–91.

so in a language and idiom adopted directly from indigenous Indian rulers. If one sees in the re-erection of the iron pillar in Delhi a triumphal rejection of the pre-Islamic traditions of India, one is therefore left with the need to explain why this particular royal tradition was embraced so enthusiastically by the Delhi sultans. Even the association with a mosque finds parallels in the erection (and re-erection) of such pillars in front of preconquest temples, however different their form and function; in the case of the Firuzabad pillar, its previous association with a Chauhan temple was familiar to those who reused it. The relocation of such pillars within or near mosques may have been represented as an Islamicization in contemporary textual rhetoric, but it was clearly a practice adopted from preconquest (and mostly Hindu) kings.[56]

The peregrinations and tribulations of the antique pillars bear comparison with those of the icons and insignia that were ritually appropriated and reappropriated by medieval Indian rulers.[57] The meaning of these objects was directly related to their possession of a history, to the existence of a genealogy memorialized in contemporary narratives (both oral and textual), or even inscribed upon the objects themselves and the buildings that housed them.[58] Such relics were inalienable by virtue of an indexical relationship with kingship and their consequent possession of the power to define the historical identity of those who deployed them. Possessing the ability to "attract new meanings, fictitious memories, altered genealogies, and imagined ancestors," inalienable objects are ideally suited to confer legitimacy on those associated with them.[59]

The potential for legitimation inherent in these inalienable fragments of antiquity was obvious to the Muslim rulers that reused them, for the Ta'rīkh-i Fīrūz

Shāhī tells us that in setting up the iron pillar, Iltutmish, like every great king, wanted to establish a lasting memorial to his power.[60] Although it has been suggested that this entailed a shift in emphasis in the meaning of these antique columns, "from an exclusively cosmological role to one that encompassed ideas of kingship and legitimacy,"[61] the neglected epigraphic evidence discussed above suggests that Iltutmish was following a precedent rather than establishing one, even if subsequent Islamicate historiography saw otherwise.

The association of the pillars with earlier Indian kings (historical and mythical) was not only stressed in medieval Persian sources,[62] but in some cases was literally legible. A keen interest in the original cultural context of the reused pillars is suggested by attempts to decipher the inscriptions on the pillars reused in the fourteenth century by Firuz Shah Tughluq, an interest in antique epigraphy that recalls the response of earlier Persian rulers to the relics of the pre-Islamic past.[63] Sanskrit inscriptions were evidently read with a high degree of accuracy, for the *Sīrat-i Fīrūz Shāhī*, the Persian text that records the removal of the Firuzabad pillar, reports quite correctly that the writing on the

56. Page (see note 43), p. 34. See also notes 66 and 92. On the association with temples see Irwin (1987, see note 21), p. 134; idem., "Islam and the Cosmic Pillar," *South Asian Archaeology* (London, 1985) p. 397, fig. 3.

57. Richard H. Davis, "Trophies of War: The Case of the Chalukya Intruder," in *Perceptions of South Asia's Visual Past,* ed. Catherine B. Asher & Thomas R. Metcalf (New Delhi: Oxford & IBH Publishing Co. Pvt. Ltd., 1994), pp. 162–174. See also D. Dayalan, "The Role of War-Trophies in Cultural Contact," *Tamil Civilisation* 3, nos. 2–3 (1985): 134–137.

58. See, for example, the golden image that came to rest in the Lakshmana Temple at Khajuraho after twice being looted and once given as a gift, facts recorded in the foundation inscription of the temple that housed it: F. Kielhorn, "Inscriptions from Khajuraho," *Epigraphia Indica* 1 (1888–1891): 134; Richard H. Davis, "Indian Art Objects as Loot," *Journal of Asian Studies* 52, no. 1 (1993): 29.

59. Annette B. Weiner, "Inalienable Wealth," *American Ethnologist* 12 (1985): 224.

60. 'Afif (see note 12), p. 314; Elliott & Dowson (see note 13), vol. 3, p. 353.

61. McKibben (see note 13), p. 113. See also Brand (as in note 14, p. 219), where the use of "captured pillars" in mosques is said to have been a concept developed by the early sultans of Delhi.

62. In addition to the historical kings, a widespread popular tradition identified the pillars with Bhim, one of the legendary Pandava brothers who once ruled India. The pillars appropriated by Firuz Shah are said to have been the walking stick of Bhim: Elliott and Dowson (see note 13), vol. 3, p. 350. The Allahabad pillar is similarly identified, as are Ashokan pillars in Bihar and the Nepalese Tarai, and a *stambha* erected at Badoh in Madhya Pradesh in the ninth century: Burt (see note 39), p. 106; F. Kielhorn, "Pathari Pillar Inscription of Parabala; [Vikrama-]Samvat 917," *Epigraphia Indica* 9 (107–108): 248; Hultzsch (1925, see note 13), pp. xviii, xxiii; Kejariwal (see note 50), p. 170; Michael D. Willis, *Temples of Gopakṣetra* (London: British Museum Press, 1993), p. 75. While Mughal sources preserved the memory that the *lat* reused in Firuzabad was once associated with Hindu rajas (Colebrooke [see note 46], p. 177; Prinsep [see note 13], p. 566), seventeenth-century popular opinion had it that the pillars at Allahabad and Delhi were erected by Alexander the Great: Cunningham (1972, see note 7), pp. 163–164; Foster (see note 44), pp. 177, 248. On the legends that accumulated around the Delhi pillar see Vogel (as in note 7).

63. See, for example, the interest of the Buyid ruler 'Adud al-Dawla in the Pahlavi inscriptions at Persepolis, where he had two Arabic inscriptions carved to commemorate his visit in 344/955. His son, Baha' al-Dawla, later commemorated his own visit in 392/1001–1002 with an inscription located opposite a Pahlavi text: Sheila S. Blair, *The Monumental Inscriptions from Early Islamic Iran and Transoxiana* (Leiden: E. J. Brill, 1992), Nos. 6–7, 18, pp. 32–35, 60–62, figs. 10–12.

column commemorates its reinscription by prince Visala Deva two centuries earlier, and notes its previous association with a temple.[64] By contrast, the Prakrit inscriptions on the Firuzabad pillar remained elusive, connoting a mythologized antiquity. Even here the inscriptions were integral to the perceived meaning of the pillars, since monumental texts are capable of evoking power not only through their content, but also "through their location in space and the way they look."[65] That the only two pillars to be inscribed when reused in an Islamicate context (at Fatehabad [fig. 7] and Allahabad) were inscribed with genealogical texts very similar in content and nature to those that Gupta and Chauhan rajas had earlier carved on similar pillars is strong evidence for a continued association between reuse, kingship, and legitimacy.[66]

The act of epigraphic translation prefigured a physical *translatio* that was no less relevant to the issue of legitimacy, for it was not only the pillars that were palimpsests, but also the acts and practices associated with them. The very ability to move and re-erect these extraordinary relics of the Indian past echoed the original act of creation, conveying significant messages about patronage and power in a manner determined by royal precedent. Such heroic endeavors were memorialized in contemporary Persian texts, which prefigure European treatises on similar topics by several centuries.[67] The reported failure of earlier kings to move

the pillars transported by Firuz Shah Tughluq, and the demise of later attempts to repeat such feats only serve to underline the extraordinary skills needed to move the pillars, which could weigh up to thirty tons or more.[68]

The attempt to foster a sense of legitimacy by forging an association with a distinguished political lineage, and with the glories of a real or imagined past, was a common concern of those engaged in the business of state formation in medieval Iran and South Asia.[69] In both realms, the construction of genealogical histories relating the present to the glories of the past finds a visual counterpart in the patronage of archaizing art and architecture, or the reuse, recontextualization, and reworking of carefully selected relics of the past.[70]

64. 'Afif (see note 12), p. 312; Elliott & Dowson (see note 13), vol. 3, p. 352; Page (see note 43), p. 34. On the translation of pre-Islamic inscriptions in Islamic histories see Franz Rosenthal, *A History of Muslim Historiography*, 2nd ed. (Leiden: E. J. Brill, 1968), pp. 123–126.

65. Alan K. Bowman & Greg Woolf, *Literacy and Power in the Ancient World* (Cambridge: Cambridge University Press, 1994), p. 8. Although written of classical antiquity, this was equally true of many pre-modern societies. In medieval China, the presence of archaic inscriptions added to the value of antique bronzes, even when neither read nor legible: Craig Clunas, *Superfluous Things, Material Culture and Social Status in Early Modern China* (Cambridge: Polity Press, 1991). As Catherine Asher notes of the inscriptions on the Allahabad pillar, even though they were probably not accessible to early seventeenth-century viewers "they clearly were recognized as the product of an ancient Indian past": Asher (see note 11), p. 7.

66. Ibid., pp. 7–8. See also the suggestion that Firuz Shah Tughluq's decision to inscribe his memoirs on the Jami' Masjid of Firuzabad was inspired (in a general sense) by Ashoka's edict on the adjacent pillar, even if illegible: K. A. Nizami, "The Futuhat-i-Firuz Shahi as a Medieval Inscription," in *Proceedings of Seminar on Medieval Inscriptions (6–8th February 1970)* (Aligarh: Centre of Advanced Study, Aligarh Muslim University, 1974), p. 30.

67. Firuz Shah Tughluq's endeavors are memorialized in a long section of 'Afif's *Ta'rīkh-i Fīrūz Shāhī* and in the anonymous *Sīrat-i Fīrūz Shāhī*: 'Afif (see note 12), pp. 308–314; Page (see note 43), pp.

33–42; Elliott & Dowson (see note 13), pp. 350–353. For similar treatises on moving antique columns and obelisks in early modern Europe, see Domenico Fontana, *Della Transportatione dell'Obelisco Vaticano* (Rome, 1596); Francesco Bianchini, *Considerazioni teoriche e pratiche intorno all transporto della Colonna d'Antonino Pio collocata in Monte Citorio* (Rome: Stamperia della Reverenda Camera Apostolica, 1704).

68. The iron pillar in Delhi reportedly weighs over six tons, while the Ashokan stone pillars such as that moved to Firuzabad can weigh over thirty tons: Smith (see note 7), p. 4; Triveda (see note 12), p. 249; Irwin (1981, see note 39), p. 338. The *Sīrat-i Fīrūz Shāhī* reports that in the fifty years before Firuz Shah's successful appropriation of the Topra pillar (that now in Firuzabad), three Chingizid and Chaghatai rulers had tried unsuccessfully to move it: Page (see note 43), p. 34. The destruction of the iron pillar of Dhar is attributed to the attempt by Sultan Bahadur (r. 1526–1537) to carry it off to Gujarat. Jahangir later intended to carry the largest fragment to Agra to serve as a lamp-stand, but this was never carried out: Asher (see note 11), p. 8; Thackston (see note 8), p. 235. See also Garth Fowden's remarks on the political kudos accruing to Late Antique emperors from the ability to move apparently immovable Egyptian obelisks to Constantinople and Rome: Garth Fowden, "Obelisks Between Polytheists and Christians: Julian, EP.59," in *Polyphonia Byzantina: Studies in Honour of Willem J. Aerts*, ed. Hero Hokwerda, Edmé R. Smits, & Marinis M. Woesthuis (Groningen, 1993), p. 37. For a good discussion of the logistics involved in moving antique obelisks in early modern Europe see Dibner (as in note 35).

69. "The role of history in linking present rulers with past ones (whether with those of ancient Iran or with the caliphate) and thereby legitimizing the transfer of power to the current incumbents is clearly crucial": Meisami (1993, see note 53), p. 250. See also Clifford Edmund Bosworth, "The Heritage of Rulership in Early Islamic and the Search for Dynastic Connections with the Past," *Iran* 11 (1973): 51–62. For the importance of genealogies (mythological and otherwise) in medieval Indian kingship see V. Raghavan, "Variety and Integration in the Pattern of Indian Culture," *The Far Eastern Quarterly* 15, no. 4 (1956): 499; R. C. Majumdar, "Ideas of History in Sanskrit Literature," in *Historians of India, Pakistan and Ceylon*, ed. C. H. Philips, (Oxford: Oxford University Press, 1961), p. 24.

70. See the revival of Chola architectural styles by the Vijayanagara rulers of southern India, which has been read as a "visual statement of appropriation and incorporation" of the former territories of the earlier

Occasionally the textual and artifactual coincided in the articulation of genealogical claims, as when Mughal emperors reinscribed royal artifacts bearing the accumulated names of illustrious predecessors,[71] or when epic passages from the *Shāh-nāma*, the Iranian book of kings, were quoted on the walls of cities and palaces, in an endeavor "to legitimize the present through identification with the past."[72] The latter case is particularly interesting, evidencing as it does the ability of the mythologized pre-Islamic past to serve as an instrument of legitimation through the operation of a type of *isnād* paradigm. Just as the appeal to authority in contemporary Persianate histories was "linked to the appropriation of prior authoritative narratives,"[73] the epic past enshrined in texts such as the *Shāh-nāma* could be appropriated by Muslim rulers seeking to construct a genealogy by means of which the present

could be "instantly incorporated into a victorious tradition."[74]

Like the Mirror for Princes literature of the eleventh and twelfth century, the *Shāh-nāma*, reportedly inspired by an ancient Indian king's patronage of historical and allegorical texts,[75] provided a paradigm for a reframing of the pre-Islamic kingly past within an Islamicate matrix that emphasized the shared experience of kingship.[76] The use of past precedent to frame the contemporary encounter with India can be seen in the commissioning of the *Shāhrīyār-nāma* by the Ghaznavid sultan Mas‘ud III (r. 1099–1115), who was celebrated in an epic poem inscribed on the walls of his palace, giving the genealogy of the Ghaznavid sultans in the meter of the *Shāh-nāma*.[77] The *Shāhrīyār-nāma* details the Indian exploits of the great-grandson of Rustam, and was clearly intended to cast Mas‘ud's own Indian campaigns in an epic light. Slightly later, the Ghurid overlords of Iltutmish devised a lineage that related themselves both to the kings of pre-Islamic Iran and to the Arabic–Islamic past embodied in the caliphate, invoking (like many Persian kings before and after them) various material relics of that past to bolster their claims to a noble lineage.[78] When it came to royal rhetoric appropriated

Chola empire: George Michell, "Revivalism as the Imperial Mode: Religious Architecture During the Vijayanagara Period," in *Perceptions of South Asia's Visual Past,* ed. Catherine B. Asher & Thomas R. Metcalf (New Delhi: Oxford and IBH Publishing Co. Pvt. Ltd., 1994), pp. 192–193. This took place several hundred miles from where its sources of inspiration stood, offering a further parallel for the relocation of ancient monuments discussed above. The phenomenon continued until the early modern period in South India: Mary Beth Coffman Heston, "Images from the Past, Vision of the Future: The Art of Marttanda Varma," in *Perceptions of South Asia's Visual Past,* ibid., pp. 201, 204. A more literal expression of the same impulse reveals itself in the reuse of objects and architectural fragments associated with earlier dynasties: Joanna Williams, "A Recut Aśokan Capital and the Gupta Attitude Towards the Past," *Artibus Asiae* 35 (1973): 225–240. In North India, Rajput and Sikh chiefs who challenged centralized authority as Mughal power waned sometimes carried off fragments of Mughal monuments for reuse in their own buildings: Cunningham (1972, see note 7), p. 223; Janice Leoshko, "Mausoleum for an Empress," in *Romance of the Taj Mahal* (Los Angeles & London: Thames & Hudson, 1989), p. 84.

71. Sheila S. Blair, "Timurid Signs of Sovereignty," *Oriente Moderno* 76, no. 2 (1996): 571–572. There are, of course, numerous instances of the phenomenon from Late Antique and medieval Europe: Kim Bowes, "Ivory Lists: Diptychs, Christian Appropriation and Polemics of Time in Late Antiquity," *Art History* 24, no. 3 (2001): 352.

72. Sheila S. Blair, "The Ilkhanid Palace," *Ars Orientalis* 23 (1993): 243–244; Alessio Bombaci, *The Kūfic Inscription in Persian Verses in the Court of the Royal Palace of Mas‘ūd III at Ghazni* (Rome: IsMEO, 1966), p. 40.

73. Meisami (1999, see note 53), pp. 287–288. See especially the relationship between the translation of preexisting narratives in texts such as the *Shāh-nāma* and the *translatio imperii* that led to the triumph of Persianate political culture over its Arabicizing predecessor in Iran. For the role of citation in Arabic and Persian histories of the Ghaznavid period see ibid., pp. 291–292; Roberto Rubinacci, "Le citazioni poetiche nell'Al-Ta'rīḫ al-Yamīnī di Abū Naṣr al-‘Utbī," in *A Francesco Gabrieli, Studi Orientalistici offerti nel sessantesimo compleanno dai suoi colleghi e discepoli* (Rome: Dott. Giovanni Bardi, 1964), pp. 263–273; Clifford Edmund Bosworth, "The Poetical

Citations in *Baihaqī's Ta'rīkh-i Mas‘ūdī*," in *XX. Deutscher Orientalistentag vom 3. bis 8. Oktober 1977 in Erlangen,* ed. Wolfgang Voigt (Wiesbaden: Franz Steiner Verlag GmbH, 1980). On the relationship between literary citation and other forms of cultural production in medieval Europe, see Cutler (see note 4), p. 1064; Umberto Eco, "Riflessioni sulle tecniche di citazione nel medioevo," in *Ideologie e Pratiche del Reimpiego nell'Alto Medioevo* (Spoleto: Presso la Sede del Centro, 1999), Settimane di Studio del Centro Italiano di Studi sull'Alto Medioevo 46, vol. 1, pp. 461–484.

74. Linda Seidel, "Images of the Crusades in Western Art: Models as Metaphors," in *The Meeting of Two Worlds, Cultural Exchange Between East and West During the Period of the Crusades,* ed. Vladimir P. Goss (Kalamazoo: Medieval Institute Publications, Western Michigan University, 1986), p. 386.

75. Vladimir Minorsky, "The Older Preface to the Shāh-Nāma," in *Studi Orientalistici in onore di Giorgio Levi della Vida* (Rome: Istituto per l'Oriente, 1956), vol. 2, p. 167. On the impact of the text on Persianate historiography in India see ibid., p. 167; M. Athar Ali "Ta'rīkh. 4. In Muslim India," *The Encyclopaedia of Islam,* new ed., vol. 10 (Leiden: E. J. Brill, 1998), p. 295.

76. See Meisami (1999, as in note 53, pp. 285–286 on the importance of the "great man" paradigm of Persian historiography. Bosworth (see note 73, p. 51) notes, however, the absence of quotations from the *Shāh-nāma* in Bayhaqi's history of the deeds of the Ghaznavids in India. On the use of quotations from the *Shāh-nāma* in an Anatolian Seljuq Mirror for Princes, see Julie Scott Meisumi, "The Šāh-nāme as a Mirror for Princes: A Study in Reception" in *Pand-o Sokhan,* eds. Christophe Balaÿ, Clair Kappler, and Živa Vesel (Teheran: Institut français de recherche en Iran, 1995), pp. 265–273.

77. Bombaci (see note 72), pp. 40–42.

78. Bosworth (see note 69), pp. 54–55.

for genealogical purposes, cultural boundaries were relatively fluid. Thus, Indo–Muslim sultans might claim descent from the Pandavas (to whom many of the antique pillars were attributed), while later Indo–Persian historians imagine the heroes of the *Shāh-nāma* and Indian epics such as the *Rāmāyana* as contemporaries whose colorful trajectories sometimes intersected.[79]

The paradigmatic role of the pre-Islamic past in conferring legitimacy on *parvenu* Persianate dynasts offers one potential model for the co-option of the Indian past and its material traces by Iltutmish and the newly emergent Delhi sultanate. Contemporary evidence for the role of material remains within such a paradigm may be found in Seljuq Anatolia, geographically remote from sultanate India but culturally contiguous by virtue of its shared Persianate Turkic cultural milieu. Seljuq participation in the pre-Islamic past of Anatolia was orchestrated by means of spolia, historical and mythological tales, and textual quotation. Scott Redford notes of the architectural program undertaken at Sinop after its conquest in 1214 that: ". . . Sultan Izzedin Keykavus seems to have placed himself in a mythic context, keeping company with the kings of yore, whether Caesar or Khusraw."[80] The walls of Konya erected by Alaeddin Keykubad in 1219–1221 incorporated classical and Byzantine spolia along with epigraphy, which included both religious texts and quotations from the *Shāh-nāma*. The latter functioned as a vector of appropriation that extended the mythic age of pre-Islamic Iran to Anatolia and permitted the assimilation of a pre-Islamic past instantiated in the material remains of cultures that, strictly speaking, lay outside the cultural ambit of the text.

Given this extrapolation from the mythologized past of pre-Islamic Iran to the instantiated past of pre-Islamic Anatolia, the pre-Islamic pillars reused in sultanate Delhi might be considered the material correlates of a citational practice encountered in contemporary Persianate historiography and occasionally reflected in princely practice. Although no equivalent for the *stambha*s and *lat*s of India existed in Iran, the evidence

from contemporary Anatolia suggests that they were potentially assimilable as a variant of the known.[81] The common use of the past in the self-representations of both Persianate rulers and their Rajput equivalents may have facilitated the process of assimilation, for later European encounters with India attest the fact that "symbolic representations of power could be 'translated' on the basis of cross-cultural analogy."[82] Both undertakings bring to mind Walter Benjamin's classic formulation of the translator's art as "a somewhat provisional way of coming to terms with the foreignness" of its object.[83] Such pillars may even have been familiar from preexisting descriptions of the region, for a tale preserved in the eleventh-century Egyptian compendium, the *Kitāb al-Hadāyā wa al-Tuḥaf*, refers to a mysterious iron pillar encountered during an earlier phase of Islamic conquest. According to the tale, Hisham b. 'Amr al-Taghlibi, the 'Abbasid governor of Sind, was confronted with an iron pillar seventy cubits long in "Kandahar" (probably the region of Gandhara in northeastern Afghanistan and northwestern Pakistan) during an attempt to conquer India in 768. The governor was told that the column was a victory monument erected by Tubba', the celebrated pre-Islamic ruler of Yemen, and fashioned from the weapons used by his Persian allies in gaining the victory that it commemorated.[84] The recasting of weapons to produce an indexical relationship between victory monuments and the events that they commemorate is relatively common, and similar claims made for medieval iron columns that survive in India may be relevant to the ways in which the iron column in Delhi was perceived.[85] Moreover, the

---

79. Brajadulal Chattopadhyaya, *Representing the Other? Sanskrit Sources and the Muslims (8th to 14th Century)* (New Delhi: Manohar, 1998), p. 84; Briggs, (see note 13), pp. liii–lxiii.

80. Scott Redford, "The Seljuqs of Rum and the Antique," *Muqarnas* 10 (1993): 154; idem., "Words, Books, and Buildings in Seljuk Anatolia," in *Identity and Identity Formation in the Ottoman Middle East and the Balkans: A Volume of Essays in Honor of Norman Itzkowitz,* ed. Karl Barbir & Bakri Tezcan (forthcoming). I am grateful to Scott Redford for providing me with a copy of his unpublished paper.

81. See, however, the undated *minārs* in the area around Kabul: Warwick Ball, "The so-called 'minars' of Kabul," *Studia Iranica* 13 (1988): 117–127. On the issue of equivalence see note 22 above.

82. Joan-Pau Rubiés, *Travel and Ethnology in the Renaissance. South India Through European Eyes, 1250–1625* (Cambridge: Cambridge University Press, 2000), p. 30.

83. Walter Benjamin, [Harry Zohn, tr.], *Illuminations* (London: Fontana Press, 1992), p. 75.

84. Ghāda al-Ḥijjāwī al-Qaddūmī, *Book of Gifts and Rarities, Kitāb al-Hadāyā wa al-Tuḥaf* (Cambridge Mass.: Harvard University Press, 1996), pp. 180–181. The same story is repeated with characteristic scepticism by al-Biruni, writing at the Ghaznavid court: Hakim Mohammad Said (tr.), *Al-Beruni's Book on Mineralogy: The Book Most Comprehensive in Knowledge on Precious Stones* (Islamabad: Pakistan Hijra Council, 1410/1989), p. 220. On Tubba' see A. F. L. Beeston, "Tubba'," *The Encyclopaedia of Islam*, new ed., vol. 10 (Leiden: E. J. Brill, 1999), pp. 575–576.

85. The iron pillar on Mount Abu is said to have been cast from the arms of a fleeing Muslim army: Cousens (see note 5), p. 207. For a modern parallel see the inclusion of captured Iranian helmets in Saddam Hussein's Victory Arch in Baghdad, a monument fashioned

association of the Kandahar column with a known figure from pre-Islamic Arabia sets the 'Abbasid campaign of conquest in an epic context, while demonstrating how familiar figures of antiquity could be associated with the obscure relics of Indian antiquity. In similar fashion, the pillars reused by Firuz Shah Tughluq came to be seen as relics from the time of Alexander the Great.[86] As a curiosity that hinted at a wondrous technological capacity, the iron pillar may have evoked legends concerning mythical kings such as Alexander and Solomon, whose marvelous works were represented both textually and visually in medieval Persianate culture.[87]

Such identifications suggest that what was at stake in the appropriation of the antique pillars was neither the assimilation of a living adversary nor a past characterized by a single antecedent regime, but the palimpsest of cumulative heroic pasts. It is this that distinguishes the re-erection of the pillar in the Delhi mosque from the contemporary display of recently acquired Indian loot in the same monument.[88] The commemorative value of the iron column lay not in its specific associations with the historical kings of India, but in its ability to represent "the broader notion of Indian kingship, regardless of whether specific names or deeds were known."[89] As "visual substitutes" for history, inalienable objects such as insignia, regalia, or royal pillars of fame are ideally suited to "bringing past time into the present, so that the histories of ancestors, titles, or mythological events become an intrinsic part of a person's identity."[90] The construction of identity is directly relevant to the re-erection of antique pillars by the Delhi sultans, for as William McKibben notes:

> Through the physical incorporation of the lat from its antique site to the new Islamic capital, the empires of pre-Islamic India (Dār al-Ḥarb) were symbolically incorporated into the Dār al-Islām.[91]

The translation of the Indian past into the sultanate present may have been read as a retrospective Islamicization according to existing paradigms developed in relation to other pre-Islamic pasts, but the manner in which this was achieved reveals a dependence on indigenous Indian models of legitimation.[92] If the iron pillar itself was a fragment of the distant mythic past, the reuse of similar objects during the more recent Chauhan past was conceivably within living memory when Iltutmish incorporated it into the Delhi mosque in the early thirteenth century. The potential for legitimation resided not just in the pillar itself, therefore, but in the act of translating it, which belonged in the normative realm of Indian kingly self-representation.

The stability of certain kinds of ritualized activity through periods of political change often serves to foster a sense of continuity,[93] and the benefits of conforming to type were no doubt obvious to the Ghurid conquerors of India and their *parvenu* successors such as Iltutmish. As McKibben notes perceptively, "recognition of the pre-Islamic Indian past (*jāhiliyya*) as an authoritative basis for rule and linkage to an uninterrupted line of Indian sovereigns served to legitimize the sultan's claim to power in a country where the Muslim population remained a minority."[94] Despite the undoubted political

from melted down Iranian weapons: Samir al-Khalil, *The Monument: Art, Vulgarity and Responsibility in Iraq* (London: Andre Deutsch, 1991), p. 8.

86. See note 62.

87. See, for example, a fourteenth-century representation of the metal wall built by Alexander from the Great Mongol *Shāh-nāma*: Glenn D. Lowry, *A Jeweller's Eye, Islamic Arts of the Book from the Vever Collection* (Seattle and London: Arthur M. Sackler Gallery & The University of Washington Press, 1988), No. 12, pp. 86–87.

88. For a detailed discussion of Islamicate looting practices in South Asia during the eleventh to thirteenth centuries see Flood (as in note 26), chapter 3.

89. McKibben (see note 13), pp. 113–114.

90. Weiner (see note 59), p. 210.

91. McKibben (see note 13), p. 114.

92. The later "Islamicization" of the Firuzabad pillar through its removal from a temple and reuse as a *minār* of a mosque is celebrated in the *Sīrat-i Fīrūz Shāhī*: Page (see note 43), p. 34. However, not all the pillars reused by Firuz Shah were set up in mosques, and it is not clear how widespread such attitudes regarding the Islamicization of pre-Islamic relics were, or if one can project them back into the early thirteenth century. Moreover, as noted above, even the secondary association with religious architecture has earlier Indian precedents.

93. Richard Bradley, "Ritual, Time and History," *World Archaeology* 23, no. 2 (1991): 211. For further examples of continuity with preconquest traditions in the ritual practices of Ghurid and sultanate rulers, see Richard M. Eaton, "Temple Desecration and Indo-Muslim States," in *Beyond Turk and Hindu: Rethinking Religious Identity in Islamicate South Asia*, ed. David Gilmartin & Bruce Lawrence (Gainesville: University Press of Florida, 2000), p. 269; Flood (as in note 26). Arjun Appadurai's work on the different historical narratives that have accumulated around a single structure, a Sri Vaishnava temple in Madras, highlights how the maintenance of a set of norms relating to the authority, continuity, and interdependence of different narratives concerning the past permitted "an orderly symbolic negotiation between 'ritual' pasts and the contingencies of the present." The operation of such norms served to preserve cultural continuity in the face of changes, even those wrought by the advent of colonial rule: Arjun Appadurai, "The Past as a Scarce Resource," *Man* n.s.16 (1981): 217–218.

94. McKibben (see note 13), pp. 113–114. Despite assertions that "unbelievers, especially profane idolaters" would not have been permitted entry to the Delhi mosque (Kumar, see note 12, pp. 157–158), we have little evidence for the audiences that gestures such

changes that followed in the wake of the Ghurid conquest of India, the observance of certain established norms (the maintenance of existing coin types, for example) shows a keen awareness of the benefits of projecting authority in a manner congruent with past precedents, wherever possible or useful.

Through the manipulation of inalienable objects, Iltutmish and his successors encompassed and incorporated an Indian history within which they were in their turn accommodated. That the process of articulating legitimate sovereignty was a bilateral one is clear from the well-known Palam inscription, written in 1276, eight decades after the conquest of Delhi. Enumerating the dynastic changes in the region during the eleventh to thirteenth centuries, the author of the Sanskrit text writes:

> The land of Haryānaka was first enjoyed by the Tomaras and then by the Chauhānas. It is now ruled by the Śaka kings (i.e. the sultans). First came Sāhabadīna (i.e. Shihab al-Din Ghuri), then Khudavadīna (i.e. Qutb al-Din Aybak), master of the earth, Samusdīna (i.e. Shams al-Din Iltutmish), then Pherujsāhi (i.e. Firuz Shah), lord of the earth.[95]

This seamless integration of Ghurid and early sultanate rulers into South Asian history as just the latest in a long line of conquering monarchs betrays little sense of the religious, political, and cultural rupture so often highlighted by historians and art historians alike. Such assimilation may be a product of a pragmatic urge to legitimize effective political authority,[96] but it is surely just as much a product of the ability of early Indo–Islamic sultans to engage with existing traditions, to project their authority in the expected manner. In part at least, the incorporation of the Delhi sultans into indigenous Indian histories and royal genealogies reflects the successful manipulation of semiotically charged artifacts whose power resided in the fact that they were already possessed of a distinguished history.

96. Eaton (see note 93), p. 270.

---

as the re-erection of the iron pillar addressed. See, however, Catherine Asher's comments on the likelihood that some of those dwelling in early sultanate Delhi (and presumably using its Friday Mosque) were non-caste Hindu converts to Islam: Catherine B. Asher, "Delhi Walled: Changing Boundaries," in *City Walls: The Urban Enceinte in Global Perspective,* ed. James D. Tracy, (Cambridge: Cambridge University Press, 2000), p. 255. In preconquest temples, the degree of access to the sanctuary was related to such factors as caste status: Pierre-Sylvain Filliozat, "Le droit d'entrer dans les temples de śiva au XIe siècle," *Journal Asiatique,* 263 (1975): 103–117.

95. G. Yazdani, "The Inscriptions of the Turk Sulṭāns of Delhi," *Epigraphia Indo-Moslemica* (1913–1914): 4; Prasad (see note 22), pp. 3–11. As Yazdani comments (ibid., p. 37), "the poet extols the greatness of the Mléchha king in no less flattering terms than are used in the panegyrics of the Hindu period." See also Chattopadhyaya (as in note 79), pp. 48–54. For two other similar inscriptions from Delhi, one dated Samvat 1347 (A.D. 1291), the other Samvat 1384 (A.D. 1328), see Prasad (as in note 22), pp. 15–18, 27–30. The corollary to this is the inscription of the Ghurids and other "Muslim" conquerors into medieval lists of those vanquished by successful Indian rulers. The vanquished are incorporated into such lists by means of dynastic or ethnic appellations (such as *Turushka*), not on the basis of religious affiliation: Cynthia Talbot, "Inscribing the Other, Inscribing the Self: Hindu-Muslim Identities in Pre-Colonial India," *Comparative Studies in Society and History* 37, no. 4 (1995): 692–722, especially p. 701. Similarly, it has been pointed out that the connotations of "Hindu" in pre-Mongol Persian literature "were primarily ethnic": Carl W. Ernst, *Eternal Garden: Mysticism, History, and Politics at a South Asian Sufi Center* (1992: State University of New York Press, 1992), pp. 24, 30–31.

Crossing lines

Architecture in early Islamic South Asia

MICHAEL W. MEISTER

The architecture of early Islamic South Asia shows in clear material terms multiple layers of reception, local marking, and subversion. That local aspects of construction and ornament were incorporated into early Islamic monuments is an increasingly accepted concept, yet substantive incorporation of local beliefs has hardly been approached. Both Hindu and Muslim monuments from early Islamic Pakistan suggest that such an issue should be raised.[1]

Multan

In the sixth and seventh century A.D. perhaps the best known pilgrimage temple in India's northwest was that dedicated to a solar deity at Multan (Punjab Government 1926:272–277), yet other cults, not all of them canonically "Hindu," could also have been discovered (Meister 2000b).[2] Some of the complexities of crossing lines in the two millennia before Islam reached South Asia in the eighth century are suggested by words of the French Vedic scholar, Louis Renou (1953:5–6), which can give a sense of the processes of in-migration in this region from a much earlier period: "The Vedic clans . . . surrounded by the hostile mass . . . themselves were divided. There were the *aris* or 'strangers.' . . . There were the *vrtyas,* whose religion Vedism tried to absorb." There need have been little homogeneity, but rather substantial diversity, among populations filtering in at any time.

Under Arab Muslim hegemony in the eighth century A.D. the importance of Multan as a pilgrimage center remained. Abu Zayd al-Hasan, who traveled there in the ninth century, recorded that (Renaudot 1733:68):

there is a famous Idol called *Multan,* whither they report in Pilgrimage from the remotest parts, even from distances of several Months. Some of the pilgrims bring with them the odoriferous Wood *Hud al Camruni* . . . which they offer to this Idol; delivering it to the Priest of the Temple that he may burn it before his God.[3]

S. M. Ikram (1964:14, 17–18), reporting on conditions in the Indus valley in the eighth century, wrote that "soon after the conquest of Sind and Multan the killing of cows was banned in the area" and that the Arab ruler's dress soon became "similar to that of the Hindu rajas, and, like them, he wore earrings and kept his hair long." Only "through a *coup d'état*" in 997 was Multan "captured" by the Ismailis, who "destroyed the old historic temple . . . which Muhammad ibn Qasim had left in charge of the Hindus." In 1005 Mahmud of Ghazni "compelled the ruler of Multan to recant his Ismaili beliefs," and in 1175 "Sultan Muhammad Ghuri captured Multan and appointed an orthodox Sunni governor." I cite these facts from Ikram in part to suggest the degree to which territorial disputes could involve intra-Islamic contestation.

Multan had also become a major Muslim pilgrimage center at least by the time the tombs of Rukn-i 'Alam and other *pīrs* were built there by the fourteenth century (fig. 1) (Punjab Government 1926:278–282). Yet, in spite of its previous "destruction," the Sun temple at Multan continued to have a presence. According to the Multan *Gazetteer* (ibid.:274, 279–280), "[i]t was apparently destroyed in the 11th century, but it was again restored, and it seems to have been still standing in Thevenot's time (after 1666 A.D.)." Its latest iteration on the hill, the Pralādpuri temple behind the tomb of Bahā-ud-din Zakaria, was finally de-ritualized only by partition in 1947 and its body wrecked in response to the destruction of the Bhabri masjid in north India in 1992.[4]

---

1. Variants of this paper were presented at a UNESCO-sponsored "Colloquium on Indus Civilization: Dialogue Among Civilizations," Islamabad, Pakistan, April 2001, and a symposium "Exploring the Frontiers of Islamic Architecture" organized by the Aga Khan Program for Islamic Architecture at MIT, Cambridge, Mass., May 2001.

2. Eliade (1969:302) wrote of "a convergence for a large number of religious, magical, and alchemical traditions and practices, most of them Śivaistic, but some of them Buddhist."

3. The Chinese pilgrim Hiuen Tsang had also visited Multan and written a description of the Sun temple in 641 A.D. (Punjab Government 1926:24).

4. The Prahlādpuri temple, in close proximity to the tombs, remains a protected monument under the Government of Pakistan. The site of the ancient Sun temple has not been archaeologically

Figure 1. Multan, tomb of Rukn-i 'Alam, ca. fourteenth century (restored, twentieth century).
Photo: Michael W. Meister.

Figure 2. Khatti Chor (Kabirwala), tomb of Khalid Walid, ca. twelfth century, view from south. Photo: Michael W. Meister.

Multan's great tomb architecture combined elements and materials of the constructional traditions of the Indus with forms of ornament that conspicuously mark this region's contact with elsewhere in the Islamic world (Hillenbrand 1992; Khan 1987–1988). Yet we can see these tombs as part of a continuum of experience with sacrality that goes far back in the history of the region.[5]

determined, although Alexander Cunningham's excavations of a well next to the Prahlādpuri shrine (Punjab Government 1926:272–273) showed continuous habitation from the sixth century B.C., and "ashes in the 8th century A.D." that may "represent the capture of Multán by Muhammad Kasim in A.D. 702."

5. Eliade (1969:302) remarked that with ascetic traditions "we are dealing with a movement of considerable importance that seems to have been highly popular after the twelfth century of our era. . . . These mythologies and folklores . . . represent extremely archaic contents."

I have found useful R. A. Jairazbhoy's (1995:v) observation in his book on *Foreign Influence in Ancient Indo–Pakistan* that

[o]nce technologies of civilization have been learned or fashioned . . . , once an idiom has been learned by the native craftsman from the limited horizons within his purview, there follows a period of entrenchment and assimilation. If after this there should be no further contact with a world of different values, then there is a process of hardening in which innovation gives way to repetition, and elaboration is preferred to invention.

The "Frontier"

Certainly the rapid expansion of Islam across Eurasia in the seventh to twelfth centuries offers one of the great case studies for testing processes of innovation produced by contact. Yet we must challenge the creation of any

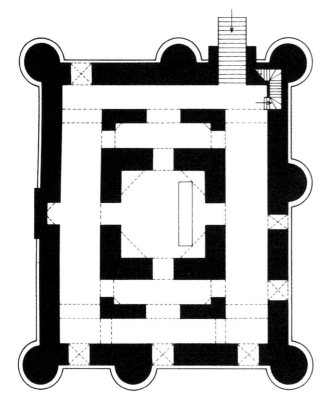

Figure 3. Khatti Chor, *ribāṭ* of Khalid Walid, ground plan. Drawing: Michael W. Meister, after Khan (1990) and Ali (1991).

Figure 4. Khatti Chor, tomb of Khalid Walid, *miḥrāb* in west corridor. Photo: Michael W. Meister.

single canon to define all art under Islam. It would seem too much to claim, for example, that among all territories into which Islam initially spread, it was *only* South Asia that was "a clear slate" requiring "the entire range of Islamic institutions" (Blair and Bloom 1994:149).[6]

Oleg Grabar's seminal book on *The Formation of Islamic Art* in 1973 both helped frame a defining canon and began to destabilize it. As an art historian he found (Grabar 1973:39) that only "for Western Iran, in the areas under the direct and continuous influence of the Sasanian empire, is it possible to talk of a fairly clear artistic style," but wrote eloquently of the broad multicultural worlds and communities across which

Islam as a religion quickly extended itself in the seventh century:

> The result of this religious and ethnic variety was twofold. On the one hand, it brought the Muslim world into contact with a far wider set of ways of life, beliefs, and artistic traditions. On the other hand, it meant the Muslim world lacked a single predominant artistic koiné such as the Roman. . . .[7]

In addition to this focus on continuities of Sasanian and Roman conventions in early Islamic west Asia (Grabar 1967), Grabar (1973:128) also offered a significant preliminary insight into formative contributions of other regions, particularly the east:

> It is a feature of the Islamic frontier, of the peculiarly fascinating world of the edges of the empire where a Muslim elite sought to convert others and mixed with an

---

6. Blair and Bloom (1994:149) continue "virtually all of [these] were fundamentally different in spatial concept from most Hindu and Jain structures." The temple they view as never "designed for congregational worship, the sole requirement of the mosque," overlooking both evolving functions of the temple and the semiotic value of a mosque.

---

7. Grabar (1973:39) continued ". . . in most other areas, especially the northeast, the variety of forms is impossible to define in unified stylistic terms."

Figure 5. Kallar (Salt Range), brick temple, ca. eighth century, view from west. Photo: Michael W. Meister.

Figure 6. Kallar, brick temple, dome and pendentive on the interior. Photo: Michael W. Meister.

astounding variety of ethnic and cultural groups. Although we know very little about the formation and history of a Muslim frontier spirit, it shaped much of the mind and forms of later Islamic culture, and it is perhaps not an accident that original functions first developed there quite early.

In particular, as Grabar (1973:38) had written earlier in his study,

> The predominance of Central Asia in the growth of the special religious form of the mausoleum to holy men should probably be explained by the frontier spirit of the *ghazi*, warriors for the faith. Thus it would appear that the islamization of eastern and northeastern Iran was more rapid, more profound, and more original than that of the western Iranian world.

Tomb or *ribāṭ* of Khalid Walid

Perhaps no monument could better be used to represent the "frontier spirit" Grabar talked of—and the response of local craftsmen—than the ca.-twelfth-

century fortified brick tomb attributed to Khalid Walid near the village of Khatti Chor (Kabirwala tehsil) southeast of Multan in Pakistan (figs. 2–4) (Khan 1990:75–78; Edwards 1990, 1991).[8] Should this, with its bastions, court, and corridors, also be considered a *ribāṭ*, "dedicated to the monastic and missionary fighters for the faith," (Grabar 1973:128) in addition to a tomb for one of them?[9]

Islamization in the northeast of Iran, as Grabar (1973:38) wrote:

> was the work of a comparatively small number of Arabs . . . military men who settled in or near . . . ancient cities with

---

8. The tomb was "built under the orders of 'Ali Karmakh, who acted as governor of Multan under Shahab u'd–Din Ghuri" (Khan 1990:75).

9. Grabar (1973:38) also comments that "it is not accidental that [in northeastern Iran] . . . we hear of ribats, although no certain instance of the monuments themselves have been preserved." Hillenbrand (1996a:512) refers to this monument as the "*ribāṭ* of 'Ali ibn Karmakh near Multan," citing Edwards (1991).

Figure 7. Nandana (Salt Range), brick temple, late
tenth–eleventh century, view of domes in ruined interior.
Photo: Michael W. Meister.

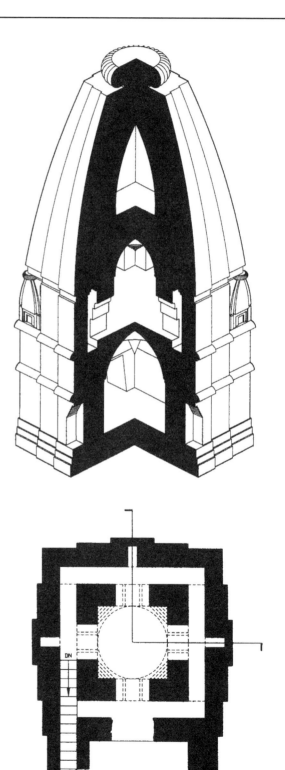

a rich and impressive Zoroastrian, Manichaean, and
Buddhist heritage. . . . [T]hat these cities were on or near
the frontier as guardians of the Muslim world . . . greatly
affected the character of the faith found there.

Within the massive structure of Ali bin Karmākh's
ribāṭ, with its surrounding vaulted corridors and central
domed chamber (fig. 3), the *miḥrāb* placed at the center
of the west wall of the inner court was decorated by
cut-brick ornament that carefully combined an Islamic
message with patterns marking the South Asian location
of the tomb (fig. 4) (Akbar, Rehman, & Tirmizi 1991).[10]
As Ahmad Nabi Khan (1993:266) phrased it, "Islamic art
[in Pakistan] learnt a great deal from the Hindu way of
construction and decorative embellishment."

It is not difficult to compare the Indic arch (*candraśālā*)
and vase-and-foliage (*pūrṇa-ghaṭa*) pillarets of this

---

10. The inscription carved on bricks framing this *miḥrāb* (Ali 1991)
was removed by smugglers but recovered by customs officials some
years ago.

Figure 8. Nandana, brick temple, axonometric section and
ground plan of second story. Drawing: Hasina Choudhury,
© Michael W. Meister.

Figure 9. Taxila, Shrine of the Double-headed Eagle, façade detail, ca. second–third century. Photo: Michael W. Meister.

miḥrāb to source forms on a Hindu–Shahi-period temple such as the brick structure at Kallar from the eighth century (fig. 5) (Meister 1996, 2000). What we may question instead is the way and for what reasons such forms have been received and incorporated here.[11] Are they simply borrowed local decoration, or are they rather a claim—in the name of the *fakir* or *ghazi*—on the locality of South Asia itself?

To represent such arched decoration as a variant on "Islamic" patterns found elsewhere masks the point.[12] They are, rather, empathetically understood local forms, with demonstrable antecedents from the pre-Islamic period.[13]

The brick construction of the half-dome of the *miḥrāb* also parallels local building conventions known from Hindu–Shahi and previous periods (Meister 1996). Such domes had begun much earlier in the traditions of Gandhara and the northwest. Examples of interior domes with plain triangular pendentives come from sixth- and early-seventh-century stone temples at north Kafirkot and Bilot as well as the eighth-century brick temple at Kallar (fig. 6).[14] Such local conventions evolved and were passed on from late Kushan through Shahi periods, to those of early Islamic patronage in the region. The large domed chambers and vaulted corridors inside temples built by the Hindu Shahis in the tenth century at Amb, Bilot, and Nandana (figs. 7–8), for example, can

11. See categories of interaction posited in Meister (1972).

12. Hillenbrand (1996b:168) writes that the "most common form of arch was the horseshoe, distinguished from its counterpoint in Western Islamic architecture by a pointed apex."

13. Hillenbrand, ibid., states that "arches could be cusped, whether with three cusps ('tomb' of Khalid ibn Walid) or more commonly five or seven, a form found extensively on contemporary gravestones and mosques as far away as India [citing Delhi and Ajmer

mosques]" without acknowledging the existence of indigenous pre-Islamic sources. See Meister (2000a:1331), "[t]he [5-]cusped entrances to the small temple at Amb . . . continue a line of evolution begun with the simple triple-arched vaulted entrance of temple B at Māri."

14. Some of these pendentives still are crowned by structural wood beams, a combination of wood and brick found later in the construction of the tombs at Multan (Khan 1990).

Figure 10. Lal Muhra (North–West Frontier Province) brick tomb no. 4 with blue-tile ornament, ca. thirteenth century. Photo: Michael W. Meister.

remind one of similar spaces in local brick structures of the following Islamic period that take on a much different modality (Meister 1996, Khan 1997–1998).

In the late-tenth-century temple at Nandana, the hill fort from which Hindu–Shahi rulers lost control of their territory to Mahmud of Ghazni, for example, large interior dome covered chambers on each of two stories (fig. 7). A stairway built into the outer wall led to a vaulted corridor surrounding a central chamber on the upper level.[15] Much the same interior construction was used for the tomb of Shah Gardez at Adam Wahan (Bahawalpur)—a domed tomb with no curvilinear "*śikhara*" as at Kallar and Nandana (figs. 5, 7–8).[16] That is, the sign value marked by the exterior form of the building could change independent of the constructional system used.

Domes go back well beyond "Islamic contact" in this region, at least to such Buddhist-period monuments as cells of the monastery of Takt-i-bhai north of Peshawar, and may seem to represent both a response to constructional conventions of nearby central Asia and the Roman world and to the semantic suggestion of a

Figure 11. Lal Muhra, brick tomb no. 4, dome and squinch on the interior. Photo: Michael W. Meister.

15. See also the temples at Amb and Bilot (Meister 2000a:figs. 14, 15).
16. Compare Khan (1990:fig. 26 & pl. 82).

Figure 12. Sadan (Muzaffargarh), tomb of Shaikh Sadan Shahid, west view, ca. thirteenth century. Photo: Michael W. Meister.

Buddhist ascetic's thatch-domed hut (Coomaraswamy 1988; Renou 1998). In this early period, most notably on the façade of the Shrine of the Double-headed Eagle at Taxila (fig. 9), architectural forms could be used to signify the variety of community cross-currents present: the classical pediment of a fire temple, the arched façade perhaps of an ascetic's retreat, and the *toraṇa* gate of a Buddhist shrine. In similar fashion, the tomb of Khalid Walid also signed its location by its ornament (fig. 4).

Tombs at Lal Muhra and Sadan

Many other sources also interacted, of course, as models for the architecture of early Islamic South Asia; remarkable tenth-century Samanid tombs survive at Bukhara,[17] twelfth-century tombs at Chhist, a minaret at Jam, an arch at Bust (Grabar 1973; Hillenbrand 1996a, b; Maricq & Wiet 1959).[18] Local craftsmen who built for

Muslim merchants along Gujarat's coast before political hegemony was established also built temples (Shokoohy 1988). The monuments of Ghurids and Ghaznavids, slave dynasty and later sultans, become markers of where people had come from and where they had arrived (Meister 1972, 1993).

Questions of plunder or patronage, craft guilds and contact, of assimilation, innovation, stagnation, and change need to be parsed with care.[19] The little-known brick tombs at Lal Murha (figs. 10–11), south of Dara Ismail Khan in the North-West Frontier Province, for example, have precursors at Bukhara and Chhist as well as being local constructions with brick and blue-tile ornament that can seem antecedent to those more famous local tombs of the fourteenth century at Multan (fig. 1) (Ali 1988; Ali, Durrani, & Sehrai 1997; Khan 1990:167–173).[20]

---

17. Of the Samanids Grabar (1973:38) remarked "by the end of the ninth century the rise of the Samanids can serve as a convenient point in time at which a fully formed culture of Islamic Iran can be assumed, at least for the northeastern provinces. . . ."

18. Excellent photographs of the tombs and ornament at Chhist appear in Niedermayer (1924:pls. 182–184).

19. Reuel Marc Gerecht (*The New York Times,* Mar. 8, 2001) wrote of "the tolerance of traditional Islam, which in Central Asia and the Indian subcontinent even made its peace with polytheists and idol worshipers."

20. Khan (1990:167) wrote that "the tombs are unique in design and construction, inspired and executed by local masons."

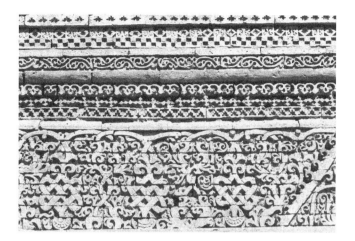

Figure 13. Sadan, tomb of Shaikh Sadan Shahid, detail of cut-brick ornament. Photo: Michael W. Meister.

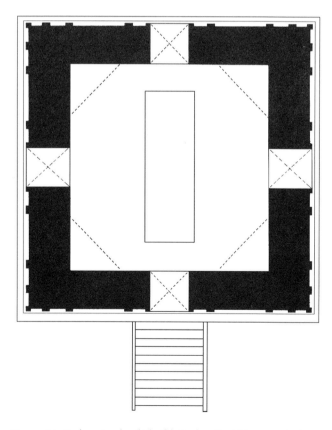

Figure 14. Sadan, tomb of Shaikh Sadan Shahid, ground plan. Drawing: Michael W. Meister.

Figure 15. North Kafirkot (N.W.F.P.), sculpture of a transubstantiating sage excavated in front of temple B, ca. sixth–seventh century. Photo: Michael W. Meister.

Yet southwest of Multan, near a small village known as Sadan or Jalaran, also in the thirteenth century, a tomb for a saint known as Sadan Shahid had been built of exquisitely made thin bricks, carved across the surface with precise ornament (fig. 12–14).[21] This tomb combines local with constructional and decorative conventions brought from Central Asia (Ali 1993; Khan 1990:82–86). Compared with the contemporary tombs at Lal Murha, however, it has been intentionally indigenized by its decoration, which conspicuously

---

21. Ali (1993:133) identifies the village as Jalaran. The cut-brick ornament, he remarks (136), "refers to the continuation of pre-Muslim architectural decoration" but "proper attention is also given to calligraphic decoration," largely the name of Allah and Muhammad repeated on the outer walls.

continues and elaborates the niche forms and foliage found a century earlier on the *miḥrāb* in the *ribāṭ* of Khalid Walid (fig. 4). Did this ornamentation, perhaps, suit the local—as well as transnational—power of the *pîr*?[22]

Dome and spire

Ettinghausen and Grabar (1994/1987:216–217) had already raised the issue: "Why the earliest consistent group of Islamic mausoleums should appear in tenth-century Iran is not altogether clear." They concluded that "[d]ynastic pretensions, worshipping the burial places of Ali, and attempts to attach a Muslim meaning to traditional holy sites must all have played a part in a phenomenon . . . which may have spread westward from Iran."

I might wonder if the *idea* may also have spread westward from lands where Alexander's first encounter with sages became so important an Islamic trope for kingship.[23] Certainly *ṛṣis* continued to play an important role in the seventh century in India's northwest, as the image recently excavated at north Kafirkot can attest (fig. 15)—as also in the distant past and today (Meister 2000b; Meister & Rehman in press).[24] In Islamabad I suggested that seals from the Indus Valley civilization with figures seated in yogic posture (fig. 16) "might be seen as marking a line of sages and followers in the northwest as much a part of the heritage of Pakistan as of India."[25]

Grabar (1973:128) postulated that, more important than the conversion of old building types to new functions, "is the appearance of new, particularly Islamic functions that acquired a monumental form"; using that frame, he also put forward that "[c]ommemorative buildings, especially mausoleums to holy men," were thus "less uniquely Islamic." For northeastern Iran, he "suggested that . . . the original impetus for mausoleums derived from princely constructions," but also significantly noted that:

Figure 16. Moenjo-daro, Indus Valley, steatite seal perhaps showing a yogic shaman (so-called proto-Śiva seal), second millennium B.C. Photo: Gregory Possehl.

the widening of the patronage and changes in religious and cultic habits (here related more precisely to the importance of semi-religious orders guarding the frontier and of social organizations with mystical overtones) led to the wider use of the monumental tomb.

What Grabar was playing with at the time was that monumental forms could both have and acquire multiple and concurrent Islamic and non-Islamic functions.

J. Spencer Trimmington's (1971:22) study of Sufism asserted that "Indian Islam seems to have been essentially a holy-man Islam" and continued that "[t]hese migrants in the Hindu environment acquired an aura of holiness, and it was this which attracted Indians to them, rather than formal Islam." To understand the role of the saint's tomb in South Asia, Trimmington's (ibid.:22, 26) further observations seem particularly apropos (although they might apply nearly as well to the temple and its icon [Maxwell 1982, 1984]):

As in other aspects of Sufi thought and practice there is an essential distinction between the way in which the genuine Sufi approached a saint's tomb and the practice of the people. The mystic . . . find[s] in the material symbol an aid to meditation. But the popular belief is that the saint's soul

---

22. As one believer said to me at the ruin, were a person to take even a brick away, "the power of the *pîr* would strike him dead."

23. Michael Barry, "The King and the Hermit—the Visual Transmission of a Theme from Alexander and the Brahmin to Thangir," presented at the UNESCO "Colloquium on Indus Civilization," Islamabad, April 2001.

24. The sculpture was found in two pieces above and in front of the stairway to temple B and is of a scale appropriate to have been placed in that temple's sanctum.

25. See note 1.

Figure 17. Thila Yogiyan, domed tomb of an ascetic, post Mughal. Photo: Michael W. Meister.

lingers about his tomb. . . . At such places his intercession can be sought.[26]

Certainly the acts of those who visit the tomb of Shaikh Sadan Shahid today—tying threads and miniature baby-swings to the gnarled tree in front of it—confirm his observation.

In South Asia, then, did the tomb become a temple, or its rival? Does the transcending image of the sage in part explain the building of Sikandra or the Taj?[27] It may seem too large a leap to move to the defining royal monuments of Mughal India, yet it was with the mental image of the Taj Mahal that Grabar began his search for

the "earliest Islamic commemorative structures" in 1966.[28] Were they regal or sacral, for king or saint?[29]

In the late Mughal period and after we can test that question in part by citing the burial practice of one much patronized sect of ṛṣis, the Gorakhnāth or Kānphata Yogîs. On a forested hill at Thila Yogiyan, north of Rotas fort in the Punjab, for example, this wealthy and powerful group over time built a number of almost royal tombs for its holy men (fig. 17). These take the form of square-domed chambers; the body of the sage is buried upright under the floor; a liṅga is placed above his head at the center of the shrine.[30] The

26. He (Trimmington 1971:23, 26) also commented that "[t]here were two categories of Sufis, those associated with khānaqāhs and the wanderers. . . . Indian khānaqāhs grew up around a holy man"; "dervishes . . . acted as cultural agents in spreading and stabilizing Islam."

27. That a long tradition of holy–men's tombs preceded the development of royal tombs in South Asia was not addressed by Begley (1979); the interdiction against monumentalizing graves was also circumvented in other regions of the Islamic world, drawing on other models and "new functions"; and Grabar (1966:7) had demonstrated how many and varied the names were to "illustrate the multiple facets of memorial construction in the minds of Muslims."

28. Grabar (ibid.) began: "One of the most characteristic buildings of Islamic architecture is, without doubt, the monumental tomb. The Taj Mahal or the great Mamluk mausoleums in Cairo are visited by thousands of casual tourists, while every traveler in North Africa or the Near East has seen along the roads, on top of hills, . . . hundreds of small shrines usually assumed to be the resting place of some saint or hero. . . ."

29. "Siddhas . . . understood liberation as the conquest of immortality" (Eliade 1969:302).

30. Ibid.:307, 402: "they are not cremated but are buried in the posture of meditation. . . . Above the tomb are set symbols of the liṅga and yoni"; "[a]scetics were buried in the posture of meditation, and liṅgas were set up on their tombs. Many of these tombs later became temples."

symbolism of the dome above is both shared by Islam and transformed (Coomaraswamy 1938).[31]

Permeability of borders

My tentative supposition on the permeability of borders in South Asia has been that mechanisms at work make separation and survival as possible as assimilation (Meister 1994a). They have seemed to me to involve the capacity to integrate a variety of cultural patterns within a shared social system—a social compact. It is this compact that architecture itself can signal in its forms and ornament, its layered and multiple uses over time and territory (Meister, 2000b). Architecture can share communities as well as differentiate them.

BIBLIOGRAPHY

Akbar, Siddiq–a–, Abdul Rehman, and Muhammad Ali Tirmizi
1991   (ed.) *Sultanate Period Architecture.* Lahore: Anjuman Mimaran.

Ali, Taj
1988   *Anonymous Tombs in the Gomal Valley, and the Beginning of Tomb Architecture in Pakistan* (Memoirs of the Department of Archaeology no. 4). Peshawar: Department of Archaeology, University of Peshawar.
1991   "The Mihrab-Inscription of the So-Called Tomb of Khalid Walid Near Kabirwala (Khanewal District)," *Ancient Pakistan* 7:39–46.
1993   "Tomb of Shaikh Sadan Shaheed, its Decoration," *Ancient Pakistan* 8:133–139.

Ali, Taj, Mukhtar Ali Durrani, and Ziaullah Sehrai
1997   "Earliest Islamic Monuments in Pakistan: The Construction of their phase of Transition, An Analytical Study," *Āthāriyyāt (Archaeology)* 1:61–70.

Barry, Michael A.
in press   "The King and the Hermit—the Visual Transmission of a Theme from Alexander and the Brahmin to Thangir," UNESCO "Colloquium on Indus Civilization," Islamabad, 2001.

Begley, Wayne
1979   "The Myth of the Taj Mahal and a New Theory of Its Symbolic Meaning," *The Art Bulletin* 61:7–37.

Blair, Shiela S., and Jonathan A. Bloom
1994   *The Art and Architecture of Islam, 1250–1800.* New Haven and London: Yale University Press.

Coomaraswamy, Ananda K.
1938   "The Symbolism of the Dome." *Indian Historical Quarterly* 17:1–56 [reprinted in *Ananda K. Coomaraswamy: Essays in Architectural Theory,* ed. Michael W. Meister, 9–37. New Delhi: Oxford University Press, 1995].
1988   "Early Indian Architecture, IV: Huts and Related Temple Types," ed. Michael W. Meister. *Res* 15:5–26.

Edwards, Holly
1990   "The Genesis of Islamic Architecture in the Indus Valley." Ph.D. diss., New York University.
1991   "The Ribāṭ of 'Alī b. Karmākh," *Iran* 29:85–94.

Eliade, Mircea
1969   *Yoga: Immortality and Freedom,* 2nd ed. Princeton: Princeton University Press.

Ettinghausen, Richard, and Oleg Grabar
1994   *The Art and Architecture of Islam, 650–1250.* New Haven: Yale University Press [first published London: Penguin Books Ltd., 1987].

Grabar, Oleg
1966   "The Earliest Islamic Commemorative Structures, Notes and Documents," *Ars Orientalis* 6:7–40.
1967   *Sasanian Silver, Late Antique and Early Mediaeval Arts of Luxury from Iran.* Ann Arbor: University of Michigan Museum of Art.
1973   *The Formation of Islamic Art.* Princeton: Princeton University Press.

Hillenbrand, Robert
1992   "Turco-Iranian Elements in the Medieval Architecture of Pakistan: the Case of the Tomb of Rukn-i 'Alam at Multan." *Muqarnas* 9:148–174.
1996a   "Ghaznavid," in *The Dictionary of Art,* vol. 12. New York: Grove.
1996b   "Islamic Art (c) Afghanistan, Pakistan and western Central Asia, c. 1050–1250," in *The Dictionary of Art,* vol. 16. New York: Grove.
1997–1998   "Gandhāra-Nāgara Temples of the Salt Range and the Indus." *Kalā, the Journal of Indian Art History Congress* 4:45–52.

Ikram, S. M.
1964   *Muslim Civilization in India.* New York: Columbia University Press.

Jairazbhoy, R. A.
1995   *Foreign Influence in Ancient Indo–Pakistan,* expanded edition. Karachi: Sind Book House.

---

31. Akbar's tomb at Sikandra and his Diwan-i-Khass at Fatehpur Sikri, in my view, invert this borrowing.

Khan, Ahmad Nabi
1987–1988   "Naked Brick Architecture of the Early Islamic
            Period of Pakistan: An Analytical Study." *Pakistan
            Archaeology* 23:303–325.
    1990   *Islamic Architecture of Pakistan: An Analytical
            Exposition.* Islamabad: National Hijra Council.
    1993   "Architecture," in *Islam in South Asia,* ed. Waheed-
            uz-Zaman and M. Saleem Akhtar, pp. 265–314.
            Islamabad: National Institute of Historical and
            Cultural Research.

Maricq, A., and G. Wiet
    1959   *Le Minaret de Djam, la découverte de la capital des
            sultans Ghorides (XIIe–XIIIe siècles).* Paris: C.
            Klincksieck.

Maxwell, T. S.
    1982   "The Five Aspects of Śiva (In Theory, Iconography and
            Architecture)," *Art International* 25/3–4:41–57.
    1984   "Nānd, Parel, Kalyānpur: Śaiva Images as
            Meditational Constructs," in *Discourses on Śiva,* ed.
            Michael W. Meister, pp. 62–81. Philadelphia:
            University of Pennsylvania Press.

Meister, Michael W.
    1972   "The Two-and-a-Half Day Mosque." *Oriental Art,* new
            series 18:57–63.
    1993   "Indian Islam's Lotus Throne," in *Islam and Indian
            Regions,* ed. A. Dallapiccola. Stuttgart: Franz Steiner
            Verlag, pp. 445–453.
    1994a   "Art Regions and Modern Rajasthan," in *The Idea of
            Rajasthan, Explorations in Regional Identity,* ed.
            Karine Schomer, Joan Erdman, Deryck O. Lodrick,
            and Loyd Rudolph, vol. I, pp. 143–176. New Delhi:
            Manohar, 1994.
    1994b   "The Membrane of Tolerance: Middle and Modern
            India," in *Art, the Integral Vision,* ed. B. N. Saraswati,
            S. C. Malik, and Madhu Khanna, pp. 289–298. New
            Delhi: D. K. Printworld.
    1996   "Temples Along the Indus," *Expedition* 38.3:41–54.
    2000a   "Chronology of Temples in the Salt Range, Pakistan,"
            in *South Asian Archaeology* 1997, ed. Maurizio
            Taddai and Giuseppe De Marco, pp. 1321–1339.
            Rome: Istituto Italiano per l'Africa e l'Oriente.
    2000b   "Discovery of a New Temple on the Indus."
            Expedition 42.1:37–46.

Meister, Michael W., and Abdur Rehman
in press   "Archaeology at Kafirkot." *South Asian Archaeology
            2001,* Paris.

Niedermayer, Oskar van
    1924   *Afganistan.* Leipzig: Verlag Karl W. Hiersemann.

Punjab Government
    1926   *Gazetteer of the Multan District 1923–24.* Lahore:
            Superintendent, Government Printing, Punjab.

Renaudot, Eusebius
    1733   *Ancient Accounts of India and China, by Two
            Mohammedan Travellers, Who went to those Parts in
            the 9th Century.* London: printed for Sam. Harding.

Renou, Louis
    1953   *Religions of Ancient India.* London: The Athlone
            Press.
    1998   "The Vedic House," ed. Michael W. Meister. *Res*
            34:141–161.

Shokoohy, Mehrdad
    1988   *Bhadreśvar: The Oldest Islamic Monuments in India.*
            Leiden: E. J. Brill.

Trimmington, J. Spencer
    1971   *The Sufi Orders of Islam.* Oxford: Oxford University
            Press.

Transformation of words to images

Portraits of Ottoman courtiers in the Dîwâns *of Bâkî and Nâdirî*

ZEREN TANINDI

Artists and artisans of all kinds were employed at the Ottoman court and regarded as an integral part of its organization. They formed a body known as the *Ehl-i Hiref,* whose members produced a vast range of works of art and artifacts for the sultan and his court.[1] The number of palace artists and craftsmen varied from 600 to 900 in the sixteenth century. Expenditure on articles made by them and on wages paid to them amounted to huge sums annually, and the fact that the court was prepared to pay such sums for the production of works of art shows that this was seen as a function of the state and a display of power. Qur'ans and manuscripts on religious, historical, and literary subjects with illumination, illustrations, and finely crafted bindings, and albums (*muraqqa*) comprising works of calligraphy, miniature painting, and illumination are among the arts of the book produced by the *Ehl-i Hiref.*

Although Ottoman rulers were the main patrons of the arts of the book, leading statesmen and bureaucrats also commissioned such items from the beginning of the fifteenth century. Umur Beg (d. 1461), a prominent statesman during the reigns of Mehmed I (1413–1421) and Murad II (1421–1444; 1446–1451) was an Ottoman intellectual and bibliophile, as demonstrated by the list of the books which he endowed to the *medrese* he established in his own name in Bergama, and to the *zaviya* and mosque established by his father Timurtaş Paşa in Bursa.[2] The similarity of the binding decoration of these books to that of the tiles, woodwork, stone carving, and mural painting of early Ottoman buildings in Bursa suggests that the first organized Ottoman art studios were situated in Bursa.[3]

The most intensive period of interest displayed by courtiers in the arts, particularly those of the book, coincides with the reign of Sultan Süleyman I (1520–1566). Grand vizier İbrahim Paşa (d. 1536) and finance minister (*defterdar*) İskender may be said to have initiated intervention by Ottoman statemen in artistic activity at the palace by launching projects intended to display the power of Sultan Süleyman.[4] The collection of books which Rüstem Paşa acquired while serving as grand vizier (1544–1553; 1555–1561) and the Qur'ans which he donated to his mosque in Tahtakale, Istanbul, reveal him to have been a bibliophile.[5] It was during his period that Matrakçı Nasuh wrote and illustrated history books;[6] that Ârif Çelebi, a writer of offical memoranda (*tezkireci*), was appointed şehnâmeci and wrote the five volumes of *Şehnâme-i Âl-i Osman* that was illustrated by the court artists;[7] and that an outsized Qur'an project was started and its 220 folios transcribed by Ahmed Karahisari between the years 1545–1555.[8] But it was grand vizier Sokullu Mehmed Paşa who can really be said to have pioneered major projects by court artists of the book. His interest in such projects seems to have begun in 1555 when he was appointed third vizier, since it was probably no coincidence that the history of

1. R. M. Meriç, *Türk Nakış Sanatı Tarihi Araştırmaları,* vol. 1, vesikalar (Ankara, 1953); R. M. Meriç, *Türk Cilt Sanatı Tarihi Araştırmaları,* vol. 1, vesikalar (Ankara, 1954); F. Çağman, "Behind the Ottoman Canon: The Works of the Imperial Palace," *Palace of Gold and Light: Treasures from the Topkapı Istanbul* (Istanbul: Palace Art Foundation, Inc., Washington D.C., 2000), pp. 46–56.

2. J. Raby and Z. Tanındı, *Turkish Bookbinding in the 15th Century: The Foundation of an Ottoman Court Style,* ed. T. Stanley (London: Azimuth, 1993), pp. 33–37.

3. Ibid., pp. 118–125.

4. G. Necipoğlu, "Süleyman the Magnificent and the Representation of Power in the Context of Ottoman–Hapsburg–Papal Rivalry," *The Art Bulletin* LXXI, no. 3 (1989):401–427.

5. Z. Tanındı, "13–14. Yüzyılda Yazılmış Kur'an'ların Kanuni Döneminde Yenilenmesi," Topkapı Sarayı Müzesi Yıllık I (1986):144–145; Z. Tanındı, "The Manuscripts Bestowed as Pious Endowments by Rüstem Paşa, The Grand Vizier of Süleyman the Magnificent," *Soliman le Magnifique et son Temps. Actes du Colleque de Paris Galeries Nationales du Grand Palais 7–10 Mars 1990,* ed. G. Veinstein (Paris, 1992), pp. 265–267.

6. H. Yurdaydın, *Nasûhü's-Silâhî (Matrâkçî), Beyân-ı Menâzil-i Sefer-i Irâkeyn-i Sultân Süleymân Hân* (Ankara: Türk Tarih Kurumu, 1976).

7. E. Atıl, *Süleymanname: The Illustrated History of Süleyman the Magnificent* (Washington, D.C. and New York: National Gallery of Art and Harry N. Abrams Inc., 1986).

8. F. Çağman, "The Ahmed Karahisari Qur'an in the Topkapı Palace Library in İstanbul," *Persian Painting from the Mongols to the Qajars: Studies in Honour of Basil W. Robinson,* ed. R. Hillenbrand (London and New York: I. B. Tauris, 2000), pp. 57–73.

the events of 1551–1552 in which Mehmed Paşa, then *beylerbeyi* of Rumelia, played such an important part, was written by the chronicler Ârif Çelebi in 1557 and illustrated by a court painter in the same year. This elegantly designed book, known by the name *Fütuhat-ı Cemîle,* is regarded as the first example of the *gazanâmes,* which were works written in verse and illustrated. It may have been written for Sokullu Mehmed Paşa as a propatory trial for Arifî's Süleymannâme.[9] The poet and bureaucrat Seyyid Lokman was appointed *şehnameci* (1569) during Mehmed Paşa's term in office as grand vizier (1565–1579).[10] The design and production of the illustrated history books known as the *Şehinşahnâme, Şehnâme-i Selim Han, Hünernâme,* and *Zübdetü't-Tevarih,* and of *Şemailnâme-i Âli Osman,* a portrait album of the Ottoman sultans which was to serve as a guide for these works, were carried out by *şehnâmeci* Seyyid Lokman and the painter of miniatures *nakkaş* Osman.[11] The unexpected death of Mehmed Paşa did not bring such projects relating to the arts of the book to an end; on the contrary, they now gathered momentum. An increasing number of books on a widening range of subjects were produced in both verse and prose, and the number of artists and writers increased until the end of the sixteenth century. Patronage of the arts of the book at the Ottoman palace continued with texts in verse and prose eulogizing the achievements of military commanders written by a secretary (*kâtib*) in the service of those in command of the Ottoman–Safavid wars which began in 1578.[12] These texts were illustrated at a time when the events were still fresh in people's minds, by contemporary artists who were probably eye witnesses of the events described. In some cases the illustrations include portraits of the authors.[13] Works in

the *gazanâme* genre include the *Nusretnâme* of Mustafa Âli, *Şecaatnâme* of Dal Mehmed (Âsafi), *Kitab-ı Gencine-i Feth-i Gence* of Rahimîzâde İbrahim Çavuş, *Gazavat-ı Osman Paşa* of Talîkîzâde, and one other work on the *Tarih-i Feth-i Yemen* of Mustafa Rümûzî.[14]

In the prefaces or epilogues of such books—some of them illustrated, produced in the court art studio during the last quarter of the sixteenth century—and sometimes in the inscriptions on their bindings, we find dedications to chief black eunuch (*darüssaade aga*) Mehmed Ağa, chief white eunuch (*babüssaade ağa*) Gazanfer Ağa, and the dwarf Zeyrek Ağa as patrons who commissioned the books and in some cases are portrayed in the illustrations. This demonstrates that following the death of Mehmed Paşa, patronage of the arts of the book took on a new configuration.[15]

When we look at the illustrations of accounts of chroniclers who wrote histories in verse and of secretaries who were prose writers by profession but became skilled at verse, we find the historic events they describe presented with almost photographic visual clarity. In the transformation of words into images, the observations of eye witnesses come to the fore. Through their images the artists reveal contemporary historic personalities and topographies with which they were familiar. We see that the artists had no difficulty in illustrating individuals with whom they were acquainted and events which they themselves had witnessed, even when the text itself is enigmatic. Thus the image takes precedence over word, without any of the intermixture of imagination found in the contemporary Safavid illustrations. The artist visualizes the events in realistic and dignified images, conveying many elements that the written texts fail to mention; complementing the word with interpretive and objective visual material; adding historical details that can only be read between the lines, his own experiences in the private and social sphere, his worldview and cultural legacy, and a knowledge of events either personal or heard from others, in the process of presenting the reality contained in the word.

9. Topkapı Palace Museum Library, no. H.1592. See: F. E. Karatay, *Topkapı Sarayı Müzesi Kütüphanesi Farsça Yazmalar Kataloğu* (İstanbul, 1961), no. 161; H. Sohrweide, "Der Verfasser der als *Suleymân-nâma* bekannten İstanbuler Prachthandschrif," *Der Islam* 47 (1971):p. 289; N. Atasoy and F. Çağman, *Turkish Miniature Painting* (İstanbul, 1974), pp. 29–30, pl. 10.

10. B. Kütükoğlu, "Şehnâmeci Lokman," Vekayi'nüvis Makaleler (İstanbul: İstanbul Fetih Cemiyeti, 1994), pp. 7–15.

11. F. Çağman, "İstanbul Sarayı'nın Yorumu: Üstad Osman ve Dizisi," *Padişahın Portresi. Tesavir-i Âli-i Osman* (İstanbul, 2000), pp. 164–187.

12. B. Kütükoğlu, *Osmanlı-İran Siyasi Münasebetleri (1578–1612)* (İstanbul: İstanbul Fetih Cemiyeti, 1993).

13. *Nusretnâme,* Topkapı Palace Museum Library, no. H.1365, fol. 43b. See: C. Fleischer, *Bureaucrat and Intellectual in the Ottoman Empire: The Historian Mustafa Âli (1541–1600)* (Princeton: Princeton University Press, 1986), fig. 11; *Şecaatnâme,* İstanbul University Library, no. T.6043, fol. 153a. (This miniature is unpublished.)

14. C. Woodhead, "From Scribe to Litterateur: The Career of a Sixteenth-Century Ottoman Kâtib," *Bulletin of the British Society for Middle Eastern Studies* 9, no. 1 (1982):pp. 55–74; I. Stchoukine, *La peinture turque d'apres les manuscrits illustres Ier partie. De Suleyman Ier a Osman II, 1520–1622* (Paris: Librarie Orientaliste Paul Geuthner, 1966), pp. 75–76, 80, 82–83, 122–123, 128–129, pls. LIX–LXXV; Fleischer (see note 13), pp. 110–111, figs. 4–5, 8–21, 24.

15. The author is currently preparing an article on the patronage of arts of the book by court eunuchs for the J. M. Rogers festschrift.

Some renowned Ottoman professional poets reflect in almost all their poems the historicism which dominated Ottoman literary life. Among these are Bâkî, who was writing in the second half of the sixteenth century, and Nâdirî, who was writing in the late sixteenth and early seventeenth centuries. They were not only poets who addressed praises, complaints, and requests to Ottoman aristocrats and bureaucrats, but also members of the elite ranks of the clergy who served in the Ottoman state organization. As such their lives were closely connected with palace officialdom. The praises, complaints, and requests these poets expressed might take the form of a single word, a sentence, or several lines. Where just a word alludes to a significant contemporary event, usually one which the poet himself has witnessed, it is difficult for the ordinary reader today to recognize these allusions and ascertain the events or people to whom they refer with certainty, since they are like ciphers slipped in between the sentences. But where these lines have been transformed into images by the hand of an illustrator working in the Ottoman palace art studio, enabling the researcher to accurately identify them by comparison with historic sources, the veil of mystery is lifted, revealing historical facts. This study will examine a miniature (New York: Metropolitan Museum of Art, no. 45.174.5)[16] illustrating Bâkî's *Dîwân,* the folios of which are dispersed among several collections, and miniatures from the only illustrated copy of Nâdirî's *Dîwân* (Istanbul: Topkapı Palace Museum Library, no. H.889)[17] in the light of the relationship between word and image.

Bâkî was the penname of Mahmud Abdülbâkî (d. 1600), whose poetry attracted attention while he was still a *medrese* student. Between 1561 and 1575 he taught at famous *medreses* in Istanbul, and between 1579 and 1586 served as *kadı* in Mecca, Medina, and Istanbul. At intervals between 1586 and 1597 he served as *kadı asker* of both Anatolia and Rumelia.[18] Like his close friend the poet and historian Mustafa Âli, he was a respected bureaucrat and successful spokesman of refined Ottoman culture, and as such numbered among the ranks of notable figures at court.[19]

While still a successful *medrese* student he accompanied his teacher to Aleppo in 1555–1556, where he met and became friends with the painter and poet Sâdikî Beg, who was later to become palace librarian to the Safavid Sah Abbas I (r. 1587–1629). This literary friendship between the two poets is reflected in Turkish poems by Sâdikî Beg. The fame of Bâkî's poems reverberated beyond the boundaries of the Ottoman Empire to reach the Safavid court.[20] Bâkî's close relations with palace circles is reflected in his poems, which frequently make laudatory reference to the four sultans he served under: Süleyman the Magnificent (r. 1520–1566), Selim II (r. 1566–1574), Murad III (r. 1574–1595), Mehmed III (r. 1595–1603), their viziers, and other eminent bureaucrats including his patron, author of *münşe'at* Ahmed Feridun Beg (d. 1583), and the latter's splendid palace at Ahırkapı in Istanbul.[21] In addition he occasionally makes allusion in a single word to western and eastern envoys who came to the Ottoman capital and were given audience by the sultan.[22]

For many years it was thought that the single-page miniature from Bâkî's *Dîwân* depicted an Ottoman sultan entering a city (fig. 1). However, reading of the

---

16. Page size: 26 x 15 cm. Miniature: 19.4 x 11.8 cm. *The Metropolitan Museum of Art Bulletin XXXVI/2* (1978): 48; R. Milstein, *Miniature Painting in Ottoman Baghdad* (Costa Mesa: Mazda, 1990), p. 99, fig. 8; *Arte Islamico. Del Museo Metropolitana de Arte de Nueva York. Colegio de San Ildefonso Septiembre de 1994–enero de 1995* (Mexico, 1994), pp. 88–89.

17. F. E. Karatay, *Topkapı Sarayı Müzesi Kütüphanesi Türkçe Yazmalar Kataloğu* (İstanbul, 1961), no. 2372. The covers of the binding (26 x 15 cm), which includes a flap, are of dark cherry-colored leather, decorated with gold-tooled medallions and corner pieces filled with stamped cloud bands and *hata'i* flowers. It is thought that the doublures, also of dark cherry-colored leather, have lost their original character in subsequent repairs. In the center of these doublures are medallions filled with *Rumî* motifs executed in gold brushwork. There is illuminated decoration in two places; one on fol. 1b, consisting of an illuminated heading with triangular projections adorned with resplendent large *Khatai* flowers and clouds. This illumination is reminiscent of the early seventeenth-century Safavid-period Isfahan style. The second illuminated heading is on fol. 33b, and consists of a plain design of small *hatai* flowers in gold on a dark blue ground. For the miniatures in this manuscript: Stchoukine (see note 14), p. 95, pl. C–CI; Atasoy and Çağman (see note 9), pp. 68–69, pl. 44; E. J. Grube, F. Çağman, and Z. Akalay, *Islamic Painting. Topkapı Sarayı Collection* (Tokyo: Heibonsha, 1978), no. 107; E. Atıl, "Ahmed

Nakşi: An Eclectic Painter of the Early 17th Century," *Fifth International Congress of Turkish Art,* ed. G. Feher (Budapest, 1978), pp. 104–106; F. Çağman and Z. Tanındı, *Topkapı Palace Museum. Islamic Miniature Painting* (İstanbul, 1979), no. 176, fig. 61.

18. M. F. Köprülü, "Bâkî," *İslam Ansiklopedisi* 2 (1961):243–253.

19. Fleischer, (see note 13), p. 31.

20. T. Gandjei, "Notes on the Life and Works of Sâdiqî: A Poet and Painter of Safavid Times," *Der Islam* 52/1 (1975):114–115; T. Gandjei, "Turkish in the Safavid Court of Isfahan," *Turcica XXXI–XXXII* (1991):311–318. It is evident that Bâkî's poems were also read by intellectual literati in the provinces from the time they were written onward: Köprülü (see note 18), p. 251. F. Köprülü relates seeing a fine, highly decorated copy produced in Baghdad in the year 1591 in an antiquarian bookshop (probably in Istanbul): Köprülü (see note 18), p. 251.

21. S. Küçük, *Bâkî Dîvânı* (Ankara: Türk Dil Kurumu, 1994), pp. 73–74.

22. Ibid., p. 20.

lines at the top of this miniature and close examination of the picture itself revealed that it depicted a very different event. The lines at the top of the picture read: Let the Persians be happy, let their eyes be illumined, Mir Heydar, light of the eyes of the Persian sultan, comes (*Şâd-mân olsun 'Acemler gözleri aydın yine, Mîr Heydar nûr-ı çeşm-i husrev-i İran gelür*).[23] The five couplets which follow these lines in the complete text of the *Dîwân* are missing here, and the sixth couplet is written at the lower edge of the picture.[24] The picture is an illustration of the upper couplet only, in which the phrase "Mir Heydar comes" refers to an event which preoccupied Ottoman–Safavid political relations between 1588 and 1590. Mir Heydar was son of the younger brother of the Safavid ruler Sah Abbas I. According to an agreement reached between the Safavids and Ottomans, the ten-year-old prince Heydar Mirza was sent as a hostage to the Ottomans as a guarantee of peace, and he set out from Qazvin for Istanbul in October 1590. He was accompanied by an envoy, Mehdi Kulu Han, the governor of Ardabil; two trusted companions, Şah Kulu Halife and Ali Han; his physician Abi Talib; Safavid soldiers carrying gifts sent by the Şah to the Ottoman palace; and Veli Ağa, the Ottoman official sent to Qazvin to take charge of the hostage. The convoy was met on its arrival in Erzurum by the Ottoman commander Ferhad Paşa. Banquets were given in their honor and gifts presented to the prince. Meanwhile, preparations were being made to accommodate the prince and his retinue in Istanbul. Pertev Paşa Palace in the district of Vefa was chosen, and Selânikî Mustafa Efendi, who was later to write a famous history, was charged with furnishing the palace. Heydar Mirza arrived in Istanbul in January. He and his entourage were met at Üsküdar by Hasan Paşa, *beğlerbeği* of Anatolia and son of the celebrated grand vizier Sokullu Mehmed Paşa (d. 1579), and from here crossed the Bosphorus by ship. The prince and his retinue entered the city in a splendid procession that drew huge crowds, since the people of Istanbul had not seen a spectacle on this scale for many years. The procession lasted until nightfall, and many women spectators who lived at a distance were unable to return

home after dark and were stranded in the city. Some went to the homes of acquaintances, but around four hundred women were obliged to spend the night in Bayezid Baths, causing anxiety to their families. Some husbands divorced their wives for arriving home late. All these details were recorded by Selânikî Mustafa Efendi (d. 1600?) in his work *Tarih-i Selânikî*.[25]

The separation of a ten-year-old child from his family to be sent as hostage to a foreign country left a deep impression on the people of Istanbul and the Ottoman court. The only known visual depiction of this event is on the page bearing the above-mentioned lines by Bâkî. This miniature shows the entry into Istanbul of Heydar Mirza and his retinue. In the upper part of the picture we see the walls of Istanbul and the city behind. At the upper right edge are the dome and two minarets, one

23. Ibid., p. 21. In one copy of the *Dîwân,* the heading at the top of this and previous lines reads: "Praise be to the merciful Sultan Murad who welcomed with kindliness the setting foot [in his own country] of the beloved cousin of the Persian shah." That the poet put such a heading to his lines demonstrates the importance which he attached to this event: Ibid., p. 19.

24. Ibid., p. 21, line 22.

25. Selânikî Mustafa Efendi, *Tarih-i Selânikî*, prep. M. İpşirli (İstanbul, 1989), pp. 216–220. Ferhad Paşa's secretary Rahimizade İbrahim Çavuş describes the journey of Heydar Mirza from Iran to Istanbul, his audience with Sultan Murad III, and the gifts he presented to the sultan in his book *Kitab-ı Gencine-i Feth-i Gence* (Topkapı Palace Museum Library, No. R.1296, fols. 45b–54a. Karatay [see note 17], no. 706), which is illustrated with miniatures portraying the prince: Z. Tanındı, "Safavid Princes and Envoys in the Ottoman Court," *Interactions in Art* (Ankara, 2000), pp. 239–240. Ottoman *Şehnameci* Seyyid lokman describes the reception ceremonies given to this prince in his work *Şehname-i Âl-i Osman* (The British Library, no. Add.7931, fols. 138b–147b). G. Necipoğlu, *Architecture, Ceremonial, and Power. The Topkapı Palace in the Fifteenth and Sixteenth Centuries* (Cambridge, Mass., and London: The MIT Press, 1991), p. 68. This manuscript is left unfinished and it has only three Ottoman sultan portraits, of Sultan Osman I (r. 1299–1326), Orhan I (r. 1326–1362), and Mehmed I (r. 1413–1421). The Austrian album drawing (ca. 1590) shows the arrival of Heydar Mirza in Istanbul (Vienna Österreichische Nationalbibliothek, Cod. 8626. F. Babinger, "Drei Stadtansichten von Kostantinopel, Galata ("Pera") und Skutari aus dem ende des 16. Jahrhunderts," *Österreichische Akademie der Wissenschaften Philogisch-Historische Klasse,* Denkschriften, 77, Band 3 (1959): p. 8. I would like to thank an outside reader of Res for giving me the last-mentioned information.

The prince was circumcized in 1593 during his stay in Istanbul with a magnificent ceremony at the palace of the late Sokullu Mehmed Paşa in Kadırga: Selânikî (see note 25), p. 313; İ. H. Danişmend, *İzahlı Osmanlı Tarihi Kronolojisi* 3 (İstanbul, 1971), p. 127. The prince died in 1596 and was buried in Eyüb İstanbul: Selânikî (see note 25), p. 547. In December 1599 the Safavid court sent the nursemaid Güliter Hanım and envoy Hüseyin Beg to Istanbul to visit the prince's grave. They were welcomed with a ceremony as required by Ottoman law and brought to the palace: Selânikî (see note 25), p. 841. Subsequently, however, the prince's body was secretly disinterred and probably taken to Ardabil: Danişmend (see note 25), pp. 160–161. Also see: Kütükoğlu (see note 12), pp. 195, 215–217. There is very little information in Safavid sources about Heydar Mirza being sent to the Ottomans: Eskandar Beg Monshi, *History of Shah Abbas the Great* II, tr. R. Savory (Boulder, Colo.: Westviev Press Inc, 1978), p. 707.

Figure 1. Arrival of Safavid prince Heydar Mirza at Istanbul. Bâkî's *Dîwân,* ca. 1600.
19.4 x 11.8 cm. Metropolitan Museum of Art, bequest of George D. Pratt, no. 45.174.5.
(Photo: courtesy of the Metropolitan Museum of Art, New York)

broad and the other slender, of Haghia Sophia Mosque, a building which served as a kind of code identifying the city depicted as Istanbul. At the upper left-hand edge is the city gate, with a band of musicians playing in the gallery above the gateway. Inside the walls men and women watch the procession eagerly. The figure leading the procession is thought to be Hasan Paşa, beğlerbeği of Anatolia, who is advancing alongside the city walls toward the gate with his honor guard. Right in the center, below this row of figures, rides the ten-year-old Heydar Mirza on horseback, flanked protectively by two elderly Safavid statesmen, who are perhaps the prince's atabey Şah Kulu Halife and the Şah's head of the threshold (eşik ağası) Ali Ağa. Behind his horse come mounted Safavid noblemen, perhaps Mehdi Kulu Han, governor of Ardabil, and his men, and before his horse march Safavid infantrymen. The row of figures along the lower edge of the picture, whose lower left corner is missing, includes a high-ranking Ottoman bureaucrat on horseback, perhaps Veli Ağa, with Ottoman peyks, solaks, and other guardsmen. At the center of the left edge are two women gazing at the procession.

From the stylistic characteristics of the painting it is evident that special attention was paid to the preparation of this manuscript. The style of the figures in particular recalls that of illustrated manuscripts produced in Ottoman Baghdad between 1590 and 1603.[26] This style, which originated in Baghdad, acquired a dominating influence toward the end of the sixteenth century, since Hasan Paşa (d. 1602), the son of Sokullu Mehmed Paşa, was an active patron of the arts in Baghdad between 1598 and 1602, when he served as governor of that city.[27] Throughout the second half of the

sixteenth century Hasan Paşa and the poet Bâkî both moved in the same bureaucratic circles. When the Safavid prince Heydar Mirza and his retinue arrived in Istanbul, Hasan Paşa was beğlerbeği of Anatolia and Bâkî was military judge (kadı asker) of Anatolia. Both numbered among the foremost eye witnesses of this event, Hasan Paşa having met Heydar Mirza and his delegation at Üsküdar. Hasan Paşa is not mentioned in the lines inscribed on the miniature illustrating this event, but the words "excellency Hasan" (hazret-i Hassan) in the fourth line which follow these in the full text seem to refer to Hasan Paşa, even though at first sight they might seem to refer to Hasan, son of the caliph 'Ali b. Abi Talib.[28] This is reinforced by the fact that it is the portrait of Hasan Paşa, governor of Anatolia, which appears in the miniature. As governor of Baghdad, Hasan Paşa must have commissioned an illustrated copy of Bâkî's Dîwân from the book decorators who were active in the city at that time, and the evidence points to the Dîwân containing the miniature in question being this copy. Since Hasan Paşa had been present at the arrival in Istanbul of Heydar Mirza and his companions, the event would have been fresh in his mind, and he probably described this to the illustrator, thus enabling him to include details in the image that were absent in the written work.[29]

Mehmed b. Abdülganî (Ganî-zâde), the other poet who is the subject of this article and who wrote under the cognomen of Nâdirî (d. 1626), came from an educated family. He began his working life as a müderris in 1591, and remained in this post until 1601. Between 1602 and 1612 he served as kadı of Salonica, Edirne, and Istanbul, and on several occasions until the end of his life held the high-ranking posts of kadı asker of Anatolia and Rumelia, respectively.[30] Nâdirî, who was also a fine calligrapher, followed a career comparable to that of Bâkî, and shared a similar degree of intimacy with eminent figures at the court. Indeed, he married the

26. F. Çağman, "XVI. Yüzyıl Sonlarında Mevlevi Dergahlarında Gelişen Bir Minyatür Okulu," I. Uluslararası Türkoloji Kongresi (İstanbul, 1979), pp. 651–677; K. Ruhrdanz, "Zwanzig Jahre Bagdader Buchillustration-zu Voraussetzungen und spezifiz Zwiges der Turkischen Miniaturmalerei," Mittelalterliche Malerei im Orient, 22 (1982), pp. 143–162; Milstein (see note 16).

27. M. T. Gökbilgin, "Hasan Paşa," İslam Ansiklopedisi 5 (1964):323–329; Çağman (see note 26), pp. 662–664. An ornate copy of Bâkî's Dîwân was produced in Ottoman Baghdad in 1591, presumably because the intelligentsia of Baghdad wished to see his poems in a manuscript of artistic excellence: Köprülü (see note 18), p. 251. This interest of Baghdad's intellectuals in precious manuscripts is also evidenced by an ornately decorated copy of Tacü't-Tevârih, written in 1574 by Bâkî's fellow student Hoca Sa'düddin Efendi who served as tutor to several Ottoman sultans, produced in Baghdad in 1590 (Paris Bibliotheque Nationale, no. T.150). Vers l'Orient . . . , Galerie Mazarine 16 mars–30 avril 1983, Paris Bibliotheque Nationale (Paris: Bibliotheque Nationale, 1983), no. 46. This unillustrated manuscript has a fine illuminated heading on fol. 1b.

28. Küçük (see note 21), p. 21, line 20.

29. No copies of Bâkî's Dîwân illustrated by miniatures of court quality are known to have been produced at the Ottoman palace studio. Two copies of the Dîwân with miniatures in Ottoman style dated ca. 1595 are of indifferent quality: Milstein (see note 16), p. 99. A third copy of Bâkî's Dîwân with carefully produced miniatures does not contain the full text of the Dîwân. Dated 1636, it was illustrated in the Isfahan style, perhaps for a Turkmen bey of Afsar descent, at Nacaf near Baghdad: S. R. Canby, The Golden Age of Persian Art: 1501–1722 (London: British Museum Press, 1999), p. 122, fig. 111; N. M. Titley, Persian Miniature Painting (London: The British Library, 1983), p. 121, pl. 18.

30. N. Külekçi, Ganî-zâde Nadirî ve Dîvânından Seçmeler (Ankara: Kültür Bakanlığı, 1989), pp. 1–7.

daughter of Sunullah Efendi, who in 1599 succeeded Hoca Sa'düddin Efendi as *şeyhülislam*. Sa'düddin Efendi had been tutor to the sultans and to Nâdirî. His close connections with palace circles is evident from poems which he wrote to the Ottoman sultans Murad III (r. 1574–1595), Mehmed III (r. 1595–1603), Ahmed I (r. 1603–1617), and Osman II (r. 1618–1622); to palace officials *Ağas* such as Gazanfer, Server, and Ali, who were influential in Ottoman politics and palace government in the late sixteenth and early seventeenth centuries; and to grand viziers.[31] From Bâkî's poems it appears that, unlike Nâdirî, he maintained his official dignity and never struck up acquaintance with officials of the royal household or asked them to intercede for the advancement of his career.

Copies of Nâdirî's *Dîwân*, particularly those dating from the early seventeenth century, are almost all of the same size, bound in fine leather, and in some cases beautifully illuminated. The poems are diversely arranged in these copies. However, as already mentioned, only one is illustrated with miniature paintings, and this is the copy which concerns us here. It contains no copying date. The first miniature is situated on folio 4a between lines in praise of Murad III[32] and depicts the sultan leaving Topkapı Palace (*Saray-ı Cedid*) through the first gate (fig. 2).[33] The three figures on horseback following him are three principal officials of the Privy Chamber, the *silahdar ağa, ibrikdar ağa,* and *çuhadar ağa*. He is preceded by *solak* and *peyk* guardsmen. Along the lower edge of the picture is a crowd of both Muslim and non-Muslim spectators, as evident from their costumes. Some of these are holding out scrolls of paper, probably petitions, to the sultan. Behind the battlemented wall next to the palace gate rises the dome of Haghia Eirene, and in front of the wall is a row of palace officials. At the left-hand edge is Haghia Sophia Mosque, and on the side of the buttress between the main dome and the minaret is an owl. The lines praising the sultan which precede and follow this miniature are so florid that it is extremely difficult to draw connections between words and picture. However, we do gather from these lines that the sultan is joyful on the occasion of a holy feast day, that he is wearing red clothing and smiling at the populace, and that his horse is richly caparisoned. We can conclude from this that

the miniature probably depicts Sultan Murad III proceeding to the mosque for feast day or Friday prayers. As the poet says, the sultan's horse is richly furnished and the sultan's under-robe is red. The illustrator has read between the lines of poetry to depict an event he himself had witnessed, and portrays the sultan as a portly figure of advanced age.

The second miniature (fig. 3) is a double spread depicting a battle scene (fols. 6b–7a). Apart from the name Sultan Mehmed Han Gazi and words concerning the conquest of an unnamed fortress situated between

Figure 2. Murad III leaving the first gate of the Topkapı Palace. Nâdirî's *Dîwân*, ca. 1605. 18.7 x 12.5 cm. Topkapı Palace Museum Library, no. H.889, fol. 4a. (Photo: courtesy Topkapı Palace Museum, Istanbul)

31. Ibid., pp. 49–59; 69–70; 80–87; 79, 164, 174, 266–267.

32. Ibid., p. 44, line 18–19.

33. Stchoukine (see note 14), pl. C; Atıl (see note 17), fig. 5; Grube, Çağman, and Akalay (see note 17), no. 107; Necipoğlu (see note 25), fig. 14.

Figure 3. Battle of Haçova. Nâdirî's *Dîwân,* ca. 1605. 18.9 x 10.9 cm. Topkapı Palace Museum Library, no. H.889, fol. 6b–7a. (Photo: courtesy of the Topkapı Palace Museum, Istanbul)

lines of eulogy preceding and following this picture, and the word *Erdel* (Transylvania) mentioned in each of the lines inscribed on the miniature, there are no clues to what it represents. However, when we closely inspect details in the picture and evaluate them in the light of historical information, it is possible to identify the event. Both from the mention of his name in the text and the resemblance to his known portraits, we can identify the imposing figure on horseback in the upper part of the left-hand page as Mehmed III. Sultan Mehmed III was the first sultan after Süleyman the Magnificent to lead his army into battle; and this battle took place in 1596 between the Ottomans and Austrians at Haçova north of Erlau in Hungary, following the conquest of the latter fortress in Hungary by the Ottomans. During this battle the Ottoman army was unable to halt the Austrian advance. Some of the Christian troops got as far as the

sultan's own tents and plundered their contents, some climbing onto the treasury chests. The unarmed officials who were in camp at the time attacked the invaders with anything they found to hand, such as tent poles and axes, while the cooks chased them away with saucepans and frying pans. The sultan, observing this from a distance, lost hope and wished to call a retreat, but his tutor Hoca Sa'düddin Efendi spoke words of encouragement and held up the mantle of the Prophet Muhammed for the sultan to lay his face against (or, according to some historians, actually garbed the sultan in it).[34] The Banner of the Prophet (*Sancak-ı Şerif*) had also been taken on campaign for the first time, and

34. Selânikî (see note 25), p. 641; Peçevi İbrahim Efendi, *Peçevi Tarihi,* II, prep. by B. S. Baykal (Ankara, 1982), pp. 180–189; Danişmend (see note 25), p. 174.

during the battle the sultan rode close to it.[35] Eventually courage and morale were restored, and the Ottomans won the battle.[36] The miniature incorporates all the details of this battle as described by historians. At the top left, to the right of Sultan Mehmed we see Sa'düddin Efendi, and to the left of the latter, behind the sultan, is the eunuch Gazanfer Ağa, who was one of the principal companions of the sultan in this battle, and about whom we find detailed information in subsequent lines of the poem. The figure walking at the sultan's left hand carries a bundle of floral patterned cloth on his head that probably contains the mantle of the Prophet (*Hırka-i Serif*).[37] In this part of the miniature the artist has drawn portraits of three leading figures in Ottoman government at the end of the sixteenth century: Sultan Mehmed, Hoca Sa'düddin, and Gazanfer Ağa, all of whom are watching the progress of the battle with anxious expressions.[38] In the lower part of the left-hand page are depicted Christian soldiers attacking the tents in the Ottoman camp. Some of them are shown climbing onto the treasure chests, and camp servants are shown attacking them with sticks, saucepans, and frying pans. At the center right of the page are topographical features mentioned in historic texts: a river and a ruined church. In front of this church are two soldiers in armor with outstretched arms. The fact that they are given an empty space to themselves on the surface of the painting suggests that the artist was depicting specific individuals to whom he attached special importance.

On the right-hand page are depicted Muslim soldiers chasing Christian soldiers off the battlefield. Close examination reveals that the names of the generals are inscribed. The tall, slender Ottoman commander on the left-hand side of the page, with a long thin face, wearing a white turban and mounted on a horse, is grand vizier Cağalazade Sinan Paşa, who is identified as Cağalazade on the red flag at the left edge. The stout man with the thick beard and white turban at center left is identified on the flag held by the armored soldier to his right as

Hasan Paşa; that is, the son of the late grand vizier Sokullu Mehmed Paşa, whose portrait we see in the above-mentioned miniature depicting the arrival of Heydar Mirza in Istanbul. At lower left we see Crimean troops coming to the aid of the Ottomans. Their commander is the figure at their head who has drawn his bow. His name, Feth Giray, is written on the flag held by the soldier at his right hand. The names of some of the Christian generals are written on their hats. The figure wearing a tall black hat among the commanders being pursued by Cağalazade at top right is identified as *Maksimliander* (Maxmilien), who was commander of the Habsburg forces at Haçova. The name of the figure with a white beard to his left is identified by his Turkish nickname *Gümüş Ayaklı* (silver-footed), and the name of the third named figure at the lower right edge who wears a cape and carries a mace is *Erdeloğlu* (Transylvanian-son). This is probably Sigismond Bathory, the Transylvanian general known to have fought at the Battle of Haçova; so presumably the mention of *Erdel* in the lines at the top of the miniature is a reference either to him or to the lands that he owned.[39] Among the fleeing soldiers at the top of the picture is a rabbit looking back as it runs up the hill. This probably has symbolic meaning, as the rabbit has sometimes signified good or bad fortune. Therefore the rabbit shown abandoning the battlefield may convey the idea that good luck has deserted the Christian army.[40] While depicting all the complex details of the battle in the narrow compass of these two pages, the painter has still managed to find space for this symbolic motif. He has meticulously observed cultural differences between those engaged in the battle, and lent individuality to their faces. These aspects of the painting strengthen the hypothesis that the painter may have been an eyewitness to this event. Although the poet Nâdirî's words do not correspond to the image here, the painter has inserted a

---

35. M. Tayyib Gökbilgin, "Sancak-ı Şerif," *İslam Ansiklopedisi*, 10 (1966):190.

36. Danişmend (see note 25), pp. 172–176.

37. Another miniature depicting Sultan Mehmed III at the Battle of *Haçova* illustrates *Eğri Feth-i Tarihi*, thought to date from 1598. This miniature is the work of Nakkaş Hasan, who was present at the battle, and portrays Sultan Mehmed accompanied only by Gazanfer Ağa. The bundle containing the *Hırka-i Şerif* is here carried on the head of a mounted man to the sultan's left. The green *Sancak-ı Şerif* is carried before the sultan by the official appointed for this purpose, the *Sancak-ı Şerif şeyh'i*: Z. Akalay, "Nakkaş Hasan Paşa," *Sanat* 6 (1977):115.

38. The historian İbrahim Peçevi, who was also an eyewitness at the Battle of Haçova, writes that a year later one of the infidel lords sent Tiryaki Hasan Paşa a portrait of Sultan Mehmed and Hoca Sa'düddin on horseback watching the outcome of the battle with worried expressions, and that he himself had seen this portrait: Peçevi (see note 34), pp. 187–188. This suggests that there may have been some connection between the artist who painted the portrait seen by Peçevi and the miniature painter, or that the latter had seen this portrait.

39. Those names were mentioned in the history of Mustafa Âli: *Kühnü'l-Ahbar*, Nuruosmaniye Library. No. 3409, fol. 453b.

40. A. Daneshvari, *Animal Symbolism in Warka wa Gulshah*. *Oxford Studies in Islamic Art*, II (Oxford: Oxford University Press, 1986), p. 20.

very crucial event relating to Mehmed III between the lines of poetry.[41] Either he was illustrating an event which he had witnessed, or was basing his illustration on the writings of an eyewitness, İbrahim Efendi of Pecz (d. 1649?), author of *Tarih-i Peçevi*. He may even have consulted İbrahim Efendi, who was a member of the same intellectual circle as himself and the poet Nâdirî, and listened to an oral account of the event which had taken place around two decades earlier but still remained fresh in people's memories.[42]

The third picture shows Sultan Mehmed III at a musical entertainment in a pavilion whose windows have a sea view (fol. 8b).[43] The sultan is seated on the throne to the right, with three officials of his household, musicians at the left, and dwarfs clowning to the right (fig. 4). The palace eunuch nearest to the sultan is almost certainly Gazanfer Ağa; the bearded and moustachioed figure behind him, who is explained in detail on folio 22a, is probably the poet Nâdirî, and the other eunuch at the far left is thought to represent the *mirahur* Ali Ağa, whose name is frequently mentioned by the poet in his *Dîwân,* and who will be discussed in detail further on.[44] Apart from the sultan there are no clues to the identity of the figures depicted here in either the lines inscribed at the top and bottom of the page, or in those preceding and following this page.[45]

The fourth illustration (fol. 10a) is clearly identifiable, both from the poet's words and the details in the picture itself (fig. 5). The name Ahmed occurs in the lines inscribed on this page[46] and on folio 9b. The lines which precede and follow this miniature tell us that with the arrival of Sultan Ahmed I (r. 1603–1617) in Edirne spring also arrived, and the crowds of spectators were finally able to see the sultan as he proceeded on horseback along a path of satin cloth.[47] Sultan Ahmed is depicted on horseback at the right of the page, riding along a colorful runner. To his right are two *solak* and two *peyk* guardsmen. In front of them is a white horse,

Figure 4. Mehmed III entertained at the shore pavilion. Nâdirî's *Dîwân,* ca. 1605. 14.4 x 12 cm. Topkapı Palace Museum Library, no. H.889, fol. 8b. (Photo: courtesy of the Topkapı Palace Museum, Istanbul)

probably carrying the sultan's canopy, led by another horseman. Along the lower edge of the picture is a crowd of spectators. At the upper right of the picture is a retinue of palace officials accompanying the sultan to Edirne: three officers of the Privy Chamber, and figures who are probably officials of the Enderun or Inner Palace household, bureaucrats, and high-ranking officials. Above them can be seen the heads of men and women of Edirne, and in the top left corner is the city's landmark, Selimiye Mosque, designed by the celebrated architect Sinan. During his reign Sultan Ahmed visited Edirne twice during the winter months for hunting. During his first visit in 1605 Nâdirî was *kadı* of Edirne, and during his second in 1612 Nâdirî was *kadı asker* of Anatolia, and as holder of these posts Nâdirî witnessed the sultan's

41. The poet Bâkî also wrote eulogies relating to Sultan Mehmed III's participation in the Battle of Haçova in his *Dîwân,* but these lines are not illustrated: Küçük (see note 21), pp. 33–35. The historian Selânikî tells us that when Sultan Mehmed III returned from Haçova to his palace in Istanbul in December 1597, the poet Bâkî wrote a *kaside* of conquest and a *zafername:* Selânikî (see note 25), p. 654.

42. Peçevi (see note 34), pp. XVII–XXIII.

43. Stchoukine (see note 14), pl. CI; Atıl (see note 17), fig. 7.

44. Külekçi (see note 30), pp. 190, 248.

45. N. Külekçi, "Gânî-zâde Nâdirî. Hayatı, Edebi Kişiliği, Eserleri, Dîvânı ve Şeh-nâmesinin Tenkidli Metni," (Ph. D. dissertation. Erzurum Atatürk University, 1985), p. 118.

46. Külekçi (see note 30), p. 52, line 12.

47. Ibid., p. 50, lines 4–8.

Figure 5. Arrival of Ahmed I at Edirne. Nâdirî's *Dîwân,* ca. 1605. 19 x 11.5 cm. Topkapı Palace Museum Library, no. H.889, fol. 10a. (Photo: courtesy of the Topkapı Palace Museum, Istanbul)

Figure 6. The siege of Kavkaban fortress by Sinan Paşa at Yemen. Nâdirî's *Dîwân,* ca. 1605. 19.3 x 12.1 cm. Topkapı Palace Museum Library, no. H.889, fol. 14a. (Photo: courtesy of the Topkapı Palace Museum, Istanbul)

visits to Edirne. In the lines of poetry before and after the picture there is no clue as to which of the two visits is represented. However, in two lines which are not included in this *Dîwân,* the date 1612 is given in the form of a chronogram.[48] Sultan Ahmed acceded to the throne at the age of fourteen, was circumcised the same year, and died at the age of twenty-eight. He was sixteen years old at his first visit to Edirne, and twenty-three at the second. In this miniature he is depicted as a young man without beard or moustache, full cheeked and of slender build,[49] indicating that the miniature portrays him during his first visit to Edirne.

In the lower part of the fifth miniature (fol. 14a) an elderly commander is shown seated in front of his tent, and prisoners of war are being presented to him. Above, Ottoman troops are besieging a castle (fig. 6).[50] The sentence "He subjugated Kavkaban in Yemen" (*Yemen'de Kevkeban'ı teshir eyledi*) among the couplets at the upper edge of the picture, and the name Sinan in the bottom line on folio 13a are sufficient to confirm his identity. Yemen was conquered by the Ottomans in the

48. Ibid., p. 270, line 8.
49. In other portraits of Sultan Ahmed I executed in the early seventeenth century he also has the youthful appearance of the early

years of his reign: B. Mahir, "Portrenin Yeni Bağlamı," *Padişahın Portresi. Tesavir-i Âl-i Osman* (Istanbul: Türkiye İş Bankası, 2000), figs. 67, 74.
50. Atıl (see note 17), fig. 8. In this publication, the commander is erroneously identified as Mehmed Paşa. Also see: Çağman and Tanındı (see note 17), fig. 61.

sixteenth century, and Sinan Paşa (d. 1599) was sent to crush a rebellion there in 1569, and remained until 1571. His military successes in Yemen led to his being known as Koca Sinan Paşa, Conqueror of Yemen, and he served as grand vizier three times in the late sixteenth century.[51] Sinan Paşa's army attacked the city of Kavkaban in Yemen, but it was a long time before they managed to take possession of the hilltop stronghold of Kavkaban Castle.[52] This miniature shows the castle before it was captured, and the surrounding landscape is true to life. However, the architecture of the castle perched on an inaccessible mountain is reminiscent rather of medieval European fortified cities. Presumably the artist, since he had not seen the castle in Yemen for himself, drew upon either his memories of a European castle that he had seen, or depictions of castles on maps available to him. On the hills facing the citadel Ottoman gunners are firing cannon, while janissaries behind emplacements are firing rifles. The commander seated in front of his tent is Sinan Paşa, and the figures brought into his presence are Yemeni prisoners. Sinan Paşa was about fifty years old when he came to Yemen, but he is portrayed in his old age here. Probably the painter, like Nâdirî, only saw Sinan Paşa in his later years and portrayed him accordingly.

The sixth miniature in the *Dîwân* (fol. 18b) shows a large two-storyed house (fig. 7).[53] The lower story of the house opens on to the street through an arched colonnade covered by a sloping roof. Through one of the windows can be seen the heads of two horses, and behind them is a glimpse of the city beyond. At the top of the flight of steps leading up to the door stands an official who is talking to a group of people and receiving their written petitions. At the far right a young man stands in front of the other door of the house. The upper story has numerous windows and balconies with railings.

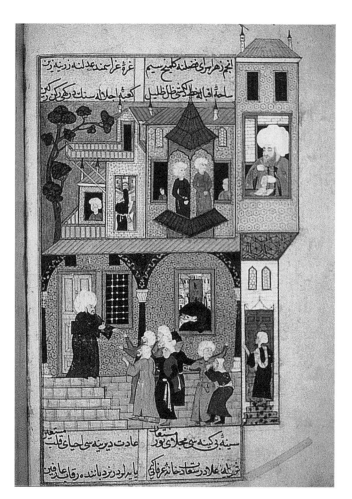

Figure 7. The house of Şehülislam Mustafa Efendi. Nâdirî's *Dîwân*, ca. 1605. 17.8 x 12 cm. Topkapı Palace Museum Library, no. H.889, fol. 18b. (Photo: courtesy of the Topkapı Palace Museum, Istanbul)

Through one of the windows can be seen a city street winding into the distance. The house seems to be crowded, with numerous people looking through the windows. In the upper right section of the house, which is perhaps a third story, is seated an important personage, possibly the owner of the house, who is examining some writing which he holds in his hand. Among the lines of poetry on the pages preceding and succeeding this miniature (fols. 18a, 19a) the reference to the office of jurisconsult (*müfti*) and the name Mustafa help to identify the scene.[54] The man is Mustafa Efendi (d. 1606), who served as military judge of Anatolia, and was twice appointed as *şeyhülislam* for brief periods in

51. Ş. Turan, "Sinan Paşa," *İslam Ansiklopedisi*, 10 (1966):670–675.

52. While he was in Yemen Sinan Paşa had Mustafa Rümûzî, who was treasurer (*defterdar*) in Yemen, write an account of his achievements there: H. Yavuz, "İslam Sanatları Bakımından Rümûzî'nin Futuh-ı Yemen'i," *Marmara Üniversitesi İlahiyat Fakültesi Dergisi* IV (1986):53–65. This book entitled *Tarih-i Feth-i Yemen* was illustrated with miniatures in 1595, when Sinan Paşa was serving as grand vizier for the last time. These miniatures, too, depict the conquest of Kavkaban Castle in detail, and give a realistic representation of the topography: İstanbul University Libraray, T.6045, fols. 513a, 518b, 522a, 527a: Stchoukine (see note 14), pp. 83, 129. For the topographic views of Midland of Yemen see: F. Varanda, *Art of Building in Yemen* (Cambridge, Mass., and London: The MIT Press, 1982), pp. 31, 33, 172, 180.

53. Atıl (see note 17), fig. 9.

54. Külekçi (see note 45), pp. 191–193.

1603 and 1606, during the reign of Sultan Ahmed I. Nâdirî may have written his long eulogies of Mustafa Efendi in order to gain the good opinion of the man who succeeded Nâdirî's own father-in-law, Sunullah Efendi. In depicting the house of a bureaucrat in Istanbul, the artist has drawn the portrait of the *şeyhülislam,* whom he probably knew well, although his name is not mentioned in the poem.[55] He has used the window as a kind of picture frame and, as if hanging up a picture, placed Mustafa Efendi in the jutting bay, the most prominent part of the house. The seventh miniature in the *Dîwân* (fol. 22a) depicts *Medrese* of Gazanfer Ağa, as we learn from the writing above the door of the building (fig. 8).[56] This *medrese* is still standing in Istanbul today, located at the foot of the Bozdoğan Aqueduct near the district of Fatih. It was built in 1596 and includes a fountain (*sebil*) for the distribution of drinking water as well as the mausoleum of the *medrese*'s founder Gazanfer Ağa.[57] That same year the poet Nâdirî took up the post of professor at this *medrese.*[58]

Gazanfer Ağa (d. 1602) was *babüssaade ağası* at the imperial palace.[59] He had served the future Selim II in Kütahya, accompanied him to Istanbul, and served at the palace for thirty years. His close friendship with the famous Ottoman writer, intellectual, and bureaucrat Mustafa Âli must date from the time when they were both in Kütahya.[60] During the reigns of Murad III and Mehmed III, Gazanfer Ağa was a man of influence over both sultans and their mothers, and recent research has revealed that in conjunction with the sultans' tutor Sa'düddin Efendi, Gazanfer Ağa almost ruled the palace from behind the scenes and was the foremost patron of illustrated manuscripts produced at the palace studios between 1584 and 1602.[61] As explained above, he and Hoca Sa'düddin were with the sultan at the Battle of Haçova (fig. 2), and because he was a eunuch he had

Figure 8. Arrival of Gazanfer Ağa at his *madrasa*. Nâdirî's *Dîwân,* ca. 1605. 18.2 x 12.1 cm. Topkapı Palace Museum Library, no. H.889, fol. 22a. (Photo: courtesy of the Topkapı Palace Museum, Istanbul)

the appearance of a slender youth without beard or moustache.[62]

Nâdirî wrote *kasides* for Gazanfer Ağa and speaks words of praise about him in the preface to the *Dîwân.*[63] The seventh miniature is placed between lines lauding him and his *medrese.* A row of students is depicted in the domed classroom of the *medrese* facing their professor Nâdirî. On the basis of this identified portrait

55. İ. H. Daniçmend, *İzahlı Osmanlı Tarihi Kronolojisi,* 5 (İstanbul, 1971), p. 120.

56. Atasoy and Çağman (see note 9), pl. 44; Atıl (see note 17), fig. 6.

57. Semavi Eyice, "Gazanfer Ağa Külliyesi," *Türk Diyanet Vakfı İslam Ansiklopedisi,* 13 (1996):432–433.

58. Külekçi (see note 30), p. 3.

59. Mehmed Süreyya, Sicilli Osmani, 3, prep. A. Aktan, A. Yuvalı and M. Hülagu (İstanbul, 1996), p. 731; M. P. Pedani, "Safiye's Household and Venetian Diplomacy," *Turcica* 32 (2000):9–32. I would like to thank E. Fetvacı for bringing to my attention the last-mentioned article.

60. Fleischer (see note 13), pp. 31, 73, 110, 126, 169, 172.

61. Filiz Çağman, "Illustrated Stories from a Turkish Version of Jami's Baharistan," *Turkish Treasures* 2 (1978): pp. 21, 26.

62. Another portrait of Gazanfer Ağa can be seen in three miniatures illustrating *Eğri Fethi Tarihi.* He is either the figure standing beside Sultan Mehmed III or the figure riding on horseback: Akalay (see note 37), pp. 114–115, 118–119.

63. Külekçi (see note 30), pp. 80–86, 158; Külekçi, Ph.D. diss. (see note 45), pp. 196–200; 205–208; *Dîwân-ı Nâdirî,* Topkapı Saray Museum Library, no. H.889, fol. 2b.

of the poet we can identify him in other miniatures in the same manuscript. The first of these portraits is the second figure from the right among the horsemen arrayed along the battlemented city wall in folio 4a (fig. 2), and the second portrait is the figure standing second from the left in folio 8b (fig. 4). Flanking the classroom on either side of the miniature are the domed cells which housed the *medrese* students. In the lower left-hand corner is the *sebil,* and at the top behind the *medrese* is the wall of the Bozdoğan Aqueduct. The mounted figure wearing a turban of the *selimi* type in the lower right-hand corner of the miniature, outside the *medrese* gate, we can identify as Gazanfer Ağa from the known portrait already identified. In this way the artist, probably in consultation with the poet Nâdirî, included in his illustrations of the poetry significant elements connected to Gazanfer Ağa; bringing together the *medrese* building, the portrait of the *medrese*'s founder, and the portrait of the poet Nâdirî who was teaching there. While in earlier times public institutions of this kind had been founded by sultans, imperial women, and grand viziers, toward the end of the sixteenth century we find that a *babüssaade ağası* wielding influence in the palace government now possessed the authority to found an institution in his own name, and that this building was documented by an artist a few years following its construction.

The last miniature in the *Dîwân* (fol. 26b) depicts a battle (fig. 9). The Ottoman troops are arrayed on the right of the picture. The mounted figure wearing the large white *selimi* turban at the center-right edge is the army commander. To the left are Christian soldiers, whose commander is the figure dressed in a cape at the upper-left edge. The artist has distinguished the cultural differences of the figures by their facial features and apparel. The lines on the previous page refer to a battle and praise the commander, comparing him to Rüstem, Isfandiyar, and Afrasiyab, heros of Firdausi's *Sehnâme* (fol. 25b). A person called Ali is mentioned, probably with allusion to the heroism of 'Ali b. Abi Talib, son-in-law of the Prophet Muhammad (fol. 26b). The *kaside*s in this illustrated copy of Nâdirî's *Dîwân* have not been given titles, unlike some unillustrated copies of the same work. From the latter, therefore, it is possible to learn for whom the *kaside* was written. When we compare the lines preceding this miniature with those in copies without miniatures but with headings, we discover that these lines were written to Mirahur Ali Ağa.[64] Nâdirî wrote other poems to Ali Ağa, including some to both

Figure 9. Battle of *Hadım* Hafız Paşa at Niğbolu. Nâdirî's *Dîwân*, ca. 1605. 18.6 x 11.7 cm. Topkapı Palace Museum Library, no. H.889, fol. 26b. (Photo: courtesy of the Topkapı Palace Museum, Istanbul)

Ali Ağa and Gazanfer Ağa.[65] Moreover, Nâdirî writes in his preface to the *Dîwân* that it was compiled at the desire of Ali Ağa.[66] There is little information about Ali Ağa in historical sources. At present we know that in 1597 he was employed carrying commands issued by the sultan and grand vizier, and that in the same year he was promoted to the rank of equerry-in-chief (*büyük mirahur*), the officer in charge of the palace stables and those of the sultan.[67] In June 1598, when Sultan

64. Külekçi, Ph.D. diss. (see note 45), pp. 203–204.

65. Ibid., pp. 201–202, 206–208.
66. Ibid., p. 32.
67. Selânikî (see note 25), pp. 656, 686. For the duties of the *mirahur* see: İ. H. Uzunçarşılı, *Osmanlı Devletinin Saray Teşkilatı* (Ankara: Türk Tarih Kurumu, 1988), pp. 488–510.

Mehmed III, accompanied by grand vizier Mehmed Paşa and Hoca Sa'düddin Efendi, visited the palace at the royal estate of Davud Paşa near Istanbul, *Mirahur* Ali Ağa had given a banquet for him in his tent as required by the regulations governing his post.[68] In October of the same year *Mirahur* Ali Ağa and *Kapıağası* Gazanfer Ağa sent the best of the troops under their command to assist *Hadım* Hafız Paşa, *voivode* of Wallachia and commander of the Battle of Nicopolis.[69] *Mirahur* Ali Ağa was also chief among those charged under Ottoman law with meeting the nursemaid Güliter Hanım and envoy Hüseyin Beg upon their arrival from Iran in 1599 to visit the tomb of the Safavid prince Heydar Mirza, as explained in detail above.[70] Both of these crumbs of information taken from the historian Selânikî and Nâdirî's poems reveal that Ali Ağa and Gazanfer Ağa acted in concert, and that both wielded influence in the palace administration at the end of the sixteenth century. The battle scene depicted in this last miniature and placed between lines of a poem written for Ali Ağa probably represents the battle commanded by Hadım Hafız Paşa to which Ali Ağa and Gazanfer Ağa sent reinforcements. Although no detailed information is known about the past life of *Hadım* Hafız Paşa, his cognomen *Hadım* tells us that he, like Ali Ağa, must have risen from the ranks of the palace eunuchs, which would explain why they sent assistance to him. We can therefore conclude that the commander in the white turban in this battle scene is *Hadım* Hafız Paşa, and that the enemy commander wearing a cape facing him is Mihal, voivode of Wallachia.

The artists who illustrated the poems of Bâkî and Nâdirî constructed pictures of historical accuracy that are in contrast to the florid style of the poetry itself. They have included realistic details that are absent from the poems. Despite the lack of written descriptions, important figures and buildings have been depicted on the basis of observation, resulting in recognizable images. The name of only one of these artists is known: the illustrator of Nâdirî's *Dîwân*. He was Ahmed Nakşi, who is identified as the illustrator of a biographical work in its concluding lines.[71] When the miniatures executed by Ahmed Nakşi for the latter biography are compared with those illustrating Nâdirî's *Dîwân*, it is evident that he was the painter of both. Nâdirî is thought to have been a member of the *Nakşbendi* mystic order, and it should not be regarded as coincidence that the second name of the painter was Nakşi; thus we can conclude that the painter, too, was a member of this order and took the name for that reason. The way the artist, who was active during the first quarter of the seventeenth century, draws buildings in perspective in western style and his skillful portrayal of differences in cultural identity (as seen in his representation of Christians and their commanders—for example in his picture of the Battle of Haçova), suggest that he may have spent his youth in the European territories of the Ottoman Empire. The absence of any portrait of Sultan Osman II in the miniatures of the *Dîwân*, and his portrayal of Sultan Ahmed I as the young man he would have been at his first visit to Edirne, suggest that the manuscript may have been produced in the year 1605. The painter Ahmed Nakşi lived through the events that the poet refers to only cryptically in his poems, and shared the same cultural environment. Therefore he had no difficulty in transforming the written word into visual form, skillfully inserting his own observations, which were mostly fresh in his mind, between the poet's lines.

---

68. Uzunçarşılı (see note 67), p. 749.

69. Ibid., pp. 774, 772.

70. Ibid., p. 841.

71. *Tercüme-i Şekaik-i Numaniye:* Topkapı Saray Museum Library, no. H.1263. See: S. Ünver, *Ressam Nakşi: Hayatı ve Eserleri* (İstanbul, 1949); Atıl (see note 17), pp. 103–104; Z. Tanındı, *Türk Minyatür Sanatı* (Ankara: Türkiye İş Bankası, 1996), pp. 55–57.

Figure 1. Lovers Celebrate with Poetry, Music, and Wine. Hafiz, *Divan.* Bukhara ca. 1525. The Art and History Trust Collection on loan to The Arthur M. Sackler Museum, Smithsonian Institution.

Interpreting the *ghazal*s of Hafiz

PRISCILLA SOUCEK

For many Persians, the poet Muhammad b. Muhammad Shams al-din Shirazi known as Hafiz (ca. 1320–ca. 1390) and his *Divan* epitomize Iran's rich poetic and cultural tradition. The esteem with which he is held is represented concretely by the effort expended over the centuries to collect, edit, and analyze his poetry, making him easily the most closely studied and widely known Persian poet. Many of the questions surrounding his *Divan* derive from the fact that he does not seem to have prepared a definite edition of his own poems, and only a handful of them are contained in literary or historical texts copied in his lifetime. The adulation accorded to the *Divan* of Hafiz prompted interest in his biography, but very few facts about his life are recorded in contemporary sources.

The intersection of these twin lacunae with his great popularity had the paradoxical result that both his poetry and his biography enjoyed a substantial posthumous evolution. Over time the number of *ghazals* attributed to Hafiz increased from the 450 to 490 in the earliest known manuscripts to approximately 570 for versions used in the Ottoman world, such as the edition prepared by al-Sudi in the early seventeenth century, and reached more than 700 for copies that were circulating in the Indian subcontinent by the nineteenth century (Rehder 1974a; Schimmel 1979:11; Clarke 1984:I, v–vii). In the centuries that followed his death a close reading of his verses gave rise to anecdotes that were gradually assembled into a kind of mythologized biography (Ritter 1964). His *ghazals,* too, became enshrouded with commentaries, which stressed their allegorical or mystical character and particularly their affinities with the practices of Sufism. Most texts of this type such as the *Latifa-i Ghaybiyya,* cited by E. G. Browne in his *Literary History of Persia* (Browne 1956:III, 300–301, 315–319), remain inaccessible, but some indication of their contents can be gained by reading the ponderous commentaries supplied by H. Wilberforce Clarke in his English translation of the *Divan* of Hafiz, first published at Calcutta in 1891 (Hafiz, tr. Clarke 1984).

From the 1940s onward a new approach emerged, both in Iran and in other centers of Persian studies, which sought to recover the "true Hafiz" and to prune his *Divan* of its accretions. Literary scholars began to publish editions based on the oldest available manuscripts of his poems, and the first of these, edited jointly by

Muhammad Qazvni and Qasim Ghani, first appeared in 1941 and has been reprinted several times (Hafiz, ed. Qazvini and Ghani: 1985). The next year saw the publication of Qasim Ghani's detailed historical analysis of fourteenth-century Shiraz, and taken together these publications gave a new impetus and direction to the study of Hafiz (Ghani 1942). In 1945 R. Lescot published an essay that used historical references in Hafiz's *ghazals* to place specific poems within a chronological framework, and others have continued to investigate links between Hafiz and the milieu in which he lived (Lescot 1945:80–91; Duchesne-Guillemin 1981:142). These studies analyze topical and historical references contained in the poems of Hafiz and have served to counterbalance traditional commentaries which stressed the symbolic and mystical content of his verses.

A systematic search of libraries and private collections in various countries brought to light a few poems by Hafiz cited in literary or historical texts transcribed in his lifetime as well as copies of his *Divan* dated within a few decades of his death, and these in turn have prompted the publication of new editions of his poems (Rehder 1974a; Hillmann 1975; Duchesne-Guillemin 1981:143–44). Over the last fifty years editions of the *ghazals* of Hafiz have proliferated; some are based on manuscripts of particular importance, but many revise his *Divan* in the light of this new evidence. This study is based mainly on the edition of P.T. Khanlari first published in 1359/1981, revised in 1984 and republished with new annotations in 1996 (Hafiz, ed. Khanlari 1996). Khanlari's text was reprinted by R. Saberi in his recently published bilingual Persian and English edition (Hafiz, tr. Saberi 2002). Most of the translations of Hafiz included here are based on those of Saberi, although some have been slightly modified. The information contained in Khanlari's edition has been supplemented by that of Kh. Kh. Rahbar, which provides a short interpretation for each *ghazal* and analyzes its meter (Hafiz, ed. Rahbar 1989). His text is similar but not identical to that used by Khanlari so that references contained in this study will cite both editions. Khanlari includes 486 *ghazals* in his edition, whereas Rahbar has 494. Rahbar's text is also useful because it contains variants that appear in some Hafiz manuscripts of particular importance, such as the one inscribed with the name of the Safavid prince Sam Mirza b. Ismail now divided between various private and public collections, and a manuscript in the British Library, Or. 7573, made for the Mughal Emperor Jahangir (Stchoukine 1931; Welch 1976:20–21, 62–69).

The interpretations given to a single poem which opens with the line "Saqi, there is talk of the cypress, the rose and the tulip" (Hafiz, ed. Rahbar 1989: no. 225, pp. 305-306; Hafiz, ed. Khanlari 1996: no. 218, pp. 452-453; Hafiz tr. Saberi 2002: no. 218, p. 264) provide an index of how the traditional and recent approaches to the text of Hafiz yield divergent interpretations. This *ghazal* mentions that Hafiz's poetry is famous in Bengal and concludes with his wish to join the assemblies of a certain Sultan Ghiyath al-din. Indian commentators identified the latter with a Ghiyath al-din who ruled Bengal and used interpretations of other verses in the *ghazal* to concoct a story involving a mortal illness from which he was miraculously saved by concubines named Cypress, Rose, and Tulip. Ghiyath al-din's desire to commemorate this momentous event led him to send a request to Hafiz, who lived in faraway Shiraz, for a poem on this theme (Browne 1956:III:283–284; Hafiz, tr. Clarke 1984:no. 158, vol. I:310–311).

Persian scholars have rejected this fable, interpreting the erstwhile concubines as references to a spring garden and identifying Ghiyath al-din as a ruler of Fars. The most plausible candidate is an Injuid named Kaykhusraw who ruled in Shiraz between 734–739/1334–1339 at which time Hafiz would have been in his twenties, making this *ghazal* one of his earliest poems. This *ghazal* is notable for the absence of any mystical overtones (Duchesne-Guillemin 1981:146–148).

The search for the "true Hafiz" and its concomitant concentration on the poet, his life, and his work is logically the main concern of literary scholars, but the purpose of my essay is to view Hafiz from a different direction by focusing on the ways in which his poetry has interacted with the visual culture of the regions where it has had such a profound and enduring popularity. Despite the prodigious effort expended on the study of Hafiz, this manifestation of his prominence remains largely unexplored. Even a cursory survey of publications on the arts of Iran and related regions reveals that over the centuries the *Divan* of Hafiz was used in a variety of ways. It was inscribed on metalwork, woven into textiles, and served as the basis for illustrations in manuscripts produced from the fifteenth to nineteenth centuries. In Iran, his poems continue to inspire contemporary painters and calligraphers. The distribution and production of these objects from Turkey to Iran, Central Asia, and the Indian subcontinent appears to reflect the geographical range of his greatest popularity (Soucek 2002).

Those who seek to identify and understand the essential features of his poetry logically focus their attention on the milieu in which he lived, but anyone who wishes to examine the role of Hafiz in the visual arts must cast a wider net. This study will have two chronological divisions. The first will deal with Hafiz and the Timurids, and the second with Hafiz during the sixteenth and early seventeenth centuries. These two periods are closely related in their approach to Hafiz and quite distinct from subsequent uses of his text between the mid-seventeenth and nineteenth centuries. The contemporary use of Hafiz by painters and calligraphers also deserves a separate study. The two periods to be discussed here reflect divisions in the visual evidence but both are also recognized as distinct periods in the evolution of his text (Farzad 1968:I, 15).

Most modern literary critics stress that the *ghazals* of Hafiz contain a blend of erotic, mystical, and courtly themes that are so interwoven as to be inseparable; J. Meisami characterizes his *ghazals* as "polysemic" (Meisami 1987:289–292). D. Davis proposes that some of the variations in his verses spring from a deliberate cultivation of ambiguity:

> If there are alternate social or political roles to be played, Hafiz can usually be counted on to be on both sides, like one of those elusive subatomic particles Heisenberg talks about, which as soon as you locate them in one place reassemble themselves in another
>
> *Davis 1999:280*

When those verses are inscribed on an object or illustrated in a manuscript, one or another of these meanings often predominates. Thus, the examination of objects and manuscripts produced in different settings and for diverse audiences over several centuries should provide a number of "readings" of the *Divan* of Hafiz that will add to an understanding of the broader importance of the poet and his work. Given the scope of these questions, however, the present essay can be no more than an exploration of these topics by focusing on a few representative examples. Although this quest is, in many ways, the inverse of that undertaken by literary historians, it will make use of the findings about Hafiz and his poetry that have emerged from their work.

Any evaluation of Hafiz and his poetry must rest on the understanding that his primary vehicle of expression, the *ghazal,* is a highly stylized poetic form that by his time had acquired a formal structure and a well-defined group of themes expressed by means of a specific vocabulary. At its most basic the *ghazal* is a short poem composed of varying numbers of *bayts,* each of which is divided into two *misra*s or hemistiches. The *ghazals* of Hafiz can have as few as six *bayts* or as many as twelve. Although *bayt* is often translated as "line," it is functionally more equivalent to a stanza in English poetry, because usually each is syntactically and conceptually complete in and of itself.

The *bayts* of a given *ghazal* are linked to each other by their shared meter and rhyme, but the opening and closing ones have a special status. The opening *bayt,* both halves of which rhyme, establishes the meter and the rhyme scheme of a particular *ghazal.* The initial *bayt*'s first *misra*, known as the *matla* (beginning), serves as a de facto title for identifying the *ghazal* as a whole. By the fourteenth century, the *maqta*, or final *bayt* of a *ghazal,* usually incorporates the poet's *takhallus,* or identifying epithet, in this case "*Hafiz,*" and serves as both a conclusion for and a "signature" to a *ghazal* (Rehder 1974b:73–75).

The semantic and syntactic integrity of each *bayt* has led literary scholars to debate whether the *ghazal* as a whole possesses a definable identity. Some scholars prefer to stress the independence of each of Hafiz's *bayts* and maintain that their order is often arbitrary, an approach epitomized in the phrase "orient pearls at random strung" that appears in the earliest English translation of Hafiz by Sir William Jones, published in 1772 (Arberry 1946; Bausani 1958; Meisami 1995a:55–56). More recently, scholars have preferred to focus on various ways in which his *bayts* are thematically linked and subordinated to a broader concept that provides a measure of unity to the *ghazal* as a whole (Rehder 1974b; Hillmann 1974; Bashiri 1979a).

As early as the thirteenth century the character and content of the *ghazal* had become conventional. It was generally devoted to an exploration of love by using a defined set of themes and images that described both the beauty and attraction of the beloved and the state of mind of the lover when united with or separated from the object of his affections. The lips, face, hair, and body of the beloved were often described or evoked through metaphors, many of which are drawn from the imagery of the garden. Blossoming flowers, swaying trees, and fragrant herbs are among the favorite sensory analogs employed (Meisami 1987:237–256; Meisami 1995b). The lover's mood ranges from pleasure at meeting the beloved and the exaltation of passion, to despair over separation or estrangement, but these sentiments are often expressed indirectly through figures of speech or by allusion to the travails of legendary lovers of the past such as Layla and Majnun, Shirin and Farhad, or Yusuf and Zulaykha (Meisami 1987:286–290; Rehder 1974: 73–83). The inclusion of the poet's *takhallus* or "pen-name" in the last verse of a *ghazal* makes it appear self-referential, but this use of authorial voice was also conventional and need not mean that most such poems are autobiographical in content (Hillmann 1974:131–145).

By the time of Hafiz the *ghazal* was used not only to describe romantic, and often erotic love, but also the quest of the mystic for a spiritual union. The same vocabulary and imagery came to be used to describe both experiences and there was often considerable ambiguity about which constituted a poet's major focus. This intertwining of the erotic and the mystical came to be characteristic of the *ghazal* as a poetic form, but Hafiz himself interjects further ambiguities into his verses. He was renowned as a poet who used the *ghazal* with its distinctive structure and vocabulary as a vehicle for panegyrics that praised prominent figures of his own time, such as the rulers of Shiraz or their high officials. The efforts of literary historians in recent decades have led to a clearer understanding of Hafiz's role as a court poet, and about one quarter of his *ghazals* contain implicit or explicit references to specific individuals (Lescot 1945:59–80; Duchesne-Guillemin 1981:146–150). In so doing Hafiz is often said to have substituted the *ghazal* for the *qasida* which was the traditional vehicle for encomiastic verse, although he was not the first author to have done so (Meisami 1987:277–281).

This study will mention the appearance of Hafiz's verses on objects, but its main aim is to analyze the paintings in manuscripts of his poetry. It will seek to identify their salient features and to consider the ways in which they are related to the poet's text. The vast majority of Persian illustrated manuscripts contain narrative texts and these differ from Hafiz's *ghazals* in several respects. In narrative poems such as the *Shahnama* of Firdausi or the *Khamsa* of Nizami stories unfold in a linear fashion and the most memorable incidents occur only once. In contrast, the *ghazals* of Hafiz usually contain a succession of images that lack any overt narrative sequence. They frequently have a dream-like fluidity that erases the boundaries of time and space, and the same few themes are repeated in hundreds of these poems. Despite this relative thematic homogeneity of Hafiz's *Divan,* the various *bayts* of a given *ghazal* can differ from one another in the images or associations that they evoke. Citation of the first *bayt,* and particularly its *matla^c*, was probably often sufficient to recall the *ghazal* as a whole, whereas use of the final *bayt* and its *maqta^c* would have drawn attention to Hafiz himself who was also frequently the implicit narrator of the poem as a whole. The diction of his *ghazals*, which often has the cadence, emotional directness, and simplicity of speech, reinforces the immediacy of his authorial presence.

The challenge that such poetry presents to a would-be illustrator has some similarities to the problems posed by the illustration of the Psalms in Medieval Europe. Both are fundamentally non-narrative and explore "feelings" rather than describing events. A solution to this challenge found in some copies of the Psalms was to depict those aspects of the texts "that admitted of literal illustration," creating what has been termed *imagines verborum* or "word-pictures" (Sandler 1996:87; Horst 1996:64). The fundamental goal of such depictions was "to provide a visual gloss" for the text which explained or reinforced its meaning (Sandler 1996:87). Sometimes these "word-pictures" were constructed by combining elements drawn from separate places in the text to create a new whole. They could also draw upon well-established iconographic models linked to the Psalms by commentaries (Ibid.:95).

Although in many cases paintings belonging to manuscript copies of the *Divan* of Hafiz have been published, this often occurred without noting the particular *ghazal* they illustrate. This habit has obscured their relationship to the text, particularly since many *ghazals* touch on several subjects and a poem containing only a few lines can be interpreted or illustrated in a variety of ways. In this study, the precise location of paintings will be noted as a necessary prelude to a more satisfactory analysis of their relationship to his text.

Hafiz and the Timurids

The variety of rulers to whom Hafiz dedicates his *ghazals* demonstrates that Hafiz was known outside of Shiraz during his lifetime, but it was during the fifteenth century that his verses reached a wider audience (Lescot 1945:70–73, 79–80; Rehder 1970:84–248, esp. 245–246). The poet's rising importance during that epoch is manifested in a variety of ways. Numerous fifteenth-century manuscripts of his poetry survive, some written within a decade or two of his death, and a few of them were illustrated (Karatay 1961: nos. 628–629, pp. 216–217; Rehder 1974a). His verses were inscribed on fifteenth-century metalwork (Komaroff 1992:156–158, 176–177, 201, 216–217). Poets of that period

imitated his *ghazals*, and several other fifteenth-century authors mention him in their texts (Yarshater 1955:76, 79–80; Rehder 1970: 245–246). The perception of Hafiz that emerges from these fifteenth-century sources appears to have laid the foundation for the ways in which his poetry was interpreted and illustrated in the sixteenth and seventeenth centuries not only in Iran but also in the Indian subcontinent.

Hafiz spent almost his entire life in the city of Shiraz, which was also the most important center for manuscript production in Iran during the fourteenth through sixteenth centuries. Thus it is only natural that the scribes of that city produced many copies of his *Divan*. Shiraz manuscripts are also of particular importance for the text of Hafiz, for three of the earliest and most complete examples were copied there for the Timurid prince Iskandar b. Umar Shaykh b. Timur, who ruled that city between 1410 and 1414. One of these, Add. 27261, is in the British Library and two others, Aya Sofya 3945 and Aya Sofya 3857, now housed in the Süleymaniye Library, Istanbul, once formed part of the Ottoman imperial library. The most important of these, Aya Sofya 3945, which contains 486 *ghazals*, belonged to the library of Mehmet II (r. 1451–1481) (Ritter 1942: 239–242; Rehder 1965:109; Rehder 1974a:151–152; Duchesne–Guillemin 1981:143–145). The manuscripts made for Iskandar Mirza are of high quality, produced by professional scribes and embellished with illuminated headings, but none is illustrated.

Two of Iskandar's Timurid successors as rulers of Shiraz are also linked to Hafiz. The latter figures in a text entitled *Anis al-Nas* (The Good Companion) composed ca. 1426 by a certain Shuja^c and dedicated to Ibrahim Sultan b. Shah Rukh b. Timur, who served as governor of Shiraz between 1414 and 1435. Shuja^c, who was distantly related to the fourteenth-century ruler of Shiraz Abu Ishaq Inju, intended his text to offer moral and ethical guidance to its readers, but it also demonstrates the importance of Hafiz and his heritage for the educated person of his time (de Fouchécour 1998:48–51). Shuja^c is the first author to describe an encounter between Timur and Hafiz said to have occurred just after the former had conquered Shiraz in 1393. Shuja^c recounts that Hafiz pleaded poverty in order to evade the payment of his portion of the tribute imposed by Timur on the households of the city. Timur is said to have recited the following verse by Hafiz:

> My Shiraz Turk if she but deign/ to take my heart within her hand,
> I'll barter for her Hindu mole/ Bukhara, yea, and Samarkand.

Arberry 1946:711

Timur is said to have commented that a destitute individual would not exchange those cities for a beauty mark, whereupon Hafiz retorted that he was bankrupt precisely because he had given them away. The cleverness of his reply supposedly led Timur to forgive Hafiz's debt (Shujaᶜ 1971:317).

Whether or not this episode ever occurred, Shujaᶜ's text displays an intimate knowledge of Hafiz's poetry, not only citing it but using the latter's ideas as the basis of a chapter on the etiquette of love (ᶜishq) (de Fouchécour 1998:48–51). According to Shujaᶜ, the proper conduct of amorous adventures requires a refined temperament and revolves around seeing the face of the beloved and exchanging glances with him (Shujaᶜ 1971:142, 155–156). This belief that love should be manifested through "the play of the glance" (nazarbazi) must have been current in Iran during the fourteenth to sixteenth centuries because it not only underlies many poems by Hafiz but also helps to explain the way lovers are depicted in contemporary paintings, including those illustrating the *Divan* of Hafiz.

Another Timurid governor of Shiraz, Abu'l Qasim Babur b. Baysunghur who ruled Shiraz in the 1450s, is credited with being the first to build a structure over the grave of Hafiz (Dawlatshah [n.d.]:344). This suggests that the grave of Hafiz had, by that time, become an object of veneration. The scribes of Shiraz continued to produce manuscripts of Hafiz's *Divan* throughout the fifteenth century and some of them were illustrated, but none of these has yet been published (Karatay 1961: nos. 627–631, pp. 216–217).

Various kinds of evidence show that during the fifteenth century Hafiz's fame was not confined to Shiraz or the region of Fars, but quickly spread eastward to Herat where his *ghazals* were clearly appreciated by that city's cultural elite. His popularity during the fifteenth century in eastern Iran and adjacent regions is shown by the transcription of his poetry on metalwork objects produced in Timurid Khurasan during the second half of the fifteenth century. The most important of these are jugs and bowls inscribed with verses about wine drinking, a theme which Hafiz treats in many of his *ghazals* (Melikian-Chirvani 1982:233, 246, 248–250; Komaroff 1992:156–158, 176–177, 201, 216–217).

The earliest among them is a silver-inlaid brass jug (mashraba) dated to 866/1461–2, signed by Habib Allah ibn Ali Baharjani and now in the Victoria and Albert Museum (Melikian-Chirvani 1982: no. 109, pp. 248–250; Komaroff 1992: no. 4, 156–158). This vessel is of particular interest because its silver-inlaid decoration includes two complete *ghazals* by Hafiz, related in theme but distinct in meter, and they are inscribed in a

clear and legible fashion in horizontal bands that ring the vessel at its widest point (Hafiz, ed. Rahbar 1989: nos. 65 & 176, pp. 91–92, 237–238; Hafiz, ed. Khanlari 1996: nos. 66 & 172, pp. 148–149, 340–341). Their text is virtually identical with that found in recent editions of Hafiz, which suggests that Habib Allah had at his disposal a high-quality manuscript of the *Divan*. Each *ghazal* contains eight *bayt*s. They are inscribed on this vessel in four distinct groups of four lines each. Rather than inscribe them sequentially, Habib Allah used two groups of four *bayt*s from one *ghazal* to frame the two horizontal zones bearing the text of the other poem (Hafiz, ed. Rahbar 1989: no. 176:1–4, no. 65:1–8, no. 176:5–8; Hafiz, ed. Khanlari 1996: no. 172:1–4, no. 66:1–8, no. 172:5–8). These two poems are also made visually distinct by the way in which the artist has transcribed them. Each *misra*ᶜ or hemistich of the central text is surrounded by its own frame, an arrangement which was customary when transcribing poetry, but in the *ghazal* that is transcribed in the upper and lower zones, every *misra*ᶜ is divided into two sections, each of which has its own frame, so that a single poetic line occupies four consecutive compartments.

These two poems contain complementary justifications for wine drinking suggesting that this is the purpose the vessel would have served. The framing text describes how Hafiz was awakened at dawn and was told to rise and take a cup of wine so that he might be properly inebriated when united with his beloved, who was returning to him after being with an anonymous rival who is dismissed as "a pigeon." It concludes with a reference to the recitation of the poem itself and to the fame of Hafiz (Hafiz, ed. Rahbar 1989: no. 176; Hafiz, ed. Khanlari 1996: no. 172; Hafiz, tr. Saberi 2002: no. 172, p. 209). The middle poem, which interrupts the first, is a meditation on the evanescence of life and the need to enjoy the moment rather than wait for paradise because the water of eternal life is likely to be nothing more than a cup of wine. It concludes with the question of whether God will prefer the ascetic who pines for the water that will be available only in Paradise, or Hafiz who prefers the wine cup (piyala) (Hafiz, ed. Rahbar 1989: no. 64; Hafiz, ed. Khanlari 1996: no. 66; Hafiz, tr. Saberi 2002: no. 66, p. 79). Both the content and arrangement of these verses suggest the vessel was intended to be used at a celebration which combined the drinking of wine and the recitation of poetry, particularly that of Hafiz.

A wine bowl now in the Hermitage Museum, St Petersburg, is inscribed with verses from three different *ghazals*, all of which describe wine drinking (Komaroff 1992: no. 29, pp. 216–217). They are composed in different meters and are physically separated from each other on the vessel. One runs around the rim on the interior of the bowl and two encircle its exterior (Hafiz, ed. Rahbar 1989: no. 394:1a–2b, 3b; no. 144:1a–2b, 10a–b; 391:1a–2b, 4a–b; Hafiz, ed. Khanlari 1996: no. 388: 1a–2b, 3b; no. 137:1a–2b, 10a–b; no. 383:1a–b, 2a–b, 4a–b). The verses on the interior urge the *saqi* (cup-bearer) to make haste and fill the cup with wine, and those on the exterior extol the pleasures and benefits of drinking through a selection of verses rearranged to suit the context. The upper citation alludes to looking into the "cup of Jamshid" and the lower one presents wine drinking as a cure for the pains and sorrows of life. These verses could be given subsidiary interpretations but they appear to have been chosen for their celebration of wine drinking and to enhance the object's intended function. In each case the text consists of a sequence of verses different from that contained in printed copies of the *Divan,* but one that is appropriate to the vessel's intended use.

Comments about Hafiz in various texts composed in Herat during the second half of the fifteenth century suggest that many of his fifteenth-century admirers preferred to stress esoteric interpretations of his *ghazals* and to emphasize his affinity with the doctrines and practices of Sufism, both of which were much in vogue there at that time. These views about Hafiz are contained in several texts written in Herat. The earliest of these is the *Nafahat al-uns* (The Breath of Divine Intimacy), a biographical compendium devoted to the lives of important Sufis and mystics, composed at Herat between 1476 and 1479 by the poet and scholar Nur al-Din Abd al-Rahman Jami. His description of Hafiz is much more cursory than that he accords to either Farid al-Din Attar or Jalal al-din Rumi, whose espousal of Sufism is clearly documented, but Jami acknowledges the strength of Hafiz's connection to the spirit of Sufism (*tasavvuf*). His description of Hafiz as *lisan al-ghayb ve tarjuman al-asrar,* "the tongue of the invisible and the translator of secrets" who uses *libas-i majaz,* "the garment of allegory," in order to communicate *ma'ni-i haqiqat,* "the significance of true reality," lays the foundation for most later statements about Hafiz (Jami 1958:614; Rehder 1970:167–171).

Other Herati authors echo Jami's comments. In his compilation about the lives and works of poets, entitled *Tazkira al-Shuara,* which was probably composed in the 1480s Dawlatshah Samarqandi notes that although Hafiz's diction is simple, his verses are very popular among the Sufis, stating that "the seekers of truth have an inexpressible desire for the words of Hafiz" (Rehder

1970:184; Dawlatshah [n.d.]:338). Two slightly later texts written in Herat amplify these descriptions of Hafiz as a poet whose verses are particularly popular among Sufis. The hidden meanings in Hafiz's poetry are linked to his cultivation of homoerotic love in the *Majalis al-Ushshaq* (The Assembly of Lovers), composed by Jami's disciple Husayn Gazurgahi between 1503 and 1504. The latter repeats and amplifies Jami's statements about the esoteric content of the *ghazals* of Hafiz and also ascribes amorous adventures to him without providing any specific details about the identity of the poet's beloved (Gazurgahi 1997:202–205).

The other source, the preface to a new edition of Hafiz's poems prepared at Herat in 907/1501–1502 by a group of scholars at the instigation of the Timurid prince Abu'l Fath Faridun Husayn Khan, gives a more overtly religious interpretation to the hidden meanings in Hafiz's poetry by comparing his text to the Qur'an (Roemer 1952: no. 116, pp. 134, 141, pls. 65 & 67, fols. 97a, 100b–101a). The author of the preface, Abdallah Marvarid, who probably also formed part of the editorial group, describes how they worked to purge Hafiz's text of accumulated errors and to give it a new arrangement (Ibid.:138–139, pls. 66–67, fols. 99a–100a). Or. 3247, in the British Library, has been identified as a copy of this edition, which reduced the number of *ghazals* included to 182 (Rehder 1974:147).

The characterization of Hafiz as a poet who understood hidden truths by Jami and other Timurid authors has been interpreted by modern scholars to mean that the practice of using Hafiz's *Divan* for prognostication was already underway by the second half of the fifteenth century (Burke 1992:140). The strongest textual support for this practice comes in the remarks made by Abdallah Marvarid in his preface to the *Divan* discussed above, where he compares Hafiz's poetry to the *Quran,* which by the sixteenth century was widely used for prognostication. The fact that this new edition was prepared at the Timurid court is also consonant with evidence about later rulers who turned to Hafiz as a source of consolation and support in times of personal or dynastic crisis. This habit is documented for the Mughal rulers of India and also attributed to various members of the Safavid dynasty by the *Latifa al-ghaybiyya* ([Khan Bahadur] 1992; Browne 1956:III, 315–319).

Hafiz in the sixteenth and early seventeenth centuries

The sixteenth and early seventeenth centuries comprise the period in which illustration of the *Divan* of

Hafiz was most widespread. Published examples include copies made by court painters for members of both the Safavid and Mughal dynasties (Stchoukine 1931; Welch 1976). In addition to their intrinsic quality of execution, these manuscripts may also reveal the ways in which the perspective of their royal owners could have affected their illustration. Anonymous manuscripts can also contain paintings that reflect Hafiz's text in subtle and idiosyncratic ways, demonstrating that those responsible for their creation had an intimate knowledge of, and appreciation for, his poetry. Rather than attempting to survey all known illustrated manuscripts from the sixteenth and early seventeenth centuries, the focus here will be on the ways in which individual paintings reflect the themes or the text of the particular *ghazals* that they illustrate.

Interpretations attached to the poetry of Hafiz by Timurid authors probably underlie the way his poetry was viewed among the Safavids, the Mughals, and the Shaybanids. The impact of Timurid culture was particularly strong in sixteenth-century Bukhara, and the pair of paintings in a manuscript of the *Divan* of Hafiz probably made there in the 1520s, and now in the Soudavar Collection, echo themes expressed in Timurid sources such as Shuja'ʿs *Anis al-Nas* and Gazurgahi's *Majalis al-ushshaq*. One shows amorous couples engaging in "the play of the glance" (see fig. 1) while poetry is being recited and music played, and the other uses a well-known compositional type depicting a group of turban-clad ascetics or scholars (see fig. 2) to create a subversive endorsement for the pleasures of inebriation (Soudavar 1992: no. 77a & b, pp. 208–209).

In the first instance, the painting illustrates one of the *ghazals* in which Hafiz celebrates the joys of gatherings for wine drinking, poetry recital, and music in the presence of handsome youths (Hafiz, ed. Khanlari 1996: no. 14, pp. 24–25; Hafiz, tr. Saberi 2002: no. 14, p. 18). The theme of both this *ghazal* and its illustration is encapsulated in the final *misraʿ* of its second verse:

> It is the season of joy, the time for wine and the age of youth.
>
> *Hafiz, tr. Saberi 2002: no. 14:3, p. 18*

The painting is placed after the poem's concluding couplet in which Hafiz describes the recital of his own poetry to a musical accompaniment as a love offering to a handsome youth:

> If that moon be the buyer of Hafiz's pearls, at every breath
> The rebec's pleasant sound will reach Venus' ear
>
> *Ibid.: no. 14:6*

The painting shows a group of men expressing their affection for one another in a variety of ways and several of them appear to be intoxicated. The poem's theme is particularly well articulated by the pair depicted in the painting's upper zone; a bearded older man who recites poetry from a manuscript held in his hand, and a handsome youth who prepares to hand him a cup of wine. The older man's placement just below the text in which Hafiz extols his own poetry makes him the author's visual surrogate.

This painting of amorous couples recalls the double-page composition which celebrates the interrelated pleasures of intoxication, homoerotic friendship, music, and poetry recitation that appears on the opening pages

Figure 2. A Group of Clerics Enjoy Wine. Hafiz, *Divan*. Bukhara ca. 1525. The Art and History Trust Collection on loan to the Sackler Museum, Smithsonian Institution.

of a copy of the *Gulistan* of Saꞏdi, dated to 1488, made at Herat for the Timurid ruler Husayn Mirza and now in Cairo (Lentz & Lowry 1989:no. 146, pp. 260–261, 286). The postures of the five lovers in the foreground of the Soudavar illustration echo those of the figures in the foreground of the left page of the Cairo painting. The latter's focal point is a portrait of Husayn Mirza who offers a flower to the handsome youth seated beside him, even as the latter appears to be on the verge of a drunken stupor. The Cairo frontispiece and the Soudavar illustration exemplify the pursuit of love described in the *ghazal*s by Hafiz and viewed through the prism of Herati authors including Gazurgahi. The latter devotes the final chapter of his *Majalis al-Ushshaq* to a celebration of Husayn Mirza's devotion to love (Gazurgahi 1997:343–353).

The other painting in the Soudavar manuscript illustrates one of Hafiz's most famous *ghazal*s and celebrates the accession of a ruler who allows the public consumption of alcohol (fig. 2). Its last two lines underscore its panegyric function and wish this ruler a long and successful reign (Hafiz ed. Rahbar 1989: no. 285, p. 385; Hafiz, ed. Khanlari 1996: no. 280, pp. 576–577; Hafiz, tr. Saberi 2002: no. 280, p. 336). The Soudavar painting immediately follows the *ghazal*'s satirical opening lines that describe how outwardly abstemious religious leaders reacted to this change:

> In the age of the guilt-forgiving and fault-covering king,
> The Hafiz drank from a flask and the *Mufti* from a cup.
> The Sufi moved from the monastery to the wine-vat's side,
> When he saw the *Muhtasib* carry a wine jug on his
> shoulder
>
> *Hafiz, trans. Saberi 2002: no. 280, p. 336*

The painting employs a well-known composition, popular in Timurid Herat, in which scholars or ascetics, seated in the open air, are engaged in conversation or disputation. Their religious or scholarly credentials are emphasized by their serious demeanor and plain clothing and by the presence of books and writing implements (Lentz & Lowry 1989: figs. 93 & 155, pp. 263, 281). In the Soudavar painting, the venerable ascetics are conducting their conversation with the aid of wine, represented by flasks at their side and wine cups held discretely in their hands (fig. 2). Later illustrators of this *ghazal* usually prefer to depict these religious authorities as denizens of a tavern (see fig. 3), a characterization that gives such paintings a broader humor (Stchoukine 1931: fig. 9; Schmitz 1997: fig. 74).

Another idiosyncratic yet telling image (see fig. 4) belongs to a manuscript that is dated to 1537, produced

Figure 3. A Group of Clerics in a Tavern. Hafiz, *Divan*. Shiraz, ca. 1580. The Arthur M. Sackler Museum, Smithsonian Institution, no. S86.0048, fol. 114a.

in Shiraz and now in the Pierpont Morgan Library (PML15, Schmitz 1997: no. 6, pp. 32–33). It illustrates a *ghazal* which is closely identified with Hafiz himself, in which he speaks of his own death and invites future visitors to visit his grave and celebrate there with wine drinking and music (Hafiz, ed. Rahbar 1989:no. 336, lines 1, 4, 5, 6, p. 456–457; Hafiz, ed. Khanlari 1996: no. 328, lines 1, 4, 5, 6, pp. 672–673). In the Morgan manuscript the order of the *bayt*s in this *ghazal* has been manipulated so that this illustration is bordered by lines directly related to its theme. The lines over and under the painting read:

> Sit beside my grave with minstrel and wine,
> So that by your fragrance, dancing from the tomb, I rise.
> O idol, sweet of motion, rise and show me your stature,
> So that dancing, from life and the universe I may rise.
>
> *Hafiz, tr. Saberi 2002: no. 328:4–5, p. 392*

Although it is rarely illustrated, this *ghazal* is inscribed on the cenotaph erected over Hafiz's grave in 1773 by Karim Khan Zand (Sami 1971:84–90; Hafiz, tr. Clarke 1984:II:732–733). The Morgan painting appears to be a "word-picture" of this verse because it shows a youth seated beside a tomb, drinking wine, and a group of musicians are clustered in the painting's foreground (Schmitz 1997: fig. 51).

Although many scholars stress the differences between commercial and court manuscripts, there are important parallels between the way Hafiz's poetry is illustrated in copies made for Safavid and Mughal patrons and in a group of manuscripts produced for sale at Shiraz during the 1570s and 1580s. In all cases their paintings are few in number and usually reflect the principal themes treated in the *ghazals* of Hafiz: wine drinking, amorous encounters, and a critique of religious hypocrisy, although the placement of illustrations within his text can vary from one copy to another. Polo playing, an activity popular with princes and rulers, and mentioned in some of Hafiz's panegyric verses as a metaphor for sovereignty, is also illustrated in both royal and commercial manuscripts.

To date, most discussions of sixteenth-century Hafiz manuscripts have been focused on a single copy that bears an inscription to the Safavid prince Sam Mirza b. Shah Ismail. It once contained four illustrations, of which three remain. The key publication on this manuscript, S. C. Welch's *Persian Painting: Five Royal Safavid Manuscripts of the Sixteenth Century,* reproduces the now lost "Polo Game" along with the three surviving paintings. His comments about the three paintings include translations of sections from the *ghazals* that they illustrate and further translations of the relevant *ghazals* are included in his 1979 catalogue, *Wonders of the Age* (Welch 1976:20–21, 62–69; Welch 1979:118–129). Several subsequent studies have republished these same paintings that are presently divided between private and public collections (Soucek 1990; Soudavar 1992:159–161).

Although the manuscript made for Sam Mirza is in certain respects unique, and questions about its origin and patronage remain unresolved, this essay will consider two other aspects of its paintings: parallels between its compositions and those in later manuscripts, and the manner in which two of its paintings utilize the content, structure, and diction of Hafiz's text. The Sam Mirza manuscript shares three compositions with several other illustrated copies of Hafiz's *Divan,* the now lost "Polo Game," the scene set in a mosque, and the depiction of a tavern. It is this last example which

provides the most useful index of the relationship between the copy dedicated to Sam Mirza and other illustrated Hafiz manuscripts.

Most of the illustrations in Hafiz manuscripts from the sixteenth and seventeenth century are adaptations of well-established compositions to this new context, but the theme of the tavern is so closely associated with the poetry of Hafiz that such paintings may well have been

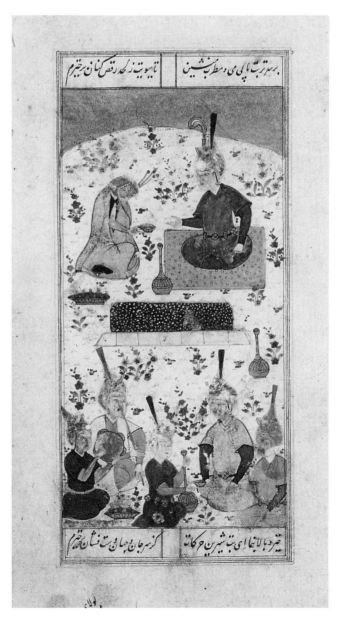

Figure 4. Celebrating at the Grave of Hafiz with Music and Wine. Hafiz, *Divan.* Shiraz, 1537. The Pierpont Morgan Library, Ms. M. 15, fol. 115b.

designed specifically for his text. Just as descriptions of taverns occur in several of his *ghazals*, so too there are several compositional variants on this theme. The best known and most frequently illustrated such *ghazal* is the one used in the Bukhara illustration of ca. 1520 discussed above in which religious leaders demonstrate their enthusiasm for tavern life (Hafiz ed. Rahbar 1989: no. 285, p. 385; Hafiz, ed. Khanlari 1996: no. 280, pp. 576–577; Hafiz, tr. Saberi 2002: no. 280, p. 336). Illustrations of this *ghazal* occur in Shiraz manuscripts from the 1570s and 1580s as well as in an early seventeenth-century Mughal manuscript made for the emperor Jahangir (Stchoukine 1931: fig. 9; Lowry & Beach 1988: no. 160, fol. 114a).

When the opening lines of this *ghazal* are depicted in Shiraz manuscripts of the 1570s and 1580s the resulting images are often more literally descriptive than was the case in the Soudavar illustration discussed above. A painting now in the Sackler Museum of Asian Art is representative of this type (figs. 2 & 3). The *ghazal*'s first two couplets are inscribed over the painting and several of the characters mentioned in those lines are easily identified in the image. The "guilt-forgiving and fault-covering King" looks down on the revelry from the painting's upper left corner and the *muhtasib* carrying a flask on his shoulder is shown just below him. A man seated near a wine vat may represent the Sufi described by Hafiz.

This literal and detailed connection between the wording of the *ghazal* and its depiction found in Shiraz manuscripts appears to have provided a model for the illustrators of Jahangir's copy of the *Divan* (Stchoukine 1931: fig. 9). The middle ground of the Moghul illustration is occupied by the sufi seated beside his wine vat and the *muhtasib* carrying a flask on his shoulder. A princely figure in the background, who dispenses drinks, may represent the benevolent ruler celebrated in this *ghazal*.

Another *ghazal* describing a tavern that was illustrated in Shiraz during the 1570s focuses on the image of the magical cup of Jamshid (Hafiz, ed. Rahbar 1989: no. 143, pp. 193–194; Hafiz, ed. Khanlari 1996: no. 136, p. 288). This text is depicted in a Hafiz manuscript now in Paris, suppl. persan 1477 (Richard 1997: no. 134, p. 196). The *bayts* inscribed over this painting refer to the Magian sage who offers this magical cup to Hafiz, or his poetic persona:

Last night, I took my questions to the Magians' Pir;
Who solved problems by his powerful insight,
I saw him joyful and happy with a cup of wine in his hand.
Hafiz, tr. Saberi 2002: no. 136, lines 3a–4a, p. 166

The illustration in the Paris manuscript shows a group of men before a tavern, some standing, others seated and inebriated. One man appears to be conversing with the white-bearded tavern keeper who holds a cup in his outstretched hand. In this case the image appears to have been constructed as a visual rendering of Hafiz's text.

The best known of such tavern depictions is the painting in the manuscript dedicated to Sam Mirza (see fig. 5) which S. C. Welch has entitled "Worldly and Otherwordly Drunkenness" and "Allegory of Drunkenness" (Welch 1976, pp. 68–69; Welch 1979: 128–129). The same *ghazal* by Hafiz was illustrated in both Shiraz manuscripts of the 1570s and 1580s and in the copy of Hafiz made for the Mughal emperor Jahangir (Stchoukine 1931: fig. 3; Hafiz, ed. Rahbar 1986: no. 421, pp. 571–572; Hafiz, ed. Khanlari 1996: no. 413, pp. 842–843; Uluç 2000: pl. 146). The manuscript made for Sam Mirza and the commercial copy from Shiraz share the same version of this *ghazal* and both paintings are situated after the same verse. The *bayt* inscribed over both of these paintings describes an angel whose face has become flushed from wine drinking. Its initial *misra*[c] is included in the edition of Rahbar but not that of Khanlari:

The angel of mercy took the cup of reveling,
Put a twist on her locks and rose-water on rose petals.
Welch 1976:69; Hafiz, ed. Rahbar 1986: no. 421, line 5, p. 572; Hafiz, tr. Saberi 2002: no. 413, line 5, p. 488

Of these illustrations, the one in the manuscript of Sam Mirza appears to be the more literal of the two. This painting's uppermost section, situated just below the text panel, shows a group of angels offering each other cups of wine. The face of a drinking angel on the painting's left side is visibly flushed. The lower portion of this painting recalls later lines in this *ghazal* that describe drinking youths and music making, but those components lack the clear literal quality found in its depiction of angels. Welch stresses the manner in which "the romantic passion of Hafiz's mysticism" and his "visionary Sufi spirit" are embodied in this painting, which he feels bridges the divide between "the effects of wine and divine ecstasy." (Welch 1976:20–21).

The Shiraz manuscript, dated to 1581, now Hazine 1014 in the Topkapy Saray Museum, Istanbul, provides a less elevated interpretation of this *ghazal*. L. Uluç has identified its setting as a tavern in a brothel (Uluç 2000:129–131). The painting's foreground shows two

Figure 5. The Allegory of Drunkenness. Hafiz, *Divan*. Herat or Tabriz, ca. 1525. Harvard University Art Museums.

men engaged in a violent confrontation over the attentions of a young woman, an incident not directly alluded to in Hafiz's text, but the painting's upper portion that shows two men conversing, one seated inside the tavern and the other standing in its doorway, may provide a more literal depiction of the *ghazal*'s opening verse:

> The doorway of the Magians' house was swept and washed,
> The Pir sat welcoming the young and the old
> *Hafiz, tr. Saberi 2002: no. 413, pp. 488–489*

In its rendering of a tavern, the painting in the manuscript of Sam Mirza appears to be more literal in its rendition of Hafiz's text than the Bukhara painting but less closely tied to its text than is true of some later paintings from Shiraz or of those found in the manuscript prepared for Jahangir. Other illustrations in Sam Mirza's manuscript demonstrate, however, that their creators paid close attention to the poetry of Hafiz.

The painting in his manuscript most closely linked to Hafiz's text is the delicately executed scene of a princely couple in a spring garden accompanied by attendants and musicians (see fig. 6) that S. C. Welch has entitled "Lovers Picnicking" (Welch 1976:62–63). The painting is carefully balanced in terms of both its composition and the actions of the figures within it. Its focal point is a couple seated on a carpet under a canopy; they look toward each other and touch discreetly. Their left hands are joined and the fingers of the woman's right hand clasp the man's right shoulder; his right hand is extended to grasp a wine cup held by a kneeling attendant. This couple's actions are echoed in the trio of men seated on the left side of the foreground. A youth extends his left hand to take a wine cup from an attendant while at the same time looking at the bearded man seated to his right who both gazes at him and offers him a pomegranate.

This painting is a finely executed example of a well-established type, and the poem in question uses conventional language and symbolism. It describes a springtime garden where amorous pursuits are combined with wine drinking and music. Hafiz compares the cheek of the beloved to roses and tulips, and his/her kisses have the sweetness of sugar (Hafiz, ed. Rahbar 1989: no. 163, pp. 220–221; Hafiz, ed. Khanlari 1996: no. 159, p. 334; Hafiz, tr. Saberi 2002: no. 159, p. 195).

What makes this painting memorable is the harmonious rapport that is established between the image and the text which it illustrates; both are enlivened by a similar rhythm. The hexameter *hazaj*

meter used for this *ghazal* is associated with dances and marches (Hillmann 1971:111–116). This *ghazal*'s rhythmic power is enhanced by its combination of a short, six-foot line and an unusually long rhyme scheme that encompasses six out of eleven syllables in each line's second hemistich. The poem's pulsating rhythm and its rhyme, which serves as a refrain linking each line to the others, is visually embodied in the musicians and dancers in the painting's foreground and echoed in the swaying trees and flying birds of the garden.

The other painting from Sam Mirza's manuscript uses a different technique to reinforce its bonds with Hafiz's text. This scene of royal celebration, often entitled "The Feast of ʿId," and now in the Soudavar Collection, depicts an enthroned prince surrounded by his courtiers. The façade of the building behind him is bordered by four cartouches inscribed with the first and fifth lines from the *ghazal* which it illustrates (Hafiz, ed. Rahbar 1989: no. 246, lines 1 & 5, pp. 333–334; Hafiz, ed. Khanlari 1996: no. 241, lines 1 & 5, pp. 498–499):

> Friends eagerly wait, for it is the time of 'Id and roses,
> Saqi! Behold the refulgent moon in the king's resplendent
>   face and bring wine!
> We have good government and a generous king,
> Oh God, spare him from the evil eye.
> *Soudavar 1992:159; Hafiz, tr. Saberi 2002: no. 241*

The juxtaposition of these non-sequential lines, within the painting, parallels the modification of Hafiz's text in the metalwork inscriptions noted above and was probably intended to enhance the painting's encomiastic role. Since these verses of praise are applied to a royal patron, however, they may also have had the added function of an augury that celebrates and enhances his rule.

The practice of consulting the *Divan* of Hafiz in times of personal crisis was popular not only in Iran but also in other areas where Persian was used as a literary language. The enthusiasm of the Mughal emperor Jahangir for the poetry of Hafiz is documented in his memoirs, where he notes:

> I have had recourse to the *Divan* of Hafiz on many an occasion, and the way things have turned out have usually been in accordance with results he predicts. Rarely has it been otherwise.
> *Jahangir 1999:222*

A Hafiz manuscript now in the Khuda Baksh Library, Patna, contains marginal notations made by the Mughal emperors Humayun and Jahangir when they used it for prognostication (Hafiz, Khuda Baksh Ms. 1992). These nine inscriptions were partially destroyed when

Figure 6. Lovers Entertained in a Garden. Hafiz, *Divan.* Herat or Tabriz, ca. 1525. Private Collection on loan to the Harvard University Art Museums.

the manuscript was rebound but they have been painstakingly reconstructed by Abdul Muqtadir Khan Bahadur, who has also linked those notes to specific events in the emperors' lives ([Khan Bahadur] 1992:7–35). In the case of Humayun, the auguries were taken at times of military crisis and are connected with the need to defend his domain ([Khan Bahadur] 1992:14–15).

The reasons which led Jahangir to have recourse to Hafiz are more varied in character and occurred at intervals over most of his reign. Some of them are seemingly minor problems such as the loss of a diamond amulet during a hunting expedition, but others are linked to major personal and dynastic crises (Ibid.:18–19). One augury encouraged him to visit his dying father, a gesture that secured his right of succession to the Mughal throne, and another was taken to relieve his anguish during a period of separation from his own son Khurram Shah, the future Shah Jahan (Ibid.: 14–15, 25–26).

A manuscript of the *Divan* of Hafiz now in the British Library, Or. 7573, that was copied and illustrated for Jahangir, reveals another side of his attraction to this poet. I. Stchoukine, who published this manuscript, divides its paintings into two groups—three of which depict events from Jahangir's life but have no connection with the text, and five that present "images de saints derviches et de graves docteurs" and illustrate Hafiz's *ghazal*s (Stchoukine 1931:160).

Those scenes containing Jahangir's portrait may well have a more directly personal importance than the remainder of the manuscript's paintings, but given the fact that he was intimately familiar with, and deeply attached to, the *Divan* of Hafiz, there is little doubt that all of the illustrations in Or. 7573 are directly related to the message and content of that text. This small but important manuscript deserves a fuller study than is possible in the context of this essay. Many of its "ordinary" paintings are linked to the theme of wine drinking or intoxication, well known enthusiasms of Jahangir. Scenes which reveal the hypocrisy of religious authorities such as "The Drunken Faqih Issues a Fatwa against Wine Drinking," must have carried a special meaning for him because he was repeatedly reprimanded by the pious for his own consumption of wine (Ibid.: fig. 1).

Both groups of paintings illustrate the intervention of angels in human affairs. One of them shows angels performing the *sama*[c], or ritual dance of the Sufis in harmony with the human participants who fill the painting's foreground (Ibid.: fig. 7). The text over the image reads:

When the Friend begins his *sama*[c]
Angels dance in the Empyrean.
Hafiz, ed. Rahbar 1989: no. 197, lines 6, 8;
Hafiz, ed. Khanlari 1996: no. 192, lines 3, 10;
Hafiz, tr. Saberi 2002: no. 192

The second example to include an angel is one of three in Or. 7573 that contains a portrait likeness of Jahangir (Stchoukine 1931: fig. 3). This painting is linked to a *bayt* from the *ghazal* discussed above that describes the intoxication of angels and is illustrated by "The Allegory of Drunkenness" in the manuscript made for Sam Mirza. The very different painting in Jahangir's manuscript illustrates a *bayt* that praises a certain Shah Nusrat al-din. The line over the painting reads:

The sky pulls the led-horse of Shah Nusrat al-din.
Come see how the angel holds his stirrup.
Hafiz, tr. Saberi 2002: no. 413, line 9, p. 489

The Mughal illustration appears to reflect the wording of Hafiz's text. The emperor on horseback holds a falcon on his wrist and is surrounded by courtiers on foot who have their gaze focused on him. The small angel who rushes in to seize the emperor's stirrup appears to be unnoticed by his attendants. Jahangir's interest in angels, manifested in these paintings, is also evidenced by their prominence in the architectural decoration of his palaces. Jahangir's enthusiasm for angels has been linked by E. Koch with his attraction to Solomonic imagery (Koch 1982:177–178).

The popularity of the *ghazal*s of Hafiz appears to have expanded rapidly in the years following his death and to have spread throughout the area where Persian flourished as a literary language. In contrast to this broad enthusiasm for his poetry, visual renditions of his *ghazal*s are relatively rare but they can still provide insight into the ways in which his poetry was understood in a particular place and at a specific time. Literary scholars have expended considerable energy to establish a critical edition of his *ghazal*s. They have also debated about whether the *ghazal*s of Hafiz are best understood line by line or whether they are constructed around unifying themes and about the degree to which he should be considered a court poet.

This examination of the ways in which specific *ghazal*s by Hafiz were used in metalwork or visualized in paintings suggests that those responsible for their creation were aware of the broad unifying themes that many of his poems contain but it also demonstrates that close attention was paid to the meaning, wording, and sound of specific *bayt*s. The multifaceted character of his text offered considerable programmatic flexibility to anyone who sought to transcribe his verses on objects or to give them a pictorial form. The examples studied here demonstrate that the sequence of *bayt*s in his *ghazal*s was sometimes changed to better suit the needs of a patron or to clarify the intended message of an object or painting. Despite these occasional alterations in line order, most of the *ghazal*s inscribed on metalwork or illustrated in manuscripts produced between the late fifteenth and early seventeenth centuries are included in modern critical editions of Hafiz's poems, a circumstance which suggests that they belong to the earliest preserved stratum of his text. Some of the most widely used compositions appear to have been inspired by specific lines, or even a few words, from a particular *ghazal*.

The widespread belief that Hafiz's poetry provides a bridge between the present and the future, and serves as a link between the visible and invisible realms, may well have inspired its esoteric interpretation in Sufi circles, but probably these same qualities also served to enhance the importance of a more literal understanding of his *ghazal*s. Manuscripts made for, or belonging to, royal patrons demonstrate that they were particularly attracted to the panegyric facet of his verses, a reaction that confirms the importance accorded to this aspect of his poetry in recent scholarly studies.

Illustrated copies of the *ghazal*s of Hafiz are not as numerous as those of more standard narrative texts, but their paintings are also less formulaic. They often appear to be inspired by a close reading of his text and they are normally sited with considerable exactitude. This essay has focused on the place of Hafiz within literary and visual traditions between the fifteenth and early seventeenth centuries in Iran, Central Asia, and India. An examination of his importance for later centuries would no doubt reveal new ways of reading and visualizing his text, even as the contents of his *Divan* continued to evolve.

BIBLIOGRAPHY

Arberry, A. J.
1946 "Orient Pearls at Random Strung," *Bulletin of the School of Oriental and African Studies* 11:699–712.
1962 ed., trans., *Fifty Poems of Hafiz,* 2nd ed., The University Press, Cambridge.

Bashiri, I.
1979a "Hafiz's Shirazi Turk: A Structuralist Point of View," *Muslim World* 69:178–197.
1979b "Hafiz and the Sufic Ghazal," in *Studies in Islam,* 16:34–64.

Bausani, A.
1958 "The Development of Form in Persian Lyrics," *East and West,* ns. 9:145–153.

Browne, E. G.
1956 *A Literary History of Persia: The Tatar Dominion,* vol. III of IV, The University Press, Cambridge.

Burke, A. K.
1992 "The Contribution of Hafiz of Shiraz to Secular Aspects of Humanism," *Indo-Iranica* 45:132–143.

Clarke, H. Wilberforce
1984 "Preface," in *The Divan-i Hafiz,* trans., comm. H. Wilberforce Clarke, 3 vols., Calcutta, 1891, reprinted in 2 vols., Nashr Avaran Journalistic Institute, [Tehran], 1984, I: v–xliv.

Davis, D.
1999 "Sufism and Poetry: A Marriage of Convenience?," in *Edebiyat* 10:279–292.

Dawlatshah S.
[n.d.] *Tazkirat al-Shuʿara,* ed. M. Abbas, Barani, Tehran.

Duchesne-Guillemin, J.
1981 "Pour l'Étude de Hafiz," in *Acta Iranica,* vol. 21, *Monumentum Georg Morgenstierne,* Brill, Leiden, I:141–163.

Farzad, M.
1968 *Jami-i nusakh-i Hafiz,* 9 vols., Pahlavi University, Shiraz.

de Fouchécour, C.-H.
1998 "'The Good Companion' (*Anis al-Nas*): A Manual for the Honest Man in Shiraz in the 9th/15th Century," in *Iran and Iranian Studies,* ed. K. Eslami, Princeton, N.J., Zagras, 42–73.

Gazurgahi, H.
  1997 *Majalis al-ushshaq,* ed. Gh.-R. Tabataba'i Majd, 2nd
        printing, Zarin-Bahar, [n.p.].

Ghani, Q.
  1942 *Tarikh-i 'Asr-i Hafiz,* Zavvar, Tehran.

Hafiz, tr. Clarke, H. W.
  1984 *The Divan-i Hafiz,* trans., comm. H. Wilberforce
        Clarke, 3 vols. Calcutta, 1891, reprinted in 2 vols.,
        Nashr Avaran Journalistic Institute, [Tehran], 1984.

Hafiz, ed. Qazvini, M., and Q. Ghani
  1985 *Divan-i Khvaja-yi Hafiz Shirazi,* 3rd printing, Iqbal,
        Tehran.

Hafiz, ed. Rahbar, Kh.
  1989 *Divan-i Ghazaliyyat,* ed. Kh. Kh. Rahbar, 5th printing,
        Safi Alishah, Tehran.

Hafiz, Khuda Baksh ms.
  1992 *Diwan-e Hafiz: The Royal Mughal Copy,* Khuda
        Baksh Oriental Public Library, Patna, Maktaba Jamia
        Ltd., Delhi.

Hafiz, ed. Khanlari, P. N.
  1996 *Divan-i Hafiz,* ed. ann. P. N. Khanlari, 2nd ed. of
        1362/1984, with the addition of later notes, 2 vols.,
        Nil, Tehran.

Hafiz, tr. Saberi, R.
  2002 *The Divan of Hafez, A Bilingual Text: Persian–English,*
        University Press of America, Lanham, Md.

Hillmann, M.
  1971 "Sound and Sense in a *Ghazal* of Hafiz," in *Muslim
        World,* 61:111–121.
  1974 *Unity in the Ghazals of Hafez,* Biblioteca Islamica,
        Minneapolis.
  1975 "The Text of Hafiz: Addenda," *Journal of the
        American Oriental Society,* 95:719–720.

Horst, van der, K.
  1996 "The Utrecht Psalter: Picturing the Psalms of David,"
        in *The Utrecht Psalter in Medieval Art,* ed. K. van der
        Horst et al., HES Publishers BV, Westrenen, The
        Netherlands, 22–84.

Jahangir
  1999 *The Jahangirnama: Memoirs of Jahangir, Emperor of
        India,* trans. W. M. Thackston, Smithsonian Institution
        and Oxford University Press, Washington, D.C.

Jami, A. al-R.
  1958 *Nafahat al-uns min hadrat al-quds,* ed. M. Tawhid-
        pour, Mahmudi, [Tehran].

Karatay, F. E.
  1961 *Topkapy Sarayy Müzesi Kütüphanesi Farsça Yazmalar
        Kataloğu,* Topkapy Sarayy Müzesi, Istanbul.

Khan Bahadur, A. M.
  1992 ["Comments"] in *Diwan-e Hafiz: The Royal Mughal
        Copy,* Khuda Baksh Oriental Public Library, Patna,
        Maktaba Jamia Ltd., Delhi:7–35.

Koch, E.
  1982 "Jahangir and the Angels: Recently Discovered Wall
        Paintings under European Influence in the Fort of
        Lahore," in *India and the West, Proceedings of a
        Seminar Dedicated to the Memory of Hermann
        Goetz,* ed. J. Deppert, *South Asian Studies*
        15:173–195.

Komaroff, L.
  1992 *The Golden Disk of Heaven: Metalwork of Timurid
        Iran,* Mazda and Biblioteca Persica, Costa Mesa,
        Calif.

Lentz, T. W., & G. D. Lowry
  1989 *Timur and the Princely Vision: Persian Art and Culture
        in the Fifteenth Century,* Los Angeles County Museum
        of Art, Los Angeles.

Lescot, R.
  1945 "Essai d'une chronologie de l'oeuvre de Hafiz,"
        Bulletin D'Etudes Orientales, 9:57–100.

Lowry G. D., & M. C. Beach
  1988 *An Annotated and Illustrated Checklist of the Vever
        Collection,* Sackler Gallery and University of
        Washington Press, Washington, D.C.

Meisami, J. S.
  1987 *Medieval Persian Court Poetry,* Princeton University
        Press, Princeton, N.J.
  1995a "Hafiz in English: Translation and Authority," in
        Edebiyat, ns. 6:55–80.
  1995b "The Body as Garden: Nature and Sexuality in
        Persian Poetry," in *Edebiyat,* ns. 6:245–274.

Melikian-Chirvani, A. S.
  1982 *Islamic Metalwork from the Iranian World: 8th–18th
        Centuries,* Her Majesty's Stationery Office, London.

Rehder, R. M.
  1965 "New Material for the Text of Hafiz," in *Iran,*
        3:109–119.
  1970 "Hafiz: An Introduction," unpublished Ph.D.
        dissertation, Princeton University.
  1974a "The Text of Hafiz," in *Journal of the American
        Oriental Society* 94:145–156.

1974b   "The Unity of the Ghazals of Hafiz," in *Der Islam*
51:55–96.

Richard, F.
1997   *Splendeurs persanes: manuscrits du xiie au xviième
siècle,* Bibliothèque Nationale, Paris.

Ritter, H.
1942   "Philologica XI: Maulana Dalaladdin Rumi und sein
Kreis (Fortsetzung und Schluss)" in *Der Islam,*
26:221–249.
1964   "Hâfiz," in *Islâm Ansiklopedisi,* M. E. Basimevi,
Istanbul 5:65–71.

Roemer, H. R.
1952   tr., *Staatsschreiben der Timuridenzeit,* F. Steiner,
Wiesbaden.

Sami, A.
1971   *Shiraz,* tr. R. N. Sharp & M. A. Cantab, 2nd ed.,
Musavi Printing Office, Shiraz.

Sandler, L. F.
1996   "The Word in the Text and the Image in the Margin:
the Case of the Luttrell Psalter," in *Essays in Honor of
Lilian M. C. Randall, Journal of the Walters Art
Gallery,* 54:87–99.

Soudavar, A.
1992   *Art of the Persian Courts,* Rizzoli, New York.

Schimmel, A.
1979   "Hafiz and his Critics," in *Studies in Islam,* 16:1–33.

Schmitz, B.
1997   *Islamic and Indian Manuscripts and Paintings in The
Pierpont Morgan Library,* The Pierpont Morgan
Library, New York.

Shujaᶜ
1971   *Anis al-Nas,* ed. I. Afshar, Tehran, B.T. N. K., Tehran
University, Tehran.

Soucek, P.
1990   "Sultan Muhammad Tabrizi: Painter at the Safavid
Court," in *Persian Masters: five centuries of painting,*
ed. S. Canby, Marg, Bombay, 55–70.
2002   "Hafiz and the Visual Arts," in *Encyclopaedia Iranica,*
s. v. in press.

Stchoukine, I.
1931   "Quelques images de Jahangir dans un Divan de
Hafiz," in *Gazette des Beaux-Arts,* 6th ser.,
6:160–167.

Uluç, L.
2000   "Arts of the book in sixteenth century Shiraz," 4 vols.
Ph.D. dissertation, New York University, Institute of
Fine Arts.

Welch, S. C.
1976   *Persian Painting: Five Royal Safavid Manuscripts of
the Sixteenth Century,* George Braziller, New York.
1979   *Wonders of the Age: Masterpieces of Early Safavid
Painting, 1501–1576,* Fogg Art Museum, Harvard
University.

Yarshater, E.
1955   *Shiᶜir-i Farsi dar ᶜahd-i Shah Rukh,* Tehran University
Press, Tehran.

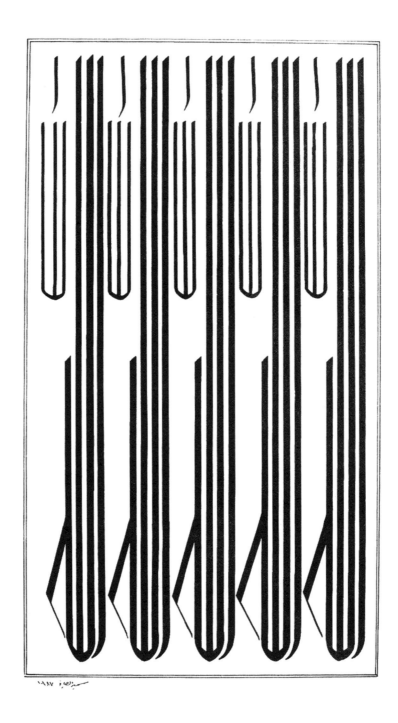

Figure 7. Samīr al-Ṣā'igh (Lebanon), *Composition,* 1987.

Reexploring Islamic art

Modern and contemporary creation in the Arab world and its relation to the artistic past

SILVIA NAEF

Introduction

This article will try to outline how and why "Islamic art" was replaced by Western art between the end of the nineteenth and the beginning of the twentieth century, then rediscovered in the second half of the twentieth century when it became an identity issue in the art production of the Arab world. To avoid confusion, I would like to specify what I mean by "Islamic art." In the last decades, scholarship has rightly criticized this term as too vague and too general to describe a reality extending through fifteen centuries and through an immense and varied geographic area.[1] Here the expression "Islamic art" will be used in the sense many artists in the Arab world have given it (mostly without defining it explicitly), i.e. as meaning the art production of their countries before the strong impact of Western civilization in the nineteenth century. In order to stress this specific meaning, it will be put in quotes.

The Arab Orient, or *Mashriq,* will be taken as a peculiar case of a general evolution which can be observed throughout the Islamic world. Thus, European arts began to influence Ottoman miniature painting as early as the eighteenth century: Western painting had been taught in Istanbul's military schools since the nineteenth century and an Academy of Fine Arts, directed by Osman Hamdi, a disciple of the French Orientalist painter Jean-Léon Gérôme, was opened there in 1883.[2] In Iran, one finds copies of Western paintings made as early as the sixteenth century, and the Western tradition is perceptible in Qajar painting.[3]

The situation in what we now call the Arab world was slightly different from what happened in the capital of the Ottoman Empire or in independent Persia, even if

it is difficult to generalize. The Arab lands were provinces, often lacking the necessary infrastructure for the development of a high standard of art production. The earliest centers of Western-type art production in the Arab East are found in areas such as Egypt and Mount Lebanon, where contact with the West was more developed due to historical reasons that I will not elucidate in this paper.

In the Christian communities of Greater Syria, Western art had an impact as early as the seventeenth century, when icons were painted in an Italianate style;[4] however, this painting did not affect secular art production. In the nineteenth century, when oil portraits became very fashionable in Beirut, the new bourgeoisie liked to be portrayed by Western-trained artists who did not have any ties with the ecclesiastical painters of previous times.[5]

In Egypt, the change in art production came from above. It was, as in other fields, an autocratic change. Although a few young Egyptians were sent from Egypt to Europe as early as 1835–1836 to study drawing, sculpture, and etching,[6] and many Orientalist painters chose Egypt as their place of residence, the date of birth of "modern," i.e. Western-style art (al-fann al-ḥadīth), is generally considered to be May 13, 1908, when the School of Fine Arts (sponsored by Prince Yūsuf Kamāl and directed by the French expatriate Guillaume Laplagne)[7] opened in Cairo.

1. For a discussion of this question, see for instance Oleg Grabar, *The Formation of Islamic Art,* New Haven and London, 1973, pp. 1–18.

2. Cf. Günsel Renda [et al.], *A History of Turkish Painting,* 2nd ed., Geneva, 1988.

3. Cf., for example, two recent catalogues: *Royal Persian Paintings: The Qajar epoch, 1785–1925,* ed. by Layla S. Diba with Maryam Ekhtiar, Brooklyn, 1998, and *Qajar portraits,* catalogue written by Julian Raby, London, 1999.

4. Cf. Bernard Heyberger, "Entre Byzance et Rome: l'image et le sacré au Proche-Orient au XVIIe siècle," in *Histoire, Economie et Société,* 4 (1989), 527–550; Sylvia Agémian, "Ne'meh al-Musawwir, peintre melkite, 1666–1724," *Berytus,* 34 (1991), pp. 189–242 and, by the same author, "Œuvres d'art melkite dans l'Eglise des 40 Martyrs d'Alep," *Etudes Arméniennes,* 1 (1973), pp. 91–113.

5. Cf. John Carswell, "The Lebanese Vision, A History of Painting," in *Lebanon, The Artist's View, 200 Years of Lebanese Painting,* London, 1989, pp. 15–19.

6. Gaston Wiet, *Mohammed Ali et les Beaux-Arts,* Cairo, n.d., p. 409 mentions Ḥasan Wardānī, Muḥammad Murād, and Muḥammad Ismā'īl. After their return to Egypt in the 1830s, Wardānī taught drawing, Murād etching and drawing and Muḥammad Ismā'īl sculpture and drawing (Wiet, p. 409).

7. Very little is known about this sculptor. Bénézit does even not give a birth date.

The adoption of Western art

Before analyzing how and why "Islamic art" became relevant as an element in the art production of the Arab world during a period grossly circumscribed between 1950 and 1990, we have to explain why it first disappeared.

To introduce this question, we will start with a quote from one of the major modernist leaders of the Middle East in the first half of the twentieth century, Mustafa Kemal Atatürk. Though not an Arab, he indirectly influenced many thinkers in the Arab world and his way of thinking is representative of that time. In 1923, the founder of the Turkish Republic declared: "A nation that ignores painting, a nation that ignores statues, and a nation that does not know the laws of positive sciences does not deserve to take its place on the road of progress."[8] Herewith Atatürk clearly formulated what many thought: adopting modern art was a necessary condition to become a "civilized" nation. Adopting it was equivalent to studying the sciences, a compulsory step on the way to progress, a point almost all intellectuals of the East would have subscribed to at that time. Western art symbolized progress, Islamic art did not.

Another point is perceptible only implicitly in Mustafa Kemal's statement: for him, the East at that time ignored painting and, more generally speaking, "art." This idea was very broadly shared, not only in Turkey, but also in the Arab lands. Most painters of the first generation, symptomatically called "pioneers" (ruwwād), were deeply convinced that they came from a surrounding in which not only painting, but art in general, simply did not exist. We shall quote here from the writings of two of the major artists of this generation, the Lebanese Muṣṭafā Farrūkh (1901–1957) and the Egyptian Muḥammad Nāǧī (1888–1956). In his memoirs, Farrūkh reports the astonishment of his teachers at the Royal Academy of Fine Arts in Rome in the 1920s when they discovered that their talented young pupil was a Muslim, a native of a country that was, as Farrūkh himself put it, "devoid of any form of artistic stimulation."[9] Originating from such a desolate environment, Farrūkh interprets his desire to become an artist as resulting from "inspiration" and devoid of any rational explanation since, as he says, until the age of ten, he had seen images only on playing cards.[10] In the same mood, in one of his writings, Muḥammad Nāǧī

expressed his despair about the faculty of the Egyptian fellah to produce art, saying "the Nigger [sic] in Congo and the Aboriginals of the Sundae Islands have more to tell us about this topic."[11] Islamic art had been internalized as a "non-art" by this generation of artists because it did not fit Western conceptions.[12]

If Islamic art did not belong to the category of art, there was another point which particularly touched the Arab East. At the end of the nineteenth century the debate about the congenital capacities of "Aryans" and "Semites," theorized by intellectuals like Ernest Renan,[13] led to the conclusion that the Arabs, as "Semites," had a somehow natural "repulsion" for figuration, i.e. art in the West at the time. Therefore, art pupils first had to prove their physical capacity to produce figurative art in the Western way. The debate arising a few years after the foundation of the School of Fine Arts in Cairo, reported by the French-language periodical L'Egypte contemporaine, is an illustration of this.[14]

The French sculptor Guillaume Laplagne, the first director of the Cairo School of Fine Arts, rejected the idea of a natural incapacity of the Egyptians in producing art, arguing that some of the students he had been teaching for two years had "a real talent" and that what they had been missing until then was adequate teaching. In his eyes, pretending that there were no

8. Quoted in Klaus Kreiser, "Public Monuments in Turkey and Egypt, 1840–1916," Muqarnas 14 (1997), p. 114.

9. Muṣṭafā Farrūkh, Ṭarīqī ilā al-fann, Beirut, 1986, p. 109.

10. Farrūkh, op.cit., p. 31.

11. Mohamed Naghi, Un impressionniste égyptien/Muḥammad Nāǧī, Al-fannán al-ta'thīrī al-miṣrī (French/Arabic), Cairo, 1988, p. 47.

12 This idea was very widespread and resisted for a long time. Thus, the 1960 edition of the Encyclopaedia Britannica, in an entry written by Hermann Goetz, a specialist of India and director of the Baroda Museum and Picture Gallery from 1940 to 1953, stated: "Islamic art is essentially an art of ornament," vol. 12, p. 708. Even Claude Lévi-Strauss during a trip to the Indian subcontinent at the beginning of the 1950s, reported this idea of Islamic art as a "non-art": "Sur le plan esthétique, le puritanisme islamique, renonçant à abolir la sensualité, s'est contenté de la réduire à ses formes mineures: parfums, dentelles, broderies et jardins." In Claude Lévi-Strauss, Tristes tropiques, Paris, Collection Terre Humaine, 1955 (1st ed.), p. 481.

13. Too many of Renan's writings treat this question to be listed here; however, the opening lecture he gave at the Collège de France in 1862 gives a good general overview of his thought: Ernest Renan, "De la part des peuples sémitiques dans l'histoire de la civilisation," in Ernest Renan, Mélanges d'histoire et de voyages, Paris, n.d., pp. 4–25.

14. The idea of modernization through art in the case of Turkey has been studied by Deniz Artun in a DEA-thesis with the title "Politiques de modernisation/Pratiques d'art, Une approche anthropologique des artistes boursiers de l'Etat impérial et républicain de Turquie à l'Académie Julian," Paris, Ecole des Hautes Etudes en Sciences Sociales, 2001; for Lebanon, Kirsten Scheid is preparing a Ph.D. thesis at Princeton on the same theme. Scheid presented a paper on the use of landscapes at the 2001 MESA: "Borrowed Locality: Landscapes Made Lebanese and Lebanon Landscaped," Presentation for MESA, non-circulating, November 20, 2001.

artists in Egypt was like affirming that there were no poets in a country where children could not learn to speak.[15] Max Herz, a Frenchman in charge of the conservation of the monuments of Islamic Cairo, and Aḥmad Zakī, one of the personalities of the local "Renaissance" movement, saw things in a different way. Every nation had a different character, each of them said, and art was the expression of this very character. Therefore, teaching Egyptians European art was a waste of time; it would be more useful to introduce them to the authentic principles of their local arts, to make artisans and not artists out of them.[16]

However, the modernization process proved to be stronger than individual reluctance. "Islamic art" (or, more generally speaking, the traditional art production of the region) would be replaced by Western figurative art.[17] Western academic art produced by local artists became a sign of progress, as a 1932 report about the Cairo Salon, which had become the yearly institutional exhibition, states: the French teacher Morik Brin, secretary general of the "Association des Amis de la Culture Française," spoke of the "progress" made by Egyptians in this field, in a country where "everything had still to be created."[18]

Changes in paradigms

Thus, by the middle of the twentieth century, the major centers in the Arab region had adopted Western forms of art. Academies or schools had been founded all over the region: in Lebanon in 1937 (Académie Libanaise des Beaux-Arts, ALBA), in Iraq in 1941 (Ma'had al-Funūn al-Jamīla; an Academy would follow in 1962), and in Syria in 1959 (Kulliyyat al-Funūn al-Jamīla). Before the foundation of these institutions, scholarships had been granted to young artists who went to study in Europe, mostly France and Italy. These

institutional changes signaled the adoption of the Western way of conceiving art, art production, and teaching.

During the 1940s and 1950s some artists began to question the dominating trends of the time: the prevailing old-fashioned representation of landscapes, genre painting, and still lives. Two occurrences lead to this change: first of all, the new experiences of Western artists since the beginning of the century became better known. These experiences rejected academicism and integrated, among other elements, traditions and forms inspired by the artistic traditions of the Islamic world. Matisse and Klee are the most famous examples. Therefore, local traditions—formerly rejected as "non-art"—recovered the status of art for most actors on the scene.

Another contributing factor was the explosion of nationalisms and the building of new identities after the post-World War II independence of most states in the region. In all cultural fields, this required modernity to be compatible with the cultures of the region. Modernity (ḥadātha) and authenticity (aṣāla) became the two terms of a difficult equation. The concept of "modernity" in itself was also evoked for the first time: whereas in the first half of the century, being modern meant essentially to adopt Western forms and concepts, now a real reflection on this topic started. In opposition to the Western experience, where modernity was perceived as a break with the past, in the Arab world (as in other non-European countries) modernity was, from the beginning, a way of reconquering the past.[19]

I will give here two examples which arose independently from each other. In Egypt, the first challenge to institutionalized academic art came in 1946, when the Group for Modern Art (Jamā'at al-Fann al-Ḥadīth) exhibited in Cairo's Lycée Français. The group included young artists who had studied under the instruction of Ḥusayn Yūsuf Amīn, an art teacher who had lived in Europe and Latin America. 'Abd al-Hādī al-Jazzār (1925–1966) and Ḥāmid Nadā (1924–1990), the two main artists of the group, had a new style and used elements taken from popular arts of the country.[20] The same procedure was adopted, a few years later, by the Baghdad Group for Modern Art (Jamā'at Baghdād li-l-Fann al-Ḥadīth), which exhibited for the first time in

15. Guillaume Laplagne, "Des aptitudes artistiques des Egyptiens d'après les résultats obtenus à l'Ecole des Beaux-Arts," L'Egypte contemporaine, 1 (1910), p. 434.

16. For a more detailed presentation of this debate, see S. Naef, "Peindre pour être moderne? Remarques sur l'adoption de l'art occidental dans l'Orient arabe," in B. Heyberger/S. Naef (eds.), La multiplication des images en pays d'Islam (17e–21e siècles), De l'estampe à la télévision, Istanbul/Beirut, 2002 (forthcoming).

17. Therefore, Louis Massignon had to explain to his Parisian audience, in a conference he gave in 1920, that "art" as such existed in the Islamic world (L. Massignon, "Les méthodes de réalisation artistique des peuples de l'Islam," Syria, 2 (1921), p. 47.

18. Morik Brin, Peintres et sculpteurs de l'Egypte contemporaine, Cairo, 1935, p. 53. The Cairo Salon was created in 1922.

19. For a more detailed discussion, cf. Silvia Naef, A la recherche d'une modernité arabe, L'évolution des arts plastiques en Egypte, au Liban et en Irak, Geneva, 1996, Chapter 4.

20. On Jazzār, see Alain and Christine Roussillon (eds.), Abdel Hadi Al-Gazzar, Une peinture égyptienne/An Egyptian Painter (French/English/Arabic), Cairo, 1990.

Figure 1. Jawād Salīm (Iraq), *Water Melon Eaters,* 1950s.

the Iraqi capital in 1950. Its founder, Jawād Salīm (1919–1961), a knowledgeable man and a polyglot, who had studied art in Italy and England, thought Iraqi art could not earn the international consideration it deserved until it had developed a character of its own. This peculiar character had to reveal itself through the modern art language of the West combined with what he called the "local character" (*al-ṭābi' al-maḥallī*). How should this principle be expressed through art? First, art was, at that time, figurative. Very few painters went into abstraction before the 1960s. Secondly, some of the newly created Arab states were aiming to build a secular or even socialist national identity. Therefore, the religious aspects of the local cultures were put into the background; the heritage of pre-Islamic civilizations, e.g. Pharaonic in Egypt and ancient Mesopotamian in Iraq, were reevaluated.

Jawād Salīm was a painter and a sculptor and the author of the Freedom Monument (*Naṣb al-ḥurriyya*), erected in Baghdad in 1962 to celebrate the fourth anniversary of the Republic. He went back mainly to the folkloric patterns that could be found in carpets, tapestries, ceramics, and tattoos. Another "Islamic" motif was the half-moon he abundantly used as a basic element through which he structured bodies, heads, and palm trees in his compositions. From the tradition of

miniature paintings, he took the black ink pen stroke (fig. 1). In Egypt, Ḥāmid Nadā also borrowed from the popular tradition, in addition to open references to the Pharaonic heritage shown clearly in the painting *The Liberation of the Suez Canal* (1956), fig. 2.

"Islamic art" as such was not yet popular. One could question why, for instance, there was no reference to miniatures. The only example of such a use is found in colonial Algeria, where since the 1920s Muḥammad Rāsim (1896–1975) successfully painted miniatures representing scenes of Ottoman Algiers. And Algeria never had a tradition of miniature painting! Nevertheless, in the early thirties he was the only Arab–Algerian recruited as a teacher to the Academy of Fine Arts in Algiers, which did not otherwise accept Muslims.[21] In Iraq, where the thirteenth-century miniaturist Yaḥyā al-Wāsiṭī was an often-quoted reference for many artists, miniatures were never a viable means of expression. Possibly this was due to the peculiar esthetic concept of this painting genre, probably considered incompatible with modern art.

Subsequently, we can conclude with the following statement: as long as art remained figurative, the reference to "Islamic art" was not a real issue. This was due to technical reasons, but was also because this heritage was not considered compatible with modernity.

The rediscovery of "Islamic art": *Ḥurūfiyya* and calligraphy

In the 1960s, abstraction became a larger trend in the Arab world. The first painters who dedicated themselves to it pursued a Western-inspired abstraction, but found it difficult to be accepted by an audience who had just discovered and started to appreciate figuration.

Since the late 1940s, artists like the two Iraqi expatriates Jamīl Ḥammūdī (b. 1924) and Madīḥa 'Umar tried to exploit in their paintings the esthetics of calligraphy, the major art in the Islamic tradition. In the 1960s, the Lebanese Ethel 'Adnān (b. 1925) began to draw Arabic poems on what she called "Japanese exercise books."

In 1970, another Iraqi, Shākir Ḥasan Āl Sa'īd (b. 1926), who had earlier belonged to the Baghdad Group for Modern Art, issued a manifesto with the title "The One Dimension" (*Al-Bu'd al-Wāḥid*). Āl Sa'īd had explored Sufism and had discovered what he thought to

---

21. Cf. *Mohammed Racim, Miniaturiste algérien,* exhibition catalogue, Paris, Institut du Monde Arabe, 1992.

Figure 2. Ḥāmid Nadā (Egypt), *The Liberation of the Suez Canal,* 1956.

be the essential modernity of Arab script.[22] This could, in his eyes, become *the* form around which Arab artists could build their work. Until then, the manifesto explained, artistic expression had been understood only through the technical aspect. Through the use of the letter, which was form and content at the same time, art would once again become the expression of a philosophical concept, of the artist's attitude toward existence. Together with the arabesque, the calligraphic ornament had been the major form of expression of Arab civilization. Its re-employment in modern art would therefore reconcile the Arab artist with his most important and significant heritage.[23]

Nevertheless, there was no thought of going back to the patterns of "Islamic art." On the contrary, the use of the Arabic script (not of the art of calligraphy) should give to the works a fundamentally contemporary *and* Arab character. The artists using Arab writing considered themselves artists rather than calligraphers, in the modern sense given to this word (in Arabic, *rassām*). They called themselves *ḥurūfī* (and not *khaṭṭāṭ*, the Arabic word for calligrapher). The term plays with the Arabic word *ḥurūf* (letters) but also refers to the adherents of a mystical movement of the Islamic Middle Ages. The recovering of heritage took a double meaning that was both formal and intellectual.

At the same time, as the manifesto already pointed out, the use of Arabic letters in modern abstract works of art was not an Iraqi concern alone, but extended to the Arab world as a whole. In fact, the movement launched by Āl Saʿīd became the only pan-Arab art movement since the beginning of the century. Artists everywhere adopted the *ḥurūfiyya* to express their identity.

What is the relation of *ḥurūfiyya* to Islamic heritage? As previously mentioned, the artists referring to it did not want to go back to the art of calligraphy, but aimed at being painters in the full sense of the word. Therefore, they have to be distinguished from artists like the Paris-based Iraqi Hassan Massoudy or the Tunisian Lassaâd Métoui,[24] who practice what they call a modern form of calligraphy.

---

22. For the work of this artist, cf. *Croisement de signes,* exhibition catalogue, Paris, Institut du Monde Arabe, 1989.

23. For the Arabic text, see Shākir Ḥasan Āl Saʿīd, *Al-Bayyānāt al-Fanniyya f ī l-ʿIrāq,* Baghdad, 1973, pp. 39–40. French translation in Silvia Naef, *L'art de l'écriture arabe, Passé et présent,* Geneva, 1992, pp. 58–59. Another text by the same author has been translated in *Croisement de signes,* op. cit., pp. 55–58.

---

24. Both have published several books, for instance : Hassan Massoudy, *L'ABCdaire de la calligraphie arabe,* Paris, Flammarion, 2002 (with Isabelle Massoudy); *Calligraphie arabe vivante,*

Figure 3. Nja Mahdāwī (Tunisia) with Wolfgang Heuwinkel (Germany), *Composition*, 1991.

Hurūfī can mean different things. The Tunisian Nja Mahdaoui [Najā Mahdāwī] (b. 1937) focuses on form: his purpose is to reproduce the "gesture" of the calligrapher. His paintings are built on shapes that resemble Arabic letters but are not Arabic letters. In a more recent exhibition that he held in Paris in 2000, he started to explore Japanese writing.[25] In spite of its fundamental difference, in the sense that the signs Mahdaoui uses are not letters of the alphabet but mere strokes of the pen, most of his work is close to traditional calligraphy (fig. 3).[26]

Other artists play with the letter and take it simply as a basic form of composition, like the Egyptian Ṣalāḥ Ṭāhir (b. 1912)[27] or the previously mentioned Jamīl

Ḥammūdī, who sees himself as the father of the *ḥurūfiyya*—his first compositions with letters date from the 1940s. With the exception of some early works, most of his production—the bulk of which was painted in the 1970s and 1980s—was basically figurative, with some forms developing into Arabic letters. Sometimes, the presence of letters seems quite forced: the feeling given by the composition is that of a juxtaposition of heterogeneous elements. The relation to the visual tradition of Islamic art is almost completely lost. Ḥammūdī has a thoroughly Western conception of the work of art, in spite of his reference to the miniatures of al-Wāsiṭī[28] (fig. 4). Ḥammūdī sees himself as one of the major exponents of this trend, which was very popular in Arab art production of the 1970s and 1980s—popular to the extent of becoming inflationary, or, as the Algerian painter and art critic Muḥammad Khadda remarked, an easy recipe and fashionable on both sides

republished in 1999 (1st ed. 1981). On Massoudy: Jean-Pierre Sicre, *Hassan Massoudy, Le chemin d'un calligraphe,* Paris, 2001 (1st ed. 1991). Lassaâd Métoui, *Danse avec le vent, Calligraphie arabe contemporaine,* Paris, 2001; *L'atelier du calligraphe,* Paris, 2000; *Calligraphie arabe: dans le sillon du calame,* Paris, 1998, with a preface by the former minister of culture Jack Lang. Their calligraphies illustrate many books on poetry and other subjects published in France.

25. In an exhibition held at Comptoir des Ecritures from November 4, 1999 to January 8, 2000.

26. On Mahdaoui, cf. *Nja Mahdaoui* (French/Arabic), Tunis, 1983.

27. Cf. Sobhi El-Charuni, *Salah Tahir,* Cairo, 1985.

28. It was after he happened to see the work of Yaḥyā al-Wāsiṭī while reading a French magazine in Paris that Hammūdī had the idea to use letters in his paintings: André Parinaud, *Jamil Hamoudi,* Paris, 1987, p. 6.

of the Mediterranean: easy, but including a danger, the danger of exoticizing Arab painting.[29]

In other words, *ḥurūfiyya* could be defined as the use of forms inspired by Arab letters and employed in order to "arabize" painting. It has to be distinguished from the revival of calligraphy initiated in recent years by the IRCICA, the Istanbul-based Research Center for Islamic History, Art and Culture, founded in 1976 as a "subsidiary organ" of the Organization of the Islamic Conference. The center aims at the research and organization of activities on the "Islamic legacy," as well as the establishment of "training courses to promote skills and techniques relevant in the fields of Islamic arts and culture."[30] The IRCICA organizes exhibitions and courses in calligraphy[31] as well as international calligraphy contests. The first of these contests was held in 1986, the fifth in 2001.[32] Prizes ranged in 2001 from $2500 to $150 (a book about calligraphy). Participants came from all over the world, as an article claimed,[33] but most of them belonged to countries of the Islamic world, as the list of prizes by nationalities shows.

The IRCICA sponsors traditional styles and has an agenda that focuses on conservation rather than innovation, as the categories—one for each of the most important classical styles—in the calligraphy contest show.[34] Modern calligraphers like Hassan Massoudy are looked at with suspicion: the director of IRCICA, Ekmeleddin Ihsanoğlu, says Massoudy's work is not art.[35]

Figure 4. Jamīl Ḥammūdī (Iraq), *Gilgamesh/Ishtar*, 1971.

Figure 5. Ḥusayn Māḍī (Lebanon), *The letter 'ayn*, 1973.

29. Mohammed Khadda, "Calligraphie et modernité," in *Nouveaux enjeux culturels au Maghreb* (Annuaire de l'Afrique du Nord 1984), Paris, 1986, p. 135.

30. http://www.oic-oci.org/english/main/ircica.htm.

31. Cf. for instance *Bulletin d'information de l'IRCICA*, 53 (December 2000), "Présentation de diplômes en calligraphie," pp. 40–41.

32. "Le cinquième concours international de calligraphie au nom du calligraphe égyptien Sayyed Ibrahim et le prix de l'IRCICA pour la distinction dans la calligraphie," *Bulletin d'information de l'IRCICA*, 54 (April 2001), p. 22. The IRCICA also publishes catalogues reproducing the winner plates (1987, 1993, 1995, 1997).

33. "Le jury a noté que des œuvres avaient été reçues de certains pays où cet art venait de commencer à se développer, et décidé d'exprimer [sic] son encouragement aux artistes de ces pays, recommandant que des prix d'encouragement soient accordés aux auteurs de certaines bonnes œuvres reçues de Corée, du Japon, de la Thailande et en particulier de la Chine, d'où cinq calligraphes ont participé . . ." Ibid., p. 23.

34. The categories are: *jali thuluth, thuluth, naskh, jali talik, ta'lik, jali divani, divani, koufi, muhaqqaq, reyhani, ijaza, riqaa, magrebi, khurde ta'lik*. Ibid., pp. 27–31. I use the spelling adopted in this publication.

35. Quoted in Paul Amman, Roger Canali, and Thomas Widmer, *Meisterschreiber, Zeitgenössische arabische Kalligraphie und ihre Künstler*, Berne, 1998, p. 97.

Seeking the "spirit" of "Islamic art"

A few artists tried to go back to what they considered to be the "spirit," or the essence of "Islamic art." For them, the mere reproduction or quotation of forms borrowed from Islamic heritage was not satisfactory. They wanted to give back the basic concept of Islamic art in a modern shape, compatible with our age. This

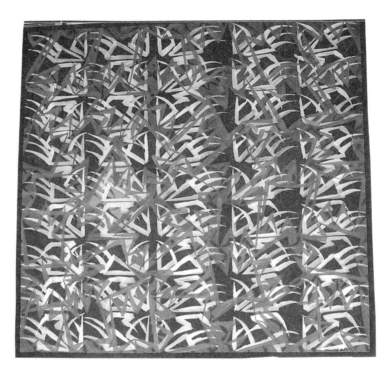

Figure 6. Ḥusayn Māḍī (Lebanon), *Composition,* 1997.

was the case with Ḥusayn Māḍī and Samīr al-Ṣāigh, both Lebanese.

Ḥusayn Māḍī (b. 1938), who lived in Italy for many years, started to paint shapes of birds or women in a continuous repetition, like arabesques. In 1973 he created a series of etchings called Arab alphabet, in which he drew the twenty-eight letters (plus the word *Allah* and the combination *lām alif*). In this work, his reference to the concept of "Islamic art" was strong: the letter was embedded in an inner circle, then surrounded by others (fig. 5). Māḍī sees himself as a modern artist trying to revive, in a form more suitable to our age, what he considers to be the intrinsic force of "Islamic art" (fig. 6).

Samīr al-Ṣāigh (b. 1945) aimed at going back to the esthetic understanding of Islamic art by trying to seize its peculiar ways of expression. In his critiques of the attempts to create an Arab modernity by going back to the past, to the "heritage," al-Ṣāigh noted that the disappointment generally prompted by this type of work comes from a superficial understanding of Islamic art. This disappointment, he said:

> originates from a limited and superficial understanding, in which heritage has been read through disconnected esthetical pieces and factors. The works which sought

inspiration from the Arabic script, or from icons and miniatures or the ones which came back to ancient civilizations, stopped at the formal aspects of these vestiges and creations and forgot or ignored the esthetical point of view, as well as the comprehensive artistic view they conceal. [. . .] The esthetical or artistic value of the letters in calligraphy exists only with its proper logic which derives from a comprehensive Arab view of the world and of art.[36]

Samīr al-Ṣāigh also was one of the advocates of a modernity not only rooted in the Western tradition, and of an art independent of Western concepts. Indeed, in 1992, when the concept of plural modernities was not as current as today, he rejected the capability of the West to be the only source capable of defining the criteria of modernity[37] (fig. 7).

As we said in the beginning, this article concentrates mainly on the Arab world; however, parallel experiences, developing at about the same period, can be found elsewhere reflecting what we think to be not specifically an "Islamic" trend, but rather part of a

---

36. Samīr al-Ṣā'igh, "Thamānīnāt al-fann al-lubnānī wa-l-as'ila al-ṣa'ba," *Funūn 'Arabiyya* 1 (1981), p. 52.

37. Samīr al-Ṣā'igh, "Al-ḥadātha āb khā'in," *Al-Mulḥaq,* no. 10, 16 May 1992, p. 10.

Figure 8. Nadīm Karam (Lebanon), *The Archaic Procession*, downtown Beirut, 1997. These shapes accompanied the reconstruction of downtown Beirut and moved from one spot to the other.

global "back to the roots" movement.[38] In Iran, for instance, the "Saqqakhaneh" group of artists, who became famous in the 1960s, used talismans, script, and other items taken from folk art.[39] Hossein Zenderoudi (b. 1937) and Mohammad Ehsai (b. 1939) made calligraphic compositions in the 1960s and 1970s. Even in Turkey, where the reform of 1928 had reduced the Arab alphabet to a mere relic of the past and where Atatürk ordered the closing down of several calligraphy schools,[40] Erol Akyavaş (1932–1999) introduced the Arabic script among other references to Islamic art. Like Ḥusayn Māḍī and Samīr al-Ṣāigh, Akyavaş's reference to Islam as a cultural tradition was very strong. He made a series of lithographs inspired by the *Mirājnāmeh* (*Miracname*), which was a big success when it was exhibited in Ankara in 1987. Akyavaş considered his painting to be religious, breaking with the Sunni tradition of non-representation.[41]

Islamic references in contemporary art since 1990

With the beginning of the 1990s, new media such as video and installations appeared. At the same time direct reference to "Islamic art" as a means of cultural affirmation diminished. This had less to do with the new media than with a change in priorities. Younger artists were less interested in identity questions. Even if some artists now strongly refer to "Islam" and incorporate cultural symbols taken from the heritage, they do not use them to express a concern with a national character or to show a national specificity, but rather to report the daily reality of life in countries where culture is permeated by "Islamic" elements. Art has become a particular, individual experience in a given context. Artists today express their reality, their life in an Islamic society—whatever this might mean—as a reflection on self within this society (figs. 8 and 9a & b).

To conclude, we could say that the specific references to Islamic art in the Arab world coincided with a precise period. To relate it to some historical references, we could say that this period was between 1967 (June War) and 1991 (Gulf War). It was a time of the radicalization of nationalism after the Arab defeat in the Six-Days-War. Artists, like other intellectuals, pleaded for stronger ties with tradition, with "Arab" culture, and

38. On contemporary art in the Islamic world, cf. Wijdan Ali, *Modern Islamic Art: Development and Continuity,* Gainesville, 1997, as well as *Contemporary Art from the Islamic World,* ed. by Wijdan Ali, London, 1989.

39. Rose Issa, "Borrowed Ware," in *Iranian Contemporary Art,* exhibition catalogue, Barbican Centre, London, 2001, pp. 17–19.

40. *Die Meisterschreiber,* op. cit., p. 14.

41. Erol Akyavaş *His Life and Works,* Istanbul, 2000, p. 150.

Figure 9a & b. Aḥmad ʻAskalānī (Egypt), *Men in Prayer,* installation, Townhouse Gallery, Cairo, April 2002.

for less influence by Western trends as a form of resistance.[42] In the 1980s, with the strengthening of religious pressure, even a secular sector like art could not escape from such an influence, and "Arabness" in art became nearly an obligation.[43] The 1991 Gulf crisis marked the end of this sort of nationalism. Globalization on the one hand and the new interest in art from outside the West on the other hand also concurred in orienting artistic production in the Arab world in another direction.

If contemporary art has abandoned its concern for the Islamic heritage, then what about the "rebirth" of calligraphy: is it not a lively tradition, as the success of Massoudy or Métoui in France[44] and the participation in the IRCICA contests show? In my opinion, these are only epiphenomena, the signs of the "reinvention" of a tradition that has already disappeared rather than proof of its renaissance. In 1995, the Paris-based Iraqi

calligrapher Mohammed Saïd Saggar noticed that since the introduction of printing, calligraphy had lost its vitality and was "ossified" in formal research and creativity.[45] And this is probably the status of Islamic art today: the specific contexts that produced it have disappeared, and it cannot survive in its traditional form. However, elements inspired by it will regularly appear as an expression of a cultural belonging, but through genres which are not in themselves "Islamic." Anything else is little more than folklore.

---

45. Mohammed Saïd Saggar, "Introduction à l'étude de l'évolution de la calligraphie arabe," in G. Beaugé & J. F. Clément (eds.), *L'image dans le monde arabe,* Paris, 1995, p. 106.

---

42. See the manifesto "Naḥwā al-ruʼya al-jadīda," issued by a group of Iraqi artists in 1969. Arabic text in Shākir Ḥasan Āl Saʼīd, *Al-Bayyānāt al-Fanniyya . . . ,* op. cit., pp. 31–35. French translation in Silvia Naef, *A la recherche . . . ,* op. cit., pp. 375–380.

43. For an overview of art in this period, cf. Abdelkébir Khatibi, *L'art contemporain arabe, Prolégomènes,* Paris/Rabat, 2001.

44. Their calligraphy is reproduced on postcards and sold in souvenir shops near the Centre Pompidou in Paris.

Beyond Islamic roots—beyond Modernism

FERESHTEH DAFTARI

Islamic art has long affected Western art and continues to do so today. Its impact on European modern artists has been widely recognized; Henri Matisse, Paul Klee, and Wassily Kandinsky are prime examples of artists for whom the creators of miniatures, calligraphy, ceramics, carpets, and metalwork were historical accomplices, giving them the confidence to break new ground in their iconographies and styles and helping them along in their spiritual and aesthetic choices.[1] Today, a new phenomenon is becoming apparent: many artists who draw on Islamic art actually originate in its lands but now are rooted in the West. These artists are extending the Islamic vocabulary beyond its original framework, developing new narratives that reconfigure and subvert the original idioms. At the same time, they also defy the assumptions of modernism. A complex interaction is at work, then: the platform from which artists such as Ghada Amer, Shahzia Sikander, and Shirazeh Houshiary operate involves a deviance from both the Islamic and the modernist canons. Refusing to "represent" their cultures in a Western framework, these artists also shun homogenization into a purely Western aesthetic language. They speak in a multivocal polyphony marked with a mixture of accents. Elusive or transparent, the Islamic references are retained only to be superseded or altered, sometimes unrecognizably. Importantly, gender, when addressed, creates a space of observation equally unsparing to those Islamic cultures with a narrow vision of women, as to the myopic Western perception of the veil, for instance, as well as to modernism's own sins of female exclusion. Two of the three artists considered in this study resist stereotypes fabricated in any corner of the world, and Houshiary, the third artist, steps above gender and other divisive concepts altogether toward what binds and consolidates our common humanity. To expand our sense of the meaning of their work we must examine both the places where these artists are anchored and where they break loose and wander free.

Ghada Amer

Ghada Amer's best-known works have the least apparent connection to any Islamic tradition: they are stitched and embroidered canvases that appear from a distance as drip paintings recalling Abstract Expressionism, but that invite a double reading, revealing images of female auto-eroticism when viewed at closer range (fig. 1). Amer can easily be situated with a group of artists who dismantle such modernist idioms as Abstract Expressionism and Minimalism—Janine Antoni and Sue Williams, for example. Yet to understand the extent of her audacity and the range of her references one needs to look not only within Western parameters but outside them as well.

Amer left Cairo for France when she was eleven. Her first experience of her difference concerned her appearance: desperate to fit, she has explained "I did everything to look like the others."[2] More importantly, what started her on her path as a "seamstress" artist, adopting the needle instead of a brush, were the Egyptian fashion magazines in which imported Western models were altered and Islamicized. A head scarf added here, a hem line elongated there, or a décolleté covered—changes like these transformed the European prototypes into Islam-approved models. Amer's early bifocal attention, in reality a measure of cultural distance, persists in her work to this day. Its beginnings may be sought in a series of actions she staged in Paris with an artist friend, Ladan Naderi: donning the veil, the two women surfaced in a variety of situations, attending art openings and having themselves photographed in front of iconic monuments such as the Eiffel Tower. In 1992, these photographs were exhibited as a series entitled "I Love Paris" at the city's Hôpital Ephémère.

I would like to extend my gratitude to Ghada Amer, Shahzia Sikander, and Shirazeh Houshiary for sharing their thoughts and precious studio time with me. I am equally thankful to their galleries: Deitch Projects and Brent Sikkema in New York, Lisson Gallery in London. I am especially grateful to Elly Ketsea at the Lisson Gallery. Finally my heartfelt thanks go to David Frankel who is a superb editor and a great friend.

1. On the affinities between Islamic art and modernism, see Markus Brüderlin, ed., *Ornament and Abstraction: The Dialogue between Non-Western, Modern and Contemporary Art* (Riehen-Basel: Fondation Beyeler and Cologne: Du Mont, 2001). On the influence of Islamic art in the West, and, more specifically, on the connections among Paul Gauguin, Henri Matisse, Wassily Kandinsky, and "Persian" art, see Fereshteh Daftari, *The Influence of Persian Art on Gauguin, Matisse, and Kandinsky* (New York and London: Garland Publishing, 1991).

2. Ghada Amer, quoted in an interview with Xavier Franceschi, in *Ghada Amer* (Brétigny-sur-Orge: Espace Jules Verne, 1994), n.p.

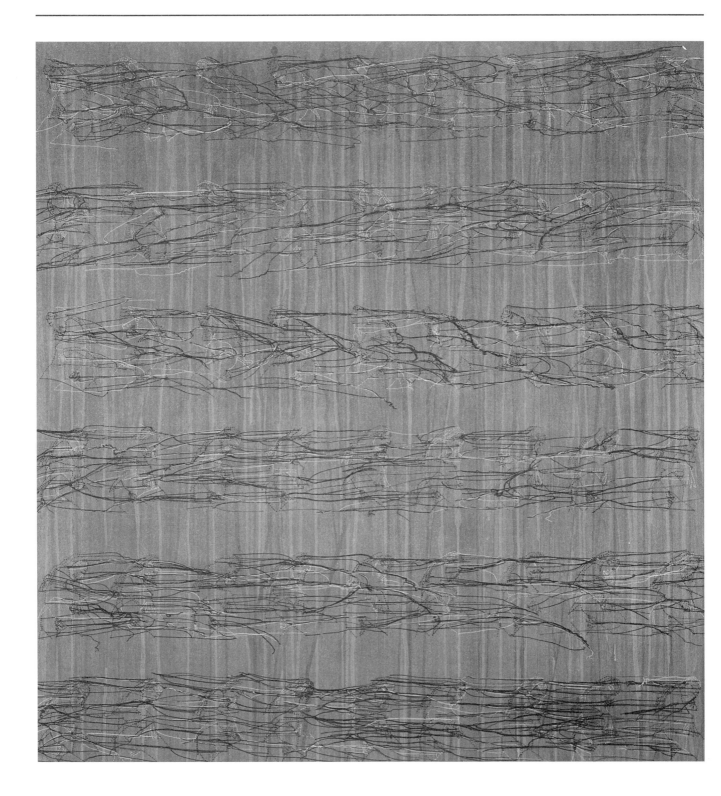

Figure 1. Ghada Amer, *The Sad Painting/Diane,* 2001. Acrylic, embroidery, and gel medium on canvas (52 x 50"). Courtesy of the artist and Deitch Projects, New York.

Figure 2. Ghada Amer, *Majnun,* 1995–1997. Embroidery on seven plastic storage closets. Each closet: 64 x 69 ″. Courtesy of FNAC & Fonds Régional d'Art Contemporain, Provence-Alpes-Côte d'Azur.

There was a guest book in which viewers could record their reactions, which were overwhelmingly negative. This gave the exhibition a conclusive point: "Muslim women were not the subject of the message," asserts the artist, "the perception of them was."[3]

It was around this time that Amer turned her attention to the written or, rather, embroidered text. She at first chose a crude, coarse, rough execution and banal material—recipes, beauty tips lifted from magazines like *Marie Claire* and *Madame,* a straightforward definition of love drawn from the Petit Robert dictionary, all stitched in shaggy capital letters. The mundanity of these texts, and of course the Roman alphabet, distanced her from the aestheticized art of Islamic calligraphy, and especially from its historical splendor when applied in the service of religion.[4] Amer's works are the antithesis to the meticulously cared-for calligraphic page. She used heavyhanded stitching and let the loose threads dangle,

evoking the allover drips of Abstract Expressionism and also, perhaps, the reverse side of a highly finished sartorial item. Neither a forum for patriarchal voices nor an arena for the usually male gestural expression of modernist abstraction, the territory Amer marks out in her work is that of an average female with modest interests. She approaches her material with the intention to elevate the disparaged and the feminine.

Beginning in 1995 Amer switched to Arabic texts. Except in a work in which the Arabic word for "fear" is embroidered on a *borqa,* the cloth garment that separates a Muslim woman's face from the world, she draws her texts from French translations of Arabic, not from the original Arabic. Translation necessarily involves a foreign, intermediary gaze into a culture, and this is a powerful element in Amer's experience; as a young Egyptian living abroad, first in France and then the United States, she has constantly had to reformulate and revise her idea of her origin, first to herself, then rephrasing it to others.

Majnun (1995–1997; fig. 2) is Amer's first venture into the use of literary sources. The tale on which it is based, *Layla and Majnun,* is "perhaps the most popular

3. Interview with author, April 2001.

4. On this subject see, e.g., Priscilla P. Soucek, "The Arts of Calligraphy," in Basil Gray, ed., *The Arts of the Book in Central Asia: 14th–16th Centuries* (Boulder, Colo.: Shambhala; Paris, France: UNESCO, 1979), pp. 7–34.

romance in the Islamic world,"[5] a passionate, tragic story of doomed and unrequited love that predates Shakespeare's *Romeo and Juliet,* to which it is often compared, and has inspired many Arab, Persian, and Turkish authors. Rather than following an erudite edition of the text, Amer has based her version on a French translation of short, digestible excerpts by an unnamed author.[6] We are still in the domain of sentimental interest recognizable to the reader of *Marie Claire.* The selections she quotes—Majnun's effusions of desire and longing for death—deliver florid medieval poetry, but she detaches them both from the venerated art of calligraphy and from traditional representations, in the numerous miniatures where the emaciated Majnun, estranged from society, roams the wilderness in the company of wild animals. In Amer's version the words are embroidered in capital letters on seven storage boxes, sites of suspended, tucked-away life that recall another kind of exile, a modern state of homelessness and deracination. Amer also asserts the rupture with the past in another way: she lodges the lyrical excesses of the Oriental Majnun within a Western modernist vocabulary, for the shapes of the storage boxes evoke the geometries of Minimalism. Anachronistically applied to white cubes, the verbiage violates and contaminates the exigencies of pure abstraction. A rebel within her culture, an intruder into another, Amer perverts all traditions, affirming her unattached alien condition.

The next text Amer approached was the Koran. Still using a French translation, she carefully searched for suras in any way relating to women. If, in *Majnun,* Layla remains absent except through Majnun's emotions, in the Koran a woman's whole existence is constructed, ruled, regulated, and defined from above. By following the representation of women through these literary and sacred prisms, Amer pursued her interest in the way gender is pieced together.

Having examined the sacred Amer moved on to the profane. Scanning love in both the Western and the Arab worlds, she has studied all shades of the spectrum from the carnal to the chaste, from Hollywood to Cairo, from pornography to serious erotic taxonomy. Her first works on this subject, a genre she continues to this day, were those involving the image of a self-stimulating

female nude (fig. 1). Then, in an installation from 1999 entitled *Love Park,* she switched to the textual counterpart of sexual explicitness, inscribing on signposts quotations from the sixteenth-century text *The Perfumed Garden,* by Shaykh Nefzawi.[7] A more recent installation, from 2001, takes its title from an Arabic text called *Jawami al-ladhdha,* or *The Encyclopaedia of Pleasure* (fig. 3). The text is now little known, but such literature was once in no way clandestine; erotic literature has enjoyed great popularity in the Arab world, and the earliest extant treatise dates back to the ninth century.[8] The text Amer had used earlier, Shaykh Nefzawi's *The Perfumed Garden,* is itself just such a treatise and begins, "Praise be given to God, who has placed man's greatest pleasure in the natural parts of woman, and has destined the natural parts of man to afford the greatest enjoyment to woman." To defer to God, or bow to established authority, and then move on to sex is a strategy that is not unfamiliar to Amer, as we shall see.

The *Jawami al-ladhdha,* written by Abul Hasan Ali Ibn al Katib, has never been published in English, only translated for a thesis by Salah addin Khawwam in Aleppo, in 1974.[9] As she did with *Majnun,* in *The Encyclopaedia of Pleasure* Amer has inscribed the text on white cubes, once again asserting a link with Minimalism but also conjuring piled-up storage boxes and evoking an atmosphere of deferred settlement or nomadism. The text's many subjects range from pederasty to jealousy, from aphrodisiacs to remedies for impotence; Amer has woven those sections that speak of women, writing in golden thread and in capital letters. From a chapter concerned with female sexuality at various ages, for example, she chooses a passage regarding a man's desire to buy a bondmaid he wishes was over twenty. The bondmaid hearing the remark answered:

> Didn't you hear the following verses:
> Pleasurable girls range from ten
> To twenty and lo! Not above twenty,
> If you want to have a girl above twenty,
> Go up only a little bit higher,

5. See Peter J. Chelkowsky's "Commentary" on "Layla and Majnun" in *Mirror of the Invisible World: Tales from the Khamseh of Nizami* (New York: The Metropolitan Museum of Art, 1975), p. 66.

6. André Miquel. *Majnûn, L'amour poème* (Paris: Sindbad [La bibliothèque arabe], 1984).

7. See Shaykh Nefzawi, *The Perfumed Garden,* trans. Sir Richard F. Burton (New York: Castle Books, 1964). Amer titled the series of signposts *Love Park* and exhibited them in SITE Santa Fe.

8. For a brief history of this subject see Abdelwahab Bouhdiba, *Sexuality in Islam,* trans. Alan Sheridan (London, Boston, Melbourne and Henley: Routledge & Kegan Paul, 1985).

9. Amer came into possession of the manuscript through a photocopy sent to her by her sister, a professor of medieval French literature.

Figure 3. Ghada Amer, *The Encyclopaedia of Pleasure,* 2001. Fifty-four cardboard boxes, embroidery on canvas. Dimensions varied. Courtesy of the artist and Deitch Projects; photograph by Tom Powel Imaging.

But avoid a forty year old woman for she is a misfortune.
Verily, it is tiring to have
Lasting company with women.[10]

Other chapters Amer copies carry titles such as "On the praiseworthy aesthetic qualities of women," "On women's desire for coition," and "On the advantages of a nonvirgin over a virgin."

The explicitness of some of these texts parallels that of Amer's masturbating nudes, which she culled from Western pornographic magazines. Serially repeated, and thereby suggesting mechanical manufacture, Amer's nudes desecrate the idea of the individual implicit in the Abstract Expressionist art that these works visually echo. Her texts, too, are mechanically reproduced; honor the lewd in a golden script; and transgress the grand aspirations of calligraphy, its range of styles, and cult of

beauty. Produced by a team of assistants in Cairo and New York the *Encyclopaedia* testifies to a range of broken traditions both Eastern and Western.

Amer interferes in the visual language of the West and in the calligraphic traditions of Islamic cultures. Armed with minimalist regimentation and predictable repetition she disrupts the gesturally free art of Abstract Expressionism. The minimalist tool itself is dismantled by the use of its nemesis, the figuration of the body. Amer pursues a similar strategy with her texts. Debased into printed scripts, shaggily or mechanically executed, they commit the pleasures of the body to the print, and deflate the aesthetic pretensions of calligraphy.

Amer, however, strikes her blows from within the cocoon of tradition. Just as she maintains the appearance of Abstract Expressionism or Minimalism while eroding their tenets from inside, she engages in embroidery without espousing its innocence, and invokes the canon of calligraphy while narrating what remains unspeakable and what calligraphers would find unwritable. Subversion escalates in her work from the aesthetic to the cultural. Operating within the

10. Abul Hasan 'Ali Ibn al-Katib, *The Encyclopaedia of Pleasure,* Salah addin Khawwam, ed. Adnan Jarkas and Salah addin Khawwam, transls. (Toronto, Ontario: Aleppo Publishing, 1977), p. 214. Photocopy of this manuscript given to the author courtesy of Ghada Amer.

boundaries of a variety of different traditions, Amer ultimately exerts a simultaneous attachment to and distance from them.

Shahzia Sikander

Shahzia Sikander, like Amer, is detached from local parochialism, wherever in the world it occurs. She lets herself blend with traditions and in doing so perverts them, erasing their boundaries and affirming the undesirability of hierarchies, limits, and polarized separations. Sikander, who now lives in New York, was born in Lahore, Pakistan, where she obtained a B.F.A. in studying the art of the miniature. At the time this pictorial language was considered moribund and survived degenerately as kitsch. It was an anomaly in Pakistan and irrelevant to any modernist discourse. With Sikander, though, miniature painting attains a new, global status. Manipulated, its codes transgressed, it is resuscitated not to survive in isolation but to befriend, contaminate, and challenge the course of another tradition: the art of the West. Whether retaining its traditionally intimate format and paper support or enlarged to mural scale, intermixed with photographs, or even digitized, it always remains detectable as miniature painting even though it is never uniquely of Islamic origin.

From the vast pool of miniature styles available to her, Sikander scans idioms from the Hindu to the Muslim, from India to Iran. She has studied India's indigenous Rajput painting, dominated by subjects from Hindu myth, and also its Mughal painting, Islamic in origin, more concerned with temporal and historical events, and more naturalistic in style. Beyond India, she has looked at the Safavids in Iran—contemporaries of the Mughals and of paramount importance to the development of Mughal art in the sixteenth century. The Mughal ruler Humayun took refuge at the court of his cousin, Shah Tahmasp, in Tabriz, and when he returned to India he took with him two of Persia's finest artists. Tabriz was also a training school for Humayun's successor, Akbar, who in the 1580s moved his capital from Kabul to Lahore.

Sikander's *Mirrat I* (1991–1992; fig. 4) is among her early attempts to graft disparate idioms. Kangra miniature painting, in itself a cross-fertilized hybrid of Hindu mythology and Mughal naturalism, provided the perfect source for her early interest in disclaiming homogeneity. In this work Sikander addresses the themes of romantic love, revolving around Krishna, that characterize Kangra painting, but she omits the divine,

Figure 4. Shahzia Sikander, *Mirrat I,* 1991–1992. Vegetable color, dry pigment, watercolor, gold leaf, and tea on hand-prepared paper, 11 x 8″. Courtesy of the artist.

except indirectly in the depiction of peacocks, the traditional companions of the love god.[11] Executed in Lahore, where according to the artist Muslim Mughal paintings were available but Hindu Kangra paintings were not,[12] Sikander takes the Hindu myth and turns it into a contemporary reality: the protagonist was a friend of hers, the Mughal architecture a fort in her native Lahore. The frame, a purely ornamental matter, remains traditional. The work accordingly oscillates among aesthetic systems: the perspectival structure is Western, the framing border is Arabesque, the portraiture is contemporary and realistic, the convention of repetition—

---

11. See M. S. Randhawa, *Kangra Paintings on Love* (New Delhi: National Museum, 1962).

12. Interview with the author.

the simultaneous representation of separate moments within a narrative—is Hindu. In the process of making these combinations Sikander fuses the anticipation of love as experienced by her friend in real life with its nostalgic representation in Hindu art. These mixed codes belie Western realism just as they defy the traditional spirit of miniature painting, which is rarely an index of mundane realities but lies somewhat closer to fairy tales,[13] even when it attempts to capture the shadows and gravity of the real world. Even at this early juncture in her artistic career, Sikander was conceptually distancing herself from her craft, creating a kind of parody of the miniature.[14]

At this stage, however, craft still superseded concept, and Sikander maintained a traditional meticulousness of execution throughout the picture. Later, when she moved to the United States, this unified treatment broke down, perhaps an indication of Sikander's refusal to be typecast as a predictable exotic entity. The new vision might have been fueled by personal experience related to her ethnicity. Studying for her M.F.A. at the Rhode Island School of Design in 1993–1995, she was confronted for the first time with a perception of herself that confined her within a framework: the "Muslim woman." It was at RISD that she wore the veil for the first time, in a performance not unlike Amer's, and watched people's reactions. The performance was ephemeral but the notion of the veil has persisted in her work, both literally and conceptually.

It first appears in *Separate Working Things II* (1993–1995; fig. 5), a miniature that Sikander executed with precision and high finish only to violate it with a loose, unrefined vocabulary, an almost graffiti-like mode of mark making so that a detailed realism vies for attention with an abstract voiceover. The generic landscape is defaced with transparent, ghostlike creatures, some Indian and recognizable (one figure silhouetted against the architecture faintly echoes the portraits of Shah Jahan), some fictional, or purely abstract. A number of these, a clustered composite of human and animal forms, have taken refuge under what appears to be an intimation of the veil—not a dark, ominous shroud, and not opaque but shredded into flowing white strings. Another figure on the periphery wears a veil as a windswept wedding crown. This

Figure 5. Shahzia Sikander, *Separate Working Things II*, 1993–1995. Vegetable color, dry pigment, watercolor, tea on hand-prepared "wasli" paper, 10 x 7". Whereabouts unknown.

transparent all-over layering, reminiscent of the work of Sigmar Polke, supports an iconography also centered on levels of opacity and transparency, in other words on the concealing and revealing properties of the veil.

It is in a light note that Sikander introduces the veil. She does not dwell on it. The picture is mostly about a certain kind of tension, the contrapuntal relation of differing modes of expression. But Sikander does not lose sight of the veil. In other works such as *Who's Veiled Anyway* (1994–1997) she throws it on a polo player, a familiar character in Persian miniatures.[15] In

13. It is not surprising that Shahzia Sikander would eventually turn for her themes to Western fairy tales such as the story of Red Riding Hood.

14. Zahoor-ul-Ikhlaq is another conceptual painter from Pakistan who, like Sikander, has deconstructed traditional miniatures.

15. For illustration, see Shahzia Sikander (Chicago: The Renaissance Society at the University of Chicago, 1998), pl. 20.

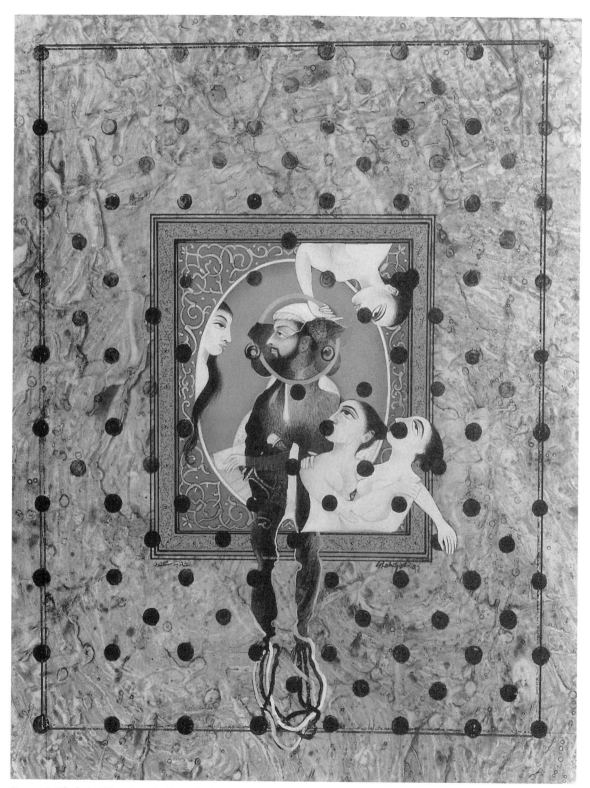

Figure 6. Shahzia Sikander, *Perilous Order,* 1997. Vegetable pigment, dry pigment, watercolor, and tea-water on paper, 10 3/8 x 8 3/16″. Whitney Museum of American Art, New York. Purchased with funds from the Drawing Committee.

those, however, the rider is always a male; Sikander switches genders, letting her female polo player gallop freely in this Safavid-inspired miniature.[16] Another example appears in the "Extraordinary Realities Series I" (1996)—originally a readymade miniature made for tourists Sikander found in a Houston market—in which she includes a picture of herself wearing a red bridal veil, an Indo-Pakistani custom.[17] In every case the veil resists a fixed interpretation as a sign of repression. Not necessarily filtered through the Islamic religion, it is multifaceted, becoming a sign and metaphor for fluctuating meanings.

The process of layering and hybridity, part and parcel of the same vision, reaches a new level in *Perilous Order* (1997; fig. 6). The female figures in this image are plucked from a Basohli painting, an early eighteenth-century illustration of the Bhagavata Purana, showing maidens whose clothes Krishna has stolen.[18] These naked women flutter around a male figure, a friend of the artist, who is portrayed as a Mughal prince or ruler. Among these Hindu, Islamic, and contemporary references Sikander inserts the shadow of an invented figure often recurring in her work, and completes the image with regimented dots conveying a Minimalist grid.

This signature image of an uprooted but self-nourishing female is of special interest in the hybrid scenarios Sikander concocts. Always hovering in transit, she is an alter ego. Barely sketched out in the left corner of *Separate Working Things II*, included but made of shadows in *Perilous Order*, she is fully present in *Fleshy Weapons* (1997), and voluptuously modeled as a multiarmed goddess.[19] Half naked, half veiled, Hindu–Muslim hybrid, wishful invention, mutation, the figure in *Fleshy Weapons* reflects the artist's profound desire to erase boundaries, preach fusion, merge adversaries, and intimately link differences.[20] Purity and homogeneity have no place in Sikander's vision; she is no accomplice to the exotic vision of a woman

excluded, dismissed, and banished under a veil. Instead she expands the associations of the veil, lacing it with humor in miniatures, layering it into installations as translucent sheets of paper, multiplying its incarnations from representation to ethereal abstraction.

Shirazeh Houshiary

Unlike Sikander, Shirazeh Houshiary buries every point of departure that might define an origin. "I set out to capture my breath," she says, to "find the essence of my own existence, transcending name, nationality, cultures."[21] Born in Shiraz, Iran, Houshiary enrolled at the Chelsea School of Art in 1976 and has lived in London ever since. Presented as a figurehead for new British art in the 1980s and then pressured to do the same for Iranian art in the identity-driven exhibitions of the 1990s, she shunned categorizations and withdrew from events that would have cast her in their light. Unconcerned with gender or ethnicity, perpetually trying to move beyond, she seeks a passage to a condition free of divisions, a space shared by all humanity. Yet she is profoundly sustained in this quest by Eastern mysticism, and specifically Sufism, which has allowed her to propose paradoxes and conquer them, dismantle binary thoughts, merge the spiritual with the scientific, and test and overcome easy categorizations and conceptual ghettos.[22]

The process of taming polarities, paradoxically, begins with polarities. For instance, in *Licit Shadow* (1992–1993; fig. 7), a series of sculptures in six parts, Houshiary draws formal vocabularies from diverse and specific origins, then lets them flow into a common geometry. The grid structures and serial productions of Minimalism come to mind, but only to provide a nest for honeycomb patterns that may hark back to the *muqarnas* of Islamic architecture. The materials, ranging from lead to gold, carry their own hierarchical symbolism, referring to the alchemic struggle to overcome base matter. The juxtaposition of the cold, dead weight of the cube with flickers of bright copper and gold create further antagonisms within a cohabitation in which Houshiary above all attempts to breathe life into the rigid will of

16. In information given to the author Sikander explained her source to be the *Polo Player*, a 1642 Safavid miniature from Riza-I Abbasi Album, illustrated in Esin Atil. *The Brush of the Masters: Drawings from Iran and India.* (Washington D.C.: The Freer Gallery of Art, Smithsonian Institution, 1978), p. 78.

17. For illustration, see *Shahzia Sikander*, (see note 15) pl. 10.

18. For an illustration of the source, see M[ohindar] S[ingh] Randhawa, *Basohli Painting* (Calcutta: Ministry of Information and Broadcasting, Government of India, 1959), pl. 9.

19. For illustration, see *Shahzia Sikander*, (see note 15) pl. 3.

20. On a discussion regarding the "nearness of difference" see "Chillava Klatch: Shahzia Sikander Interviewed by Homi Bhabha," in *Shahzia Sikander*, (see note 15) pp. 16–21.

21. Shirazeh Houshiary, quoted in Ann Barclay Morgan, "From Form to Formlessness: A conversation with Shirazeh Houshiary," *Sculpture* 19, no. 6 (July–August 2000), pp. 26–27.

22. On Houshiary and Islamic and Sufi thought and symbolism, see Jeremy Lewison, "Light of Darkness," in *Isthmus: Shirazeh Houshiary* (Grenoble, Munich, Maastricht: The British Council, 1995), pp. 65–92.

Figure 7. Shirazeh Houshiary, *Licit Shadow,* 1992–1993. Lead, copper, and gold leaf; six parts, dimensions varied. Weltkunst collection, Switzerland. Installation view at Le Magasin, Grenoble. Photograph by Georg Rehsteiner.

the geometry. By stretching outward and compressing inward the cores of her structures, she hints at the pulmonary rhythms of expansion and contraction. The sense of breathing remains central to Houshiary's iconography.

With time, the dualities in her work have blended into more seamless wholes. Site-specific brick sculptures such as *Loom* (2000; fig. 8), for example, once again point to both an icon of modernism—Constantin Brancusi's *Endless Column* (1937–1938)—and Islamic architecture, with its earthbound tomb towers or soaring minarets. Among the latter, the Malwiya (848/49–852), the "snail shell" or ramped minaret tower of the Great Mosque of al-Mutawakkil, in Samarra, stands out as a possible antecedent.[23] The feeling of simultaneous lightness and weight, previously conveyed through materials, here emanates from the sense of corkscrew rotation, which seems at once to be tightening its grip on the earth and whirling to be released from it.

A gyrating, spiral movement like this one reverberates in Sufi rituals such as the dance of the whirling dervishes, in which the dance is intended to lead to a state of altered consciousness, a surpassing of the self. The movement in Houshiary's *Loom,* then, is simultaneously downward and inward, upward and outward. In visual terms it also relates directly to the double helix, the twinned spirals of genetic material encapsulated in DNA. Fusing the artistic vocabularies of East and West, *Loom* also weaves spirituality and science into a tightly unified expression.

Houshiary's monochrome paintings go still farther in communicating the meeting of opposites, the commingling of cultures, the acceptance of not only all but also none in particular—a process leading to a new order which is neither Islamic nor modernist but something new to both. The imagery of the paintings may be traced back to the works in graphite on paper, mounted on aluminum, that she executed in the early 1990s.[24] Soon after, in 1993, she moved from paper to

23. For illustrations of both the Great Mosque and *muqarnas,* see John D. Hoag, *Islamic Architecture* (New York: Harry N. Abrams, 1977), pp. 54–55, 108, 157, 257.

24. For illustrations see *Dancing around my ghost: Shirazeh Houshiary* (London: Camden Arts Center; Dublin: The Douglas Hyde Gallery, 1993).

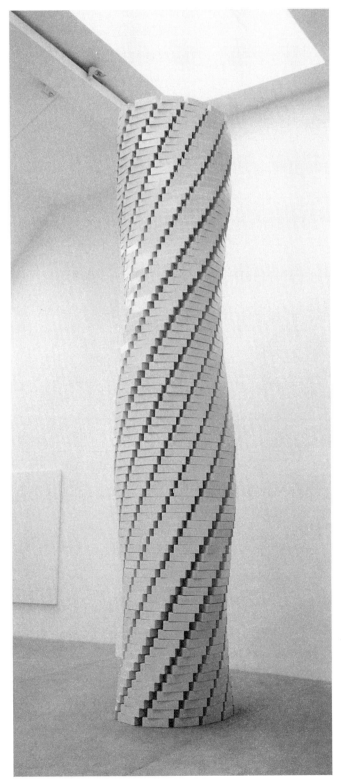

Figure 8. Shirazeh Houshiary, *Loom,* 2000. Glazed brick.
17'3" x 43". Courtesy of the Lisson Gallery, London.
Photograph by Dave Morgan.

canvas, working on top of a canvas she laid on the floor, a position loaded with history in that it recalls the balletic choreographies of gestures performed by the New York School artist Jackson Pollock. Houshiary, on the other hand, moves with the meticulousness and intimacy of a miniature painter.

The earlier drawings show the marks of Arabic calligraphy. In the paintings too, Houshiary begins by tracing a word whose identity she does not divulge, preferring to keep the mystery of its origin. Then in a process of detachment she dissolves form and meaning through repetition—a device central to both Western Minimalist practice and to *zikr,* a Sufi method of meditation. Alternating writing with erasure, or veiling the writing with color, Houshiary moves from form to formlessness, from the word to the unutterable, from legibility to invisibility, from text to an abstraction bearing an activity's generalized trace. *Presence* (2000; fig. 9)—a painting in the collection of The Museum of Modern Art—at first sight resembles a blank canvas painted a monochrome white, then intimates a horizontal shadow when viewed from a distance, a web of barely visible cracks when scrutinized up close. The form looks like an accident of nature more than the product of intense manual labor. Houshiary's paintings are elusive, barely visible, and they change in our vision over time—they refuse to be frozen into a finite moment, of the kind that could be captured by a camera. They intentionally stand at the very edge of perception, the signs both emerging from nothingness and simultaneously melting back into it. Yet these paintings painstakingly record a process of obstinate mark making, of personal gestures inscribing time, of checking the pressure of one's presence, the precision of one's vision, against the resistant surface. It is as if Houshiary were trying to capture the self in its least material form, as force, breath, or energy. What remains is the ghost of the activity.

Ideas of the transcendence of the self appear in Sufism, which also deals with its annihilation, and reemergence transformed, through the twin concepts of *fanā* and *baqā.*[25] Like a Sufi's quest for the divine, Houshiary's apparent self-effacement is founded on grand ambition. It encompasses the sublime while engaging the material. It is within this circular spectrum that the works reveal their mystical foundations, while also pointing to the Western monochrome tradition. Restricted mostly to the colors of night and day—

25. See Annemarie Schimmel, *Mystical Dimensions of Islam* (Chapel Hill: The University of North Carolina Press, 1975).

Figure 9. Shirazeh Houshiary, *Presence,* 2000. White acquacryl with silverpoint and graphite on canvas, 6'1" x 6'1". The Museum of Modern Art, New York. Committee on Painting and Sculpture Funds. Photograph by Dave Morgan.

another opposition Houshiary complicates by drawing light into darkness and casting shadows on the pristine whiteness of her canvases—the paintings set up a zigzagging sequence of references, from the white monochromes of Robert Rauschenberg, which do not demand attention as precious objects, to those of Robert Ryman, which relish their materiality, to the spiritual dimension of modernist abstraction, beginning with Kandinsky and Kasimir Malevich and moving on to Mark Rothko and Ad Rheinhardt. Silencing the calligraphic element of the text, Houshiary veils its Islamic origin but turns up the volume of a transcendental message. And to the roster of modernist abstraction she adds a visual conundrum whose building blocks are words.

If there is anything these three artists share, it is their refusal to inhabit a ghetto either Western or Islamic. They have invented new orders alien to both. Amer's work relates to translation, which exists in a space between and above different cultures. Sikander's is a melting pot accommodating a spectrum of shades; and Houshiary's suggests an amniotic fluid, a stage prior to and beyond differences, in which everyone finds something they can recognize—the pulse of life, the trace of a self, something akin to the visualization of human presence. The signposts leading these artists to new territories and destinations are both Eastern (and not only Islamic) and Western (modernist). It may well be their nomadic condition—premised on both intimacy and distance, from the self and from others—that has given Amer, Sikander, and Houshiary the wisdom and the ability to step beyond the cocoons of both their native cultures and their host countries. Their work allows us a glimpse of a rapprochement still unfulfilled at the dawn of the third millennium.

On wings of diesel

Spiritual space and religious imagination in Pakistani truck decoration

JAMAL J. ELIAS

Of course, one doesn't need anything
on the truck—faith in God is sufficient
Bahadar Ali, truck painter

This article deals with the tradition of truck decoration in Pakistan. My purpose in presenting and analyzing the data put forward here is twofold. At the narrower level, I wish to present the tradition of vehicle decoration in Pakistan as an important popular art form with a very particular set of significations. At a wider level, I am exploring the nature of response to religious imagery in popular Islamic culture. In this essay I am not particularly concerned with explaining the responses themselves, but rather with analyzing their syntax, symptoms, and signification, and examining the signs that elicit these responses. Underlying this analysis is the belief that images elicit responses, and that these responses might be dulled as a consequence of familiarity through overexposure, but that this familiarity does not eradicate the response itself. By the term response, I imply the significations and symptoms of the relationship between a visual object and the one who views it. The nature and significance of this response necessarily extends beyond the linear equation of object and viewer, as stated succinctly by David Freedberg:

> We must consider not only beholders' symptoms and behavior, but also the effectiveness, efficacy, and vitality of images themselves; not only what beholders do, but also what images appear to do; not only what people do as a result of their relationship with imaged form, but also what they expect imaged form to achieve, and why they have such expectations at all.[1]

In the case of vehicle decoration in Pakistan, the relationship becomes particularly complicated since, as I will clarify later, the creation of the visual object is a corporate enterprise in which the truck designer (artist) shares with the truck driver who is the primary audience for this form of art. As such, the expectations of what the viewer will receive from the imaged form guides the

process of artistic creation, though (and this is not at all surprising) the finished product has significations that are not predicted by either the artist or the primary audience.

Vehicular art

The decoration of vehicles is, of course, a common practice in a number of countries in addition to Pakistan and Afghanistan. Minor decoration of vehicles is common throughout the world, and ornately decorated ones are seen in several countries, such as the Philippines, Indonesia, and countries in Central and South America. What makes the case of Pakistan (and Afghanistan) unique, however, is the pervasiveness of vehicle decoration, since ornamentation of a variety of sorts is heavily employed on virtually all privately and fleet-owned commercial vehicles. These include not only the well-known trucks and buses, but also minivans, share taxis (referred to as *Suzukis,* since they are made by adding a passenger compartment with two bench seats to a small Suzuki pickup), animal carts (especially the two-wheeled horse-drawn carriages called *tongas*), and even juice vendors' push carts.

Though decoration is pervasive, with the exception of truck, bus, and Suzuki decoration all other forms of vehicular art are informal and non-systematic, in that the decoration is done by artisans who work on different kinds of vehicles and other material objects, and the vehicles themselves do not follow identifiable patterns in the decoration itself (beyond obvious similarities such as what parts of the vehicle are actually decorated). Trucks, buses, and Suzukis share motifs and materials, although they are worked on in different coachwork shops and by different artists, and there are important differences in the decorative motifs involved.

It is worth noting that vehicle decoration is an expensive undertaking. It generally costs up to four hundred thousand rupees (U.S. $7000) to have the coachwork done on a truck; the lowest figure mentioned by any truck painter was 125,000 rupees (over $2000 in 2001). This begs the question of whether or not there is any direct economic gain from getting a vehicle

---

1. David Freedberg, *The Power of Images: Studies in the History and Theory of Response* (Chicago: University of Chicago Press, 1989): p. xxii.

decorated. In the case of buses the gain is obvious, since if two buses are departing on the same route at the same time (as they often do), passengers are likely to choose the more attractive (i.e. more decorated) one. This observation only holds true for buses on major or metropolitan routes, however, since routes connecting smaller towns are frequently traveled by buses belonging to the same company, thus negating any economic advantage to the fleet owner (although the incentive to decorate still applies to the bus operator).[2]

In the case of trucks, there is no obvious economic factor to the decoration. The overwhelming majority of Pakistani trucks are not owner-operated but rather belong to fleets. Furthermore, many trucks are contracted sight unseen, as a result of which the appearance of the truck would seem to be of no consequence to the person who hires it. Despite this lack of obvious economic benefit, it is the norm for fleet owners to authorize the driver to take the vehicle to a coachwork shop at company expense and have it decorated according to his own taste (although in the case of many fleets all trucks have similar lettering and color schemes).

Given the lack of direct economic benefit in decorating a truck to the owner or operator, and the absolute pervasiveness of this form of art (it is safe to say that, with the exception of trucks belonging to multinationals such as Federal Express, every intercity privately owned truck in Pakistan is decorated), it becomes obvious that the motivation to decorate lies somewhere else. The motifs represented on trucks display not only aesthetic considerations, but also attempts to depict aspects of the religious, sentimental, and emotional worldviews of the individuals employed in the truck industry.

Study of truck decoration

Attention was first focused on the study of truck decoration in the early 1970s in Afghanistan. Following the Soviet invasion and subsequent civil war in that country, the center of both the truck decorating industry and its study has shifted entirely to Pakistan. For the most part, publications on truck decoration consist of coffeetable-type books and journal and magazine articles with photographs and very little text. The notable exceptions are a doctoral dissertation written in Paris in 1978 by Marie-Bénédicte Dutreux; a picture book with a good introduction published in 1990 by Jürgen Grothues; a monograph written by Anna Schmid to accompany an exhibition at the Museum of Folk Art in Hamburg; and two academic articles, one of which is an extremely brief essay on the semiotics of truck decoration, and the other an examination of truck painting as an artisanal trade.[3]

Dutreux's monograph attempts a systematic study of the motifs used in truck design, but it suffers on account of serious errors in translating Pashto, Persian, and Urdu writing on trucks, thereby coming to erroneous conclusions as to the significations of truck decoration. Schmid's monograph remains the best piece of writing on Pakistani trucks; she focuses on the world of trucks and trucking (not on the details or symbolism of design), and includes a brief discussion of the religious world of the truck drivers. No one has engaged in a systematic history of truck decoration in Afghanistan and Pakistan.

Some writers have suggested that the tradition of truck decoration derives directly from the adornment

---

2. The question of bus decoration is more complicated than I have space to address in this article and I plan to deal with it at length elsewhere. A clear class distinction has emerged in Pakistani buses over the last decade: intercity buses catering to the middle class are completely distinct from the traditionally decorated buses which charge lower fares. The new intercity buses are closer to those in Europe or other countries in Asia in their level of amenities, and also resemble them in the simplicity of their graphic decoration and lack of other forms of adornment. The striking differences between buses catering to the middle and lower classes reinforces the Pakistani bourgeois's viewing of vehicle decoration as kitsch.

3. M.-B. Dutreux, *La peinture des camions en Afghanistan* (Paris: Paris I Sorbonne: Section Arts Plastiques, 1978); J. Grothues, *Automobile Kunst in Pakistan* (Suderburg: Schrader, 1990); A. Schmid, *PakistanExpress: Die Fliegenden Pferde vom Indus* (Hamburg: Dölling und Galitz Verlag, 1995); A. Lefebvre, "The Decorative Truck as a Communicative Device," *Semiotica* 75, no. 3–4 (1989): 215–227; G. W. Rich and S. Khan, "Bedford Painting in Pakistan: The Aesthetics and Organization of an Artisan Trade," *Journal of American Folklore* 93 (1980): 257–275.

There are several other articles and books that deal with truck decoration in Afghanistan and Pakistan, though these tend to focus entirely on presenting pictures of the vehicles and provide no analysis or other relevant information. Examples of these are: J.-C. Blanc, *Afghan Trucks* (New York: Stonehill Publishing Co., 1976); "Camions afghans," *Zoom* 40 (1976):48–53; *Lastwagenkunst in Afghanistan: Bilder die fahren* (Frankfurt: Dieter Fricke, 1976); M. Centlivres-Demont, "Les peintures sur camions en Afghanistan," *Afghanistan Journal* 2 (1976):60–64; J. Grothues, "Lastwagen-Kunst in Pakistan," *Südasien* 8 (1993):62; S. Hallet, "Afghanistan's Hot Roads," *Revue Architecture Plus,* New York (1973):27–32; R. von Oppen, *Art on Wheels* (Lahore: Ferozesons, 1992).

There are also several websites with good images of trucks, including Martin Sökefeld, *Colours on the Road: Truck Painting in Pakistan* (http://www.asienhaus.org/galerie/lkws/english/lkw.htm), and my own *On Wings of Diesel: Vehicle Decoration in Pakistan* (http://www.amherst.edu/~jjelias/truck_site/trucks.html).

of animal carts and camel litters, although this is undocumented and a cursory glance shows that there is little similarity in the motifs and their location on the vehicle. Photographic data would suggest that there has been an evolution from very basic decoration as early as the 1960s to the complete riot of color and design that modern Pakistani truck art has become. Techniques and motifs have evolved and changed, but certain basic elements of design have remained constant.

My own data has been collected in northern and southern Pakistan. I have focused my attention on three areas of the country: (i) the commercial center of Karachi; (ii) the Rawalpindi–Islamabad area, where the land route to China splits from the east–west route to Afghanistan and India (under normal trade conditions); and (iii) the Karakorum Highway, the main commercial artery which connects Pakistan to China.[4] I have conducted extensive interviews with truck drivers on the road and at rest stops, and while they are having their trucks built up in design workshops. At the workshops themselves, I have conducted interviews with the master artists and their apprentices, as well as the artisans who manufacture the smaller ornamental pieces that are attached to the truck after the main designing is done. I have, as yet, not conducted extensive interviews with fleet owners, the last group of people directly involved in the trucking industry who have input in the nature and form of truck decoration.

Pakistani truck design: Five regional styles

There are a number of different artistic styles in truck design, although truck artists tend to be extremely dynamic in modifying styles and motifs, as well as unself-conscious, so that motifs are added and removed from the repertoire with great rapidity. Nevertheless, most truck drivers and designers assert that there are at least four basic regional styles of truck design. On the basis of my own research, I have identified five primary regional styles, at least two of which have secondary design categories. That specific styles are identified with a particular region is hardly surprising, since Pakistan is a large and populous country with substantial cultural and linguistic diversity.

The commonest variety of truck design is the Punjabi style, which accounts for most of the trucks built up in

northern and central Punjab, Pakistan's most populous and prosperous province. Truck design workshops are dotted all across the province, but they are concentrated around Rawalpindi and Sargodha. Rawalpindi, twin city to the capital of Islamabad, is located at the intersection of the two main traffic arteries in Pakistan: the north–south route connecting the sea and all the major industrial and agricultural areas to the northern part of the country and China, and the east–west route connecting the center of the Punjab to the western city of Peshawar and on to Afghanistan. Sargodha (together with towns like Gujranwala and Gujrat) are major centers of agriculture and small-scale industry and, perhaps as a consequence, have many design workshops (this area has the highest concentration of workshops doing coachwork for buses). Trucks of the Punjabi style are the most elaborate: they have ornate metal cowling (called a *tāj*, or crown) above the windshield, and rely heavily on hammered metal work and plastic applique in their decoration. These trucks are then decorated with patterns made out of colored reflective tape. They are also the most likely of all trucks to have smaller ornamental pieces attached to the front of the truck after the main decoration is done (see figs. 1, 2, and 7).

The trucks of the Swati style are distinctive for their carved wooden doors, which are normally left unpainted, and their very limited use of plastic and hammered metalwork (see fig. 5). This style takes its name from the valley of Swat in northwestern Pakistan, which has a long tradition of wood carving. Many of the artists designing trucks in the Swati style have relocated to other places, particularly Rawalpindi and its environs, because of better employment opportunities there.

Trucks of the Peshawar style fall somewhere in between the Punjabi and Swati styles. They often have carved wooden doors although, unlike the trucks of Swat, their doors are likely to be painted, and they use a metal cowling, only it tends to be simpler than that of a Rawalpindi truck. I am inclined to view the Peshawar style not as a school of design, but as a hybrid form combining elements of Swati and Punjabi trucks.

The Baluchi style accounts for the majority of trucks from Baluchistan where workshops are centered on the towns of Quetta and Zhob, although there are also Baluchi workshops in and around Karachi. The Baluchi style is easily identifiable because the trucks themselves are distinctive: while the majority of trucks in Pakistan are Bedfords, built in plants set up by British Leland shortly after Pakistan achieved its independence, over the last two decades there has been a dramatic increase in the popularity of more powerful and larger

4. For information on the economic and anthropological significance of the Karakorum Highway, see H. Kreutzmann, "The Karakorum Highway: The Impact of Road Construction on Mountain Societies," *Modern Asian Studies* 25, no. 4 (1989):711–736.

Figure 1. Truck in the Punjabi style. Photograph by the author.

Figure 2. Truck in the Punjabi style. Photograph by the author. (See front cover.)

turbodiesels, some of which are imported from Japan and Korea while others are assembled locally. These larger trucks tend to be used for longer hauls as well as for business that relates to the seaports of Karachi and the Baluchistan coast. As an indirect consequence, larger trucks are mostly of the Baluchi style. In design terms, these trucks use more geometric patterns on side panels than do other trucks, and frequently have chrome modifications made to their bumpers, in the form of extensions and grill guards (see fig. 6). They are also the most expensive: the commonly seen Hino Cargo costs 2.1 million rupees ($35,000) as a new chassis, and between 1 and 1.6 million rupees ($16,000 to $26,000) are spent to build up and decorate the truck (2001 figures).

The Karachi style is difficult to define, and I am inclined to see it not as one style at all but an amalgamation. Karachi, as Pakistan's major sea and land port as well as its primary metropolitan area, has more trucks than any other place in the country. It also has truckers from every other region, many of whom choose to decorate their trucks in the tradition of the area to which they belong. The only distinctive Karachi design I have been able to identify has the wooden panel above the windshield carved in relief with vegetative and floral motifs and colored with iridescent paints. This design is most common in water tankers, a kind of truck ubiquitous in Karachi because the municipal water supply is hopelessly inadequate, and entire neighborhoods get their water from independent suppliers who deliver it in tankers. A variant of this style of truck comes from the eastern desert of Thar, and is similar except that the carved front wooden panel is not painted.

Decorative motifs and their meaning

I would identify six categories of motifs within the general scheme of ornamentation on a Pakistani truck.[5] In my categorization I am departing from established analyses that are sign-based, distinguishing (for example) between the figural and the calligraphic. Instead, I am

attempting to focus on the signification of all the visual symbols on the truck, and to undertake an analysis of visual decoration that suspends, for the moment, my suspicion of visual images as a linguistic system and treats the picture like the pattern, like the text.[6] I am, however, distinguishing between the merely decorative (color choice for the most part, and the geometric and floral patterns which cover most of the truck) and the decorative with obvious symbolic value, or what might better be referred to as the ornamental.[7]

The six categories of signifiers in the decorative motifs on the Pakistani truck are as follows:

1. *Explicit religious symbols and images.* These include the majority of the calligraphic program of the truck as well as explicit religious symbols such as the celestial horse, Buraq, that carried Muhammad on his Miʿrāj ascension to heaven. Some of these religious symbols are mixed in their signification, such as the star and crescent which simultaneously represent Islam and Pakistan.

By far the commonest religious symbols appearing on trucks are pictures of the Ka'ba in Mecca and the Prophet's Mosque in Medina. These images almost invariably appear on the front of the truck (never on the sides or the back), somewhere toward the top. With very few exceptions, the image of the Ka'ba appears on the left side and that of the Prophet's Mosque on the right. The purpose of this arrangement is almost certainly to be

---

5. A. Lefebvre's article mentioned above makes an attempt to evaluate the message of a Pakistani truck's decorations, but some of his assertions are so cursory and erroneous as to be nonsensical. He explicitly describes the average Pakistani trucker as a Pashtun from an alpine village who smokes hashish, has sex with young boys, and drives his truck too fast. The majority of truck drivers are not Pashtuns, and most Pashtuns do not come from alpine villages. The most likely explanation for his errors is that all his information is derived from a Pakistani informant with no real knowledge of the trucking industry or its culture, and not from actual fieldwork.

6. "We know that linguists refuse the status of language to all communication by analogy—from the 'language' of bees to the 'language' of gesture—the moment such communications are not doubly articulated, are not founded on a combinatory system of digital units as phonemes are. Nor are linguists the only ones to be suspicious as to the linguistic nature of the image; general opinion too has a vague conception of the image as an area of resistance to meaning— this in the name of a certain mythical idea of Life: the image is re-presentation, which is to say ultimately resurrection, and, as we know, the intelligible is reputed antipathetic to lived experience. Thus from both sides the image is felt to be weak in respect of meaning: there are those who think that the image is an extremely rudimentary system in comparison with language and those who think that signification cannot exhaust the image's ineffable richness." (Roland Barthes (1977), "Rhetoric of the Image" in *Image-Music-Text,* trans. by Stephen Heath (New York: Hill and Wang, 1977): p. 32.

7. The most erudite theoretical discussion of the concept of ornament as a mediator of meaning in the Islamic context is found in Oleg Grabar, *The Mediation of Ornament,* Bollingen Series, no. 38 (Princeton: Princeton University Press, 1992). In a recent article John Renard has attempted to develop Grabar's ideas and apply them to architectural themes in ornamentation in a comparative religious context (John Renard, "Picturing Holy Places: On the Uses of Architectural Themes in Ornament and Icon" in *Religion and the Arts,* no. 5 (2001):4:399–428).

representational of what they symbolize—Allah and Muhammad—and mimic the way in which their names would be written or (more accurately) read: the name of God always precedes the name of His Prophet, and an individual reading in the Perso–Arabic script would read from right to left while facing the truck.

2. *Talismanic and fetish objects.* These include a variety of amulets and other objects believed to possess powers that are talismanic, most often in the prophylactic sense of protecting the driver, his livelihood, and the truck from evil. These include animal horns, yak tails, flags of various kinds acquired from the shrines of Sufi saints, as well as other objects of personal significance.

3. *Talismanically or religiously loaded symbols.* This category is distinct from the preceding one in that it is not the ornamental object itself that possesses talismanic or prophylactic power, but the thing that it represents. Such symbols account for the majority of ornamental motifs on the truck, and are both painted on during the initial design as well as added later in the form of stickers and smaller ornamental pieces attached to the body of the truck. Common symbols are fish, which represent good fortune, and eyes, though the latter are very ambiguous in their symbolism because they appear to serve multiple purposes. Eyes often represent protection from the evil eye (*naẓar*), but the eyes on the truck are exaggeratedly feminine, thereby serving not only as symbols of beauty but also as active elements in attributing a feminine personality to the truck.

Other such symbols are the names of prominent or regional Sufi saints who are invoked for protection, although arguably these could be seen as part of the religious calligraphic program of decoration. One popular symbol is the chakor partridge, a bird commonly kept as a pet in Pakistan and Afghanistan because of a belief that it functions as a supernatural miner's canary: if anyone casts the evil eye on a household or individual, the spell is deflected onto the bird which then dies. The death of the bird serves as a warning to its owner to take immediate preventive measures to avert misfortune. A representation of the chakor partridge, therefore, possesses a clear prophylactic purpose.

4. *Idealized elements of life.* These include naturalistic paintings of landscapes, women, and pleasing animals, particularly birds. Idealized alpine landscapes and romanticized villages that the driver never gets to visit figure prominently in this category of motifs.

Figure 3. Detail of the side panel of a truck in the Karachi style. Photograph by the author.

Figure 4. Rear view of a truck in either the Punjabi or Peshawar style. Photograph by the author.

5. *Elements from modern life.* A wide spectrum of motifs come together in this category, and, at first glance, it may seem that they do not share very much by way of signification. There are relatively common images of modern vehicles such as ships and (more frequently) aircraft, pictures of celebrities from the entertainment industry (e.g the late popular Punjabi singer Nur Jahan), as well as politically significant representations such as the Pakistani flag or pictures of the late military ruler, General Ayub Khan. What all these images share is an overall representation of modernity through the Pakistani state. Viewed in this way, popular ex-dictators, the flag, revered singers, and representatives of high technology (the aircraft are invariably those of the Pakistan Air Force or the national airlines) all belong together in defining a sense of national social identity.

6. *The non-religious calligraphic program of the truck.* This category includes the romantic poetry, pithy aphorisms, and humorous quips written on the truck, as well as primarily utilitarian lettering, such as the writing of the name of the transportation company to which the truck belongs. I am not fully convinced that this constitutes one category at all. It is quite possible that the lettering related to the truck and its routes belongs in the previous category, while the romantic and philosophical poetry—what the driver and his comrades would view as high art—belong in one category and the humorous anecdotes in another, thus dividing the non-religious calligraphic program into the serious and the whimsical.

Many of the motifs categorized above occupy predictable places on the truck. Explicit religious symbols and images are always located on the front of the truck; talismanic objects and symbols may be found on the back and occasionally on the sides, but the preponderance of such signs is on the front of the truck. Motifs from the idealized or imagined life as well as from modern life appear mostly on the sides and the back; they are very rarely seen on the front. The name of the truck company normally appears on the sides, which is also where most naturalistic pictures are likely to be, though occasionally the name also appears on the front. Humorous statements are almost invariably on the back of the truck and serious ones (particularly poetry) on the front, although witticism and examples of folk wisdom do appear on the rear, but very rarely on the sides.

Two decorative programs

To illustrate the above discussion, I provide a detailed description of the primary decorative program of the trucks in figures 1 and 2. The first truck (fig. 1) was photographed in Gilgit in the far north of Pakistan; it has Gilgit registration and plies the Karakorum Highway from the Chinese border to Rawalpindi–Islamabad. The second truck (fig. 2) is registered in Quetta, in southwestern Pakistan. It was photographed in Rawalpindi and, at the time, was carrying produce between Baluchistan and the wholesale market serving Rawalpindi–Islamabad. Both trucks are of the Punjabi style.

Figure 1: Gilgit truck

The first truck is distinctive because of the extensive nature of the explicit religious signs on it. The Ka'ba and the Prophet's Mosque appear twice (panels 1 and 2).

Accompanying their iconic representation, the names of God and His Prophet appear four times as "Yā Allah! Yā Muḥammad!," in each case from right to left as one faces the truck: on the extreme ends of panel 1 (the "Yā Muḥammad!" is damaged); on panel 2 just outside the medallions with the Ka'ba and Prophet's Mosque; toward the outside of panel 3; and in very small writing on the central medallion of panel 2. To either side of this medallion is the phrase *sapurd-e khudā* (In God's protection). Both central medallions invoke the names of saints, the top one that of Shah Bilawal Nurani, *nūrānī nūr har balā dūr* (luminescent light, all afflictions stay away), and the lower one of Lal Shahbaz Qalandar, the most popular Sufi saint in all of Pakistan.

In addition, there is extensive calligraphy, some religious, some what the driver would regard as high-art poetry, and still more descriptive of the truck itself. The religious writing is above the windshield and the high-art poetry beneath it, the descriptive writing appearing both above and below. Across the top of the truck is a couplet describing Muhammad's status as the primordial human being:

*banē sārī khudāī mēñ muḥammad muṣtafā pahlē
na ādam thā na farishtē thē na ẓahir thā khudā pahlē*

In all God's creation Muhammad was made first
There was no Adam, there were no angels, God was not apparent

At the bottom of panel 1 is the inscription *Tājdār-e ḥaram hū nigāh-e karam* (Crown-bearer of the sanctuary, he is, vision of grace), an honorific title given to Muhammad by the classical Persian poet Sa'di, but popularized in modern Pakistan in a qawwali song by the Sabri Brothers.

The medallions at the bottom of panel 2 have the names of the owners on either end (Anjum Khan and Nadim Khan), and the name of the truck in the middle: *Lāhūtī Kārvān* (Divine Caravan).[8] The word *Fayẓān* appears right above the windshield, and is most likely another name for the truck.

The grill on either side of the central medallion on the main cowling (panel 3) has two couplets, the first asserting that Muhammad, his daughter Fatima, her husband Ali, and their sons Hasan and Husayn are the best of human beings (thereby advertising the Shi'i sympathies of the owner or driver). The lower couplet is particularly significant because I have observed it on

Figure 5. Truck in the Swati style. Photograph by the author.

several trucks in various parts of the country including the truck in figure 2.

*kī muḥammad sē vafā tū nē to ham tērē hēñ
yē jahān chīz he kyā luḥ-o qalam tērē hēñ*

If you are faithful to Muhammad, then I am yours
What is this world after all, the pen and the tablet are yours[9]

At the bottom of the radiator (panel 4), under the name Bedford, is a non-religious couplet:

*jal jāo khāmushī se karī dhūp mēñ lēkin
apnōñ sē kabhī sāya-e dīvār na māngo*

---

8. It is possible that this name is a reference to yet another Sufi shrine, Lāhūt-e Lāmakān, from Lasbela in Baluchistan. There is a shrine near that of Lāhūt-e Lāmakān of a saint named Bilal Nurani, who could be the same as the Sakhi Bilawal Nurani invoked on the truck.

9. The pen and tablet refer to the divine pen with which God wrote the Qur'an on a protected divine tablet (*al-lawḥ al-maḥfūẓ*) where it remains as the eternal word of God.

Burn away in silence under the blazing sun, but
Never ask your relatives for the shade of a simple wall

Below that is the registration number, and two small panels on the ends of the bumper advertising the route. Directly under the oval registration plate is the name of the truck company (Pak China Goods, Gilgit). At the bottom is another non-religious couplet:

shabnam kē ānsū ko kab dēkhtī hē dunyā
kartē hēñ sab hī nazzāra hanstī hūī kalī kā

Who ever notices the tears of the morning dew
Everyone is busy looking at the smiling rosebud

Figure 2: Quetta truck

The second truck is very different in the specific signs, though the syntax (in terms of arrangement) is very much the same. The Ka'ba and the Prophet's Mosque appear only once, nestled in clamshells on panel 2. On panel 1 they have been replaced by twin images of the King Faisal Mosque in Islamabad, symbolizing an increased emphasis on God at the expense of Muhammad. This message is repeated in the religious calligraphy: the written pair "Ya Allah! Ya Muhammad!" appears only once, on the ornamental medallions hanging from the ends of panel 2. In other places it has been replaced by references solely to God, mostly by epithets from the list of God's ninety-nine names: Yā Raḥīm! Yā Karīm! (Oh Merciful One! Oh Generous One!) appear on the ends of panel 1. The formula Yā ḥayy! Yā qayyūm! (Oh Living One! Oh Eternal One!) appears in small lettering on the central medallion of panel 2 and again on the lowest pair of panels on either side of the central medallion on panel 3, right above the windshield.

The higher emphasis on God as opposed to Muhammad would imply a lack of faith in the power of human intercession. It is therefore not surprising that no saints are invoked in the central medallions on panels 2 and 3. In both cases, the space is occupied by the formula Mā shā'llāh! (As God wishes), the commonest Muslim utterance used to guard against the evil eye and misfortune in general.

Below the large medallion in the center of the main cowling (panel 3) there is a smaller medallion—almost invisible in this illustration—with the name of the truck company (Muhammad Farid Transport). The middle pair of panels on either side of these medallions bear the identical religious couplet appearing in the same location of the truck in figure 1.

The bottom of the truck has an exaggeratedly feminine pair of eyes above a hanging gravel guard,

Figure 6. Trucks in the Baluchi style. Photograph by the author.

which is more ornamental than functional and bears a striking resemblance to a *niqāb* veil. Talismanically loaded symbols also appear on the hammered metal panel separating panels 2 and 3, which has fish running its length, and in what most likely is a representation of ibex horns in the middle (this is a very common metal and plastic object attached to the front of trucks).

At the bottom of the truck (panel 4), there is a non-religious romantic couplet reminiscent of the one in the same location on Truck 1:

jis lab pe hansī ā na sakē vo gul khilānā kyā jānē
jis ānkh mēñ ānsū reh na sakē vo rāz chupānā kyā jānē

Lips that cannot smile—what do they know of blooming flowers?
Eyes that cannot cry—what do they know of keeping secrets?

Other decorative motifs

A hybrid style, typical of Karachi, with elements of the Baluchi and Punjabi styles predominating, can be seen in figure 3, which depicts a detail of a side panel from a truck in the finishing stages of design at a workshop in Karachi. The center of the photograph has the name of the trucking company in both English and Urdu (M. Amjad Goods Transport Company), above which is a list of city names from southern Pakistan where the company operates (Karachi, Sukkur, Jacobabad, Larkana). There are two naturalistic paintings at the bottom, each flanked by pictures of birds (the right one has the Chukor partridge mentioned earlier). The painting on the left, of a cave man fighting a bear, is part of a group of images appearing on both sides of the truck which are inspired by pictures from a children's storybook and have little significance beyond pure decoration. The painting on the right depicts a romanticized village: the architecture is foreign to Pakistan, although the woman sitting in the foreground is clearly Pakistani, as is the design of the empty cot beside her. The major signification of the woman by the side of the cot is apparent when one looks at the painting closely: she is very well dressed, heavily made up, and wears jewelry. At the same time, she is sitting on the ground beside an empty cot, waiting for the arrival (or return) of someone who is absent, undoubtedly a man.

The truck in figure 4 was photographed between Peshawar and Islamabad shortly after Pakistan conducted nuclear weapons tests in May 1998. The portrait on the top panel (composed of four wooden slats) is of Abdul-Qadeer Khan, "father" of the Pakistani nuclear bomb. The written message, translated, says "Uncle Qadeer, be well!"[10] Directly under the portrait are the names of the painters and body makers.

The writing on the end panels at the botton of the truck is not legible because of the black banners fluttering in front of them. The central panel at the bottom says *Jīyō bābā* (May you live long, old man!) and "Toman is my home." The panels attached on either side have the truck's registration number written in English and Urdu, and the phrase *naṣīb apnā apnā, pasand apnī apnī* (To each their own fortune, to each their own pleasures).

Conclusion: Decoration as message

In the profusion of their numbers and the lavishness of their adornment, Pakistani trucks transform the landscape into a checkwork of moving religious and cultural tableaus, mobile talismans through which the truckers protect themselves and their livelihood, and itinerant homes which bear visual testimony to the truckers' sense of place and belonging.

It is not clearly established that either the truckers or the truck designers are entirely clear on what the significations actually are of the motifs used in truck design. In fact, many truckers with whom I have spoken plead ignorance of all the symbols and claim that they are either purely aesthetic choices, or else were put there at the sole discretion of the truck designer. The truck designers, for their part, assert that even though the overall aesthetic planning is their domain, truckers quite normally express preferences for what motifs should appear on the vehicle. Despite the fact that the truckers do not admit to any intentional messaging through the choice and placement of words and images on their trucks, I would argue that religious images, even at their least denotative, or most abstract, are images nonetheless. They are perceived and—as David Chidester has so succinctly paraphrased a central idea of Paul Ricoeur—perception gives rise to symbols, and symbols give rise to thought.[11]

---

10. The English word "uncle" is a commonly used term of respect in Pakistan, since it conveniently sidesteps the complicated significance of designating someone who bears no kinship to oneself as a maternal or paternal relative.

11. David Chidester, *Word and Light: Seeing, Hearing, and Religious Discourse* (Urbana: University of Illinois Press, 1992), p. 1.

I do not see the truckers' refusal to admit to any great significance in the choice of design as truly representative of their beliefs in this regard, but as an unavoidable and limiting aspect of my fieldwork. Pakistani society has strict class distinctions in which truck drivers

Figure 7. Detail of the side panel of a truck in the Punjabi style. Photograph by the author. (See inside back cover.)

Margaret Miles has argued that religious images, at their most denotative, are iconic, in that they are organized in a traditional way and are responded to by the individual in terms of very specific religious and historical significances. Images can also be representational, encouraging the viewer to relate the image to an element of their own experience or belief. At the other end of the spectrum from iconic imaging and response is impressionistic or highly ambiguous representation, what Miles terms "antirepresentational," which only minimally designates its sacred and experiential content.[12]

The question of whether or not the religious symbolism on Pakistani trucks elicits a standard, predictable response is related to a second point, one I raised at the beginning of my paper, which is that responses might be dulled as a result of familiarity through overexposure. Though this is indeed true, I believe that the symbol elicits a response nonetheless. In fact, with progressive loss of a symbol's status as an active figure of speech, a piece of language, or a metaphor, it becomes not less but more like literal truth. To quote Nelson Goodman's *Languages of Art,* "what vanishes is not its veracity but its vivacity."[13]

Thus, I would argue, one can make sense of the Pakistani truck which, at first glance, appears to be an explosive expression of popular or folk art. The side panels are used to depict the imagined home, thereby situating the driver, who by definition is never at home, in a social geography. The role played by the writing of the trucking company's name and routes is self-apparent in situating the driver, but other images, particularly romanticized or idealized naturalistic paintings, are equally significant. The nomadic nature of the driver is critical to his self-conception, consciously articulated by him in conversation as well as in the music to which he listens. He pines for an imagined home from which he is absent by definition, an imagined home perfectly captured by the beautiful woman sitting beside the empty cot in the bucolic village in figure 3. In his perpetual absence from a physical, geographically grounded home, the truck functions not only as his

home away from home, but also his means of livelihood as well as his partner. The last concern explains the general motivation to decorate the truck as well as to feminize it and endow it with bridal symbols.[14]

The symbolism connected with safety of person and livelihood dominates the truck and also the trucker's behavior. The interior of the truck is heavily adorned with religious stickers, and the majority of truck drivers build visits to important shrines into their regular itineraries. The need to avoid misfortune and gain good fortune provides a simple explanation for the talismanic objects, symbols, and explicit religious motifs on the truck. However, their specific nature and placement signify more messages about the worldview of those involved in decorating the vehicle, and provide more evidence for my assertion that truck decoration functions linguistically, and that the choice of motifs and their location are the syntax through which varying messages can be conveyed (fig. 8).

One important piece of evidence in this regard is the difference between how the front and the back of the truck are decorated, in that, unlike the front, the back is whimsical (often humorous), and predominantly has motifs from modern life. I find three main factors explain this. First, there is the practical consideration that the back of the truck suffers much wear and tear from the constant loading and unloading of goods. This not only makes it impractical to have too much detailed (and expensive) ornamentation on the back, but would also potentially imply a disrespectful attitude if one were to have explicit religious ornamentation which was then subjected to abuse. Second, there are important semiotic differences between the front and the behind in general, in that one's "face to the world" is one's serious expression, and one's behind is the butt of jokes.[15] Third, the back of the truck is normally seen by those stuck behind it on the road. Keeping them entertained is therefore a viable use of the back of the vehicle (bumper stickers normally go on the back of the car in the U.S. as

---

would see a member of the urban, western-educated class (which I would represent to them) as disapproving of their tastes in several registers: as coarse, backward, and superstitious. It is not surprising, therefore, that they actively chose to underemphasize tastes and beliefs that they presume would make me, as the interviewer, look at them less favorably.

12. Margaret Miles, *Image as Insight: Visual Understanding in Western Christianity and Secular Culture* (Boston: Beacon Press, 1985), p. 34.

---

13. Nelson Goodman, *Languages of Art: An Approach to a Theory of Symbols,* 2nd ed. (Indianapolis: Hackett Publishing, 1976), p. 68.

14. I plan to address this issue at length in an upcoming article.

15. The semiology of the behind is an important topic awaiting serious study. There are numerous works on buttocks and behinds, but very few make even the most limited attempt to discuss the signification of the behind, and none that I am aware of compare it to the face (cf. Mérou and Fouskoudis, *La fanny et l'imagerie populaire* (Grenoble: Terre et mer, 1982); and J. L. Hennig, *Brève histoire des fesses* (Cadeilhan, France: Zulma, 1995), translated into English as *The Rear View: A Brief and Elegant History of Bottoms through the Ages* (London: Souvenir Press).

Figure 8. Cabin interior of a truck in the Punjabi style. Photograph by the author.

well). More importantly, the only group of people other than other truckers to be stuck behind a truck are travelling in cars and, in a very poor country such as Pakistan, almost by definition belong to a class of people with whom the trucker has little contact and therefore do not represent the social context in which he draws status.

The driver's sense of personal standing in his own social circle derives from presenting his best face to the world, that being the front of the truck. When parked at truck stops, the vehicles are pulled into parking spaces face first, and truckers gather in front of the vehicles to eat, drink tea, and chat. Given that the detailed decoration of the front of the truck can only be seen

fully when the truck is stationary, and when it is stopped the people around it are normally only truckers (or laborers and mechanics), it is to them that the trucker presents his serious face. This face is one that he partly creates and partly acquires or inherits—inasmuch as he has only partial control of the ornamental program of the truck—but at the moment of display it is *his* face since *he,* the truck driver, is inseparably identified with the truck, not the truck's owner or the dozen or so people who have a hand in its design.

The truck driver may not even be aware of the specific messages given off by his vehicular face, or that the design of the truck functions as a language system, but the truth of this is clear when one compares the two trucks in figures 1 and 2. The general layout of the trucks is the same; in other words, they have the same syntactical structure as communicative devices. The differences lie in the specific ornamental motifs: the truck in figure 1, with the repetitive pairing of Allah and His Prophet, both in words and in the iconic representation of those words (pictures of the Ka'ba and the Prophet's Mosque), displays a pious veneration of Muhammad. That this veneration is part of a greater belief in the power of human intercession before God is made clear by his invocation of the names of the Prophet's family and of two Sufi saints. The truck in figure 2, in contrast, shows requisite respect to Muhammad, but in several locations where the first truck invokes Muhammad in word or image, the second invokes God, suggesting that the driver subscribes to a different Muslim sensibility which does not allow for human intercession. The message is clarified further by the absence on the second truck of any reference to Sufi saints. Very importantly however, the medallions where Sufi saints are invoked on the first truck to guard against evil are occupied on the second truck by a formulaic invocation of God (*Mā shā'llāh*) that also guards against evil. Thus the syntactic structure of the truck, where the central medallions and the explicit religious motifs at the top of the truck guard against evil, remains constant, but the religious message (that human intercession is or is not accceptable) is variable.

Built into the sign, as a perceptual metaphor, is the capacity to pattern responses concerning how the individual relates to the world or to the divine.[16] Thus the symbols used in truck decoration, even when they

16. "The consistent development and deployment of perceptual metaphors within a field of discourse may usefully be considered as symbolic models. As an extended metaphor, a symbolic model in religious discourse may organize and pattern conceptual relations—

Figure 9. Punjabi style truck being painted in Rawalpindi. Photograph by the author.

are not consciously representative of a particular religious message in the iconic sense I have mentioned above, are still shaped by a notion of the religious place of the individual, by a religious worldview, and they provide messages and elicit responses which are framed within the parameters of that particular sensibility.

BIBLIOGRAPHY

Apter, David E., ed.
  1964 *Ideology and Its Discontents*. Macmillan: New York.

Barthes, Roland
  1967 *Elements of Semiology*. Hill and Wang: New York.
  1989 Image-Music-Text. (1977). Trans. by Stephen Heath. Hill and Wang: New York.

Beaugé, Gilbert, and Jean-François Clément, eds.
  1995 *L'image dans le monde arabe*. Collection Etudes de l'Annuaire de l'Afrique du Nord. CNRS: Paris.

Blanc, Jean Charles
  1976 *Afghan Trucks*. Stonehill Publishing Co.: New York.
  1976 "Camions afghans." *Zoom* 40:48–53.
  1976 *Lastwagenkunst in Afghanistan: Bilder die fahren*. Dieter Fricke: Frankfurt.

Centlivres-Demont, Micheline
  1976 "Les peintures sur camions en Afghanistan," *Afghanistan Journal* 2:60–64.
  1994 *Images populaires islamiques au Moyen-Orient*. Encyclopedia Universalis: Paris, 385–387.

Centlivres, Pierre, and M. Centlivres-Demont
  1997 *Imageries populaires en Islam*. Geneva, Georg Editeur.

Chidester, David
  1992 *Word and Light: Seeing, Hearing, and Religious Discourse*. University of Illinois Press: Urbana.

Dutreux, Marie-Bénédicte
  1978 *La peinture des camions en Afghanistan*. Ph.D. diss., Paris I Sorbonne, Section Arts Plastiques: Paris, 231.

Elias, Jamal J.
  2002 "Queens of the Road." *Art India* 7 (3):20–21.

such as the relations between self and world or between human beings and the sacred—in terms of consistent symbolic associations built into the model" (Chidester, see note 11, p. 29).

Freedberg, David
1989 *The Power of Images: Studies in the History and Theory of Response.* University of Chicago Press: Chicago.

Geertz, Clifford
1964 "Ideology as a Cultural System," in *Ideology and Its Discontents,* ed. D. E. Apter, Macmillan: New York.

Goodman, Nelson
1976 *Languages of Art: An Approach to a Theory of Symbols,* 2nd ed. Hackett Publishing: Indianapolis.

Grabar, Oleg
1973 *The Formation of Islamic Art.* Yale University Press: New Haven.
1992 *The Mediation of Ornament,* Bollingen Series, no. 38. Princeton University Press: Princeton.

Grothues, Jürgen
1990 *Automobile Kunst in Pakistan.* Schrader: Suderburg.
1993 "Lastwagen-Kunst in Pakistan." *Südasien* 8:62–62.
1993 "Pakistanische Kunstwerke." *Das Deutsche Lackiererblatt,* Stuttgart, 2:10–15.

Hallet, S.
1973 "Afghanistan's Hot Roads." *Revue Architecture Plus,* New York:27–32.

Isenberg, Arnold
1973 *Aesthetics and the Theory of Criticism: Selected Essays of Arnold Isenberg.* University of Chicago Press: Chicago.

Kreutzmann, Hermann
1989 "The Karakorum Highway: The Impact of Road Construction on Mountain Societies." *Modern Asian Studies* 25(4):711–736.

Lefebvre, Alain
1989 "The Decorative Truck as a Communicative Device." *Semiotica* 75(3–4):215–227.

Meddeb, Abdelwahab
1995 "La trace, le signe," in *L'image dans le monde arabe,* ed. G. Beaugé and J.-F. Clément, pp. 107–124. CNRS: Paris.

Miles, Margaret R.
1983 "Vision: The Eye of the Body and the Eye of the Mind in Saint Augustine's *De trinitateu* and *Confessions*" *Journal of Religion* April:125–142.
1985 *Image as Insight: Visual Understanding in Western Christianity and Secular Culture.* Beacon Press: Boston.

Renard, John
2001 "Picturing Holy Places: On the Uses of Architectural Themes in Ornament and Icon." *Religion and the Arts* 5(4):399–428.

Ricoeur, Paul
1974 *The Conflict of Interpretations: Essays in Hermeneutics,* ed. Don Ihde. Northwestern University Press: Evanston.

Rich, G. W., and S. Khan
1980 "Bedford Painting in Pakistan: The Aesthetics and Organization of an Artisan Trade." *Journal of American Folklore* 93:257–275.

Schmid, Anna
1995 *PakistanExpress: Die Fliegenden Pferde vom Indus.* Dölling und Galitz Verlag: Hamburg.

von Oppen, Renata
1992 *Art on Wheels.* Ferozesons: Lahore.

Abject to object

Colonialism preserved through the imagery of Muharram

REBECCA M. BROWN

The month of Muharram, the first in the Islamic calendar, marks the anniversary of the famous seventh-century battle at Karbala, the defining moment for the then nascent Islamic faith. At Karbala, Husain, the grandson of the Prophet, died on the battlefield, precipitating the split of Islam into two major sects. The majority Sunni sect centered its faith on the Qur'an, with secondary emphasis on the Hadith, or the sayings of the Prophet. The Shi'i sect, while still acknowledging the Qur'an as the word of God, included the family of the Prophet and the Prophet's sayings as a major aspect of Shi'i theology. Particularly in Shi'i majority regions, but also in the Islamic world more broadly, every year during the month of Muharram the death of Husain and the earlier death of his brother Hasan are mourned in a ten-day-long set of ceremonies. These ceremonies take on different characteristics in different historical and cultural contexts, based in part on whether the region is majority Shi'i (Persia, for example) or, in the case of India, minority Muslim *and* minority Shi'i.

This paper focuses on a British colonial representation of one part of the northern Indian Muharram observances, the procession, or *julus,* which serves as the most public of the various elements of Muharram in this region (fig. 1). The image of the Muharram *julus* in question was painted for a British patron by an Indian artist in the first quarter of the nineteenth century. This is thus a Company painting, and from stylistic and provenance information, it belongs to the Patna School. The artist was most likely from the Bihar region, as the school is named for Patna, Bihar's major city along the Ganges.[1]

This image represents a key part of a larger pattern of Muharram representations by and for the British in both text and image. For the British in northern India, the annual Islamic rituals of Muharram served as a primary moment of intersection and interaction between the colonized and the colonizer. The form of those interactions appears in the imagery commissioned for the British and painted by Indian artists, while simultaneously the procession is also the subject of extensive textual description that, from the early nineteenth century through the twentieth century, characterized Muharram processions as primary examples of spatial and social transgression in colonized India. This paper explores the tension between a British fascination with the processions, demonstrated by lengthy and detailed descriptions, and a simultaneous circumscription of the *julus* in colonial discourse, demonstrated by images of Muharram which omit major elements of the procession.

The British, for whom ceremony became increasingly important over the course of their rule of India,[2] were even at this early stage fascinated by the visual and cultural spectacle of Muharram—its mourning of the martyrdom of Husain, its community-centered, politically savvy speechmaking, its inclusion and exclusion of Hindus, Sikhs, Sunni Muslims, and Christians. That fascination, however, is marked by a concurrent rejection of and horror at Muharram—its self-flagellations, its transgressive movements across the city, its disregard for delineated cultural, religious, and ethnic categories. Rather than a colonialism of dichotomous colonized and colonizer, or a colonialism of a controlled European or British Self opposed to a chaotic Islamic or Indian Other, the colonialism

Earlier versions of this paper were presented at the annual meeting of the Middle East Studies Association and the Cross-Cultural Poetics Conference. My thanks to my colleagues who offered suggestions and a critical eye, especially Deborah Hutton, Pika Ghosh, Samuel Chambers, Ruth Feingold, W. John Archer, Frederick Asher, Catherine Asher, and the writing group at St. Mary's College of Maryland. The research for this work was undertaken with support from the University of Minnesota, the Council for Overseas Research Centers, and St. Mary's College of Maryland.

1. Taking form during the rise of the East India Company to power in the subcontinent, this categorization derives its name from the patrons—those associated with the Company. One finds these works as individual paintings as well as in sets of images bound together in albums.

2. Bernard Cohn's work on Victorian India's ceremony details the development of ritual for the preservation of British India, but at a much later (post–1858) period. See Cohn, "Representing Authority in Victorian India," in Eric Hobsbawm and Terence Ranger, *The Invention of Tradition* (Cambridge: Cambridge University Press, 1992), pp. 165–210.

Figure 1. Anonymous, *Julus,* ca. 1820. Mica. Paul F. Walter Collection.

produced in paintings of Muharram is instead a colonialism of fascination and horror—hence a colonialism struggling with and negotiating the abject. Thus, this paper contributes to the growing literature problematizing colonial relations on a variety of axes.[3]

_____

3. The dichotomous notion of the colonial as Indian versus British has long been the subject of deconstructive analysis, a project which marks almost all of postcolonial theory. This paper enters the debates through psychoanalysis (see below), a method shared by early analyses of colonialism, in particular Franz Fanon, *The Wretched of the Earth,* trans. Constance Farrington, (New York: Grove Press, 1963). Homi Bhabha and others, following Fanon, have articulated a variety of concepts which attempt to break down the colonized/colonizer duality. Bhabha, *Location of Culture* (New York: Routledge, 1994). Studies outside of postcolonial theory have also analyzed the relationship of colonized/colonizer in ways that refuse the notion of an

I argue that as the images demonstrate the repulsion and attraction that the British grappled with in a struggle to represent and to know Muharram, they also direct us to the threat felt by the colonizer from this religious, community observance: not a threat caused merely by the physicality of the events, or a fear generated by the movement of the processions across the city, but a deeper challenge to the very stability of colonialism. In the image of the *julus,* this threat is defused, with crucial elements of the textual descriptions erased in favor of a controlled, decorous movement through an undefined

_____

antagonistic dualism, most recently David Cannadine, who argues that the British saw the colonized in similar terms to British society: *Ornamentalism: How the British Saw their Empire* (Oxford: Oxford University Press, 2001).

space. Despite the differences between the textual and visual descriptions of the Muharram procession, these two coexistent representations together constitute colonial discourse, and they represent a negotiation of the threat of the procession for the British position in early nineteenth-century India.

The impetus for this paper lay in my own surprise at the staid, quiet appearance of a particular painting of Muharram from the early nineteenth century, today housed in the Paul F. Walter Collection (fig. 1). Having read a great deal about South Asian Muharram processions in scholarship and literature, and seeing contemporary *juluses* in India, with their activity and sound, I did not expect such a static, controlled, decontextualized image. Indeed, images of Muharram from the early nineteenth century are consistent in exhibiting this quiet distancing from the ceremonies.[4] It is the sorting out of this anonymous Company painting—hereafter called the Walter *Julus*—which has led to this paper.[5]

This painting includes most but not all of the elements of a *julus,* which forms a central, public element of the ten-day Muharram ceremonies. The procession is only the most visible of the activities comprising Muharram in the northern Indian context.[6] In addition to the processions, participants hear sermons, or *majlis,* on the martyrdom of the two grandsons of Muhammad, which relate the story of the battle at Karbala in which Husain and his followers died.

Participants include those in the Shi'i community, but also Sunni Muslims, Hindus, Sikhs, Jains, and others of the region, making the observance of Muharram one which encompasses the entire Indian community in one way or another. This should not be read as a utopic coming together of all peoples, as different groups participate on different levels, some assisting with the construction of the procession, and some merely

witnessing the ceremonies. In many cases, the various groups participating in Muharram in South Asia divide not on religious lines but on class or caste lines, drawing different community connections across the city.[7] The alternate vision of Muharram in which only Shi'i Muslims participate is also inaccurate for northern India, where Shi'as do not represent a majority population.[8]

The painting of the procession depicts a series of *ta'ziyehs,* or replicas of the tombs of Husain and his brother Hasan, surrounded by groups of people, including musicians and soldiers, who process with animals of various sorts, most prominently elephants.[9] The variety of decoration depicted on these tombs indicates that different groups created these replicas for the procession, as is normal for this region, with different communities competing across neighborhoods for the biggest and most lavish *ta'ziyeh. Sipars,* or the shield-like elements carried on poles, reference the battle at Karbala; more specifically, the shield symbolizes Hussein's shield. The flags, generally bearing the image of two swords, and *'alams,* or posts topped by a sculpted hand and carrying the battle standard of Husain, also underscore the historical context of the procession, referring both to the battle itself and the family of the Prophet through the five fingers representing the

---

4. Procession images share a controlled, quiet quality with the *majlis,* or sermon, images. See examples in Mildred Archer, *Company Paintings: Indian Paintings of the British Period* (London: Victoria and Albert Museum, 1992).

5. As this image has no official title, I have named it after the collection in which it currently resides: The Paul F. Walter Collection. The painting is on mica, and was likely part of a set of images sold together, representing various Indian festivals and ceremonies. An image of hook-swinging, part of the Charak festival, also on mica, comes from the same set (fig. 2). See Pratapaditya Pal and Vidya Dehejia, *From Merchants to Emperors: British Artists and India, 1757–1930* (Ithaca: Cornell University Press, 1986), pp. 162–163.

6. Vernon James Schubel, *Religious Performance in Contemporary Islam: Shi'i Devotional Rituals in South Asia* (Charleston: University of South Carolina Press, 1993).

7. See Nita Kumar, "Work and Leisure in the Formation of Identity: Muslim Weavers in a Hindu City," for an analysis of the Benarsi weavers' participation in Muharram, and Sandria Freitag's introduction to the same volume, "Introduction: The History and Political Economy of Banaras," which examines the multiple identities delineated through the ceremonies. Both articles in Sandria B. Freitag, ed., *Culture and Power in Banaras: Community, Performance, and Environment, 1800–1980* (Berkeley: University of California Press, 1989).

8. India's Shi'i population is a minority within a minority. For a discussion of the mixed population in Lucknow's eighteenth-century Muharram observances, see J. R. I. Cole, *Roots of North Indian Shi'ism in Iran & Iraq* (Berkeley: University of California, 1988), p. 117. For a broader picture of this facet of Indian Muharram, see David Pinault, *Horse of Karbala: Muslim Devotional Life in India* (London: St. Martin's Press, 2001), p. 14. In Persian culture, majority Shi'i since the sixteenth century, Muharram includes primarily Shi'a participants, but like India, other sects and religions also observe or participate. See Peter J. Chelkowski, ed., *Ta'ziyeh: Ritual and Drama in Iran* (New York: New York University Press, 1979) for discussion of the central Persian observance of Muharram, the *Ta'ziyeh* passion play.

9. In the Indian context, *ta'ziyeh* refers to the replicas of the tombs of Hasan and Husain created for Muharram observances. In the Persian/Iranian context, this word refers to the passion play performed during Muharram as well as the theater in which that play is held. While reenactments of the battle do take place in the Indian context, they are not as elaborate or staged as the Persian *Ta'ziyeh*. See Chelkowski (note 8).

five major members of the Prophet's family.[10] The anonymous artist includes all of these elements in the Walter *Julus*.

The artist gives the procession a slow, measured pace by turning some of the participants to look to the rear of the column and by refraining from expansive gestures of motion in any of the figures, animal or human. He shows the solemnity of the event in the slow movement of the crowd: the figures inch forward, away from the viewer, some of them pausing to look back at the *ta'ziyehs* behind. The crowd, which one *could* see as a rowdy bunch, given the variety of poses, the variation in the direction of the gazes, and the few hands up in the air reads also in a spatially controlled manner. Most notably, the prominent figure to the right of the composition with a flywhisk in his hand is lost in the crowd around him, and his gesture is overwhelmed by the tall *ta'ziyeh* above him. The participants follow a diagonal line from the bottom-right foreground back in space to the top-left middleground. Figures on the left side of the procession repeat one another in their planted stance, marking a rhythm of enclosure on that left side. The rhythm of the *ta'ziyehs*, flags, and *sipars* also echo this diagonal, moving compositionally from top right to mid-left, completing the triangular, diagonal recession in space indicated by the bottom edge of the procession. This ordering overwhelms any variation that occurs within the crowd depicted, as if the crowd were poured into an preexisting mold for easy display. The solemnity achieved by this composition might be expected in a procession meant as a mourning ritual, but the textual descriptions do not match this level of quietude.

While most aspects of the Muharram *julus* appear in this image, several do not. Conspicuously absent are two elements which are central in textual descriptions of the procession: mourning rituals, or *matam*, and the transgression of city space caused by the procession. The absence of these two elements was what drew me to the image in the first place: when one reads accounts of the procession, it becomes surprising to see the image without those key elements that dominate textual descriptions.

First, the painting provides no images of mourners who outwardly exhibit *matam*, the manifestations of suffering that can take several forms, most often verbal and physical mourning, including both verbal cries and

weeping. Also encapsulated within the term *matam* are the more (in)famous elements of Muharram: self-flagellations and other sorts of self-inflicted physical pain. This aspect of the observances, like audible cries and weeping, communicates a connection with the experience of the Prophet's family as they were defeated at Karbala. The yearly observance becomes a reliving of the events of the seventh century, in order to remind present-day Muslims of those early sacrifices and the foundational elements of the Shi'i faith.[11]

These mourning elements are absent in both the content of the Walter *Julus* and in the manner of its portrayal. The question of *manner* is crucial, for the image not only misses the physical act of matam so integral to Muharram's procession and its *majlis*, but also lacks the emotional engagement mentioned by early nineteenth-century commentators in their descriptions of the ceremonies.[12] The column moves slowly forward, with each element—elephant, drummer, *ta'ziyeh*—playing its part. But in its overall impression, the image of the ceremony lacks an emotive connection with the events commemorated. One might seek an explanation in stylistic limitations here, arguing that the northern Indian Patna style of Company painting, out of which this work comes, does not lend itself to overt scenes of emotion.[13] While this may be true in terms of facial expression and body language, the level of emotional turmoil indicated by acts of self-flagellation could be communicated via other means: a dynamic composition, details indicating such mourning (tearing of hair, rending of clothes), or similar elements. Indeed, these types of emotional imagery can be found in other contexts, for example a ca. 1810 image of a Muharram sermon, or *majlis*, in the Victoria and Albert Museum collection, which includes figures weeping.[14] None of these elements exist within this image.

Alongside *matam*, a second major element is missing from the Walter *Julus*. In the textual discussions of Muharram, including both contemporaneous narrative accounts and the scholarly writings detailing the history

10. For more on *'alams* and the symbolism of these processional elements, see Pinault (note 8), p. 78, and Schubel (see note 6), pp. 108–109.

11. Schubel, ibid.

12. See for example Emma Roberts, *Scenes and Characteristics of Hindostan with Sketches of Anglo–Indian Society* (London: William H. Allen and Co., 1835), vol. 1, p. 178 ff.

13. For more examples of the Patna School, see Mildred Archer, *Patna Painting* (London: David Marlowe, Ltd. for the Royal India Society, 1948).

14. Victoria and Albert Museum, *Asura: Ceremony of Mourning for Hasan and Husain*, by an anonymous artist, Murshidabad, about 1810. IS 11–1887, no. 1. Published but not reproduced in Archer (see note 4), p. 83.

of this observance, the transgression or violation of the city space by the procession plays a central role. The Walter *Julus,* however, altogether neglects the context of a city or town. The procession is isolated, with no architectural background or context. Visually, this isolation focuses the viewer on the foreground and the procession taking place. One can more easily see the silhouette of the *ta'ziyehs,* the variety of people, and the shapes of the flags against a plain background. The absence of context, however, becomes one charged with political and historical implications, particularly when compared to the textual descriptions of the processions.

In this case, the context could be extrapolated as the location where the painting was made, specifically Patna, or the region around that Bihari city. The Patna School of Company painting is linked stylistically with the Murshidabad School, named for the nineteenth-century seat of the Nawab (governor) of Bengal, and thus the center of patronage for the region.[15] While similar to Murshidabad paintings, the Walter *Julus* differs in both style and content from contemporary images of Muharram set in Lucknow, a city in Uttar Pradesh to the west, and the seat of the Nawabs of Oudh (Awadh), a Shi'i dynasty that traces its ancestry to Persia. For example, images from Lucknow usually include some architecture, as the cityscape is defined, in part, by its grand *imambaras.* Thus, despite the complete absence of town or even landscape setting in the Walter *Julus,* the types of *juluses* that the artist and patron would draw from are those which took place in northeastern colonial India, specifically in either Patna or Murshidabad.

The textual history of Muharram processions in this region of colonial northern India is one of conflict and tension generated by the procession's movement through the streets of a city. Most treatments of the Indian Muharram procession in text—whether fictional, travel-related, journalistic, governmental, or historical—focus on the confrontations among various groups within the city, generally instigated by the movement of the procession through the streets. Indian cities are organized into neighborhoods (called *mohallas* in Islamic communities) centered on a temple or mosque. As the procession traverses these spaces, it passes through sacred community areas, a transgression which triggers protest from the inhabitants of the neighborhood.[16] This is, of course, not unique to India.

Many religious processions cross boundaries within cities and disrupt the order of urban space in the process, such as the Catholic and Protestant conflicts in northern Ireland, which often erupt around similar processional transgression.

We see this transgressive element of the *julus* in a wide variety of textual sources. Perhaps the most famous instance of the textual illustration of Muharram appears in the fictional account given in E. M. Forster's *A Passage to India.* Forster modelled his fictional Chandrapore after Patna.

> Mohurram was approaching, and as usual the Chandrapore Mohammedans were building paper towers of a size too large to pass under the branches of a certain pepul tree. One knew what happened next; the tower stuck, a Mohammedan climbed up the pepul and cut the branch off, the Hindus protested, there was a religious riot, and Heaven knew what, with perhaps the troops sent for. There had been deputations and conciliation committees under the auspices of Turton, and all the normal work of Chandrapore had been hung up. Should the procession take another route, or should the towers be shorter? The Mohammedans offered the former, the Hindus insisted on the latter. The Collector had favored the Hindus, until he suspected that they had artificially bent the tree nearer the ground. They said it sagged naturally. Measurements, plans, an official visit to the spot. But Ronny had not disliked his day, for it proved that the British were necessary to India; there would certainly have been bloodshed without them.[17]

Written a century after the Walter *Julus* was painted, Forster here deploys his famous sense of humor in exposing one of the truths about the colonial presence in India: the British produced a frame of reference in which they were necessary for keeping the peace, and as a result the tensions created by Muharram processions are highlighted in the text. Muharram's reputation precedes it—"one knew what happened next"—and its capacity for disruption is emphasized here in order to enhance the effect of the peacemaking British colonizer. Forster makes it clear that this is a common story, and that Ronny's "day" can be considered emblematic—a model for the strife that Muharram caused among Indian communities, or more

15. Toby Falk and Mildred Archer, *Indian Miniatures in the India Office Library* (London: Sotheby Parke Bernet, 1981), p. 215.

16. While it is likely that the participants felt this element of transgression as well, and indeed the idea of crossing boundaries (of

historical time, from the mundane world to paradise, across community lines) is central to most aspects of Muharram, this paper is about the colonial discourse surrounding the ceremonies rather than a study of Muharram for its nineteenth-century participants. See Schubel (note 6) for a discussion of the liminality engendered by Muharram rituals for the participants.

17. E. M. Forster, *A Passage to India* (New York: Harcourt Brace and Co., 1984 [1924]), pp. 102–103.

properly, for the British policing those Indian communities.

It is clear that by the time Forster wrote this fictional account of a Muharram procession, the story itself was already established in colonial lore. If we look back to the early nineteenth-century context of the Walter *Julus* and examine contemporary texts, we find early versions of the need for keeping the peace and the conflict that Muharram processions engendered. Emma Roberts, who traveled to India with her sister and brother-in-law in the 1820s, visited Patna and the entire northeastern region of India and wrote about it in her serialized memoir, later published as *Scenes and Characteristics of Hindostan.* In her chapter on Patna, she spends a great deal of time describing the Islamic cemetery, primarily due to its role in the Muharram processions each year. In Patna, as in most northern Indian *juluses,* the procession of the *ta'ziyehs* ends at the cemetery, where the tomb replicas are deposited.[18] Roberts's description of this event includes many of the same elements as Forster's fictional account:

> But this cemetery displays a stirring and magnificent spectacle during the annual imposing ceremonies of the Mohurrum. [. . .] The riches of the city enable it to celebrate the obsequies of the young martyrs, Hossein and Houssein, in a very splendid manner; and this noble square is selected for the final depository of the tazees, or tombs, which are carried about in commemoration of the funeral honours paid by the followers of Ali to his slaughtered sons. The whole population of Patna, Moslem, Christian, and Hindoo, assemble to witness the procession. [. . .] The whole square rings with shouts of "Hossein! Houssein!" accompanied by deep groans and beatings on the breast, while amid the discharge of musketry, the last sad scene is enacted by groups personating the combatants of that fatal battle in which Hossein perished. Whenever the venerated martyr is beaten to the ground, the lamentations are redoubled, many being only withheld by force from inflicting desperate wounds upon themselves. Woe to any of the followers of Omar who should dare to intrude upon the mourners; the battle is then renewed in earnest. Whole companies of sepoys have been known to engage in deadly combat with each other, and numerous lives are lost in the revival of the old dispute respecting the claims of the sons of Ali, in opposition to those of Omar, who represents himself as the adopted heir of the prophet. It requires the

utmost vigilance on the part of the magistracy to prevent the recurrence of bloodshed in the fierce collision of contending parties at Patna during the festival; the Moosulman population of that place being more turbulent and arrogant, and, as it has been already remarked, more bigoted than those of any other city belonging to the Company's territories. Even the mild Hindoos are not very governable upon these occasions.[19]

The elements of the Muharram procession highlighted here involve the reenactment of the battle at the end of the procession which requires, as Roberts says, "the utmost vigilance on the part of the magistracy" in order to prevent bloodshed. Forster's description of a century later mirrors the narrative arc of Roberts's telling of the Muharram events, with both moving toward the "inevitable" conflict and the necessary presence of the British as peacekeepers. Roberts's narrative also highlights the deep emotion and turbulence of the procession and reenactment, emotion which spills over into the non-Muslim population participating in the ceremonies.

In a later chapter devoted entirely to Muharram as a cultural event, Roberts elaborates on the early nineteenth-century observances. While focused on the grand Muharram ceremonies at Lucknow, Roberts takes some care to indicate when her narrative centers on that city and when it is more generally about Muharram observances in northern India. She distinguishes the elaborate ceremonies of the Indian subcontinent from those of the Persian and Arabian regions, emphasizing the pomp with which Muharram is observed in the subcontinent:

> Imbibing a love of shew from long domestication with a people passionately attached to pageantry and spectacle, they have departed from the plainness and simplicity of the worship of their ancestors, and in the decorations of the *tazees,* and the processions which accompany them to the place of sepulture, display their reverential regard for Ali and his sons in a manner which would be esteemed scandalous if thus accompanied in Persia and Arabia, where the grief of the Sheah is more quietly and soberly manifested . . .[20]

Roberts continues her description with a specific discussion about Lucknow's observances, including several pages detailing the participation of the Hindus in the procession, the patronage of *ta'ziyehs,* and the mourning in general. She concludes this section on Hindu–Muslim amity by noting that it is not always so friendly:

---

18. Patna's procession was extensive in the nineteenth century, by some accounts incorporating approximately 14,000 *ta'ziyehs.* See Surendra Gopal, *Patna in the 19th Century (A Socio-Cultural Profile)* (Calcutta: Naya Prokash, 1982), p. 22. See also Sir William Wilson Hunter, *A Statistical Account of Bengal* (London: Trübner & Co., 1875), p. 61.

---

19. Roberts (see note 12), vol. 1, pp. 178–181.
20. Ibid., vol. 2, p. 179.

[. . .] when, as it sometimes happens, the holidays of the Hindoo and the Mussulman fall together, it requires no small exertion on the part of the authorities to prevent a hostile collision. At Allahabad, on the celebration of the Mohurrum, some of the leading persons repaired to the judge to request that the Hindoos, who were about to perform some of their idolatrous worship, should not be permitted to blow their trumpets, and beat their drums, and bring their heathenish devices in contact with the sad and holy solemnity, the manifestations of their grief for the death of the Imaums. They represented, in the most lively manner, the obligation which Christians were under to support the worshippers of the true God against the infidel, and were not satisfied with the assurance that they should not be molested by the intermixture of the processions, which should be strictly confined to opposite sides of the city. The Hindoos were equally tenacious in upholding their rights, and it became necessary to draw out the troops for the prevention of bloodshed.[21]

Again, the tension that the processions cause is central to Roberts's narrative of the ten-day ceremony. She turns for several pages to the *majlis,* or sermon, element of Muharram, and then spends the last pages of her chapter on the final day of the Muharram ceremonies and the most elaborate of the processions. She describes the participants:

> Devout Mussulmans walk, on these occasions, with their heads and their feet bare, beating their breasts, and tearing their hair, and throwing ashes over their persons with all the vehemence of the most frantic grief; but many content themselves with a less inconvenient display of sorrow, leaving to hired mourners the task of inciting and inflaming the multitude by their lamentations and bewailments.[22]

This is followed by another discussion of the conflicts that arise during the end of the procession, echoing her narrative about Patna in her earlier chapter.

Roberts's narrative of Muharram, both within the context of Patna and more broadly in the chapter devoted to the observances, proceeds through three stages. First, Roberts notes with surprise that while Muharram commemorates the deaths of two martyrs, and thus it should be somber and quiet, it is in fact an energetic, inflammatory, and spectacular show, one that might be taken for a celebratory festival. Indeed, she calls it a festival on several occasions in her text. Second, the participation of Sunnis, Hindus, and Christians in the ceremonies is elaborately detailed in her writing, again with some surprise at the capacity of Islamic mourning rituals to become broader Indian

festivals. Finally, these discussions of cross-religious interaction generally lead to an exposition on the potential for bloodshed and conflict that the processions of Muharram engender, making necessary a British peacekeeping presence.

In addition to these three narrative elements, Roberts gives us an idea of the mourners themselves, both in their level of energy and also in their specific actions and appearance. She includes the tearing of hair, the beating of breasts, and the dusting of the body in ashes as specific actions mourners take, and adds that hired mourners perform these rituals for those not willing or not able to do so themselves. In the context of more private mourning that takes place during Muharram, Roberts describes the physical beating of these hired mourners as extremely vigorous:

> After some well-wrought passage, describing the sufferings of the unhappy princes, the reader pauses, and immediately the mourners on the ground commence beating their breasts and shouting "Hossein! Houssein!" giving themselves such dreadful blows that it seems incredible that human nature should sustain them, until at length they sink exhausted on the ground amid the piercing cries and lamentations of the spectators.[23]

Thus, the physicality of the mourning, as well as the emotional engagement with the commemoration of these martyrs, takes a central role alongside the narrative arc of the various communal conflicts Muharram induces. These textual descriptions—both the conflict and the physical mourning—are not present in the representation of Muharram's procession seen in the Walter *Julus* painted the same decade as Roberts's visit to India.

On the other hand, the image gives the viewer all of the rich details of the *ta'ziyeh,* something not usually described in detail in the verbal descriptions. While the height of the tomb replicas and the basic form are described, the variety of architectural forms used in their stacked pavilions, the variety of *'alams* and *sipars,* and

---

21. Ibid., vol. 2, pp. 188–189.
22. Ibid., vol. 2, pp. 194–195.

23. Ibid., vol. 2, p. 191. Roberts's description of the mourning is not unique. On the reverse of a *majlis* image in the Oriental and India Office Library Collections, a long paragraph companion to the image on the front includes this description of the mourners: "A Machine is constructed very superbly painted and gilt, supposed to represent their Tomb—Before which is a priest reading the circumstances of their Death which in general has a most enthusiastic effect upon the audience who weep, groan and beat their breasts with the greatest violence, loudly calling upon the names of Hussein Hossein, prostrating themselves before the Tomb and offering the sacrifice of their lives in the defence of the cause of these two Saints." Add Or 938, Prints and Drawings Collection, *Muharram,* text on reverse.

the way the procession is organized—none of these elements are usually described, whereas the image shows some of these details. What is certain, however, is that neither the text nor the image represents the "true" Muharram procession narrative of the early nineteenth century. Indeed, both operate in similar ways: what is described in detail and what is left out are negotiated, historically contingent decisions made by patron, editor, writer, and artist along the way. Therefore I resist the idea that Roberts's text is the "reality" of Muharram processions and the Walter *Julus* is thus somehow merely a representation. Both the text and the image became emblematic for Muharram: these narratives repeat themselves across the nineteenth century. Thus, even in the 1820s, an emblematic description of Muharram emerged, based on British observance and description of the *juluses* and *majlises* in a variety of northern Indian communities, including Patna, Murshidabad, Allahabad, and Lucknow.

This description carried much weight, as it continued to be used into the early twentieth century and shaped Muharram observances even in post-independence India. For example, Nita Kumar, in an essay examining the weaver community in present-day Varanasi, relates a similar contemporary Muharram conflict, one that, like Forster's fictional account above, occurs with some frequency.

> . . . Many of the tazia processions pass through crowded localities in the center of the city where lanes are only a few yards wide. Common threats to the sacredness of the occasion arise from possible collision between relatively oversized tazias or absolutely oversized *'alam,* and low tree branches or telephone wires. A collision portends Hindu–Muslim conflict: the locality, the surrounding houses and porches, and the public spaces being Hindu, the "victimized" processionists Muslim, and the offending tree probably the sacred pipal.[24]

Kumar's description stems from her own interviews with police and recent observations of the processions in Varanasi; it is a contemporary recounting of the problematic procession of Muharram. Its similarity to Forster's fictional account—from the oversized *ta'ziyeh* to the pipal tree itself—points to a continued pattern both of governmental policing and, more to the point, of widely held perceptions of Muharram that stretch from pre- to post-independent India. Again, we see a pattern emerge: an emblematic image of Muharram that seems utterly opposed to that seen in the nineteenth-century

Walter *Julus,* where a calm, slow procession proceeds through a space absent of any context.

We also see this emblematic transgressive Muharram in descriptions of nineteenth-century Muharram observances in Bombay, as explored in James Masselos's work.[25] One of the major threats to the peaceful conduct of these ceremonies was the increased presence of Persian Shi'i immigrants in nineteenth-century Bombay. These newcomers incorporated fresh elements into the ceremony, including a horse procession (in honor of Husain's mount) that involved shouting abuses at those who did not participate with the Shi'i group. As these changes clashed with the mid-century custom of carrying *ta'ziyehs* in procession, the British banned horse processions in order to alleviate the tension. After the mid-nineteenth century, the British further separated the variant forms of Muharram in order to "preserve the peace"—a peace constructed through colonial discourse as well. The policing of this division meant both the physical presence of British officers in the streets as well as legislative intervention. Laws banned certain practices perceived as dangerous, and certain "safer" customs continued—often to the detriment of those perceived as more threatening, such as the horse procession.

Masselos points out that the British curtailed Muharram because of their desire to keep control over the population, most particularly because of the aspect of transgression of space involved in the processions. He makes clear that the movement through the city did not merely carve out sacred space. Rather, the process both invaded and controlled space not normally given to the group in question. This could mean crossing boundaries between two neighboring Islamic *mohallas,* or alternatively, crossing traditionally British areas on the way to the final destination of the procession.

Thus, rather than interpret Muharram in terms of a creation of the sacred alone, Masselos acknowledges and highlights the politico–religious core of these processions and as a result explains the British intervention as one centered on order:

> The issue was not merely of maintaining peace between conflicting groups or of preventing sporadic limited incidents of lawlessness or violence. It also related to the British concern over maintaining their domination given their numbers and the size of the population over which they ruled. . . . Mohurrum raised the spectre not of a

---

24. Kumar (see note 7), p. 159.

25. James Masselos, "Change and Custom in the Format of the Bombay Mohurrum During the Nineteenth and Twentieth Centuries," *South Asia* ns 5, no. 2 (December 1982), pp. 47–67.

planned or concerted revolt but of a spontaneous, contagious upsurge.[26]

Thus, the maintenance of domination over a population larger than that of the colonizer anchored the concerns of the British in Bombay; and, as a result, the policing of Muharram took on a heightened importance. The colonizers needed to stop the transgressive acts, for they threatened the very fabric of control and order that the British attempted to produce in colonized India, by making that very numerical advantage clearly apparent.

The textual examples above—Forster, Roberts, Kumar, and Masselos—all highlight the transgression and potential for violence of Muharram's procession, a transgression policed by the British to maintain or establish order. Roberts and Forster, with Kumar in the context of contemporary India, illuminate the need for Muharram's transgression in order to support the presence of a policing force. Masselos fleshes out this discussion by articulating the threat to order. The threat posed by Muharram is greater even than a planned revolt, precisely because it is spontaneous and unpredictable—it strikes against the very principle of ordering that constitutes British colonial rule.

If this disruption of order is crucial for the textual descriptions of Muharram it is not to be found in the Walter *Julus*. Instead, we find only a compositionally static, isolated scene. The viewer is expected to focus only on the procession in isolation from the well-documented conflicts and tensions which arise in relation to it. The *julus* thus occupies a space outside a city and its varying populations and neighborhoods, evacuating the transgressive elements so central to textual descriptions of the Muharram procession.

Why is this image marked by these two absences: absence of spatial, ethnic, and religious transgression within the city, and absence of *matam,* or outward mourning rituals? These are major parts of the ceremony—indeed, one could argue that they *define* Muharram for the British viewer—and yet they are missing here. Rather than read these absences as a separation of two distinct discourses—that of transgression and *matam,* as seen in the textual descriptions, versus that of isolated, sanitized parading, as seen in the image—I read these two seemingly disparate descriptions of Muharram as *together* producing a *colonial* description of the ceremonies, a discourse of transgression, isolation, and erasure all at the same time.

The Walter *Julus* gives us insight into how these two seemingly opposed descriptions work together. The absence of external architectural or urban context helps to simplify and order the composition, and the lack of any violent gestures or active displays of mourning or *matam* further contributes to the stability and calm of the scene. The painting creates an image of Muharram occurring happily within bounds, in control, and overseen by the (British) viewer. The event of Muharram is transformed into a spectacle to behold from a distance. It bears little if any resemblance to the threatening near-riot that the textual descriptions of conflict above suggest.

Rather than highlighting the various performances of mourning, and rather than communicating the conflicts caused by the height of the *ta'ziyehs* or the self-flagellations, this image presents a Muharram neatly packaged for consumption. What we see in the Walter *Julus* is not the opposite of the transgressive, *matam*-filled ceremony seen in texts, but perhaps a visual policing of the procession—an image of the conclusion to Ronny's day: a controlled, delimited, and ordered Muharram fit for viewing by the British public. Here, the image of the *julus* makes Muharram manageable within colonial discourse, renegotiating its threat to colonialism by eliminating those elements too threatening to acknowledge in an image.

Is this the end of the story, then? Does the *julus* image serve as a neat resolution for the explosion of discourse surrounding the issues of policing crowds, legislating processions, and describing bloodshed—a sort of plot closure for the colonial discourse surrounding Muharram? Here, the textual descriptions might be read as the conflict and tension between the protagonist and the antagonist, followed by the resolution and denouement of the *julus* painting. In this plot-driven model, one reads both of these images (textual and visual) as delineating and concretizing a separation between British and Indian. The painting puts the Indians on the page, isolated from any cityscape or British presence, viewed by a British controlling eye.[27] The Indian procession is ordered and controlled through this imagery: what was transgressive chaos is now under control and able to be known.

I suggest, however, that this is not the end of the story. The Walter *Julus* cannot merely serve as a closing

---

26. Ibid., p. 54.

27. The absence of British presence in these images is characteristic of colonial and Orientalizing imagery, a facet discussed in detail in the context of French imaging of northern Africa in the nineteenth century. See Linda Nochlin, "The Imaginary Orient," *Art in America* 71, no. 5 (May 1983), pp. 118–131, 187–191.

element for the disruption of the Muharram procession, an ordering moment after the chaotic transgression of the city and interruption of the colonially imposed order. This reading would highlight the return to order prevalent in the verbal narratives. In this reading, transgression is a temporary incursion across an established and legitimate border. However, with Masselos, I argue that the threat to British hegemony represented by Muharram is stronger than mere transgression. In order to examine this deeper threat to British hegemony, I turn to the art historical context of these images.

No Muharram images were produced before the late eighteenth century, despite traditions in India of the representation of public ceremony in both Hindu and Islamic courts.[28] While many subject matters show continuity from the late-Mughal era into the colonial period, Muharram emerges as a new subject within Company painting. Thus, the imaging of Muharram develops out of colonial patronage, with the Walter *Julus* a representative example. The effort to represent Muharram is intimately linked with colonial discourse and its effects, namely the consolidation and preservation of British hegemony in the subcontinent.

Examining other images commissioned at the same time—or even more specifically, an image from the same set as the Walter *Julus*—we find subject matters which seem to focus on physically graphic ritual. Hook-swinging, for example, part of the Hindu Charak festival, involves men placing hooks in their backs and swinging on a rope from a pole (fig. 2).[29] Why and how can this

image of physical ritual exist alongside the Walter *Julus* with its total lack of *matam* imagery? Clearly, not all Indian festival or ceremonial subject matter is treated the same in this genre of painting. It must not be a simple horror at the physical elements of this ritual, for there is no problem with metal hooks piercing the shoulders of participants in the Charak festival. Moreover, this cannot simply be an Indian versus British dichotomy. It must prove more complex, in which the Islamic Indian subject matter is treated with different concerns than Hindu Indian subject matter.

The threat here is not Muharram itself or the transgression of spaces. The threat stems from a different colonial problematic. We see a discursive dualism threatened by a third term: the position of the Islamic Other. Certainly this is not the only "third" term in colonial discourse, but it is a prime example of the ways in which this discourse negotiated the complexity of India's various populations.[30] One sees in both the *julus* imagery and the textual descriptions of Muharram the same goal played out: the discourse works in both cases to defuse the threat of a third term. Hindu ritual can be fully "Othered" in its strangeness, separated entirely as utterly different from British ceremony, and thus representations of hook-swinging can be depicted without threat. But Islamic ritual cannot fill that same position, as it is too close to British practice: not different enough. Furthermore, the idea of the British as heirs to Mughal rule in the subcontinent was already current in the last quarter of the eighteenth century; this complicated the othering of Islamic culture in India and led to a discourse of sameness between British Christian and Islamic cultures.[31] Thus, I argue that the proliferation of textual description regarding the British control and the policing of Muharram serves the same purpose as the extracting of dynamic elements from the *julus* imagery. Together, these elements serve to negotiate a non-threatening position for Muharram within colonial discourse.

The discourse of Muharram therefore exists between colonial categories. As a boundary it marks both the separation of colonized and colonizer *and* the point at

28. While festivals are well represented in paintings for Indian patrons during this period and earlier, Muharram rarely figures in these works, even in works patronized by Islamic rulers. Efforts to uncover examples of Muharram representations prior to the nineteenth century in any context (Indian or otherwise) have proved fruitless. Furthermore, during the nineteenth century, representations of Persian *Ta'ziyeh* performances (in Persia, the word *ta'ziyeh* refers not to the tomb replicas but to the passion plays staged during Muharram) are the only examples of other Muharram imagery found in this search. In British India, representations of Muharram include the processions, *majlis,* and various scenes of individuals with flags, *ta'ziyehs,* or lamps decorating *imambaras.* My thanks to the H-ISLAMART list for their responses to my queries on this subject, particularly Oleg Grabar, Andras Riedlmayer, Jonathan Bloom, and Ulrich Marzolph.

29. This image of hook-swinging is not an isolated one. Two Murshidabad School hook-swinging images, ca. 1800, at the Victoria and Albert Museum depict this ceremony in an active way, one with the spectators pointing at the figure swinging from the rope (IS 11:1887 nos. 11 and 37, Archer (see note 4), pp. 72, 83). A similar Murshidabad painting (ca. 1800) is reproduced in Mildred and W. G. Archer, *Indian Painting for the British, 1770–1880* (Oxford: Oxford University Press, 1955), plate 3, fig. 5.

30. In the postcolonial context the idea of a "third space" has been articulated by Homi Bhabha in order to discuss the diasporic cultures in both the metropole and throughout the formerly colonized world, but this is certainly distinct from what I discuss here. See Bhabha, "The Third Space: Interview with Homi Bhabha," in *Identity: Community, Culture, Difference,* ed. J. Rutherford (London: Lawrence and Wishart, 1990), pp. 207–221.

31. See C. A. Bayly, *Indian Society and the Making of the British Empire* (Cambridge: Cambridge University Press, 1988), p. 13.

Figure 2. Anonymous, *Hook-swinging,* ca. 1820. Mica. Paul F. Walter Collection.

which they join together. The text and image of the Indian ceremony separates the British from the Indian by creating both a chaotic Other in the text and a neatly packaged Other in the imagery. Yet simultaneously this discourse ties the two sides together. This representation of Muharram is never outside that discourse but instead helps to create it. Imagings of Muharram, textual and visual, do this because they exist as a site for representation "in between" chaos and order, riot and calm, Indian and British. These representations cannot be reduced to the actions of the British domesticating this Indian ceremony. And they are not two parts of a unified plot line. Much of the work done by these representations involves more than the last move of domestication or denouement.

Rather than simply discuss these representations as one of a subject (the British colonizer/protagonist) domesticating an object (the Indian colonized/antagonist)

through the resolution of a crisis moment in the plot, the interstices between the two must be acknowledged. The analysis must shift from the domestication and objectification of an Islamic Indian ceremony toward an understanding of the colonial relations of power as taking place in the realm of the abject—that space in between chaos and order, subject and object, Indian and British—that space within colonial discourse, marked by the Muharram procession.

For psychoanalysis, in which field the term first gained currency, the *abject* is that which borders and marks the boundaries between a subject and its other. The abject both establishes the boundary but *also* produces both the subject and the object (that is, through the constitution of the boundary between subject and object). One of the most powerful elements of the abject—one which can enhance the reading of the discourse of Muharram processions—lies in the deep interconnections of attraction and repulsion, fascination and horror situated at its core. The most well-known characterization of the abject stems from its manifestation as physical excretions from the body (excrement, vomit, menstrual blood) that emanate from the subject, and are reviled by the self but at the same time mark the individual as a subject, and therefore elicit fascination with revulsion simultaneously.[32]

By marking a space of "not me" outside of the self through these excretions, the connections between the self and the abject solidify around seeing this "not me" and the concurrent revulsion/fascination. For psychoanalytic philosopher Julia Kristeva, the corpse represents the most striking abjection: "If dung signifies the other side of the border, the place where I am not and which permits me to be, the corpse, the most sickening of wastes, is a border that has encroached upon everything."[33] The abject is more than merely the membrane that divides self and other: the abject exists as part of both. Excrement, the corpse, and menstrual blood are all a part of the self while simultaneously becoming a jettisoned, reviled exterior.

I turn to the abject here because it offers an interpretive space that acknowledges the constitutive link between the self and the rejected outside. Unlike a simple transgression, in which two "pure" elements cross paths and thereby cause tension (as in the case of the verbal descriptions of Muharram and its procession above), the abject describes an already established and constitutive interrelationship between the interior and the exterior.[34] Thus revulsion and fascination do not oppose one another so much as constitute parts of the same reaction to that which crosses the ultimate border. In crossing that border, that which is abjected (excrement, for example) performs two functions: it establishes the self as self *and* threatens the self by pointing out the shaky ground upon which it rests: the abject. That is, because the abject emanates from "me" and establishes "not me," it also forces the self to acknowledge its

existence as contingent. Muharram's seemingly contradictory representations in image and text stem from the problematic of instability caused by Muharram's threat as abject.

Thus, any reading of the *julus* image above as an indication of separation between Indian and British is not sufficient, as reading this discourse through the abject shows. The *julus* image becomes instead a marker of fascination with the Muharram rituals on the part of the British. Its absences (self-flagellations, mourning, other visual expressions of *matam*) mark the horror of the procession *in their absence*—they are suppressed in this image quite rigidly with its ordered boundaries and its movement away from the viewer, out of threatening range. The limits placed on the procession in terms of its boundaries—what I described above as the artist "pouring" the procession into a pre-given mold—point toward this rigid controlling of some threatening facet of the procession: not illustrated directly, but indicated through its absence.

An understanding of the discourse of Muharram through the logic of abjection allows us to answer some of the remaining questions from the previous analysis. Why did the British feel threatened by the self-flagellations and the movement of the Muharram procession? Muharram might be a threat in terms of its transgressive qualities—crossing boundaries of the city, disturbing peaceful neighborhoods with disruptive *ta'ziyehs*—but this pulls the reading back into the dichotomous British versus Indian mode of the first, plot-driven analysis. Furthermore, this reading based on transgression legitimates the differentiation between British and Indian, suggesting that the transgressors were merely overstepping the bounds temporarily and that order would, of course, be restored after that brief moment. Transgression is never a long-term situation. A broader psychoanalytic context for the abject helps to move us out of the orbit of these dichotomous relationships by exploring the facets of the threat which constitute the pairs in the first place.

The abject is not merely an explanation of subject formation over and against the "not me" of excrement, menstrual blood, or the corpse. For Kristeva, this formation works within a broader frame of the constitution of what she terms the symbolic and semiotic realms,[35] which produce the site of subject

32. The abject here is articulated through Julia Kristeva's exegesis in *Powers of Horror* (New York: Columbia University Press, 1982).

33. Ibid., p. 3.

34. For Kristeva this works on a very profound level: "I experience abjection only if an Other has settled in place and stead of what will be 'me.' Not at all another with whom I identify and incorporate, but an Other who precedes and possesses me, and through such possession causes me to be." Ibid., p. 10. The object or other, here, is seen as inherent in a subject which has yet to be formed. Thus, complete separation, or the preexistence of Muharram in the sense that it exists before these images and texts is impossible. The discourse surrounding Muharram does not postdate Muharram itself—it constitutes Muharram.

35. The term semiotic here is used in a manner different from its use within semiotics. Kristeva acknowledges the relationship of the semiotic to sign systems, but claims that these systems are housed within the Mother, the representative of society for the pre-oedipal being, and thus the source of those sign systems. Thus Kristeva avoids

formation. In this context, the symbolic realm, or the linguistic, masculine realm of the Father's Law, stands in counterpoint to the semiotic, pre-speech, feminine realm of the Mother's Authority.[36] This counterpoint of course relies on the oedipal scenario, in which a child comes to subjecthood through first challenging the Father for his (a necessarily masculine child) mother's affection and then separating from the Mother when the Father says "no." By passing from the semiotic into the symbolic in this way a subject is formed. In other words, only by entering the realm of the Father's Law can an individual take shape. That Law takes the form of prohibitive juridical law: the Father sets limits (says "no") for the subject, creating rules and boundaries for subject formation.

Deploying this deeper psychoanalytic framework as a metaphor to understand the colonial encounter, one sees a symbolic realm of the colonizer producing the Law through which prohibitions and restrictions are established. The Authority of the past, semiotic realm, here inhabited by the colonized (those denied subjecthood because they are unable to pass fully into the symbolic realm), must be acknowledged and controlled by this Law. This scenario depends on the two realms—semiotic and symbolic—existing as homogeneous spaces. But Kristeva and other philosophers argue that in fact the border between these two realms exposes them as heterogeneous—there is semiotic in the symbolic (Kristeva finds this in poetic language, for instance) and symbolic in the semiotic (some argue that the latter is constituted by the former).[37] The borderland between these two, the moments when they intersect or when the semiotic introjects into the symbolic—those moments question the all-encompassing Law of the colonizer, upsetting the juridical control and as a result threatening not only the logical sensibility of the symbolic but also the fabric of the symbolic itself. For,

once the symbolic is revealed as heterogeneous, its stability falters in the face of its permeable border: the abject. In the context of the colonial discourse under discussion here, the abject, bordering and constituting the two realms, disrupts the solidity of the colonizer's position (within the symbolic) and as a result, abjection as a bordering/liminal membrane threatens because it could easily break down the fabric of the Law—the very structures upon which the colonizer exists as colonizer.

Using the abject helps to explain the reasons why one sees a proliferation of discourse in the nineteenth century surrounding the policing of Muharram's spatial transgressions within the city, and yet a dearth of imagery of this transgression—marked by a lack of *matam* and a lack of even the depiction of conflict or bloodshed—in the British-sponsored representations of Indian ceremony. The transgression itself, as noted above, does not ultimately threaten the Law of colonialism; on the contrary, it underscores the need for the British presence in India. Ronny's passage in Forster's novel above demonstrates this dynamic clearly: "But Ronny had not disliked his day. . . ." What threatens British legitimacy and presence is the paired horror/ fascination of Muharram. This procession represents a moment in which the colonizer recognizes both the distance ("not me") from the Indian colonized and also the potential for breakdown of that barrier—the interconnection and constitutive dependence that the abject represents. Muharram might just be unknowable and unexplainable in the context of the symbolic realm of the colonizer, and thus the very act of *matam* threatens that symbolic fabric and the base upon which colonialism rests. Hence, in representations of the Muharram processions, British-commissioned works represent a spatially controlled, *matam*-free Muharram.

In closing, I would like to introduce another image of the Muharram procession from a different moment in colonial discourse: the late eighteenth century. Through this image, one can trace an emergence of this abject threat and the construction of Muharram to address that threat. Earlier, the pre-nineteenth-century East India Company presence in India had a very different flavor than that of the second decade of the nineteenth century. An image by an amateur British painter in the 1780s allows this distinction to become clear.

A set of paintings of festivals, marriages, and other events in the Victoria and Albert Museum is purported to consist of copies of paintings initially done by the British amateur artist George Farington (1752–1788).[38] Within

the dominant phallus of Lacanian psychoanalysis by refiguring Lacan's imagery in this way and re-centering the Mother. As Ian Craib suggests, Kristeva's semiotic differs from the Lacanian imagery, as the semiotic "is the poetic basis of our existence in the world, and the ordering of the experience in the 'chora,' as Kristeva calls it, is prior to the acquisition of identity, let alone a masculine or feminine identity . . . we have to move out of it [Kristeva's semiotic] to some degree to make civilized life possible." Craib, *Psychoanalysis: A Critical Introduction* (Cambridge: Polity Press, 2001), p. 174.

36. Kristeva's articulation places emphasis on the Mother's Authority where other psychoanalytic theorists read the semiotic without this. Kristeva (see note 31), p. 71.

37. Luce Irigaray, for example, argues that Kristeva's semiotic realm is still constituted by the symbolic, phalllogocentric language of the Father. *The Sex Which is Not One* (Ithaca, Cornell University Press, 1985).

38. Archer (see note 4), p. 78.

this set there is a Muharram processional image (fig. 3) which, while similar in many ways to the Walter *Julus* discussed above, has certain key differences that demonstrate the movement over time of these images from the late eighteenth century (and the beginning of the Company's consolidation of its colonial presence in northern India and particularly Murshidabad) to the early nineteenth century, when the Company's position in eastern India had been relatively stable for several decades.[39]

Compositionally, this *julus*, like the Walter *Julus* discussed above, moves away from the viewer in a diagonal recession through a fairly barren landscape. In this eighteenth-century painting, however, a landscape is given, with a horizon line, a hazy tent to the left, and a tree marking the left-hand border of the image. Unlike the Walter *Julus*, Farington's *julus* evidences a higher amount of motion and energy—in the center foreground a group of men gesticulate with their heads thrown back, and to the far left of the column two men engage in sword fighting. Overall, this composition is much less rigid in its form; one does not get the poured-into-a-mold sense that the later Walter *Julus* projects. The detail in Farington's *julus* of the *ta'ziyehs* and flags also heightens the movement of the column. Despite this qualitative change, the viewer still stands separate from the procession, viewing it here not only from a distance but also from the top of a small rise, as indicated both by the perspective and also by the dark earth in the foreground.

This copy of a late-eighteenth century British amateur painting offers a different view of the Muharram procession—one still separated from the viewer and therefore in some ways domesticated, but one which also acknowledges the movement and dynamism of the *julus*. The shift from this more detailed image to the later, more static one moves in an inverted trajectory vis-à-vis the verbal discourse about Muharram, which shifts from a lack of discussion altogether in the late eighteenth century to full-blown descriptions such as Roberts's above. This shift happens while the threat of Muharram increases and while a solid, ordered, symbolic space is established for the colonizer within India, necessitating a discourse of transgression and control in the written descriptions of Muharram and an imagery of closed-down, controlled procession in painted images. The descendants of the Company

painters who copied Farington's works at the turn of the nineteenth century acknowledged in the following two decades the market for depictions of festivals which were more controlled, ordered images for the British viewer in India and in the metropole. These two works demonstrate that trajectory; the later Walter *Julus* becomes, for Muharram processional imagery, an iconographical pattern repeated throughout the nineteenth century as seen in examples from the India Office Library and Records and elsewhere.[40]

What these images show us, however, is much more than simply a distancing or othering between Indian and British. For, with the absence of the procession's bloodshed and its threat to order, these images demonstrate the resultant domestication of the tension between a symbolic and an abject space, bringing the abject into the realm of object safely and solidly, defusing any threat so that all that remains is a mild fascination with this procession and others observed (from a distance) by the British colonizer. These images demonstrate the trajectory of colonial discourse as the Company presence grew in the subcontinent in the early nineteenth century, and the discursive defusing of this abject threat helped to consolidate the colonizing position.

My initial surprise, then, at finding a Muharram processional image devoid of both *matam* and an urban setting, making transgressing spaces impossible, finds its explanation in a close analysis of the threat to colonialism these discourses demonstrate. The British negotiation of the abject space of Muharram's procession in text and image runs much deeper than a mere objectification of the Indian observances into a particular shape ready for display on museum walls and in albums of festival images. More pointedly, the Muharram imagery discussed here demonstrates a dynamic threat to the position of the colonizer which, when represented by that colonizer, must not only be objectified but de-abjectified, leading to the controlled, orderly image of the mid-nineteenth century *julus* and the tales of triumphant and necessary British control of a transgressive annual ceremony.

---

39. Farington's original oil paintings have been lost, but textual evidence of the provenance of these images, as well as the clear stylistic and compositional differences between them and other Company paintings of this period and region, indicate that it is likely that these are indeed copies.

40. Siva Lal's virtual copy of the 1820s image is in the Chester Beatty collection; other images which follow this pattern include the Sewak Ram's *julus* in a landscape at the Victoria and Albert Museum (IS 74-1954). Archer (see note 4), pp. 85–86. The one image of the *julus* which incorporates the cityscape, an anonymous work on mica, still evidences the controlled feeling of the anonymous image, with relaxed bystanders seated in the foreground: V&A IS 35-1961, no. 28. Archer (see note 4), pp. 194–195. Published in Robert Skelton and Mark Francis, eds., *Arts of Bengal* (London: Whitechapel Art Gallery, 1979), no. 98.

Figure 3. Anonymous (after George Farington), *Muharram,* ca. 1795–1805 (original 1780s), Victoria and Albert Museum, courtesy V&A Picture Library, IS 11–1887, no. 12.

List of authors

OLEG GRABAR is Professor Emeritus at the School of Historical Studies, Institute for Advanced Study.

DAVID J. ROXBURGH is Associate Professor of History of Art and Architecture at Harvard University.

OYA PANCAROĞLU is currently a postdoctoral research fellow in Islamic Art at the Oriental Institute, University of Oxford.

THOMAS DaCOSTA KAUFMANN is Professor in the Department of Art and Archaeology at Princeton University.

CYNTHIA ROBINSON is Assistant Professor of Islamic and Medieval Art History in the Department of Art and Art History of the University of New Mexico.

NASSER RABBAT is Aga Khan Professor of Islamic Architecture at Massachusetts Institute of Technology.

FINBARR BARRY FLOOD is Assistant Professor in the Department of Fine Arts at New York University.

MICHAEL W. MEISTER is W. Norman Brown Professor of South Asia Studies at the University of Pennsylvania.

ZEREN TANINDI is Professor of History of Art in Uludag University, Bursa.

PRISCILLA SOUCEK is the Hagop Kevorkian Professor of Islamic Art at the Institute of Fine Arts, New York University.

SILVIA NAEF is Professeur Adjoint in the Arabic Department at the University of Geneva.

FERESHTEH DAFTARI is Assistant Curator in the Department of Painting and Sculpture at The Museum of Modern Art in New York.

JAMAL J. ELIAS is Professor of Religion at Amherst College.

REBECCA M. BROWN is Assistant Professor of Asian and Islamic Art at St. Mary's College, Maryland.

Res 44   Autumn 2003

Anthropology and aesthetics

Contents of upcoming issue

 **res** *anthropology and aesthetics*

Back issues are available from Peabody Museum Publications

11 Divinity Avenue, Cambridge, MA 02138

phone: 617-496-9922, fax: 617-495-7535

Order on line at www.res-journal.org

GOTTFRIED SEMPER London lecture of November 18, 1853: "The Development of the Wall and Wall Construction in Antiquity," edited and with a preface by Harry Francis Mallgrave • GOTTFRIED SEMPER London lecture of November 29, 1854: "On the Relations of Architectural Systems with General Cultural Conditions," edited and with a preface by Harry Francis Mallgrave • ARATA ISOZAKI Floors and internal spaces in Japanese vernacular architecture: phenomenology of floors • INGRID KÜSTER A special Baining mask named Guaradingi, East New Britain, Papua New Guinea • GEORGE A CORBIN Appendix: a short checklist of Kairak and Uramot Baining night dance masks • RAINER CRONE A critique of "objectivity" and "metaphors of things": Russian Futurism and Friedrich Nietzsche $20

RES 12 Autumn 1986
JOSEPH LEO KOERNER Rembrandt and the epiphany of the face • MICHAEL W. MEISTER On the development of a morphology for a symbolic architecture: India • KARL A. TAUBE The Teotihuacan cave of origin: the iconography and architecture of emergence mythology in Mesoamerica and the American Southwest • GIOVANNI CARERI Sortir du cadre: métamorposes de la pictographie aztèque au contact du livre européen • NANCY INGRAM NOOTER The Late Whites of Kondoa: an interpretation of Tanzanian rock art • ADALGISA LUGLI Inquiry as collection: the Athanasius Kircher Museum in Rome • JACK J. SPECTOR The avant-garde object: form and fetish between World War I and World War II $20

RES 13 Spring 1987
JOHN HAY Structure and aesthetic criteria in Chinese rocks and art • WILLIAM PIETZ The problem of the fetish, II: the origin of the fetish • SERGE GRUZINSKI Colonial Indian maps in sexteenth-century Mexico: an essay in mixed cartography • EMILY UMBERGER Antiques, revivals, and references to the past in Aztec art • URI ALMAGOR The cycle and stagnation of smells: pastoralists-fishermen relationships in an East African society • DAVID SHULMAN The scent of memory in Hindu South India • FRED THOMPSON and D'ARCY FENTON Matsuri: the binding of secular and ceremonial space in Kakunodate, Japan • MORTON FELDMAN and LA MONTE YOUNG A conversation on composition and improvisation (Bunita Marcus, Francesco Pellizzi, Marian Zazeela) $20

RES 14 Autumn 1987
PAUL MUS The iconography of an aniconic art, edited by Serge Thion • ERIK COHEN The Hmong cross: a cosmic symbol in Hmong (Meo) textile designs • MARY ELLEN MILLER and STEPHEN D. HOUSTON The classic Maya ballgame and its arhchitectural setting: a study of relations between text and image • CARLO SEVERI The invisible path: ritual representation of suffering in Cuna traditional thought • ENRICO CASTELLI Bari statuary: the influence exerted by European traders on the traditional production of figured objects • DAVID LEATHERBARROW The image and its setting: a study of the Sacro Monte at Varallo • MARCO FRASCARI The body and architecture in the drawings of Carlo Scarpa • ROSEMARY EBERIEL Clowns: Apollinaire's writings on Picasso $20

RES 15 Spring 1988
ANANDA K. COOMARASWAMY Early Indian architecture: IV. Huts and related temple types, edited and with a preface by Michael W. Meister • MICHAEL W. MEISTER and JOSEPH RYKWERT Afterword: Adam's house and hermits' huts • ROXANA WATERSON The house and the world: The symbolism of Sa'Dan Toraja house carvings • KIYOHIKO MUNAKATA Mysterious heavens and Chinese classical gardens • CHRISTOPHER S. WOOD Michael Pacher and the fate of the altarpiece in Renaissance Germany • VALENTINA MONCADA The painers' guilds in the cities of Venice and Padua • MARTIN PRECHTEL and ROBERT S. CARLSEN Weaving and cosmos amongst the Tzutujil Maya of Guatemala • ROBERT M. LAUGHLIN What is a Tzotzil? • GEORGE KUBLER Geology as panoramic vision: William Henry Holmes (1846–1933) • JEREMY MacCLANCY A natural curiosity: the British market in primitive art • MORTON FELDMAN and IANNIS XENAKIS A conversation on music $20

RES 16 Autumn 1988
KURT W. FORSTER Four unpublished drawings by Mies van der Rohe: a commentary • MASSIMO CACCIARI Mies's classics • DAVID NAPIER Bernini's anthropology: a "key" to the Piazza San Pietro • ANDREA CARLINO The book, the body, the scalpel • JOHN GAGE Black and white and red all over • YOSHIAKI SHIMIZU The rite of writing: thoughts on the oldest Genji text • CLEMENCY COGGINS Classic Maya metaphors of death and life • JOSE PIEDRA The value of paper • WILLIAM PIETZ The problem of the fetish, IIIa: Bosman's Guinea and the enlightenment theory of fetishism • SUZANNE PRESTON BLIER Melville J. Herskovits and the arts of ancient Dahomey $20

RES 17/18 Spring/Autumn 1989
REMO GUIDIERI L'esthétique engagée • JOSEPH RYKWERT Uranopolis or somapolis? • JAMES B. PORTER Olmec colossal heads as recarved thrones: "mutilation," revolution, and recarving • DEBRA HASSIG Transplanted medicine: colonial Mexican herbals of the sixteenth century • FLORINA H. CAPISTRANO Ritual mutilation of power objects: the case of some Maori feather boxes • HERBERT HOFFMANN Aletheia: the iconography of death/rebirth in three cups by the Sotades Painter • FREDERIC SCHWARTZ "The motions of the countenance": Rembrandt's early portraits and the tronie • JONATHAN HAY Khubilai's groom • VAUGHAN HART One view of a town: Prior Park and the city of Bath • BARBARA BRAUN Henry Moore and pre-Columbian art • FRANCESCO PELLIZZI Mésaventures de l'art: premières impressions des Magiciens de la Terre $30

RES 19/20 1990/1991
RAYMOND A. MACDONALD The Laocoön Group: the poetics of painting and the reconstruction of art history • DAVID CARRIER Blindness and the representation of desire in Poussin's paintings • REBECCA STONE-MILLER and GORDON F. McEWAN The representation of the Wari state in stone and thread: a comparison of architecture and tapestry tunics • CECELIA F. KLEIN Snares and entrails: Mesoamerican symbols of sin and punishment • ESTHER PASZTORY Still invisible: the

problem of the aesthetics of abstraction for pre-Columbian art and its implications for other cultures • **DEBRA HASSIG** Beauty in the beasts: a study of medieval aesthetics • **SARAH BRETT-SMITH** Empty space: the architecture of Dogon cloth • **BRIGITTE DERLON** L'objet Malanggan dans les anciens rites funéraires de Nouvelle Irlande • **DOMINIQUE MALAQUAIS** Eighteenth-century French voyages to the Northwest Coast of North America • **THIERRY DE DUVE** Authorship stripped bare, even **$30**

RES 21 Spring 1992
MARSHALL SAHLINS The economics of develop-man in the Pacific • **KATHLYN LISCOMB** A physician's defense of his incurable obsession with painting: Wang Lü's preface to his *Painting Models* album • **CLAUDE-FRANÇOIS BAUDEZ** The Maya snake dance: ritual and cosmology • **KARL A. TAUBE** The Temple of Quetzalcoatl and the cult of sacred war at Teotihuacan • **LOUISE M. BURKHART** Flowery heaven: the aesthetic of paradise in Nahuatl devotional literature • **SAMUEL K. PARKER** Contemporary temple construction in South India: the Srirangam *rajagopuram* • **DAVID LEATHERBARROW** Plastic character, or how to twist morality with plastics • **MARK FRANKO** Expressivism and chance procedure: the future of an emotion **$20**

RES 22 Autumn 1992
JOSEPH RYKWERT Organic and mechanical • **MOSHE HALBERTAL and AVISHAI MARGALIT** Idolatry and representation • **CHRISTOPHER PINNEY** The iconology of Hindu oleographs: linear and mythic narrative in popular Indian art • **MICHAEL OPPITZ** Drawings on shamanic drums: Nepal • **BRIAN STROSS** Maize and blood: Mesoamerican symbolism on an Olmec vase and a Maya plate • **FLORA CLANCY** Late-fifth-century public monuments in the Maya Lowlands • **JANET BERLO** Beyond bricolage: women and aesthetic strategies in Latin American textiles • **MARIO CARPO** The architectural principles of temperate classicism: merchant dwellings in Sebastiano Serlio's Sixth Book • **NICHOLAS ADAMS with JANET TEMOS** The speaking architecture of E. T. Potter at Lehigh University (1866–1869) **$20**

RES 23 Spring 1993
CHARLES BURROUGHS The building's face and the Herculean paradigm: agendas and agency in Roman Renaissance architecture • **CLAUDIO SGARBI** A newly discovered corpus of Vitruvian images • **VAUGHAN HART** "A peece rather of good *Heraldry*, than of *Architecture*": heraldry and the orders of architecture as joint emblems of chivalry • **PHILLIP GUDDEMI** *Mumukokolua`*: sago spathe paintings among the Sawiyanö of Papua New Guinea • **WILLIAM A. HART** The "lawyer" of Poro? A sixteenth-century West African masquerade • **SAMUEL C. MORSE** Jōchō's statue of Amida at the Byōdo-in and cultural legitimization in late Heian Japan • **HAIM FINKELSTEIN** The incarnation of desire: Dalí and the Surrealist Object **$20**

RES 24 Autumn 1993
JOSEPH LEO KOERNER The extensionless point of practice • **ALEXANDER NAGEL** Leonardo and *sfumato* • **EMILY**

UMBERGER Velázquez and naturalism I: interpreting *Los Borrachos* • **CARL SCHUSTER** Comparative studies of certain motifs in cotton embroideries from western China, edited and with a preface by Edmund Carpenter • **INDRA KAGIS McEWEN** Hadrian's rhetoric I: the Pantheon • **THOMAS McEVILLEY** The spinal serpent • **SUSAN E. BERGH** Death and renewal in Moche phallic-spouted vessels • **ANNA C. CHAVE** Pollock and Krasner: script and postscript • **RAYMOND A. MACDONALD** *Ekphrasis*, paradigm shift, and revisionism in art history **$20**

RES 25 Spring 1994
BRIAN STROSS Maize and fish: the iconography of power in late formative Mesoamerica • **VAUGHAN HART** Carl Jung's Alchemical Tower at Bollingen • **INDRA KAGIS MCEWEN** Hadrian's rhetoric II: *Thesaurus Eloquentiae*, the villa at Tivoli • **WILLIAM TRONZO** Mimesis in Byzantium: notes toward a history of the function of the image • **JEANNE FOX-FRIEDMAN** Messianic visions: Modena Cathedral and the Crusades • **FRANCES TERPAK** Local politics: the Charlemagne legend in medieval Narbonne • **RITA ASTUTI** Invisible objects: mortuary rituals among the Veso of western Madagascar • **WYATT MacGAFFEY** African objects and the idea of fetish • **BARBARA DUDEN** The fetus as an object of our time **$20**

RES 26 Autumn 1994
JOSEPH RYKWERT On the palmette • **MARIO PROSPERI** The masks of Menander • **VICTOR I. STOICHITA** Image and apparition: Spanish painting of the Golden Age and New World popular devotion • **ANDREW BUTTERFIELD** Social structure and typology of funerary monuments in Early Renaissance Florence • **DAVID BINDHAM** Am I not a man and a brother?: British art and slavery in the eighteenth century • **HELEN WESTON** Representing the right to represent: the *Portrait of Citizen Belley, ex-representative of the colonies* by A.-L. Girodet • **ELISHA P. RENNE** Things that threaten: a symbolic analysis of Bunu Yoruba masquerades • **JAMES ELKINS** The question of the body in Mesoamerican art • **ROBERTO CALASSO** *La Folie qui vient des Nymphes* **$20**

RES 27 Spring 1995
INDRA KAGIS McEWEN Housing fame: in the Tuscan villa of Pliny the Younger • **MARILYN E. HELDMAN** Legens of Lālibalā: the development of an Ethiopian pilgrimage site • **JEAN MICHAEL MASSING** Hans Burgkmair's depiction of native Africans • **ANDREA CARLINO** "Knowe thyself": anatomical figures in early modern Europe • **SERGE MAMINO** Reimagining the Grande Galleria of Carlo Emanuele I of Savoy • **DAVID R. SMITH** Inversion, revolution, and the carnivalesque in Rembrandt's *Civilis* • **ANNA LO GIUDICE** *Nage/danse, corps/écriture: de l'insularité valéryenne* • **MICHAEL W. MEISTER** Sweetmeats of corpses? Art history and ethnohistory • **PAMELA M. LEE** The aesthetics of value, the fetish of method: a case study at the Peabody Museum **$20**

RES 28 Autumn 1995
FRANCESCO PELLIZZI Songs of the material • **WILLIAM PIETZ** The spirit of civilization: blood sacrifice and monetary debt • **GIANNI VATTIMO** Postmodernity and new monumentality •

IVAN ILLICH Guarding the eye in the age of show • BEAT WYSS *The Last Judgment* as artistic process: *The Flaying of Marsyas* in the Sistine Chapel • PAULA CARABELL *Finito* and *non-finito* in Titian's last paintings • EMILY UMBERGER Velázquez and naturalism II: interpreting *Las Meninas* • DANIEL ARASSE Entre dévotion et hérésie: la tablette de saint Bernardin ou le secret d'un prédicateur • REMO GUIDIERI Res • ANNIE SUQUET Archaic thought and ritual in the work of Joseph Beuys • KIRK VARNEDOE with FRANCESCO CLEMENTE, BRICE MARDEN, and RICHARD SERRA Cy Twombly: an artist's artist • OCTAVIO PAZ The Cy Twombly Gallery at the Menil Collection: a conversation

RES 29/30 Spring/Autumn 1996 *The pre-Columbian*

FRANCESCO PELLIZZI The pre-Columbian • CLEMENCY CHASE COGGINS Creation religion and the numbers at Teotihuacan and Izapa • KARL TAUBE The Olmec maize god: the face of corn in formative Mesoamerica • BRIAN STROSS The Mesoamerican cosmic portal: an early Zapotec example • MARGARET YOUNG-SANCHEZ An Aztec gold warrior figurine (from the Cleveland Museum) • WILLIAM and BARBARA FASH Building a world-view: visual communication in Classic Maya architecture • DAVID STUART Kings of stone: a consideration of stelae in ancient Maya ritual and representation • CLAUDE-FRANÇOIS BAUDEZ Arquitectura y escenografía en Palenque: un ritual de entronización • ARTHUR SCHLAK Venus, Mercury, and the sun: GI, GII, and GIII of the Palenque Triad • EVON Z. VOGT and VICTORIA R. BRICKER The Zinacanteco Fiesta of San Sebastian: an essay in ethnographic interpretation • ALAN L. KOLATA Mimesis and monumentalism in native Andean cities • GARY URTON The body of meaning in Chavin art • MAARTEN VAN DE GUCHTE Sculpture and the concept of the double among the Inca kings • VALERIE FRASER The artistry of Guaman Poma • MARY W. HELMS Color and creativity: interpretation of themes and design styles on a Panamanian Conte bowl • JEFFREY QUILTER Continuity and disjunction in pre-Columbian art and culture • ESTHER PASZTORY Aesthetics and pre-Columbian art • BARBARA MUNDY and DANA LEIBSOHN Of copies, casts, and codices: Mexico on display in 1892 **$60**

RES 31 Spring 1997 *The abject*

JOSEPH LEO KOERNER The abject of art history • JEFFREY F. HAMBURGER "To make women weep": ugly art as "feminine" and the origins of modern aesthetics • JULIET FLEMING The Renaissance tattoo • JOAN R. BRANHAM Blood in flux, sanctity at issue • SARAH BRETT-SMITH The mouth of the Komo • WILLIAM PIETZ Death of the deodand: accursed objects and the money value of human life • JOSEPH RYKWERT The constitution of Bohemia • VICTOR I. STOICHITA Johann Caspar Lavater's *Essays on Physiognomy* and the hermeneutics of shadow • NICHOLAS GRINDLE "Our own imperfect knowledge": Petrus Camper and the search for an "ideal form" • CHRISTINE ROSS Redefinitions of abjection in contemporary performances of the female body • MEYER SCHAPIRO A critique: Pevsner on modernity (1938), translated by David Craven • MEYER SCHAPIRO and LILLIAN MILGRAM SCHAPIRO with DAVID CRAVEN A series of interviews (July 15, 1992– January 22, 1995) **$30**

RES 32 Autumn 1997 *Tradition—translation—treason*

FRANCESCO PELLIZZI Editorial • SUSAN SONTAG Being translated • ROBERT FARRIS THOMPSON Translating the world into generousness: remarks on Haitian vèvè • ESTHER PASZTORY Treason: comments to Robert Farris Thompson • MIKHAIL IAMPOLSKI Translating images . . . • SERGE GAVRONSKY On harmony: a theory of translation • VINCENT CRAPANZANO Translation: truth or metaphor • SAINT CLAIR CEMIN A comment on language, object, and translation • GIANNI VATTIMO Translation and interpretation • ARTHUR DANTO Translation and betrayal • WILLIAM PIETZ The future of treason: political boundaries in the information age • JOHN HEJDUK Sentences on the house and other sentences I and II • DAVID SHAPIRO Poetry and architecture: mistranslation and collaboration • PAULA CARABELL Image and identity in the unfinished works of Michelangelo • KATHERINE HACKER Dressing the Lord Jagannātha in silk: cloth, clothes, and status • REMO GUIDIERI Baits and traps • BARBARA MONK FELDMAN Music and the picture plane: Poussin's *Pyramus and Thisbe* and Morton Feldman's *For Philip Guston* **$30**

Res 33 Spring 1998 *Pre-Columbian states of being*

JEFFREY QUILTER Presentation • FRANK SALOMON How the Huacas were • CATHERINE J. ALLEN When utensils revolt: mind, matter, and modes of being in the pre-Columbian Andes • RICHARD L. BURGER and LUCY SALAZAR-BURGER A sacred effigy from Mina Perdida and the unseen ceremonies of the Peruvian Formative • MARY MILLER and MARCO SAMAYOA Where maize would grow: jade, chacmools, and the Maize God • STEPHEN HOUSTON and DAVID STUART The ancient Maya self: personhood and portraiture in the Classic period • ADAM HERRING Sculptural representations and self-reference in a carved Maya panel from the region of Tabasco, Mexico • ELIZABETH NEWSOME The ontology of being and spiritual power in the stone monument cults of the lowland Maya • JOHN MONAGHAN Definitions of person and the construction of difference in Mesoamerica • ROSEMARY JOYCE Performing the body in pre-Hispanic Central America • SUSAN TOBY EVANS Sexual politics in the Aztec palace: public, private, and profane • JOHN POHL Themes of drunkeness, violence, and factionalism in Tlaxcalan altar paintings • JILL LESLIE MCKEEVER FURST The *Nahualli* of Christ: the Trinity and the nature of the soul in ancient Mexico • NICHOLAS J. SAUNDERS Stealers of light, traders in brilliance: Amerindian metaphysics in the mirror of conquest **$30**

Res 34 Autumn 1998 *Architecture*

JOSEPH RYKWERT No gratification without configuration • LEONARD BARKAN The classical undead: Renaissance and antiquity face to face • ALINA A. PAYNE Creativity and bricolage in architectural literature of the Renaissance • CHARLES BURROUGHS Grammar and expression in early Renaissance architecture: Brunelleschi and Alberti • JOSEPH RYKWERT Translation and/or representation • DAVID FREEDBERG The limits of translation • VAUGHAN HART Decorum and the five Orders of Architecture: Sebastiano Serlio's military city • REBECCA WILLIAMSON The Clocktower Controversy • BARBARA KENDA On the Renaissance art of well-being: Pneuma in Villa Eolia • **RICHARD WESLEY** The idea of a house • **PATRICK GEORGE** Counting curvature: the numerical roots of North Indian temple architecture and Frank Gehry's "digital curvatures" • **LOUIS RENOU** The Vedic house, edited and with a preface by Michael W. Meister • **CHARLES CORREA** Hornby trains, Chinese gardens, and architecture • **ELIZABETH ALICE HONIG** Making sense of things: on the motives of Dutch still life • **JÜRGEN WASIM FREMBGEN** Saints in modern devotional poster-portraits: Meanings and uses of popular religious folk art in Pakistan • **FIONA MAGOWAN** Singing the light: sense and sensation in Yolgnu performance • **DANIELLE VAN DE VELDE** Existe-t-il des noms propres de temps? **$30**

RES 35 Spring 1999 *Intercultural China*
JONATHAN HAY Toward a theory of the intercultural • **ALAIN THOTE** Intercultural relations as seen from Chinese pictorial bronzes of the fifth century B.C.E. • **LOTHAR VON FALKENHAUSEN** Inconsequential incomprehensions: some instances of Chinese writing in alien contexts • **EUGENE Y. WANG** What do trigrams have to do with Buddhas? The Northern Liang stupas as a hybrid spatial model • **ANGELA F. HOWARD** The Eight Brilliant Kings of Wisdom of southwest China • **CHRISTINE M. E. GUTH** • Mapping sectarian identity: Onjōji's statue of Shinra Myōjin • **PRISCILLA SOUCEK** Ceramic production as exemplar of Yuan–Ilkhanid relations • **PETER CHARLES STURMAN** Confronting dynastic change: painting after Mongol reunification of North and South China • **DOROTHY BERINSTEIN** Hunts, processions, and telescopes: a painting of an imperial hunt by Lang Shining (Giuseppe Castiglione) • **LUCIA TRIPODES** Painting and diplomacy at the Qianlong court: a commemorative picture by Wang Zhicheng (Jean-Denis Attiret) • **JONATHAN HAY** Culture, ethnicity, and empire in the work of two eighteenth-century "Eccentric" artists • **LESLIE JONES** Sanyu: Chinese painter of Montparnasse • **JOHN HAY** Questions of influence in Chinese art history **$30**

RES 36 Autumn 1999 *Factura*
JOSEPH LEO KOERNER *Factura* • **BRUNO LATOUR** Factures/fractures: from the concept of network to the concept of attachment • **MARIA GOUGH** *Faktura:* the making of the Russian avant-garde • **GERHARD WOLF** • The origins of painting • **FRIEDRICH TEJA BACH** Albrecht Dürer: figures of the marginal • **PHILIP SOHM** *Maniera* and the absent hand: avoiding the etymology of style • **REBECCA ZORACH** Everything swims with excess: gold and its fashioning in sixteenth-century France • **BENJAMIN BINSTOCK** Rembrandt's paint • **PAULA CARABELL** Framing and fiction in the work of Paolo Veronese: a study in the structure and meaning of the image *di sotto in su* • **T. A. ANSTEY** Fictive harmonies: music and the Tempio Malatestiano • **DARIO GAMBONI** "Fabrication of accidents": *factura* and chance in nineteenth-century art • **MATTHEW SIMMS** Cézanne's unfinish • **PAMELA LEE** How money looks: Man Ray's *Perpetual Motif* and the economy of time • **HARRY COOPER** Surface as psyche: a progress report **$30**

RES 37 Spring 2000
REMO GUIDIERI The soul of the Rhizome • **ROBERT LINSLEY** Mirror travel in the Yucatan: Robert Smithson, Michael Fried and the new critical drama • **FEDERICO NAVARRETE** The path from Aztlan

to Mexico: on visual narration in Mesoamerican codices • **ZOE S. STROTHER** From performative utterance to performative object: Pende theories of speech, blood sacrifice, and power objects • **WILLIAM HART** *Kololewengoi* and the myth of the Big Thing • **BERNARD FORMOSO** A terraced world for an armored body: the symbolism of women costumes among the Yi of Yuanyang • **OLAF H. SMEDAL** Sociality on display: the aesthetics of Ngadha Houses • **WILLIAM H. DAVENPORT** Hornbill carvings of the Iban of Sarawak, Malaysia • **KATHERINE F. HACKER** Traveling objects: brass images, artisans, and audiences • **PIKA GHOSH** The story of a storyteller's scroll • **PREMA SRINIVASAN** *Ahara-niyama:* the Srivaisnava dietary regimen **$30**

RES 38 Autumn 2000
BORIS GROYS On the new • **HENRY MAGUIRE** Profane icons: the significance of animal violence in Byzantine art • **BISSERA V. PENTCHEVA** Rhetorical images of the Virgin: the icon of the "usual miracle" at the Blachernai • **NICOLETTA ISAR** The vision and its "exceedingly blessed beholder": of desire and participation in the icon • **GRAZIELLA FEDERICI VESCOVINI** A new origin of perspective • **CHRISTOPHER HEUER** Perspective as process in Vermeer • **ALBA GUADALUPE MASTACHE and ROBERT H. COBEAN** Ancient Tollan: the sacred precinct • **CLAUDE-FRANÇOIS BAUDEZ** The Maya king's body, mirror of the universe • **ANNE PAUL** Protective perimeters: the symbolism of borders on Paracas textiles • **TAMARA L. BRAY** Inca iconography: the art of empire in the Andes • **JOSEPH MASHECK** A Pre-Bretonian advocacy of automatism in art: Spare and Carter's "Automatic Drawing" (1916) • **SIMON BAKER** The thinking man and the *femme sans tête:* collective perception and self-represension • **MARK FRANKO** The readymade as movement: Cunningham, Duchamp, and Nam June Paik's two Merces **$30**

RES 39 Spring 2001
Z. S. STROTHER African works: anxious encounters in the visual arts • **SUZANNE PRESTON BLIER** Autobiography and art history: the imperative of peripheral vision • **IKEM STANLEY OKOYE** Fieldwork and the text preceding the (question) mark: prolegomena for a response to Mudimbe's "African Art as a Question Mark" • **RUTH B. PHILLIPS** "Can you go out without your head?" Fieldwork as transformative experience • **TOBIAS WENDL** Entangled traditions: photography and the history of media in southern Ghana • **SARAH C. BRETT-SMITH** When is an object finished? The creation of the invisible among the Bamana of Mali • **WYATT MACGAFFEY** Astonishment and stickiness in Kongo art: a theoretical advance • **VAUGHAN HART and RICHARD TUCKER** "Immaginacy set free": Aristotelian ethics and Inigo Jones's Banqueting House at Whitehall • **GEORGE DODDS** Body in pieces: desiring the Barcelona Pavilion • **WILLIAM W. BRAHAM** Solidity of the mask: color contrasts in modern architecture • **BRUNO LATOUR** "Thou shalt not take the Lord's name in vain"— being a sort of sermon on the hesitations of religious speech • **REMO GUIDIERI** Great and small expectations **$30**

RES 40 Autumn 2001 *Desedimenting time*
MARVIN TRACHTENBERG Desedimenting time: Gothic column/paradigm shifter • **ANNE-MARIE SANKOVITCH** The myth of the "myth of the medieval": Gothic architecture in Vasari's *rinascita*

and Panofsky's Renaissance • **ALINA PAYNE** Vasari, architecture, and the origins of historicizing art • **BENJAMIN DAVID** Past and present in Sienese painting: 1350–1550 • **JONATHAN HAY** Toward a disjunctive diachronics of Chinese history • **PRISCILLA P. SOUCEK** Walter Pater, Bernard Berenson, and the reception of Persian manuscript illustration • **NICHOLAS NEWMAN** In the name of rococo • **ERIKA NAGINSKI** Riegl, archaeology, and the periodization of culture • **MATTHEW BIRO** History at a standstill: Walter Benjamin, Otto Dix, and the question of stratigraphy • **ROBERT BORK** Pros and cons of stratigraphic models in art history • **JAMES O. CASWELL** Lines of communication: some "secrets of the trade" in Chinese painters' use of "perspective" • **SHERWIN SIMMONS** Men of nails: monuments, expressionism, fetishes, Dadaism • **JANINE MILEAF** Body to politics: Surrealist exhibition of the tribal and the modern at the anti-Imperialist exhibition and the Galerie Charles Ratton $30

RES 41 Spring 2002
DARIO GAMBONI Visual ambiguity and interpretation • **CAROLINE A. JONES** Preconscious/posthumous Smithson: the ambiguous status of art and artist in the postmodern frame • **ROBERT LINSLEY** Minimalism and the city: Robert Smithson as a social critic • **CHARLES BURROUGHS** Opacity and transparence: networks and enclaves in the Rome of Sixtus V • **MICHAEL GAUDIO** The space of idolatry: reformation, incarnation, and the ethnographic image • **MICHAEL W. MEISTER** Giving up and taking on: the body in ritual • **PIKA GHOSH** Sojourns of a peripatetic deity • **MARIO PERNIOLA** Cultural turning points in art: art between parasitism and admiration • **DAVID GERSTEN** Hunting life: a forever house: prefigure is epilogue • **HOMA SHOJAIE** The landscape of the gaze: a search to find the space and time of seeing • **REMO GUIDIERI** An art without: after the Venice Biennale, Summer 2001 $30

RES 42 Autumn 2002 *West by nonwest*
ESTHER PASZTORY West by nonwest • **MARY MILLER** The willfulness of art: The case of Bonampak • **FLORA SIMMONS CLANCY** Shield Jaguar's monuments: Esthetics and art history • **CLEMENCY COGGINS** Toltec • **EMILY UMBERGER** • Notions of Aztec history: The case of the Great Temple dedication • **THOMAS B. F. CUMMINS** To serve man: Pre-Columbian art, Western discourses of idolatry, and cannibalism • **CECELIA F. KLEIN** Not like us and all the same: Pre-Columbian art history and the construction of the nonwest • **CLAUDE BAUDEZ** History of art and anthropology of art • **JANE MACLAREN WALSH** The Smithsonian water goddess: An Aztec sculpture rediscov-ered • **ESTHER PASZTORY** Truth in forgery • **DENNIS TEDLOCK** How to drink chocolate from a skull at a wedding banquet • **CATHERINE J. ALLEN** The Incas have gone inside: Pattern and persistence in Andean iconography • **CHANTAL HUCKERT** A case of continuity: Native textile designs of the Otomi village of San Juan Ixtenco, Tlaxcala • **ALESSANDRA RUSSO** Plumes of sacrifice: Transformations in sixteenth-century Mexican feather art • **BEATRIZ DE LA FUENTE** Beneath the sign of "otherness" • **FRANCESCO PELLIZZI** North by northwest: Time lapses and monumental vertigo $30

PEABODY MUSEUM

To order these or any other titles from the Peabody Museum,
please contact:

PUBLICATIONS DEPARTMENT
PEABODY MUSEUM OF ARCHAEOLOGY & ETHNOLOGY
11 DIVINITY AVENUE
CAMBRIDGE, MA 02138
TEL: (617) 496-9922, FAX: (617) 495-7535
E-MAIL ORDERS: peabody@fas.harvard.edu
WEB SITE: www.peabody.harvard.edu/publications

Excavation at Tepe Yahya, Iran, 1967–1975: The Third Millennium
D. T. Potts
With Contributions by Holly Pittman and Philip L. Kohl
C. C. Lamberg-Karlovsky, General Editor and Project Director

Since its discovery in 1967, Tepe Yahya has proven to be one of the most important sites excavated in Iran in the modern era. Occupied from 4900 B.C. to the first centuries A.D., Tepe Yahya provides the longest cultural sequence documented to date anywhere in eastern Iran. In important third-millennium levels, the discovery of inscribed tablets of Susa II or "proto-Elamite" type along with ceramic types typical of Mesopotamia and Khuzistan has sparked debate on the political and economic integration of the Iranian Plateau around 3000 B.C. Equally significant is evidence of sophisticated carved chlorite vessels, as well as ceramic, metallurgical, and glyptic indications of interaction with southwestern Iran, Central Asia, the Indo-Iranian borderlands, and the Persian Gulf region. Situated between the Indus Valley and the Mesopotamian plains, Tepe Yahya occupies a special place in our conception of relations between these distant territories during the Early Bronze age. D. T. Potts offers the evidence of stratigraphy, architecture, ceramics, and chronology from the site, along with a full inventory of the small finds recovered. Holly Pittman contributes comprehensive illustrations and discussion of the seals and sealings, and Philip Kohl provides a retrospective analysis of the carved chlorite industry. In a foreword and afterword, project director and site excavator C. C. Lamberg-Karlovsky tells the story of the archaeological expedition and reflects on the contributions of the Tepe Yahya project.

2001   American School of Prehistoric Research Bulletin 45
388 pp., 311 b&w illustrations, map, 17 tables, appendices, biblio.
Paper   ISBN 0-87365-549-4 $69.95

Early Pithouse Villages of the Mimbres Valley and Beyond: The McAnally and Thompson Sites in Their Cultural and Ecological Contexts
Michael W. Diehl and Steven A. LeBlanc
With contributions by Roger Anyon, John W. Arthur, and Paul E. Minnis

The Mimbres Valley is best known for the stunning black-on-white pottery of the Classic Mimbres culture. However, comparatively little attention has been given to the prior inhabitants of the valley, the Early Pithouse period villagers (ca. A.D. 200–1000), who played a generative role in the cultural and historical sequence of the Mogollon region. In *Early Pithouse Villages of the Mimbres Valley and Beyond,* Michael Diehl and Steven LeBlanc publish a complete account of two important Early Pithouse village sites excavated in the 1970s by the Mimbres Foundation. The McAnally and Thompson sites are located along the Rio Mimbres in the heart of the Southwest's Upland Mogollon. The authors synthesize information about changes over time in the pithouse villagers' lifestyle and present a complete account of the extensive archaeological digs at the two sites: the excavation units, depositional contexts, architectural details, radiocarbon dates, miscellaneous artifacts, and ceramic frequency distributions. The Thompson and McAnally sites contain architecture, artifacts, and detritus of the earliest relatively sedentary horticulturists to occupy the region. The lifeways of these people—their subsistence practices, their knowledge of construction and of the manufacture of stone tools and pots, and their rules for social interaction—provided the foundation for nine centuries of continuous occupation of the Mimbres Mogollon area.

2001   Papers of the Peabody Museum of Archaeology and Ethnology 83
160 pp., 29 figures, 47 tables, appendix, biblio. Paper.
ISBN 0-87365-211-8 $30.00

PUBLICATIONS

Souvenirs of the Fur Trade: Northwest Coast Indian Art and Artifacts Collected by American Mariners, 1788–1844
Mary Malloy

American mariners made more than 175 voyages to the Northwest Coast during the half-century after the ships *Columbia* and *Washington* pioneered the route from Boston in 1787. Although obtaining sea otter pelts for the China trade was the original purpose of the voyages, the art and culture of Northwest Coast Indians so intrigued and fascinated American sailors that the collecting of ethnographic artifacts became an important secondary trade. These objects were the first examples of Northwest Coast Indian material culture to enter American museums, and they influenced perceptions of Northwest Coast Indian people and their complex cultures.

By carefully researching the records of ten institutions and the shipboard journals of more than a dozen mariners, Mary Malloy has brought details about these early collections together for the first time. These souvenirs tell a story of commerce and cultural exchange that reached across the continent during the period when Americans were first beginning to look westward.

2000 188 pp., 39 figures, 13 plates, biblio., index. Paper.
ISBN 0-87365-833-7 $35.00

The Geography of Neandertals and Modern Humans in Europe and the Greater Mediterranean
Ofer Bar-Yosef and David Pilbeam, eds.

Archaeological investigations have provided data showing that the abrupt transition from the Middle to the Upper Paleolithic, during which populations of Neandertals and modern humans met and interacted, was a fast-moving period of change for both groups.

The papers in this volume are the proceedings of a two-day conference held at the Peabody Museum in December 1997, which addressed this transition. The expansion of modern humans and their impact on the populations of Neandertals is discussed in depth, with particular focus on the lithic industries of the Late Middle and Early Upper Paleolithic.

2000 Peabody Museum Bulletin 8
198 pp., 44 line art, 24 maps, 8 tables, biblios. Paper.
ISBN 0-87365-958-9 $25.00

The Breakout: The Origins of Civilization
Martha Lamberg-Karlovsky, ed.

A transformation occurred in the third millennium B.C. from an earlier, less complex world to one with sophisticated technological innovations and social institutions, one defined as civilization. The essays in this volume, some originally published in *Symbols,* the Peabody Museum newsletter, address the role ideology played in the origins of several ancient civilizations. Two models are proposed: K.-C. Chang's absolutist China–New World model, based on the exclusive relationship between rulers and gods, and C. C. Lamberg-Karlovsky's Mesopotamian model, based on a reciprocal social contract between ruler and ruled.

2000 Peabody Museum Monograph 9
132 pp., 21 halftones, 13 line art, 3 maps, biblios.
Paper.
ISBN   0-87365-910-4 $25.00

Nyae Nyae !Kung Beliefs and Rites
Lorna J. Marshall

With style and depth, Lorna Marshall leads the reader through the intricacies, ambiguities, and silences of !Kung beliefs. Her narrative, situated amongst the !Kung Bushmen of the Nyae Nyae region of the Kalahari in the early 1950s, brings into focus a way of life that has existed for millennia. She reveals a detailed system of beliefs of one of the last hunter-gatherer societies, beliefs in which two primal forces (N/ow and N/um) infuse everything and everyone.

1999 Peabody Museum Monograph 8
320 pp., 17 halftones, 1 map, biblio.
Paper   ISBN 0-87365-908-2 $25.00
Cloth   ISBN 0-87365-909-0 $50.00

Res

Anthropology and aesthetics

Res is a journal of anthropology and comparative aesthetics dedicated to the study of the object, in particular cult and belief objects and objects of art. The journal brings together, in an anthropological perspective, contributions by philosophers, art historians, archaeologists, critics, linguists, architects, artists, and others. Its field of inquiry is open to all cultures, regions, and historical periods.

Res also seeks to make available textual and iconographic documents of importance for the history and theory of the arts.

Res appears twice a year, in the spring and in the autumn. Subscriptions are filled only on a calendar-year basis. The 2003 subscription prices are:

Individuals: $30 per year (North America); $42 per year (rest of world).
Institutions: $64 per year (North America); $74 per year (rest of world).

Orders, which must be accompanied by payment, should be sent to a bookseller or subscription agent or directly to the Peabody Museum of Archaeology and Ethnology, Publications Department, 11 Divinity Avenue, Cambridge, MA 02138, phone: 617-496-9922, fax: 617-495-7535. Orders for back issues and subscriptions can be placed online at www.res-journal.org. Claims for missing issues should be made immediately after receipt of the subsequent issue of the journal.

The publication of *Res* is made possible by a generous donation from the Fanny and Leo Koerner Charitable Trust.

We also gratefully acknowledge long-term support from the Pinewood Foundation.

Editorial correspondence should be sent to Francesco Pellizzi, *Res*, Editorial Office, 12 East 74th Street, New York, NY 10021, phone: 212-737-6109, fax: 212-861-7874, 212-744-3540, e-mail: pellizzi@fas.harvard.edu.

The *Res* web site (www.res-journal.org) provides back issue, current issue, and upcoming issue contents; an author's guide; on-line ordering; and other features.

Permission reprint requests for volumes 1–18 and 29/30 and on should be directed to the Peabody Museum of Archaeology and Ethnology, Publications Department, 11 Divinity Avenue, Cambridge, MA 02138, phone: 617-495-3938, fax: 617-495-7535; permission reprint requests for volumes 19/20–28 only should be directed to the Getty Research Institute for the History of Art and the Humanities, Publications, 1200 Getty Center Drive, Suite 1100, Los Angeles, CA 90049-1688, phone: 310-440-7452, fax: 310-440-7778.